Canada, Adieu?

Quebec Debates its Future

Canada, Adieu?

Quebec Debates its Future

Translation and Commentary by

RICHARD FIDLER

 co-published by
Oolichan Books
and

The Institute for Research on Public Policy
L'Insitut de recherches politques

1991

Copyright © 1991 by Richard Fidler and the Institute for Research on Public Policy

ISBN 0-88982-112-7
ISBN 0-88645-130-2

Canadian Cataloguing in Publication Data
   Main entry under title:
   Canada, adieu?

      Co-published by the Institute for Research on
   Public Policy.
      Translation of selected briefs presented to
   the Bélanger-Campeau Commission.
      Includes the report of the Bélanger-Campeau
   Commission.
      ISBN 0-88982-112-7 (Oolichan). — ISBN 0-88645-130-2 (IRPP)

      1. Quebec (Province)—History—Autonomy and
   independence movements.   2. (Province)—
   Politics and government—1985-   3. Federal
   government—Quebec.   4. Canada—Constitutional
   law—Amendments.   I. Fidler, Richard, 1942-
   II. Québec (Province).   Assemblée nationale.
   Commission sur l'avenir politique et consti-
   tutionnal du Québec.   III. Institute for
   Research on Public Policy.

   FC2925.9.S4C35 1991   971.4'04   C91-091548-2
   F1035.2.C35 1991
                        73635

COVER PHOTO: Canapress Photo Service/Jacques Boissinot

Publication of this book has been financially assisted by the Canada Council

Published by
Oolichan Books
Lantzville, B.C., Canda V0R 2H0
and

The Institute for Research on Public Policy/
L'Institut de recherches politiques
P.O. Box 3670 South
Halifax, Nova Scotia, Canada B3J 3K6

Printed in Canada.

FOREWORD

Across the language divide, Canadians know little of each other's concerns and aspirations. In its June 1991 report, the Citizens' Forum on Canada's Future (the Spicer Commission) underlined both the depth of the ignorance of Quebec's goals and attitudes revealed by Canadians outside Quebec, and the failure of many Quebecers to appreciate the moods and perspectives of Canadians in other regions.

Without recognition of the many differing perspectives springing from the diverse histories and cultures making up Canada, and without respect for their different traditions of governance and social organization, there is little likelihood of success in efforts to solve the technical problems of constitutional arrangements and administrative apparatus which confront Canada today.

One opportunity for Canadians outside Quebec to develop a greater appreciation of the range of objectives and concerns driving various groups in Quebec was offered by the activities of the Commission on the Political and Constitutional Future of Quebec (the Bélanger-Campeau Commission). Testimony before the Commission, and more particularly the variety of briefs and submissions to it, opened a window for Canadians on the range and diversity of issues and opinions in Quebec that only avid readers of *Le Devoir* would otherwise be likely to encounter.

This Institute therefore welcomed Richard Fidler's willingness to compile and translate a selection of extracts from submissions to the Commission, and to prepare brief commentaries designed to provide some context for the various groups and their views within the ongoing debate. Though the Commission's report itself is available in English, none of this rich background of underlying material is readily accessible, and hence the range of views to be addressed and reconciled by the Commission for purposes of its report is not easily appreciated. With the addition of introductory commentary and reference material, as well as the full text of the Commission's report itself, this present volume offers a useful introduction not only for the general reader but for the specialist following the constitutional debate more closely.

This book thus fits snugly into a tradition of Institute work on cultural diversity and Canadian nationhood. From its inception in 1972, the Institute for Research on Public Policy has attempted to provide one of the relatively few "bridges" between the English and French intellectual worlds. Francophone researchers have worked productively with the Institute, the Institute has maintained an office in Quebec, and the Institute's publications have always included books in both official languages. Over the last several years the effort to establish a presence in Quebec and stronger links with research activities there has been a particular priority in the Institute's work program. (A list of related publications is available from the Institute.)

This current volume continues that commitment to moving information and views across Canada's language divide. At no time in our history has this seemed a more crucial task. Our present lack of knowledge and understanding erodes the ties that bind us together as a country, leaving us vulnerable to prejudice and unaware of the benefits we risk losing through inaction or indifference.

The simple fact is that we can no longer afford the luxury of remaining complacent, oblivious to what is happening in other parts of this enormous country. If we are to hold together as a national community, we must penetrate behind the headlines and develop a much more sympathetic understanding of each other's concerns and aspirations.

This need was a major motivating factor in the Institute's decision to publish Christian Dufour's recent insightful study of the relationship between Quebec and the rest of the country, first in French in 1990 as *Le défi québécois* and then in English the next year as *A Canadian Challenge*. It is a key reason also for publishing the current book, *Canada, Adieu?*

We expect that most readers of this compilation will find some of the views expressed here challenging, and some possibly downright infuriating. We are also convinced, however, that those views represent a point of departure for the kind of tough-minded dialogue from which alone will emerge a renewed federation. Facts may on occasion be unpalatable, but without them, solutions are impossible.

This land itself imposes some obligations. For a few Canadians waiting in Bull Harbour, British Columbia, for the gales to subside sufficiently to permit rounding of Cape Scott at Canada's westernmost tip, Canada Day 1991 offered another opportunity to reflect on the privileges Canadians enjoy. Landing on the other side at Yuquot (named Friendly Cove by Captain Cook because of the welcome he received on his arrival) only strengthened this impression. Here, in 1792, Chief Maquinna signed with Captains Cook of England and Quadra of Spain the Nootka Convention, which established that exploration of this coast could be undertaken cooperatively and harmoniously, rather than competitively and belligerently. It is hard in that setting to believe that Canadians, so fortunate in their land and so blessed by Providence, can fail to meet their responsibility to resolve the modest differences which now divide them.

Canada is formally a relatively young nation, but it draws on ancient traditions. We as Canadians have still the potential to demonstrate that all these traditions — aboriginal and modern, European and Oriental, French and English — can still be accommodated with respect, in a cooperative and harmonious common endeavour. The Institute hopes that this volume can make its contribution to the greater understanding and recognition essential to that goal.

Rod Dobell
July, 1991

AVANT-PROPOS

De part et d'autre de la barrière linguistique, les Canadiens connaissent mal les préoccupations et les aspirations de leurs compatriotes. Dans son rapport de juin 1991, le Forum des citoyens sur l'avenir du Canada (la Commission Spicer) a souligné la profonde ignorance des Canadiens hors-Québec face aux objectifs et aux attitudes du Québec; l'étude a également souligné que bien des Québécois n'arrivaient pas à reconnaître l'humeur des Canadiens des autres régions, ni leurs points de vue.

Aujourd'hui, le Canada fait face à des problèmes d'ordre technique reliés aux accords constitutionnels et au fonctionnement de l'administration. Or, les efforts visant à régler ces problèmes ne risquent guère de porter fruit si l'on omet de reconnaître l'existence des nombreux points de vue que dictent les racines et les cultures variées qui constituent le Canada, ou de considérer les différentes traditions touchant les modes de gouvernement et d'organisation sociale.

Les activités de la Commission sur l'avenir politique et constitutionnel du Québec (la Commission Bélanger-Campeau) ont procuré aux Canadiens hors-Québec une occasion de mieux reconnaître la gamme des objectifs et des préoccupations de divers groupes du Québec. Les témoignages devant la Commission, et plus précisément, l'éventail de notes et de mémoires qui lui ont été présentées, ont offert une vision aux Canadiens d'autres régions de l'étendue et de la diversité des problèmes et des idées exprimées au Québec, lesquelles n'auraient, autrement, été disponibles qu'aux lecteurs assidus du journal *Le Devoir*.

Par conséquent, cet Institut a bien accueilli l'offre de Richard Fidler d'assembler et de traduire des extraits tirés des mémoires présentés à la Commission, et de préparer de brefs commentaires visant à fournir certaines informations de base sur les divers groupes et sur leurs points de vue dans le présent débat. Le rapport de la Commission est disponible en anglais, mais il n'est guère possible de consulter cette précieuse masse de documents de référence. Il n'est donc pas facile de juger de la diversité des idées que la Commission a dû étudier et harmoniser dans le but de rédiger son rapport. Les commentaires liminaires et les documents de référence, qui s'ajoutent au texte intégral du rapport de la Commission, font de ce livre un exposé utile qui s'adresse non seulement au grand public, mais aussi aux spécialistes qui s'intéressent de plus près au débat constitutionnel.

Ce livre s'inscrit donc parfaitement dans la lignée des ouvrages de l'Institut portant sur la diversité culturelle et sur l'identité canadiennes. Depuis sa création en 1972, l'Institut de recherches politiques s'est efforcé d'établir l'un des rares ponts entre les communautés d'intellectuels francophones et anglophones. Des chercheurs francophones ont oeuvré avec succès auprès de l'Institut; celui-ci a établi un bureau au Québec et on a toujours compté parmi ses publications des titres dans les deux langues officielles. Ces dernières années, le programme de travail de l'Institut a accordé une importance particulière aux efforts visant à établir une présence au Québec et à resserrer les liens avec les activités de recherches que l'on y mène.

Ce volume témoigne d'un engagement continu à faire circuler l'information et les idées au-delà des barrières linguistiques au Canada. Jamais cette tâche n'a semblé aussi vitale. Faute d'une connaissance et d'une compréhension adéquates, les liens qui nous unissent en tant que pays sont en voie de s'éroder. Ceci nous expose aux préjugés et nous empêche de reconnaître les bénéfices que nous risquons de perdre en raison de notre inaction et de notre indifférence.

Il apparaît tout simplement que nous ne pouvons plus nous offrir le luxe de nous complaire à ignorer ce qui se passe ailleurs dans ce très grand pays. Si nous voulons continuer de former une nation, il nous faut aller au-delà des manchettes et démontrer une plus grande ouverture face à nos préoccupations et aspirations mutuelles.

Ce besoin a été l'un des principaux motifs de la décision de l'Institut de publier l'étude éclairée produite récemment par Christian Dufour au sujet des relations entre le Québec et le reste du pays. Cette étude a d'abord paru en français en 1990, sous le titre *Le défi québécois*, puis en anglais l'année suivante, sous le titre *The Canadian Challenge*. C'est également l'une des raisons principales qui nous amène à publier ce livre, *Canada, Adieu?*

Nous nous attendons à ce que la plupart des lecteurs de ce recueil trouvent provocantes et peut-être même tout à fait exaspérantes certaines des idées exprimées. Toutefois, nous sommes également convaincus que ces opinions constituent un point de départ pour le dialogue musclé qui seul pavera la voie vers une fédération renouvelée. Les faits ont beau parfois choquer, ils n'en demeurent pas moins indispensables à la recherche de solutions.

La géographie du pays dicte aussi certaines obligations. Pour les quelques Canadiens de Bull Harbour (Colombie-Britannique) qui attendaient que les grands vents se calment suffisamment pour leur permettre de contourner Cap Scott, à l'extrême-ouest du Canada, la Fête du Canada de 1991 a offert une autre occasion de méditer sur les privilèges dont les Canadiens bénéficient. Le débarquement sur l'autre rive, à Yuquot (baptisée «Friendly Cove» par le capitaine Cook en raison de l'accueil qu'il y a reçu à son arrivée) ne fait que renforcer ce sentiment. C'est à cet endroit qu'en 1792, le chef Maquinna signa, avec les capitaines Cook d'Angleterre et Quadra d'Espagne, la Convention de Nootka. Celle-ci permettait l'exploration de cette côte dans un esprit de coopération et d'harmonie, et non de concurrence et de conflit. Dans un tel décor, il est difficile de croire que les Canadiens, si choyés par la terre et bénis des dieux, puissent manquer à leur responsabilité d'aplanir les différences plutôt modestes qui les divisent actuellement.

Officiellement, le Canada est une assez jeune nation, mais s'inspire des traditions anciennes. En tant que Canadiens, nous avons encore la capacité de démontrer que toutes ces traditions, autochtone et moderne, européenne et orientale, française et anglaise, peuvent être respectées, grâce à un effort commun empreint de coopération et d'harmonie. L'Institut espère que ce livre pourra contribuer à la compréhension et à la reconnaissance plus poussées qu'exige la réalisation de cet objectif.

Rod Dobell
Juillet 1991

TABLE OF CONTENTS

FOREWORD

GLOSSARY OF ACRONYMS

INTRODUCTION   1

1. INDEPENDENCE vs. FEDERALISM — PARTIES STAKE
   OUT POSITIONS   35
   PQ: A sovereign Quebec in a global village   35
   BQ: Full sovereignty is a precondition to any
      new agreement with Canada   45
   PLQ: A Quebec free to choose (Allaire Report)   49
   NDP (Phillip Edmonston): A possible Canada   60
   NPD-Québec: For a constituent assembly   69
   PLC (Jean Chrétien): Independence fails the
      fundamental tests   71

2. BUSINESS DEBATES COSTS, BENEFITS OF
   SOVEREIGNTY AND FEDERALISM   81
   Chambre de commerce: Canadian federalism is an
      economic failure   82
   Mouvement Desjardins: From a distinct national society
      to a sovereign State of Quebec   89
   Association des manufacturiers: We must regain
      our competitive edge   100
   Quebec Economists (ASDEQ): Globalization modifies
      role of nation-state   104
   Conseil du Patronat: The dangers of sovereignty   114

3. LABOUR, FARM GROUPS EXPLAIN SUPPORT
   OF SOVEREIGNTY   120
   FTQ: Our progression toward sovereignty   121
   CSN: A clear choice: the independence of Quebec   127
   CEQ: Canadian federalism an obstacle to Quebec   139
   UPA: Canadian federalism has had its day   150

4. WOMEN IN THE DISTINCT SOCIETY   158
   FFQ: Women need the greatest possible
      political autonomy for Quebec   159
   CSF: Women in Quebec and English Canada —
      Two different conceptions of the state   165

5. QUEBEC'S FIRST NATIONS STATE THEIR CASE 180
AFN: We have never surrendered our sovereignty 185
Attikamek-Montagnais Council: For an equal
    relationship between our peoples 191
Nunavik Constitutional Committee: For a single
    non-ethnic government in Inuit territory 195
PQ: A new social contract with native peoples 201

6. ANGLOPHONES SEEK THEIR PLACE 205
Alliance Quebec: A place for all Quebecers 209
Equality Party: Quebec has violated a
    social contract 213

7. STATUS OF FRENCH AND FRANCOPHONES IN
QUEBEC — PROGRESS AND PERILS 218
André Raynauld: The progress of Francophones 218
MNQ: Demographic decline a burning issue 229

8. IMMIGRATION AND THE CLASH OF CULTURES 235
CEQ: Goal is integration, not assimilation
    in a French but multi-ethnic Quebec 237
CSN: Integration means more than learning French 243
Minorités ethniques et raciales: Redefining Quebec
    to encompass racial and ethnic minorities 245
Jacques Henripin: Is the Constitution the problem? 248
Fatima Houda-Pepin: Give some content to
    independence 251

9. QUEBEC'S FRUSTRATING STRUGGLE FOR
 A SECULAR SCHOOL SYSTEM 253
MÉMO: Repeal of s. 93 an urgent priority 256
RSC: Sectarian schools are a fundamental right 258
MLQ: Allophones are anglicized by sectarian schools 261
CEQ favours single secular school system 265

10. FRANCOPHONES OUTSIDE QUEBEC REDEFINE
THEIR RELATIONSHIP 267
FFHQ: A new departure, as partners 269

REPORT OF THE COMMISSION ON THE POLITICAL
AND CONSTITUTIONAL FUTURE OF QUEBEC 282

Appendix: Excerpts from *Constitution Act, 1867* and
    Constitution Act, 1982 319

GLOSSARY OF ACRONYMS

ADISQ   Association du disque, de l'industrie du spectacle québécois et de la vidéo - Quebec record, performance and video industry association
ASDEQ   Association des économistes québécois - Association of Quebec economists
BCNI   Business Council on National Issues
BNA Act British North America Act (now Constitution Act, 1867)
BQ   Bloc québécois
CDP   Commission des droits de la personne - (Quebec) Human rights commission
CDPQ   Caisse de dépôt et placement du Québec - Quebec deposit and investment fund
CÉCM   Commission des écoles catholiques de Montréal - Montreal Catholic school board
CEQ   Centrale de l'enseignement du Québec - Quebec education central (teachers' union)
CFQ   Coopérative fédérée du Quebec - Federated co-operative of Quebec
CLSC   Centre local de services communautaires - Local Community Service Centre
CPQ   Conseil du Patronat du Québec - Quebec employers' council
CSD   Centrale des syndicats démocratiques - Central of democratic unions
CSN   Confédération des syndicats nationaux - Confederation of National Trade Unions
EEC   European Economic Community
FFHQ   Fédération des francophones hors Québec - Federation of Francophones outside Quebec (now Fédération des communautés francophones et acadiennes du Canada)
FTA   [Canada-U.S.] Free Trade Agreement
FTQ   Fédération des travailleurs et travailleuses du Québec - Quebec Federation of Labour

GATT	General Agreement on Tariffs and Trade
IMF	International Monetary Fund
IQOP	Institut québécois d'opinion publique - Quebec institute of public opinion
MÉMO	Mouvement pour une école moderne et ouverte - Movement for modern and open schools
MNA	Member of the (Quebec) National Assembly
MNQ	Mouvement national des Québécoises et Québécois
MQF	Mouvement Québec français
NATO	North Atlantic Treaty Organization
NORAD	North American Air Defence Command
OAS	Organization of American States
OECD	Organization for Economic Co-operation and Development
PME	Petites et moyennes entreprises - small and medium sized firms
PQ	Parti québécois
PSBGM	Protestant School Board of Greater Montreal
RADQ	Régie de l'assurance-dépôts du Québec - Quebec Deposit Insurance Board (QDIB)
RSC	Rassemblement scolaire confessionnel - Union for denominational schools
SDI	Société de développement industriel du Québec - Quebec industrial development corporation
SIDBEC	Sidérurgie du Québec - Quebec iron and steel industry
SOQUEM	Société québécoise d'exploration minière - Quebec mining exploration corporation
SOQUIA	Société québécoise d'initiatives agro-alimentaires - Quebec food and agriculture initiatives corporation
SOQUIP	Société québécoise d'initiatives pétrolières - Quebec petroleum initiatives corporation
SPEQ	Société de placements dans l'entreprise québécoise - Quebec business investment corporation
SSJB	Société Saint-Jean Baptiste - St. John the Baptist Society
UCC	Union des cultivateurs catholiques - Catholic farmers union (now UPA)
UN	United Nations
UPA	Union des producteurs agricoles - Union of farm producers (formerly UCC)

INTRODUCTION

It would be hard to imagine another moment that so aptly captured the contradictory forces in the Canadian body politic.

Hours before, the Manitoba legislature had adjourned without endorsing an agreement the country's Prime Minister had promised would bring Quebec back into the constitutional fold "with honour and enthusiasm". The Meech Lake Accord had expired, and with it the attempt to win the hearts and minds of Quebecers by inserting a few words into the Constitution identifying their province as a "distinct society".

Yet, in the streets of Montreal, tens of thousands of Quebecers joyously celebrated the Accord's demise, carrying *fleur-de-lys* flags and banners proclaiming "Quebec — Our Only Country". It was June 24, Quebec's national holiday. Meech Lake was dead, but the Quebec nationalist movement was alive and well. Polls indicated for the first time that a majority of Quebecers supported sovereignty.

The Meech Lake Accord had effectively died a few days earlier when Elijah Harper, a Manitoba Cree leader and member of the provincial legislature, lifted an eagle feather and said "No", refusing unanimous consent on a motion to adopt the Accord. There was something appropriate about a native person giving the Accord the *coup de grâce*. After all, it referred to the existence of the descendants of the French and English speaking colonizers as a "fundamental characteristic" of Canada, but gave no such recognition to the country's First Nations.

But the Accord — named after the lake at which the first ministers initially negotiated its terms — was the culmination of the so-called "Quebec round" in Canada's ongoing saga of constitutional bargaining. It was based on minimal conditions the Bourassa government had advanced for giving Quebec's formal approval to the 1982 Constitution. Now English Canada had rejected these terms, and polls suggested that a majority of Canadians outside

Quebec were unwilling to recognize Quebec as a distinct society. It was June 1990 and in Manitoba, the three-year process of provincial ratification of the Accord had finally ground to a halt.

In the following months, Quebec was plunged into a far-reaching debate on its relationship to Canada. The National Assembly appointed a Commission on the Political and Constitutional Future of Quebec, chaired by Michel Bélanger and Jean Campeau. The Commission met throughout the winter and, in late March 1991, tabled its report. It recommended that a referendum on sovereignty be held in 1992 and that, if the result were positive, Quebec should acquire the status of a sovereign state one year to the day after the date of the referendum.

Quebec at the centre of the crisis

With the demise of the Meech Lake Accord, a new phase opened in the crisis of the Canadian state. Quebec is at the centre of that crisis. An immense territory in the strategic heart of the country, it contains 25 percent of Canada's population. "A province not like the others", it is a nation with a distinct language, culture and deep historical roots going back more than a century prior to the Conquest of 1760. Over the last few decades it has been the engine behind the process of constitutional reform.

Other sectors of Canadian society are advancing claims for constitutional change. The native peoples in particular have a powerful case for constitutional recognition of their aboriginal and treaty rights. Western Canada and the Atlantic provinces are proposing changes in the parliamentary system to increase their regional weight. Others, such as the labour movement and women's organizations, are seeking to protect and extend their gains through constitutional entitlement.

But the present crisis will not be resolved short of satisfying Quebec's substantive claims for recognition as a distinct national society, whether this means the creation of a fully sovereign state of Quebec or some redistribution of powers within the existing parameters of the Canadian state.

This book is intended as a guide in helping to understand the nature and roots of this crisis. It gives a voice to those most able to articulate the concerns and issues confronting Quebec: the Quebecers themselves. It is comprised largely of selections from the written submissions to the Bélanger-Campeau Commission, with accompanying editorial notes to provide background and contextual information. As well, it includes the full text of the Commission's Report and Recommendations.

The Commission was established in September 1990 pursuant to an agreement between the governing Liberals and the opposition Parti québécois in the National Assembly. An enlarged committee of the legislature, it included Premier Robert Bourassa, Opposition leader Jacques Parizeau, 16 other members of the Assembly (9 Liberals, 6 *péquistes* and 1 from the Equality Party), and 18 non-MNAs from various sectors of the population. The latter group included the two co-chairmen — the former chairmen, respectively, of the National Bank and the province's powerful Caisse de dépôt et placement — as well as four representatives of business organizations; four leaders from the major union and farm organizations; two elected municipal officials; one representative from each of the education, cultural and cooperative sectors; and three Quebec members of the federal Parliament (one Conservative, one Liberal and Bloc québécois leader Lucien Bouchard).

In determining the composition of the Commission, the Assembly ignored widespread public demands to make it more representative of the Quebec population, in particular by including leaders of the native peoples, the ethnic communities and women's organizations. Nevertheless, the Commission was generally regarded as an authoritative selection of Quebec decision-makers, if not the population as a whole.

The Commission's mandate instructed it "to examine and analyze the political and constitutional status of Quebec and to make recommendations in respect thereof", and to report back to the Assembly by March 28, 1991. In late September the Commission issued a call for written submissions and in early November it began a series of public hearings that, over the next three months, took its members to 11 cities throughout the province.

Despite this tight schedule, more than 600 groups and individuals submitted briefs. The Commission heard oral submissions from 235 of these, as well as a further 32 presentations at a special Forum to hear the views of young people. The Commission made a point of inviting all native groups and organizations in the cultural communities that submitted briefs to appear before it. The public hearings were televised live and given extensive coverage in the mass media.

In addition, some 55 specialists in various fields contributed information at the request of the Commission. They included political scientists, legal scholars, economists, sociologists, demographers, geographers and members of the cultural, arts and literary communities. Most of these latter submissions were subsequently published in French by the Commission.

In its report, the Commission limits itself to three principal objectives: describing some of the highlights of the constitutional debate over the last three decades in particular; outlining the strategic options now facing Quebec — essentially a choice between issuing a unilateral declaration of sovereignty or seeking a renewed federal arrangement based on a negotiated redivision of powers with Ottawa; and suggesting a process by which to determine the appropriate option. Many readers will find its discussion of the options somewhat superficial. However, given the diverse composition of the Commission, the desire of most members to achieve some broad consensus, and the limited time it had available, it is doubtful that much more could have been achieved.

The presentations to the Commission covered a much broader range of concerns than is indicated in its report. The selections in this book are intended to reveal the diversity and scope of the issues discussed as well as their underlying rationales. The arguments are a striking manifestation of Quebec's evolution as a complex, highly developed and pluralistic society with a rich tradition of political debate — a distinct political culture that even now remains largely unknown to those outside the province.

Limitations of the sovereigntist-federalist paradigm

Because the Quebec debate poses such a fundamental challenge to the existing state structure, there is an understandable tendency to reduce it to a dispute between two camps of Francophone Quebecers, broadly defined as federalist and sovereigntist. Most federalists, in this paradigm or framework, argue that there is still some hope of reforming the structure of Canadian federalism to accommodate Quebec's national character. The sovereigntists argue that this objective is neither desirable nor necessary, and many submit that such an enterprise is impossible; they point to the Meech debacle as proof.

This bifurcation was reflected in the Commission's composition (almost equally balanced between "sovereigntists" and "federalists") and in the hearings, when the point of much of the questioning by both sides was to encourage witnesses to declare their sympathies for one or the other option.

However, this polarized image can be misleading. The debate within Quebec is not only about Quebec's relationship to Canada. It is also a debate over the nature of Quebec's society, and the future development of that society.

Many of the issues discussed in the briefs to the Commission, while relevant to the Constitution, do not fit neatly within the sovereigntist-federalist paradigm. Typical issues involve the native Francophone majority's relationship with Quebec's aboriginal population, its ethno-cultural minorities, the Anglophone population, and the Francophones outside Quebec. There are significant differences among both the sovereigntists and the federalists concerning the appropriate approach to these issues.

Similarly, the broad nationalist spectrum that embraces the sovereigntists and most of the federalists is not socially homogeneous; positions on the national question are coloured by social and class distinctions. For example, within the sovereigntist camp the Parti québécois' enthusiasm for unfettered markets is not fully shared by the major union centrals.

Furthermore, the respective camps are not clearly defined even on the issue of constitutional status. Breakdowns of the 1980 referendum vote indicated that a significant number of those voting Yes did not consider themselves sovereigntists but wished to reinforce Quebec's bargaining position in subsequent negotiations, while many of those voting No were responding to promises by the then Prime Minister that a No vote would result in significant constitutional changes to accommodate Quebec's needs.

Reducing the debate to a sovereigntist-federalist conflict tends to put the focus on conceptual approaches rather than substantive grievances, and can blind one to important nuances within each camp. For example, when the Quebec Liberal party released the Allaire report in January 1991, many English-Canadian commentators were shocked at its call for a fundamental redistribution of powers. Having classified Bourassa and his party in the federalist camp, they had ignored the potential impact of Quebec's powerful sovereigntist sentiment within that camp. Likewise, some were slow to perceive the essentially federalist thrust of the report.[1]*

In fact, the vast majority of Quebec Francophones are nationalist to varying degrees, and many waver in the strategic choice between sovereignty and federalism. The ambiguity is reflected in the Bélanger-Campeau recommendation that both options be explored, while maintaining sovereignty as a tenable course of action failing a satisfactory reform of the system.

Finally, a minority of Quebecers — predominantly Anglophones, but some Francophones as well — believes that the existing constitutional set-up is sufficiently responsive to Quebec's needs to obviate the need for any major constitutional change.

---

* Notes are located at the end of this Introduction, p. 32.

A discussion of fundamentals

Many non-Quebecers have expressed dismay at the apparent "escalation" in Quebec's constitutional agenda in the wake of the Meech Lake defeat. In 1985, they note, Premier Bourassa's conditions were quite limited: recognition of Quebec as a distinct society; broader powers in immigration; a limit on the federal government's power to spend within areas of Quebec's exclusive jurisdiction; Quebec participation in the appointment of judges to the Supreme Court of Canada; and changes in the constitutional amending procedure. It was the most limited list of demands Quebec had presented in more than two decades of constitutional talks. Why, then, could Bourassa come back in 1991 with a list of 22 powers to be held exclusively by Quebec, and only four to be left to Ottawa's sole jurisdiction?

The 1985 conditions, which were incorporated in the Meech Lake Accord, were of course cast in the framework of the 1982 Constitution. To most Quebecers, the lesson of the Meech defeat is the impossibility of adjusting the 1982 Constitution to incorporate even Quebec's minimal demands, let alone acknowledge and reflect Quebec's character as a distinct national society. After Meech, then, the framework of the discussion has changed. We are no longer talking about a piecemeal revision of the 1982 Constitution. It is now a discussion of fundamentals.

This might not be evident from a reading of some of the submissions to the Bélanger-Campeau Commission, which focus their critique of the federal system on specific constitutional provisions, or in some cases simply policies and priorities currently followed by the federal government. For example, many briefs, particularly those of business groups, object at length to the duplication of programs and the imposition of "national" (pan-Canadian) standards that result from joint federal-provincial jurisdiction or federal intrusion in areas of exclusive Quebec jurisdiction; many declaim against federal fiscal policies that inflate government deficits and the public debt. By themselves, these objections hardly amount to a convincing refutation of the federal system *per se*; they might, in fact, find a sympathetic echo in any government, in Quebec or English Canada, concerned with reducing its expenditures. Thus they are not to be ignored as potential points on any agenda to rework the current federal system.

But it would be a trivialization of the debate to reduce it to these specific points. The nationalist critique of the federal regime is rooted in a perception that Quebec society is evolving in a fundamentally different direction from the rest of Canada, and that the

Canadian constitution, based on an inflexible centralizing logic, is not only unable to accommodate Quebec's approach but also constitutes an intolerable fetter on its further development as a distinct nation. The analysis is part historical, part conjunctural.

An asymmetrical federal system

The constitutional basis of the federal regime as we know it is set out in the *British North America Act* of 1867.[2] A compromise between the unitary conception of government favoured by many Ontario politicians of the time, such as Sir John A. Macdonald, and the federal conception upheld by Quebecers in particular, the BNA Act indirectly recognized Quebec's distinctive character while not expressly acknowledging it or granting the province special status. For example, Quebec was allowed to retain its distinctive system of civil law; it was not subject to the federal government's power to provide for the uniformity of laws governing property and civil rights in the other constituent provinces (s. 94); and the use of French (as well as English) in the federal Parliament and the Quebec legislature was constitutionally protected (s. 133). The system established at Confederation was not a "confederal" system in the strict sense, that is, "an association in which sovereign states are joined together by a pact or treaty, or a constitution, in which they delegate specific limited authority . . . to a central agency."[3] But it was an *asymmetrical* federal system; indeed, the assignment to all the provinces of exclusive jurisdiction over specified matters of a "local or private nature" was itself a partial reflection of Quebec's insistence on maintaining limited autonomy in the new federal structure. The federal government, of course, retained key powers in such matters as trade and commerce, money and banking, the criminal law and the military.

The Bélanger-Campeau Report states: "From Quebec's standpoint, the Canadian federal regime was based at the outset on the Canadian duality and the autonomy of the provinces." This is debatable. The Constitution, in its literal terms, gave the central state paramountcy in some areas of concurrent jurisdiction (immigration, agriculture and, later, interprovincial exports of non-renewable natural resources, forestry resources and electrical energy); the central government held the residual power to occupy new fields of jurisdiction, the emergency power to enact laws in the interests of the "peace, order and good government of Canada", and the power to declare "works and undertakings" wholly within a province to be for the general advantage of Canada and hence under its jurisdiction; in addition, the central government appointed the provincial lieutenant governors, who were empowered to "reserve" provincial legislation for assent by the governor general (i.e., the federal cabinet) and held the power to disallow provincial legislation. (The powers of reservation and disallowance, once used extensively, have fallen into disuse.)[4]

In short, it was a relatively centralized system that nonetheless allowed Quebec to operate in French, with its own educational and legal systems and cultural institutions. And, over the years, the "provincial autonomy" thesis gained some currency from successive rulings of the Judicial Committee of the British Privy Council (until 1949, the highest court of appeal on constitutional matters) that tended to give an expansive interpretation to the provinces' powers in opposition to federal attempts to whittle down and restrict their jurisdiction. In Quebec, politicians, jurists and historians regarded this Constitution as a "pact" — sometimes described as an agreement between the provinces and the federal government, more often as between two distinct "races" or ethnic groups (now described as nations), the descendants of the French and English colonizers.

Adverse legal rulings notwithstanding, a trend toward centralization within the federal system became evident in the early 20th century. It was enormously facilitated by the two world wars. During the first, the federal government entered the corporate and personal income tax fields. Following the war, it instituted conditional funding programs in health and education, and later an old age pension system (Quebec being the last province to join, in 1936). Then, during the Second World War, a national unemployment insurance system was implemented, with provincial agreement, followed in 1945 by family allowances. As the welfare state took shape, Ottawa moved into such areas as natural resources, transport, agriculture and vocational training, using the administrative techniques of shared-cost programs and conditional funding. In the 1950s it introduced the equalization program as a mechanism to redistribute wealth, and a shared-cost hospital insurance program. Quebec reluctantly went along with most of these measures, while protesting the incursions and limitations on its provincial autonomy. Throughout this period the province was governed by an extremely conservative administration with a strong ideological bias against state-operated social programs.

Quiet Revolution: Quebec wields its jurisdiction

In the 1960s, under the new Liberal government, Quebec abandoned its traditional opposition to state intervention and began using its powers under the Constitution to enact the major reforms associated with the "Quiet Revolution": the modernization of its education system, the development of health and social service programs; the establishment of a limited international presence; the formation of powerful publicly owned corporations in key economic sectors that contributed greatly to the development of an indigenous Francophone capitalist class; and, not least, successively more rigorous language laws declaring French the sole official language in the province. By enhancing the status of French and Francophones in Quebec, these reforms helped to overcome some of the substantial disparities in income and economic conditions that had historically characterized French-English relations in Quebec.[5]

The Quiet Revolution spurred Quebec to seek increased constitutional powers and resist what it saw as federal incursions into its existing areas of jurisdiction. The Allaire Report describes its objectives:

> In its relations with the federal government, Québec wanted to end federal encroachment in areas of provincial jurisdiction. It demanded that residual powers not explicitly assigned to the federal government be left to the provinces. Québec also demanded greater power in agriculture, social services, regional development and immigration. It claimed jurisdiction over radio and television broadcasting and maintained that Québec's communications policy was inseparable from cultural development and education. Finally, Québec wanted to make its voice heard in the international community, particularly within La Francophonie.
>
> Clearly, Québec was not only defending its areas of jurisdiction and claiming greater autonomy, but was demanding a distinct status within the federation. In this way, it was clearly setting itself apart from the other provinces. It affirmed itself as a distinct society with a strong national state, responsible for the development of its population.[6]

Although Quebec was unsuccessful in winning new constitutional powers, Ottawa initially demonstrated some responsiveness to its needs. For example, in 1964 it introduced a formula under which the provinces could "opt out" of certain federally funded programs without financial penalty. Quebec was the only province to avail itself of this provision, opting out of no less than 28 national programs in that year alone. Instead of participating in the Canada Pension Plan, it established its own plan and administered the funds through its own Caisse de dépôt et placement, which played an instrumental role in funding many Quebec businesses.

Opting out was typical of the federal response to Quebec's demands: an administrative adjustment, formally applying to all provinces, and thus not signifying any special constitutional recognition of Quebec's particular character.

Trudeau's counter-strategy: linguistic "equality"

However, while most Francophone Quebecers were turning to the provincial "state" to affirm their identity, an alternative strategy was taking shape, designed to counter the centrifugal dynamic of Quebec's emerging nationalism with a new Canadian nationalism that sought to locate the Francophone future in a bilingual Canada. Its most prominent exponent was Pierre Trudeau, who outlined some of the main elements in his thinking shortly before entering federal politics:

> One way of offsetting the appeal of separatism is by investing tremendous amounts of time, energy and money in nationalism, *at the federal level*. A national image must be created that will have such an appeal as to make any image of a separatist group unattractive. Resources must be diverted into such things as national flags, anthems, education, arts councils, broadcasting corporations, film boards; the territory must be bound together by a network of railways, highways, airlines; the national culture and the national economy must be protected by taxes and tariffs; ownership of resources and industry by nationals must be made a matter of policy. In short, the whole of the citizenry must be made to feel that it is only within the framework of the federal state that their language, culture, institutions, sacred traditions and standard of living can be protected from external attack and internal strife.[7]

This vision of the state was firmly fixed as federal government policy by the time Trudeau became Prime Minister, in 1968. A key piece in the edifice was the policy of official "bilingualism". The *Official Languages Act* (the OLA), enacted in 1969, guaranteed the "equality of status" of the French and English languages in federal institutions and agencies. At the same time, efforts were stepped up to increase francophone representation in the federal civil service and crown corporations.

The official languages legislation was quite limited in scope. It was declaratory in nature, with no enforcement mechanism other than a commissioner, who monitored the operation of the Act and investigated complaints without power of sanction. And its focus on the language of federal services did little to assist the Francophone communities outside Quebec struggling to build and control their own schools and other institutions in the face of public indifference and opposition from provincial governments.[8] Thus, from the beginning, Trudeau linked official "bilingualism" with attempts to constrain the provinces through constitutional entrenchment of French and English minority language rights and language of education rights. This was ultimately achieved in 1982 through the patriation of the Constitution and the adoption of a *Charter of Rights and Freedoms* that incorporated language rights as well as much else.

The significance of the official languages legislation may have been primarily symbolic. But it spoke to a real problem: the historic lack of recognition of French in the federal state. It is easy to forget today just how *English* the central government was until comparatively recently. French Canadians had to fight tenaciously for such modest recognition of their existence as bilingual postage stamps (first issued in 1927), bilingual money (in 1935), and bilingual federal government cheques (in the early 1960s). The BNA Act provided no protection for French-language rights in provinces other than Quebec.[9] The only reference to language in the *Canadian Bill of Rights*, adopted in 1960, was to the right of a party or witness in court proceedings to have an interpreter.

In Quebec, affirmative action for French

Ottawa's promotion of official "bilingualism and biculturalism", and later "multiculturalism", had little appeal in Francophone Quebec, where an overwhelmingly unilingual Anglophone minority enjoyed a relatively privileged position and "bilingualism" was a requirement largely imposed on Francophones. For example, 1971 data indicated that 36 percent of the French-speaking labour force in Quebec — in Montreal 54 percent — were obliged to speak English on the job.[10] This reflected a substantial ethnic bias in Quebec society. The federal Royal Commission on Bilingualism and Biculturalism had reported that in 1961 the average income of a French-speaking Canadian was only 80 percent (and within Quebec, only 65 percent) that of a Canadian of British origin. French-speaking Quebecers experienced a higher unemployment rate and were less educated than the English. Their hospitals, schools and universities were of inferior quality.[11]

This ethnic bias reflected, of course, a national and class bias: for example, the fact that the majority of Quebec's manufacturing and resources industries were controlled by non-Quebec interests. In 1961, 38 percent of the workforce were employed by firms owned by Anglophone Canadians; another 15 percent were employed by

non-Canadian interests. About 20 percent were employed in
businesses controlled by Francophones, concentrated in such
manufacturing sectors as shoes, textiles, clothing and furniture, and
characterized by declining markets, low productivity and low wages.
The remainder were in the public sector or agriculture. Among the
members of the Canadian "economic élite", as defined by sociologist
John Porter, only 51 (6.7 percent) were French Canadians.[12]

The federal language legislation failed to address these problems
in the socio-economic structure of Quebec. Indeed, its even-handed
promotion of both French and English, which ignored the real
inequality of status between French and English in Canada, worked
to the advantage of Quebec's relatively concentrated English-
speaking minority. In 1980 the Commissioner of Official Languages
reported that "leaving aside the National Capital Region, there are
about 19,000 bilingual positions [in the federal government] to
accommodate the English-speaking minority in Quebec but less than
7,000 to look after a broadly comparable number of Francophones
in all the other provinces."[13]

In contrast to the formal equality granted French and English
under Ottawa's approach, Quebec's language legislation sought to
promote the use of French through affirmative action. The major
statute, the *Charter of the French Language* (Law 101), enacted in
1977, made French the sole official language in Quebec and
formally guaranteed the right of everyone in Quebec to communicate with public agencies and businesses in French, to work in
French, to be served in French and to be educated in French. It
applied to the private sector as well as government, and set out
specific goals and time limits for "francising" companies employing
50 or more employees — ensuring that French-speaking employees
could work in French. It contained a detailed regulatory scheme and
was enforceable by sanctions and court orders. Its exceptions (such
as for native peoples) were carefully spelled out.

Quebec's law reflected a view of language as critical to the
definition of a distinct nation. As the White Paper introducing Law
101 put it, "The French language is not just a means for expression,
but a medium for living as well."[14] The federal bilingualism policy,
in contrast, separated language from nation. It reflected a concept
of Canada as a nation of different linguistic communities, united on
the basis of a fictional equality of these communities that had little
to do with the reality.

Parts of Law 101 — in particular, provisions making French the
sole language of the legislature and courts, and the ban on signs in
languages other than French — have been ruled unconstitutional

by the courts. But key provisions such as the francization of businesses remain in force and have in some cases been extended.

Unilateral patriation: the noose tightens

Tensions ebbed and flowed between Ottawa and Quebec City throughout the sixties and seventies, but stepped up dramatically with the surprise election of the pro-sovereignty Parti québécois government in 1976. The PQ promptly enacted Law 101 and prepared for the Referendum on sovereignty-association, which was held in May 1980.

The Referendum and its immediate aftermath constitute something of a watershed in recent constitutional history. It was the first time the people of Quebec had been given a formal opportunity to express themselves specifically on Quebec's constitutional status. The question put to the voters read:

> The government of Quebec has made public its proposal to negotiate a new agreement with the rest of Canada, based on the equality of nations;
>
> This agreement would enable Quebec to acquire the exclusive powers to make its laws, levy its taxes and establish relations abroad — in other words, sovereignty — and at the same time to maintain with Canada an economic association including a common currency.
>
> No change in political status resulting from these negotiations will be effected without approval by the people through another referendum; on these terms do you give the Government of Quebec the mandate to negotiate the proposed agreement between Quebec and Canada?[15]

The No side won with about 60 percent of the vote, the Anglophone population voting in the negative almost as a bloc. Ottawa saw its opening; Trudeau could now proceed with another prong of his strategy.

Addressing a large rally in Montreal toward the end of the Referendum campaign, Trudeau had made "a most solemn commitment" that "following a 'No' vote we will immediately take action to renew the constitution."

> And I make a solemn declaration to all Canadians in the other provinces: we, the Quebec MPs, are laying ourselves on the line, because we are telling Quebecers to vote "No" and telling you in the other provinces that we will not agree to your interpreting a "No" vote as an indication that everything is fine and can remain as it was before.
>
> We want change and we are willing to lay our seats in the House on the line to have change.[16]

It was not much, but the statement was widely interpreted in Quebec as an undertaking to go some way to meeting Quebec's demands for a redistribution of powers. However, as Ottawa moved in the following months to patriate the Constitution, it soon became evident that it was prepared to proceed unilaterally if necessary — and in the face of Quebec's proposals.

Quebec, its negotiating position weakened by the Referendum defeat, formed a bloc with the other provinces in a desperate attempt to shape an outcome that would protect its interests and restrain a shift of powers in Ottawa's favour. One tactic involved referrals by some provinces to the courts to test the constitutionality of Ottawa's moves.

In the end, the Supreme Court ruled that unilateral patriation was legal although contrary to constitutional convention. Then, in the last-minute horsetrading among the first ministers, Quebec was abandoned by its erstwhile provincial partners and the deal was done. As the Bélanger-Campeau Report indicates, and a number of briefs illustrate, Quebecers had many reasons to object to the 1982 arrangements: an inflexible amending formula that removed Quebec's traditional veto; a *Charter of Rights and Freedoms* specifically designed to invalidate parts of Law 101; recognition of Canada's "multicultural heritage" but not of the French-English duality, etc. But what was most galling to Quebec was the simple fact that Canada had ratified a major change in the Constitution without Quebec's consent and despite a nearly unanimous resolution of its National Assembly opposing unilateral patriation. Whatever it had been in the past, it was now clear that Confederation was not a "pact".

Something more was involved, as well. The Bélanger-Campeau report points to a number of features in the 1982 arrangements that reflected a fundamentally different view of the country: the concept of formal equality of individual citizens and provinces that is difficult, if not impossible, to reconcile with the idea of Quebec's distinct national identity. As the Commission states:

> The vision of an exclusive national Canadian identity emphasizes the centralization of powers and the existence of a strong "national" government. This vision appears to have a levelling effect: an exclusive national Canadian identity centred on the equality of individuals actually becomes a prohibition for Quebec to be different as a society. It also overlooks the actual inequality, within Canada, of both linguistic majorities and their respective members.

Charter challenge to Quebec

The *Canadian Charter of Rights and Freedoms* was a central element in the 1982 patriation and has since been at the centre of constitutional discourse in Canada. So it is worth taking a closer look at its rationale and impact. Trudeau's overriding goal, as noted, was to reinforce his concept of a bilingual Canada as a counterweight to Quebec nationalism through constitutional entrenchment of minority language rights, immunizing them in effect from provincial interference. Unable to do this without some measure of provincial consent, he proposed to do so through a constitutionally entrenched bill of rights, which would cover much more than language and, unlike its existing namesake, would be binding on the provinces as well as Ottawa. The idea had been discussed at previous federal-provincial conferences, and a draft Charter was even adopted at Victoria in 1971. However, the patriation package then agreed to by the first ministers foundered when Premier Bourassa, faced with a tidal wave of opposition in Quebec, had to withdraw his support.

Now, a decade later, Ottawa built its patriation strategy around the Charter, using it to win public support for proceeding even in the face of provincial opposition. Its task was facilitated by the tendency of many Canadians to confuse the proposed Charter with the immensely popular human rights codes enacted by most provinces during the 1970s. These provincial statutes outlaw discrimination on specific grounds of race, sex, age, etc. by private persons — employers, landlords, suppliers of goods and services — the major offenders against civil liberties. They are enforced by independent commissions with investigations officers, mediation services and administrative tribunals (often staffed by non-lawyers) with the power to sanction offenders. Their services are easily accessed through filing a complaint.

Quebec's *Charter of Human Rights and Freedoms*, in fact, was and is one of the most progressive in the country; for example, unlike many such codes, it prohibits discrimination on grounds of sexual orientation and political belief.

Ottawa's Charter, in contrast, is aimed against government action, not private action. It empowers judges to review, invalidate and overrule legislation and government action, in most instances on grounds of general principles that leave considerable leeway to judicial interpretation. Its provisions cannot be invoked without launching costly and usually lengthy court proceedings. It does not apply to discriminatory and inegalitarian acts by private persons.

Most Charter rights are abstractly stated: "Everyone has . . . freedom of conscience and religion", etc. On one issue, however, the Charter is not at all abstract. The provisions on official languages and minority language educational rights are specific and detailed; one critic has compared them with a taxation statute.[17] The official-languages provisions in several places are explicitly applicable to New Brunswick (Ontario refused to be similarly included), and the educational provisions were specifically drafted to overrule certain provisions in Quebec's Law 101. And these provisions are not subject to the legislative override clause, s. 33, which permits a legislature or Parliament to exempt legislation from certain Charter provisions. Furthermore, under s. 41 of the *Constitution Act, 1982*, any amendment to the Constitution pertaining to the use of the English or French languages requires the unanimous consent of the provinces (unless it applies only to one province, in which case the federal Parliament has to agree). These features underscore the centrality of the language provisions in the total scheme of the Charter.

The minority language educational provisions suffered from the same conceptual flaw as the federal official-languages legislation. They treated French and English on an equal footing when in fact the respective language communities are in quite different situations. For example, s. 23 guaranteed a linguistic minority the right to schooling in its language where its numbers were sufficient. Francophone minorities in English Canada seeking to enforce their Charter right to their own schools and school boards had to go to court and convince judges that their numbers warranted such schools. In Quebec, however, the Anglophone minority already had such schools; s. 23 simply guaranteed them the right to continue using those schools, when no responsible political party in Quebec was proposing to abolish or curtail them.

But another provision in s. 23 was worded precisely to overrule Quebec's limitation of English-language instruction to the children of parents educated in English in Quebec, in other words the traditional Anglophone population of the province.[18] The Protestant school boards lost no time in using the Charter to mount a successful challenge of the Quebec provision.

There were other problems with the Charter, from Quebec's standpoint. Apart from the language provisions, its focus is on individual rights, which are difficult to reconcile (and sometimes conflict) with the collective action needed to combat cultural and national inequality. Methodologically, the Charter poses a challenge to Quebec's distinct legal system. Its abstract principles tend to elevate the judicial discretion favoured by the common law ("judge-made law") over the formal legal rules that characterize the civil law. Furthermore, it subjects Quebec's laws and government action to judicial scrutiny for compliance with a pan-Canadian Charter jurisprudence largely determined by judges unfamiliar with the civil law tradition.

In a brief to the Bélanger-Campeau Commission, Henri Brun, a leading constitutional lawyer, pointed to the Supreme Court of Canada's interpretation of the Charter as one of the reasons why, as he put it, a sovereign Quebec should, if it decided to "opt in" to some confederal arrangement with Canada, avoid entrusting the final level of judicial review to the Supreme Court of Canada. The Charter, he said, "markedly accentuated the uniformizing and centralizing role" of the Court.

> This role has now become equally judicial and political, and the Court exercises it without much restraint and without demonstrating much sensitivity to Quebec's cultural vulnerability. Its 1988 judgment on commercial signs and advertising is a good illustration of this.

Much of the commentary on the Charter has focused on the ways in which it altered the relationship between citizens and the state. But the Charter also altered the relationship between Quebec and the rest of the country. And, as a powerful weapon to constrain government action and legislation, the Charter and the legalized form of politics it exemplifies fit nicely with a developing trend toward downgrading the interventionist role of the state.

Deregulation and decentralization

The adoption of the 1982 Constitution without the consent of Quebec — Canada's only Francophone province, and the main impetus behind the movement for constitutional change — posed a major problem of legitimacy for the Canadian state. It also occurred at a time when a noticeable shift was developing in the dominant perception of the state's role in relation to the private sector in all of the major capitalist countries, including Canada. The long postwar phase of economic expansion had ended by the mid-1970s, giving way to slower growth accompanied by permanent inflationary pressures and high unemployment. Stagflation confronted governments with escalating deficits and debts and consequent pressures to cut spending on social programs, now a huge component of their budgets. Deregulation, privatization, greater reliance on "market forces" and general "downsizing" of govern-

ment were the new catchphrases. Globalization was another, as
multinational corporations shifted trade and investment between
countries in a constant search for higher profits. Countries sought
to position themselves for the new, more competitive international
environment by forming or joining trade blocs that gave them
preferred access to larger markets.

These themes have played an increasing role in Canada's constitutional debate. Over the last decade or so, Quebec's demands for
autonomy have been used to fuel support for a realignment of the
federation that would retain a key role for the central government
as the guarantor of the economic unity of the Canadian state, while
assigning a greater role in the administration and funding of social
and cultural matters to the provinces, deemed more "responsive" to
market imperatives.

These ideas were given some currency in 1979 in the report of
the Pepin-Robarts Task Force on Canadian Unity. The Task Force
called for a new Canadian constitution that would recognize "the
distinctiveness of Quebec". But it rejected giving Quebec any special
powers, preferring instead "to allot to all provinces powers in the
areas needed by Quebec to maintain its distinctive culture and
heritage. . .".[19] It also favoured granting the provinces the residual
power to occupy new fields of competence that is now held by the
federal Parliament, and recommended that government spending
powers be subject to constitutional limits. The Task Force's
proposals were ignored by the Trudeau government, but attracted
some support from then Conservative leader Joe Clark, who
borrowed from them in his vision of Canada as a "community of
communities".

Some of these ideas resurfaced in 1985 in the report of the Royal
Commission on the Economic Union and Development Prospects
for Canada (the Macdonald Commission). This time they were more
explicitly linked with a program to restructure the state to make it
more responsive to "market forces" and the quest for international
competitiveness. The Commission is remembered chiefly for its
advocacy of a Canada-U.S. free trade agreement, the cornerstone of
its recommendations. But it also outlined a strategy to overcome
"the major unresolved community issue in Canada today . . .
constitutional *rapprochement*" between Quebec and the rest of
Canada.

The Macdonald strategy involved a "symbolic" (as it said)
recognition of "Canada's basic duality" and of Quebec as "a distinct
society", largely as a way to obviate the need for further constitutional amendments: "the problems arising from Quebec's distinctive

character . . . would not, for the most part, necessitate constitutional changes. Some problems could be adequately dealt with through intergovernmental agreements, others through delegation of power." Thus, the Commission proposed that the Constitution be amended to allow the transfer of power from one level of government to another through intergovernmental accords that would be binding on successor governments.

The Commission's operative approach was based on what it called "the principle of the equality of provinces". Thus, it recommended that not just Quebec but *all provinces* be given the right to opt out of constitutional changes that transfer powers to Ottawa, and that the conditions governing shared-cost programs between the federal government and the provinces be "stated in terms of goals or ends" in order to maximize "flexibility and opportunities to innovate".[20]

At the same time the Macdonald Commission stressed the importance of the central state as the guardian of the Canadian common market, and noted the unifying ideological role of the new *Charter of Rights and Freedoms*: "[T]he Charter links citizens with the constitutional order much more explicitly than ever in our history."

The Macdonald proposals were in some ways the constitutional counterparts of free trade, deregulation and privatization. They reflected the view that the federal government's major responsibility with respect to economic development is to ensure the existence in Canada of common markets in capital, labour, and goods and services. Provincial barriers to these markets should be removed. Responsibility for the regulation of trade and commerce should be centralized as much as possible with one level of government in order to eliminate unnecessary duplication.

When Premier Bourassa listed his five conditions for giving Quebec's assent to the 1982 Constitution, they bore a close resemblance to these proposals. All of them found their way into the Meech Lake Accord. It gave symbolic recognition to Quebec as a distinct society while also recognizing the "principle of equality of all the provinces" in the proposed resolution for adoption by the legislatures. The new opting out clause was of general application. And any province choosing not to participate in a federal shared-cost program in an area of exclusive jurisdiction would receive "reasonable compensation" if it carried on a "program or initiative that is compatible with the national objectives".

Distinct society versus equality of provinces . . . and the Charter

The Accord's attempt to generalize opting out as a constitutional formula applicable to all provinces, when in the past it had been applied in practice only to Quebec, set off alarm bells among many critics. The opting out provisions were widely seen outside Quebec as a step toward the dismantling of major social programs. If a province could establish alternative programs deemed compatible with "national objectives", might it not interfere with the principle of universality, a keystone of the welfare state? Similarly, would cutbacks in one province serve as a benchmark for lowering standards in other provinces? These kinds of concerns were raised in particular in many submissions by trade unions to the Parliamentary committee studying the Accord in 1987.

For many critics, the linkage between these provisions and the "distinct society" clause lay in the principle of equality of the provinces. Because the Accord, like all previous constitutional arrangements, failed to acknowledge that Quebec was a distinct *national* entity and not just a province, it fed fears outside Quebec that any devolution to Quebec of powers over social and other programs would be matched by a corresponding increase in the fiscal liability of *all* provinces for federally-funded programs, to the detriment of "national" (federal) standards.

The concern was credible. Critics of the Accord noted that in recent years Ottawa has responded to its fiscal crisis by cutting back drastically in its annual per capita contributions to the provinces to help fund medicare and higher education programs. The 1991 federal budget extended the existing freeze on these payments to the 1994-95 fiscal year, after which payments will be 3 percentage points below increases in GNP. The National Council on Welfare estimates that by the year 2000 the federal contribution to these social programs will have been cut by close to $100 billion, and that by 2008 it will be making no cash contribution at all. The decline in Ottawa's cash payments deprives it of its most direct means of pressuring the provinces to comply with pan-Canadian "national" standards. Poorer provinces with a relatively low tax base will inevitably be inclined to lower standards and cut back on programs.[21]

Critics fear that a similar fate may befall other federal-provincial transfer programs, such as the Canada Assistance Plan, under which Ottawa assumes half the cost of public assistance expenditures, and a group of programs in such fields as social housing, native children's education, workforce training, bilingualism, student loans, the environment and regional economic development. And they point out that for almost 10 years now Ottawa has capped its annual "equalization" payments to the provinces, which are designed to allow the provinces to establish comparable public services regardless of differences in their respective resources and tax bases.

To the critics, Meech seemed to "constitutionalize" such practices. However, to Quebecers eager to "patriate" to the province full control over social programs, such criticisms had little weight.

These concerns about possible implications of the Accord intersected with those of critics who professed to see the "distinct society" clause as a threat to rights under the *Charter of Rights and Freedoms*. The Accord stated that nothing in it affected the constitutional rights of native peoples or the multicultural character of Canada. Why, it was asked, was there no such protection for the women's equality clause that women across Canada had fought for and obtained in 1981? A campaign was soon under way in English Canada to sink the Accord unless the "distinct society" clause was made subordinate to the Charter. A major feminist organization warned of the clause's "potential" for "misuse of population control in the name of preserving or promoting distinct populations".[22]

To many Quebecers, this campaign was profoundly insulting, as it seemed to imply that they were susceptible to oppressing women unless restrained by the federal constitution. It also misrepresented the reality; Quebec had probably the best record on women's rights of any province in Canada for some years before as well as after the advent of the Charter. Fundamentally, as the Quebec Conseil du statut de la femme state in their brief to Bélanger-Campeau, this dispute reflected deep differences over "the relationship between individual rights and a society's right to protect and promote its distinct character".[23]

Above all, the dispute indicated the extent to which Charter discourse had come to dominate political discourse on the national question in English Canada. In fact, the Charter has increasingly become the chosen benchmark among federalists for defining the limits to any recognition of Quebec as a "distinct society".

Supply-side sovereignty

The new emphasis on markets and "globalization" has been invoked by many Quebecers to press their case for greater autonomy. And it has given a decidedly conservative slant to the prevailing Quebec nationalism of today.

In their briefs to the Bélanger-Campeau Commission, business groups echoed many of the same themes that business sounds in

English Canada, but with a particular nationalist twist. Government deficits were denounced, but linked to the duplication of programs resulting from overlapping jurisdictions or federal invasions of provincial domains. There were demands for constitutional constraints on the spending and borrowing powers of governments, particularly the federal government. Some, like the Chambre de commerce, called for an end to equalization and transfer payments. There were many complaints that Quebec business is uncompetitive because of excessively high wages and overly generous social programs; the Liberals' Allaire report called for an "urgent reassessment of existing social programs", without being more specific.

A popular concept in Quebec, emphasized in many briefs, is *concertation*, or enduring collaborative arrangements between business, labour and sometimes grassroots community groups, with the government acting as a "facilitator" or partner. As the Allaire report puts it, "Quebeckers have succeeded in developing a unique degree of cooperation between the public and private sectors, in implementing a kind of Japanese-style cooperation between the political class, the labour movement and the business community." The Chambre de commerce sees concertation as a device to enhance competitiveness by implementing an incomes policy with labour support: "the economic partners collectively agree on acceptable annual inflation limits, which then serve as effective guidelines for wage bargaining and price increases."

Notwithstanding the right-wing bent of much of this material, the support concertation enjoys within the labour movement is striking. Two of the major union centrals, the FTQ and CSN, emphasized its centrality to their policies in their submissions to the Commission.

Concertation is a prominent fact of economic life in Quebec today. Leaders of the major union *centrales*, or federations, sit on a number of tripartite bodies and every region of the province has its concertation forums bringing together local unions, business people and municipal governments. A continuing body, the *Forum pour l'emploi* [Forum for jobs], includes the leaders of the union centrals, municipalities, the universities, and business lobbies like the Chambre de commerce on its board. It sponsors seminars to discuss how these various interests can work together.

Business interests see concertation as a vital tool to improve their competitiveness. Union leaders defend it as a means of achieving full employment. It is common now in Quebec for union leaders to hold news conferences and lobby jointly with business leaders on behalf of specific development projects or policies. A notable example is the campaign they have mounted on behalf of the giant Hydro-Québec dam construction project in northern Quebec, in the face of strong opposition from the native peoples and environmentalists.

A variation of concertation — and certainly the most striking example of business-labour-government collaboration in Quebec, and perhaps North America — is the FTQ's Fonds de Solidarité, or Solidarity Fund. Despite the name, it is actually a mutual fund that invests workers' savings in small and medium sized firms, including some venture capital operations. Contributions to the fund are tax-deductible, thanks to both the Quebec and federal governments.

National consciousness of Quebec workers

This multi-class perspective in the ideology of Quebec trade unions is a clear manifestation of the force of nationalism in Quebec society. The unions are the biggest and strongest social organizations in Quebec, representing 40 percent of the employed workforce. They have grown rapidly during the last 30 years, and have on occasion shown their capacity for militant economic struggle. But their political development has been completely independent of the English-Canadian labour movement's. For example, instead of moving to organize their own political party like the NDP (and in fact repelled by the latter's indifference or hostility to Quebec's national concerns), the Quebec unions were drawn in behind first the Liberals of the Quiet Revolution, then, after a hiatus in the late Sixties and early Seventies, the PQ. It was the PQ government's tripartite economic summits, indeed, that gave concertation its initial boost.

The nationalism of Quebec workers, which is reflected in the political positions of the unions, is, in a sense, an envelope for their democratic and social demands. It is deeply rooted in the political culture of their society, with its strong ties of kinship and community, and above all the consciousness of being a national minority in North America, and in particular Canada. Quebec workers feel the weight of the national question much more than other social classes; many feel it in linguistic exchanges with management on the plant floor, where francization programs have had only limited success, and they are well aware of the continuing importance of bilingualism to financial and social success.

After the Referendum defeat and the 1982 wage rollback of Quebec public employees by the PQ government, the unions took their distance of that party for a period. But their nationalism today appears to be stronger than ever, as demonstrated by the decisions

of all three major centrals in 1990, for the first time, to support
Quebec sovereignty.

There is today a kind of "union sacrée" — a holy alliance —
between the unions and more conservative nationalist forces within
Quebec society around the goal of sovereignty. The rather limited
social content in the unions' strategy may leave some readers
wondering what happened to the radical rhetoric once associated
with Quebec labour. The FTQ brief expresses the shift with perhaps
unintentional irony: "The *indépendantistes* of the Sixties wanted to
rid Quebec of underdevelopment. Today we want to be able to
develop in line with our interests without being obliged to discuss
each and every one of our ideas and initiatives."

A more rigorous examination of the issues, however, might
incline many Quebec trade unionists and their partners in the farm
movement to question the unbounded confidence in market forces
that has come to dominate the rhetoric of their nationalist allies.
The supply-side sovereigntists advocate wide-open markets and
complain about institutional "barriers to trade" between Quebec
and its trading partners, but it is worth asking what these barriers
comprise. Simon Reisman, Canada's chief negotiator in the 1980s
U.S. trade talks, says that among the major protectionist measures
objected to by the Americans were Quebec crown corporations such
as Hydro-Québec and the Caisse de dépôt et placement, and its farm
supply management programs.[24] The Macdonald report listed
Quebec's language laws, the Caisse's preferential subsidies to
Quebec francophone entrepreneurs, and the government's prohibition on the acquisition of a trust company by extra-provincial
interests as possible or actual barriers to trade.[25] Indeed, many of
the key measures Quebec took to promote the status of French and
Francophones during the Quiet Revolution constituted interference
with "market forces". Is it so secure now that it can envisage
dispensing with such instruments of sovereignty?

However, as long as Quebecers, as a nation, feel isolated and
unrecognized within Canadian federalism, any far-reaching debate
within Quebec society on social issues, or a *projet de société*, is
probably precluded. For the moment, at least, such issues are
subsumed within the national question and the national — not class
— polarization it entails.

Economic union/political union

Many Quebec nationalists appear to assume that sovereignty can
be achieved without eliciting major opposition from business
interests in Quebec or elsewhere. This is a questionable assumption,

to say the least. While most business people in Quebec favour greater autonomy for the province, the dominant players do not favour sovereignty.

For the most part, the business lobbies that addressed the Bélanger-Campeau Commission were decidedly reluctant to abandon the federal state framework. There is some support for sovereignty among the owners of small and medium sized firms in Quebec (the so-called PMEs, or *petites et moyennes entreprises*), who produce for a mainly local or Quebec market. But it is noteworthy that, with one exception, none of the major business organizations that appeared before the Bélanger-Campeau Commission supported sovereignty. The exception, the Mouvement Desjardins, proves the rule: it is very much a Quebec-based institution with strong grassroots community participation in its management. In addenda to the Commission's report, representatives of the Montreal Board of Trade and the Conseil du Patronat praised the federal system as a source of Quebec's high living standards and expressed doubt that a sovereign Quebec would be able to negotiate equally favourable terms under the Free Trade Agreement.

Many nationalists attempt to dispel fears of business opposition to sovereignty by arguing that English Canada and the United States will welcome doing business with a sovereign Quebec. However, they may be putting the cart before the horse.

There is certainly little question that if Quebec were to become a sovereign state, businesses on both sides of the new frontier would have a strong interest in establishing a stable trade and investment relationship. But that does not mean that business people in English Canada are favourable or indifferent to the possible breakup of the federal state. On the contrary. While some may favour devolving particular powers or attributions to the provinces, their attachment to the federal political framework is manifest.

The Canadian economic union is a function of the existence of a Canadian state. It was this political structure that ensured the building of an east-west economic structure around railroads and later airlines and telecommunications systems that countered the north-south pull of the market. Thanks to this political structure, Quebec accounts for 25 percent of interprovincial trade in Canada, second only to Ontario with 40 percent. Thus, while Canada is an important market for Quebec businesses, Quebec is an important market for businesses in the rest of Canada, which benefit from the privileged access to that market that they gain from Quebec's membership in the federation. Which may, incidentally, explain why

Quebec trades far more with Ontario than it does with New England.

Although the Free Trade Agreement increases the importance of the U.S. market to Canadian business interests, there is no evidence that the latter are prepared to abandon their own state structure, which gives them a particular weight and therefore some leverage in their relations with their major international partners and competitors. Many business people fear that, without Quebec, Canada will be in a weaker political position in the continental market, in which the United States already enjoys overwhelming predominance. (In this respect, North America is quite unlike the European Community, where no country — not even Germany — is hegemonic.) Many Canadian business people dread the prospect of a sovereign Quebec with an equal voice in the central bank, or a central bank of its own elaborating distinct, possibly conflicting, policies. And there is a general fear of the political and social instability that might accompany any radical change in the constitutional relationship between Quebec and the rest of Canada.

Already, a formidable front of opposition to Quebec sovereignty is developing in Canadian big business circles. An article in the June 15, 1991 issue of the Quebec biweekly, *L'Actualité*, describes the thinking. "To the twenty or so business leaders I met with in Toronto in April," writes Christian Rioux, "the constitutional crisis is a golden opportunity to reduce the federal deficit and do away with the welfare state." But they take a dim view of Quebec's sovereignty, Rioux points out.

He cites the Business Council on National Issues (BCNI), which represents the 150 biggest corporations in the country. It initiated and led the campaign for the Free Trade Agreement. A BCNI committee of top business executives from Toronto and Montreal has prepared a position paper that advocates a decentralization to the provinces of social programs, job training and responsibility for language and culture. But it wants to centralize control over communications, the environment, and regulation of financial institutions in Ottawa. It favours doing this through administrative arrangements, rather than amendment of the Constitution. And it is opposed to according any "special status" to Quebec.

Thus, the Association of Economists (ASDEQ) made a telling point in its presentation to the Bélanger-Campeau Commission when it pointed to the dangers in basing one's strategy, as many sovereigntists including the PQ do, on the assumption that English Canada would react "rationally" and readily accept the offer of economic and monetary union in the event Quebec opted for political independence. Notwithstanding polls that show a substantial willingness among ordinary citizens in the rest of Canada to agree to such terms,[26] there is enough opposition by business and governments to bear out ASDEQ's statement that "all signs point to confrontation." Quebec nationalists ignore these *political* factors at their peril.

Quebec self-determination the issue[27]

The Pepin-Robarts Task Force on Canadian Unity ended its report in 1979, barely a year before the Quebec Referendum, with the observation that "Canada's efforts at reaching a comprehensive constitutional settlement have been bedevilled by two highly significant factors. . . ."

> First, for several generations there has been a remarkably consistent and coherent constitutional point of view shared by a broad majority of French-speaking Québécois. This has served both to support and to limit the freedom of action of Quebec's political leaders. No Quebec politician can afford to stray far from this collective will. . . .
>
> The second significant factor . . . is the general apathy of English-speaking Canadians on the subject. This has left English-speaking Canada's political leaders with quite extensive freedom of action, but with little popular incentive or pressure to come to terms.

"Apathy" may no longer be an appropriate description of English-Canadian attitudes. If the Spicer report is any indication, many people outside Quebec are upset by the constitutional crisis, albeit confused on the issues. There is, however, an astonishing and — to the editor of this volume, at least — disturbing reluctance to address the legitimate demands of Quebecers for fundamental constitutional change.

In a sense, this reluctance is understandable. It reflects the smug self-assurance of a majority, which, secure in its majority, perceives no need to defend its status through constitutional provisions. Equally understandable, however, is the desire of the minority to protect its existence and future in the fundamental law of the land.

The impetus for constitutional change in this country comes necessarily from two major groups: the Québécois and the First Nations. Their *national* interests have inherent constitutional implications. While other groups may seek constitutional changes to advance their interests, their claims to equality and justice can be satisfied without constitutional protection, although such protection may be of assistance in advancing those claims.

It should be clear by now, however, that the native peoples need detailed constitutional provisions, binding on all the courts, spelling out their rights as sovereign aboriginal peoples if substantial progress is to be made in resolving their claims, in particular their land claims, to their satisfaction. This was demonstrated once again by the March 1991 ruling by the British Columbia Supreme Court in the "Gitksan-Wet'snwet'en" land claims case, in which the province's chief justice held that aboriginal rights had been extinguished in a substantial area of the province by the Crown's "clear and plain" intention — manifested in colonial and provincial legislation — to unilaterally extinguish that title. Unresolved native claims for sovereignty and self-government are on the agenda in both English Canada and Quebec, and the two nations must address these claims, either in a common constitutional framework or (if Quebec opts for sovereignty) independently of each other.

As the selections in this book will indicate, it is virtually excluded that the desire of the vast majority of Québécois for constitutional recognition of their national character will be satisfied with purely administrative tinkering, even if such adjustments were to involve substantial *de facto* shifts in the existing division of powers between the federal and Quebec governments. In any event, the possibility of the current crisis being resolved without constitutional change has been foreclosed by the conclusion of the Bélanger-Campeau Commission that "it is necessary to redefine the political *and constitutional* status of Quebec" — a conclusion subsequently incorporated in legislation of the Quebec National Assembly. The determination of Quebec's future status will involve constitutional change, full stop.

The "national unity" industry is now in top gear churning out proposals to solve the crisis and bring the country together. Task forces, parliamentary committees and sub-committees, government advisory committees, and groups of "concerned citizens" are producing a deluge of ideas. Some focus on procedures: referendum, constituent assembly, enlarged parliamentary committee, changes in the amending formula, etc. Others propose changes in the way power is exercised, through senate reform, redistribution of powers, and so on.

The flurry of activity is understandable, and probably positive, so long as it recognizes the legitimacy of Quebec's needs and concerns. But there is a real danger that the process will simply become another occasion to tinker with the Constitution to make it more responsive to the needs of the corporate sector, without meeting the genuine needs of most Quebecers — i.e., another Meech Lake.

The signs are not reassuring. One is appalled to read of a self-appointed "Group of 22" prominent Canadians who managed to produce a much-discussed 7,500-word document on constitutional reform that does not mention Quebec or its exclusion from the 1982 constitutional agreement.

Quebec has made a compelling case for major changes in its constitutional status, based on its common perception of itself as a mature nation with its own distinct features. It is no longer willing to be subordinate to the political will of another people with a divergent conception of the state and society. It wants the right to determine its own policies, its own future, to have full responsibility over its destiny. This sovereignty, Quebec will have — whether within or without a Canadian federation.

However, Quebecers are still very divided over the framework in which those changes should occur — a sovereign republic of Quebec, or some renewed or revised Canadian federal state that can accommodate its perceived needs. Ironically, the majority of Quebecers — all but the unconditional sovereigntists, apparently a minority — cannot choose that framework without some additional information. They need to know whether the rest of Canada is prepared to allow Quebec the autonomy it wants and will insist on as a condition to remaining in the federation. If it is not, there is little doubt that Quebecers will opt decisively for sovereignty.

The Bélanger-Campeau hearings documented Quebecers' discontent with the constitutional *status quo* and the Commission proposed a procedure to resolve these grievances. That procedure has now been enacted in law. It involves the holding of a referendum on Quebec sovereignty in 1992, as well as the establishment of a legislative committee to evaluate any offers of a "new partnership of constitutional nature" made by the federal government and binding the provinces.

There is a strong likelihood that the political leaders of English Canada will fail to come forward with proposals for constitutional change that can offer some substantive possibility of satisfying Quebec's aspirations. In that case, Quebec probably will vote on sovereignty.[28] How, then, should English Canada respond? In a word, democratically.

Responsible political leaders in the rest of Canada should publicly welcome the referendum as a means of letting the people of Quebec themselves determine their choice of a constitutional option — an expression of their democratic right of self-determination. They should declare the intention of the people and governments of English Canada to abide by the decision of the Quebec people, whatever that decision. They should publicly undertake that if Quebec opts for sovereignty they shall negotiate its separation without engaging in blackmail or otherwise attempting to undermine or reverse its democratic decision. This might mean, for example, undertaking in advance to establish a joint public commission with Quebec to investigate and resolve potentially explosive issues such as the division of assets (and liabilities) and the public debt.

And they should declare that, if the people of Quebec reject sovereignty, the people and governments of English Canada are nevertheless cognizant of the profound desire for change in Quebec's political and constitutional status, and undertake, in advance, to entertain with the utmost seriousness Quebec's specific proposals for change — as might be expressed, for example, by a Quebec constituent assembly — and to strive to accommodate and incorporate those proposals within a common state structure.

* * *

A few words are in order on how this volume was prepared. The staff of the Commission kindly made available to the Institute for Research on Public Policy the approximately 600 briefs submitted by organizations and individuals. In addition, many organizations forwarded their briefs directly to the editor in response to an earlier request. All of these briefs were consulted, as were the written submissions solicited by the Commission from various "specialists". Selecting the briefs to publish, and the particular passages to excerpt, involved making many difficult choices. Generally, the decision reflected a judgment on the representativeness of an organization within its sector of the population, and the desire to present a fair idea of the range of issues and views presented to the Commission. The emphasis is on the views of organizations, not individuals. Attempts were made — with limited success — to avoid repetition of arguments.

In a few cases organizations provided English-language versions of their briefs. These translations were checked against the original French texts, which were followed in the interests of clarity. All of the other selections from the briefs were translated by the editor.

The book opens with the political parties, to give an overview of the major issues. The following two chapters present the views of some of the major interest groups — both business and the union centrals — which to some degree reflect the polar opposites in the federalism/sovereignty paradigm. The next chapters, 4 to 6, outline the views of organizations in the women's, native peoples' and

Anglophone communities, all of them prominent in the ongoing constitutional debates in Quebec. Chapter 7 presents some data on sociological changes in Quebec society in recent years, and indicates some of the concerns nationalists have about demographic trends. Chapters 8 and 9 discuss issues related to the integration of immigrants and the ethno-cultural communities, and chapter 10 deals, last but not least, with the "orphans" of the debate: the Francophones living in the rest of Canada.

The editor's notes, in a different typeface to distinguish them from the briefs, are designed to provide the reader with some background and context. Some notes are longer and more detailed than others to compensate for a perceived lack of information on the particular subject outside Quebec. Footnotes are by the authors of the briefs, unless otherwise indicated.

Although it is placed at the end of the volume, some readers may wish to start with the Report of the Commission, which in its own way presents an overview of the debate, although it does not discuss many of the issues addressed by the submissions excerpted in this book.

Stylistic conventions are always a problem in a volume of this nature, involving in this case three levels of text: the original French, the English translation, and the editor's notes. In general, the federal government style usages have been followed (a choice that is editorial, not political in nature!): thus, Anglophone and Francophone are capitalized, but not allophone; Quebec and Montreal do not have accents, etc. Residents of Quebec are termed Quebecers, not Québécois; the latter term is used only where the reference is clearly to native French-speaking Quebecers. Organization names and titles are given in French when it is a Quebec organization, even though there may be an "official" English version. Translations are provided in the Glossary of Acronyms at the front of the book.

Finally, this introduction would be incomplete if the editor did not acknowledge the helpful assistance of the following people: Henri-Paul Rousseau, Secretary of the Commission, for providing a copy of all the briefs; Pierre Duchesne, Secretary general of the Assemblée nationale, for permission to reprint the Report of the Commission; the many organizations and individuals who authorized the publication of their briefs; Rod Dobell, Jeffrey Holmes and Lorne Brownsey, who read the draft and provided helpful advice; Peter Heap, who likewise read the materials, provided ongoing advice and encouragement, and relieved the editor of a number of administrative details; the staff of Oolichan Books; and Maguy

Robert and Christian Dufour for assistance in various ways. And a special thank-you to my wife and companion, Patricia Bégin, for her constant encouragement and thoughtful counsel. To all, the normal caveats apply.

Richard Fidler
June 28, 1991.

Notes

1. For example, *Globe and Mail* political affairs columnist Jeffrey Simpson angrily concluded that "The separation of Quebec from Canada is just a matter of time. . . ." The same columnist had blithely assured readers six years earlier, when the PQ dropped sovereignty as an immediate goal of government, that "the dream of sovereignty in our time died. . . . May it rest in peace." ("Fact meets fiction", 21 January 1985). His *Ottawa Citizen* counterpart Marjorie Nichols at first described the Allaire proposals as "inane and not worthy of serious study" by the Prime Minister. Yet a month later, Nichols was arguing that Allaire's "proposals for the massive decentralization of the Canadian state may well provide the glue to unify this country."

2. Now the *Constitution Act, 1867.*

3. Task Force on Canadian Unity, *Coming to Terms: The Words of the Debate* (Ottawa, 1979), p. 25.

4. An interesting discussion of these and other provisions is contained in the brief of the Centrale de l'enseignement du Québec, excerpted in chapter 3.

5. See chapter 7 for some of the relevant data.

6. *A Quebec Free to Choose* (Report of the Constitutional Committee of the Quebec Liberal Party), 1991, pp. 10-11.

7. "Federalism, Nationalism and Reason" (1964), in Trudeau, *Federalism and the French Canadians* (Toronto, 1968), p. 193 (emphasis in original).

8. When the Act was overhauled in 1988, it included a limited legal remedy provision (in Part X), and a more explicit commitment to "enhance the vitality of the English and French linguistic communities in Canada and support and assist their development" (s. 43).

9. In the 1890s Manitoba made English the only language of its legislature and courts, in direct defiance of the federal Act making it a province of Canada; the legislation was finally overruled by the Supreme Court of Canada in 1979, by which time the

province's Francophones, a majority in 1870, were only 6 percent of the population. The Court decision was not based on the OLA.

10. Commission of Inquiry on the Position of the French Language and on Language Rights (Gendron Commission), *The Position of the French Language in Quebec*, Book 1, "Language of Work" (Quebec, 1972), p. 23.

11. These and the data in the following paragraph are from the Report of the Royal Commission on Bilingualism and Biculturalism (Laurendeau-Dunton Commission), Book III, *The Work World* (Ottawa, 1969).

12. John Porter, *The Vertical Mosaic* (Toronto, 1966), p. 286.

13. Max Yalden, *Commissioner of Official Languages: Annual Report 1980* (Ottawa, 1980), p. 13.

14. Government of Quebec, *Quebec's Policy on the French Language* (Quebec, 1977), p. 2.

15. Quoted in René Lévesque, *Memoirs* (translated by Philip Stratford) (Toronto, 1986), at p. 301.

16. Quoted in Robert Sheppard and Michael Valpy, *The National Deal: The Fight for a Canadian Constitution* (Toronto, 1982), p. 33.

17. Michael Mandel, *The Charter of Rights and the Legalization of Politics in Canada* (Toronto, 1989), p. 103.

18. These provisions are discussed in greater detail in chapters 8 and 9 of this book.

19. See *A Future Together: Observations and Recommendations* (Ottawa, 1979), p. 87. The report added: "but to do so in a manner which would enable the other provinces, if they so wished, not to exercise these responsibilities and instead leave them to Ottawa."

20. *Report of the Royal Commission on the Economic Union and Development Prospects for Canada*, Vol. III, Part VI, "The Institutional Context" (Ottawa, 1985).

21. For a detailed discussion, see National Council of Welfare, *Funding Health and Higher Education: Danger Looming* (Ottawa, 1991).

22. National Association of Women and the Law, Testimony before the Special Joint Committee of the Senate and the House of Commons on the 1987 Constitutional Accord, August 1987.

23. Within Quebec, many nationalists initially opposed the Accord, too, but for different reasons: they argued that the "distinct society" clause failed to correct the fundamental flaws in the 1982 Constitution, and gave Quebec no significant new powers. (See the CEQ brief in chapter 3.) However, Premier Bourassa pushed the Accord through the National Assembly within days, effectively ending the Quebec debate.

24. "Reisman accuse Parizeau de mentir", *Le Devoir*, 1 June 1991.
25. *Supra*, note 20, pp. 123, 129.
26. According to an Angus Reid survey for Southam newspapers published in June 1991, 65 percent of English Canadians favoured the negotiation of an economic union with Quebec if it declared itself an independent country, 25 percent favoured the use of economic sanctions against Quebec, and 5 percent supported ignoring the declaration and using "armed force if necessary". (*Ottawa Citizen*, 7 June 1991)
27. In the following section, the editor exercises his prerogative to express a personal view on the options facing Canadians outside Quebec.
28. The "probably" is dictated by Premier Bourassa's well-known reluctance to hold a referendum exclusively on sovereignty.

1.

Independence vs. federalism —
Parties stake out positions

The Commission received briefs from the major parties in Quebec, with two notable exceptions – the governing Liberal party, which produced its own report, excerpted in this chapter, and the federal Progressive Conservative party. The latter was represented on the Commission by Montreal MP Jean-Pierre Hogue, who abstained on the Report. The submission by the Equality Party is excerpted in chapter 6.

Parti québécois:

A sovereign Quebec in a global village

The Parti québécois, riding the crest of favourable opinion polls showing majority support for sovereignty, focused its submissions on "the place of Quebec in the 'global village'".

Some might argue that globalization reduces the significance of the nation state, and that accession to sovereignty would risk erecting further barriers to international trade and investment. The PQ argues precisely the opposite. An enthusiastic advocate of the international market economy, the party sees globalization as a further rationale for sovereignty. Quebec, it says, can participate fully in the new global economy only as a nation state: "The rules of world and continental trade are established in organizations composed exclusively of countries." Having exhausted the possibilities of development within the Canadian federal structures, Quebec is now poised for the next logical step, the sequel to its Quiet Revolution: full nationhood as a sovereign state within the community of nations.

The following excerpts comprise the bulk of its brief, which was entitled "La nécessaire souveraineté" – The necessary sovereignty. Not included are three schedules to the brief analyzing, respectively, the pattern of federal government expenditures and receipts in Quebec; a history of jurisdictional disputes between Quebec and Ottawa; and statistical data comparing Quebec with countries of comparable size, population and GDP.

The Quebec people exist and have become a nation that is striving increasingly to become a country. The Quebec nation is overwhelmingly French, and wants to continue to live and function normally in French. It has developed its own cultural characteristics and a particular sense of social solidarity.

Its progression toward a country, however, was long inhibited by fears of an economic nature. These fears are now dissipating. And because of this, there is a new vision of the future: the concern is not so much language and survival as it is the most appropriate linkage between what is cultural and what is economic. We now have the resources we need to flourish and develop, and not just survive.

As the Quebec nation strives to achieve its sovereignty, it is appropriate to take notice of the major economic entities that characterize this period.

Not surprisingly, then, our brief focuses in particular on the place of Quebec in the "global village". . . .

1. **A Choice for Quebec.** The world has changed, North America is changing, and the time has come for Quebec to choose.

As a people, we have not stood aloof from world developments. We conducted our Quiet Revolution, accomplished a genuine economic *reconquista*, grew in our own esteem and accomplished a great deal to obtain recognition as a nation. The Quebec adventure, which has lasted three and a half centuries, is neither ethnic nor ethnocentric, nor has it ever been — at least no more ethnocentric than any other nation that developed on this continent in the wake of what we called the "Discovery". Nor is it inward-looking, clinging to the past. We adhere to contemporary values: the exercise and promotion of democratic freedoms, the recognition of and respect for national identities, and international solidarity and cooperation. But — entangled as we are in a deadlocked federal system — the Quebec adventure is being hamstrung as it turns toward the world and the processes of internal development that we desire and must pursue.

While the contemporary Quebec identity was emerging, a new Canadian personality also took form. We have remained largely indifferent to it, but it has had a profound effect on thinking and conduct everywhere else, from Newfoundland to British Columbia. The Canadians have adopted a national identity and a political framework to guarantee the durability of that identity. The Canadian *Charter of Rights and Freedoms* of 1982 is in this regard both the culmination of a lengthy evolution and a guarantee of cohesion in the future. It defines the Canadian citizen, establishes his rights from sea to sea, and, as a corollary, enshrines the legal equality of the provinces and the supremacy of the federal government. Quebec did not participate in this divergent evolution and declines to be a party to it today.

There lies the problem. It is clearly a political one and it requires a political response.

There are two questions facing Quebecers, and in the last analysis it is all Quebecers who will have to answer them, to make a choice: What system is now most appropriate for us? How can we establish it?

To answer correctly, we must take into account our situation, that of Canada as it is, and that of the world at present.

René Lévesque said it admirably, more than 20 years ago, in that first sentence in *Option Québec*: "We are Québécois". He was right: we form a people. To be a Québécois is to live in Quebec, whether one was born here or chose it; it is to experience a feeling of belongingness toward the territory and the society therein; it is to recognize one's history, traditions, behaviour, values and a common language, the factors of cohesion; it is to want to participate in accordance with one's aptitudes and means, in the general movement of Quebec's cultural, political, social and economic development.

As a people, we have come to the end of the autonomy — not only political, but also economic, cultural and social — that we can exercise within the Canadian federal system, yet we are far from having achieved our developmental goals. This autonomy is insufficient.

The recent failure of the Meech Lake Accord has demonstrated once again, and beyond challenge, that Quebec cannot increase its autonomy within the Canadian federal system. Designed to procure Quebec's adherence to the 1982 constitutional reform, this accord presented the most numerically and substantively limited demands ever formulated by a Quebec government up to now. But this minimum change proposed by Quebec proved impossible to obtain.

As a people, we have the undeniable right to determine by ourselves the political system that is most appropriate to us and, ultimately, to conduct all of our affairs by ourselves if we clearly so decide. We exercised this right to self-determination for the first time during the 1980 referendum. The Quebec National Assembly exercised it again in establishing the Commission on Quebec's Political and Constitutional Future.

The solution clearly proposed by the Parti Québécois is sovereignty for Quebec, achieved democratically and implemented harmoniously with our neighbours and partners.

Sovereignty, by definition, implies that:

• all taxes levied in Quebec will be levied by the Quebec state or administrative authorities subordinate to it;

• all laws applying to Quebec citizens and on Quebec territory will emanate from the Quebec National Assembly; and

• all international treaties, conventions or accords will be negotiated by the representatives of the Quebec state and ratified by the Quebec National Assembly.

This solution has two advantages. It guarantees us the conduct of all our affairs and it also gives us access in our own right to the international relations and organizations that are now redefining our world, so that we can find our rightful place therein.

Quebec's accession to sovereignty can in our opinion only occur in compliance with the democratic processes, recognized by international law, to which we are accustomed. The Parti québécois has always maintained this fundamental position. Indeed, the legality and legitimacy of the birth of a sovereign Quebec, and the recognition of our new country internationally, are dependent on it.

This requirement of democracy means:

• that the process leading to sovereignty be undertaken by the Quebec Parliament — the National Assembly and the government — as mandated by the electorate;

• that the proclamation of sovereignty follow upon its approval by the electorate in a referendum. . . .

2. Conducting our own international relations. Two significant events reflect the world in which we live, and they are both sources and signs of a new spirit.

In 1947 thirty or so countries agreed for the first time in history to systematically liberalize international trade; the signing of the first general agreement on tariffs and trade (GATT) plunged the world community into a genuine commercial revolution that was both economic and political. The generalized application of the most favoured nation clause and equal treatment of states regardless of their size or relative weight gradually undermined the economic justification for the great empires, which had forced political frontiers to coincide with the largest possible commercial space. It was now possible for nations to contemplate a direct presence and activity in the world community, free of trusteeship or domination.

Another event of equivalent scope occurred barely one year ago: the fall of the Berlin Wall and the dismantling of the Iron Curtain in Europe. An ideological and military encumbrance was to a large degree removed. International relations are being reshaped and nations freed from the burden of restrictive blocs bogged down in a cold war that threatened world security and restricted their liberty.

In this context, a nation with the possibility and the opportunity has every reason to become an international personality in its own right, for it is in the world arena that the decisions with the greatest impact, not only for the planet but also for our day-to-day lives, will now be taken. The rules of world and continental trade are established in organizations composed exclusively of countries. A society's capacity to meet the increased competitive challenges resulting from the globalization of trade and the mobility of capital will be determined by the degree to which it controls all of the developmental tools of a modern state. Far from entailing the disappearance of national measures, the growing openness of the world has accentuated their importance. . . .

3. **The economic associations of a sovereign Quebec.** Twenty years ago — precisely because of the GATT accords that already existed — it was dishonest to argue, in opposition to Quebec's sovereignty, that our major trading partners would be able to stifle our economy by erecting tariffs to price our products out of the export market. Today this economic scaremongering is even more fallacious.

As a country with a market economy, Quebec cannot be threatened in this way. Competition is the ineluctable rule. Our economy is already subject to this rule and it complies extremely well; Quebec exports more than 40 percent of its gross national product and is one of the most trade-oriented economies in the world. Our performance compares favourably with such countries as Norway and Austria. Quebec's sovereignty will not upset the general rules of trade or the conduct of our major partners. It will however give us full mastery of the economic levers that national economies normally use to increase their competitive capacity, such as scientific research, technological development and manpower training policies.

By joining the GATT a sovereign Quebec will not provoke or experience any economic upheavals. Those provisions that already

apply and serve our trade so well will remain in force once we have
become sovereign: the most favoured nation clause, non-discrimination, national treatment and the settlement of disputes by international authorities. In addition, we will obtain what we have not had
so far: the right to be represented, speak and participate in common
decisions and arbitration panels with a specifically Quebec voice.

Our continent has lived in peace for more than a century. Of
course we have had to fight on many battlefields elsewhere in the
world, but neither wars nor military boundaries have come between
us. This is an accomplishment that has long given us an immense
advantage, and it is still an asset of infinite value. However, it must
be observed that Western Europe, for example, after a number of
major conflicts, has been quicker to set about establishing new
international relationships.

The European Economic Community is a fine example; it has
established the richest, most populous common market in the world
while allowing the cohabitation of quite disparate sovereign nations.
In addition to the 12 member countries, six other European nations
grouped in the European Free Trade Association (EFTA) have also
signed free-trade agreements with the Common Market and all of
these countries have economies that are essentially the size of
Quebec's. Similar large economic entities are emerging on all
continents.

In North America we in turn have taken this road. Despite our
regime of perpetual peace and the volume of trade already achieved,
it was necessary for us to guarantee our prosperity by ourselves
forming a larger, more coherent economic space.

The free-trade treaty between Washington and Ottawa already
includes Quebec. Moreover, it is well known that Quebec played a
decisive role in its accomplishment since the major parties here
agreed to join forces behind it and support its implementation,
thereby providing Canada with some decisive political weight.

Quebec is already a part of the North American free trade area
established by the treaty and it will remain a member after its
accession to sovereignty. We will then take our place as a new
national partner within the joint institutions established to secure
its administration, such as the arbitration mechanisms that have
been established to settle possible disputes.

Let us refer again to the rules of international trade. Regional
free-trade and common-market agreements are viewed as exceptions
to the most-favoured nation clause and must be authorized by
GATT. Such agreements must not violate either the spirit or the
other underlying rules of the General Agreement. That is why

general or sectoral regional free-trade agreements are not allowed to exclude a market-economy country that wishes to belong. The free-trade agreement or the Automobile Pact therefore cannot exclude Quebec, just as the EEC could not reject Italy or Belgium without seriously violating the rules and the spirit of the GATT.

Moreover, neither Quebec nor the United States has any greater interest than Canada does in restricting mutual free trade. The general balance of trade in North America would be affected to the disadvantage of all the partners.

In fact, all serious U.S. sources who have been consulted indicate that a sovereign Quebec will be warmly welcomed within the free-trade area since the United States has an official policy of promoting the freest possible trade among those nations practising market economics.

The United States' negotiation of a similar agreement with Mexico raises the probability of a North America constituting an immense free-trade zone encompassing four sovereign states: the United States of America, Canada, Mexico and Quebec.

No specific negotiations or particular bilateral accord are required to apply the GATT rules, reinforced by the North American free-trade agreement, as the basis for an economic association that already exists between a sovereign Quebec and Canada.

This common rule, which applies to every country in the North American free-trade area, might alone suffice to prevent the erection of an economic barrier between Quebec and Canada. It is an undeniable asset that from the outset it is understood that it will be as easy for a Montreal company to do business in Toronto as it is in Boston, just as it is to our advantage to establish straight off that Quebec remains open and receptive to Canadian and U.S. businesses.

But even now we can envisage further functional economic links between Quebec and Canada.

First, the present customs union can be maintained to our mutual advantage.

Secondly, we should take a look at the geographical constraints and find a response that is both satisfactory to us and capable of guaranteeing the cohesiveness of our Canadian partner from sea to sea. Central Canada and the West cannot be separated from their Maritime provinces without suffering serious disadvantages that would inevitably undermine their unity. The natural and historical path of communications passes through Quebec. In our opinion, the association between Quebec and Canada should be complemented by the conclusion of a lasting agreement guaranteeing free movement through Quebec territory between the Maritimes and the rest of Canada by land, sea, rail and air. . . .

Thirdly, before it is raised on a continental scale — in the event of a strengthening of North American free trade — the issue of currency is immediately posed between a sovereign Quebec and Canada. Would it be in the mutual interest of Quebec and Canada to preserve their monetary union in a context of Quebec sovereignty? We say yes, although it is also quite possible to conceive of the establishment of a Quebec currency. What is involved here are considerations of practicality and convenience, not to mention psychology. The Quebec-Canada monetary union would be a formidable guarantee of mutual agreement; it would provide both Canada and Quebec with a convenient instrument for balancing the extraordinarily high flow of trade.

This monetary union would be managed, as they are everywhere else in the world (whether a national or a common currency is involved) by a determinative institution: a common issuer or a central bank under the ultimate authority of an executive power. The arrangement could be modelled on existing common central banks ultimately reporting to member governments. However, a common parliament to administer the common currency is inconceivable. No monetary policy in the world, not even the current one in Ottawa, is responsible to a parliament. The U.S. Congress does not control the Federal Reserve Bank, nor are the Bank of France or the Deutschbank controlled by the French National Assembly or the Bundestag.

A monetary union would not impose any further uniformity of fiscal and economic policies. Nor is this the case even now in the Canadian federal system, where substantial disparities in this regard may be observed between the provinces — notwithstanding the centralization of monetary policy in Ottawa, in the Bank of Canada. To suggest this as a consequence is to violate the very principle of a monetary union between sovereign states, to renounce sovereignty in favour of a more extensive political and economic centralism than exists today in the Canadian federation, and to evoke a unitary state.

Furthermore, lasting economic cooperation between Quebec and Canada may be achieved in other sectors, such as the management of air and rail transportation firms.

The European Community and its sub-group Benelux, the European Free Trade Association and the Nordic countries provide a number of models for association between sovereign states. These associations are monetary or commercial or economic in some sectors, but never political. The European Parliament does not legislate; it issues opinions. The instrument governing relationships among the countries of the Community is not a constitution but an international treaty. The common budget of the EEC is not a state budget but serves rather to secure the functioning of the common institutions. The EEC budget, if reduced proportionately to correspond to the Canadian population, would amount to five billion dollars, compared with the current federal budget of 150 billion dollars. The European model teaches us that a comparably developed economic association endowed with common administrative institutions does not involve a symmetrical political integration. Thus, 33 years after the signing of the Treaty of Rome, we can see that each of the countries that make up the European Community retains full sovereignty in foreign policy and defence, and that two of the Twelve, France and Great Britain, even today have exclusive control over their own strategic nuclear forces.

A sovereign state does not acknowledge any constitution or constituent organ above itself. A sovereign state creates common institutions that commit it to other countries through treaties or international agreements and, of course, it may also withdraw from these if it so determines.

If, in the name of an association, we were to contemplate the establishment of a superstructure in the form of some constitution overarching our own, endowed with authority to adopt laws governing us and to levy taxes on us, we would be renouncing sovereignty and possibly establishing a federal regime that would be even more restrictive for Quebec.

4. Adopting all our laws, levying and administering all our taxes.
. . . Quebec requires an effective, functional system to accomplish the second phase of its quiet revolution. To establish this, we must first repatriate and henceforth retain the power to decide by ourselves and for ourselves, the power to adopt all our own laws and the power to levy and administer all our taxes.

The federalism we have is wrongly presented as a political system that distributes responsibilities between two levels of government. This is wishful thinking. The way they interpret it in English Canada is more correct: a national government sitting in Ottawa, extended through regional governments that are closer to the population and therefore more efficient in particular aspects. These institutions entail specific ways of functioning. The Constitution grants the federal government jurisdiction over whatever is not expressly allocated to the provinces — i.e., responsibility for innovation in a world in rapid evolution falls to this national government. Thus radio, television and telecommunications satellites are under federal jurisdiction. Ottawa is provided with the general power to spend and to tax — it may therefore intervene generally and massively in any area. It determines the regional development envelopes, just as it unilaterally decides to impose a new tax as fraught with consequences as the GST. It is the federal Parliament that adopts national standards, i.e., the objectives to be attained in a particular sector of activity once that sector has been deemed significant. For example, there is a national health policy, and other policies are even now being prepared in such fields as childcare and environmental protection.

In a system like this it is not so much the sectoral distribution of responsibilities that poses the fundamental problem as it is the institutional and constitutional subordination of the Quebec government to the federal government.

English Canada essentially accepts this mode of government and recognizes that on the whole it serves it well. The people of Quebec find themselves hamstrung by the system, since they view it as a drastic limitation on the freedom of their national government, which sits in Quebec City. . . .

Listing the new powers that should be repatriated to Quebec, as some circles suggest, leads either to an unenforceable special status, which would be intolerable to Canada, or to the demand for sovereignty.

When, for example, the Union des producteurs agricoles (UPA) convention in Quebec City suggests, as it did last year, that Quebec should repatriate and exercise full and unlimited jurisdiction over agriculture, without federal interference, this is sovereigntist discourse. The next step would be for the UPA to demand its place at the GATT table to negotiate directly with other countries. . . .

It is no use for Quebec to submit a still more elaborate list of demands in future federal-provincial negotiations. There is no likelihood that any attempt of this kind would result in a satisfactory outcome. That is what history teaches us beyond the shadow of a doubt and we would be wrong to adopt the behaviour of those "who have learned nothing and understood nothing".

Quebec's need for sovereignty is clear in too many areas for us to accept some artificial limitation on its exercise. This full and unrestricted sovereignty must be sought by and for Quebec, and affirmed by Quebec. It cannot be negotiable. . . .

5. Quebec-Canada: From two nations to two countries. Quebec's withdrawal from the Canadian federation will not mean the end of Canada. On the contrary. Over the last 30 years we have seen a number of attempts by English Canada to build a country, establish national rules and objectives in education, transportation, man-power training, science policy, foreign aid or civil rights. Yet these efforts have very often been frustrated by the Québécois who either rejected the precise definition of these national objectives or proposed complicated amendments that stifled any attempt at national construction — or simply said, as in the case of language rights, that their objectives were not better or worse but different. In other words, we in Quebec have been the spoilers in this entire, and essentially Canadian, process. We should recognize that the Canadians are, after all, entitled to their own country, the country they want, just as and just as much as we Québécois are entitled to ours.

In this context, any proposal that we in Quebec might make to reform the federal structures from top to bottom in order to design a system to our advantage runs counter to the historical trend.

Since 1960 we have clearly identified ourselves as Québécois without always noticing how strongly and consistently a Canadian nationalism has developed. There is a Canadian identity, a Canadian way of conceiving and desiring a country, a genuine and profound choice by Canadians in favour of a strong central government that guarantees the political equality of every province and every citizen before the law.

Rather than opposing them in this effort, which is as legitimate as ours, we submit that two nations as divergent in their evolution and political objectives as these should each decide to provide themselves with their own country. This can be done in harmony. . . .

Bloc québécois:

Full sovereignty is a precondition to any new agreement with Canada

The Bloc québécois was formed in May 1990 at the initiative of Lucien Bouchard, a minister in the Mulroney government and former Canadian ambassador to France, who resigned from the Cabinet and the Conservative party to protest what he regarded as unwarranted concessions to the Anglophone provinces to get their agreement to the Meech Lake Accord.

Bouchard was soon joined by other Quebec MPs: five Conservatives and two Liberals. In August 1990, shortly after the Meech Lake fiasco, a Bloc candidate was elected in a by-election in Montreal. Thus, when their brief was presented to the Commission, there were nine MPs in the Bloc's caucus; since then, one has rejoined the Tories.

In their initial Manifesto, the Bloc announced that "Our national allegiance is Québécois. The territory to which we belong is Quebec, the home of a people of French language and culture, whose sovereignty we intend to promote." They had kept their seats in the House of Commons, they said, to act as spokesmen for Quebec's interests toward the rest of Canada.

The Manifesto notes that the Bloc is not subject to party discipline and its members vote according to conscience in the House. Indeed, while they agree on the objective of Quebec sovereignty, the Bloc's members appear to differ on many other issues. For example, in the House vote to support the U.S. and allied military intervention in Iraq, in January 1991, three Bloc MPs voted against while two voted for. Three others, including Bouchard, absented themselves, although Bouchard told the media that "There are Canadians from all parts of Canada involved in the war. We have to support them; we need solidarity more than ever."

The Parti québécois, which does not run federally, announced in April that it would campaign in support of the Bloc in the next federal election. Bouchard reacted coolly to this statement; he wants to keep the door open to members of the Quebec Liberal party. He and other Bloc members are calling for a "Union sacrée", a holy alliance, of sovereigntists to convince other Quebec MPs in the traditional parties to join forces with them in support of Quebec sovereignty. In mid-June 1991 the Bloc constituted itself a federal party at a convention attended by more than 900 persons.

Excerpted below is the major part of the Bloc's brief to the Commission. Omitted is a lengthy summary of the history of Ottawa-Quebec disputes since the 1940s.

Quebec's history since the Conquest has been characterized by a dual desire. On the one hand, to create and strengthen our own institutions — and they are numerous — on the other hand, to demand more autonomy within the institutions we share with English Canada.

In this regard, the state institutions substantially lag behind most of our institutions, which have already exercised their right to self-determination. In fact, some members of this Commission have been prominent participants in these transformations. For example:

• The "credit unions" and "caisses d'économie" [savings banks] in Quebec went through several periods of instability before clearly affirming their Quebec identity and, a few years later, their affiliation to the Desjardins Movement.

• The Quebec Liberal Party likewise achieved its independence of the Liberal Party of Canada more than 20 years ago.

While we have gradually provided ourselves with economic, social and to some degree even political institutions that correspond to the actual country, in terms of state institutions we are still living under a regime of dual representative legitimacy, which greatly increases the costly incoherency and sterile, painful confrontations.

Thus, when we established the initial core of our parliamentary group we stated that although we remain in Ottawa to defend the interests of Quebec within the present system we consider the National Assembly of Quebec to be the supreme democratic expression of the Quebec people. . . .

Status quo unacceptable. The constitutional crisis in the strict meaning of the term, that is, the rejection of the five minimum conditions in the Meech Lake Accord, appears relatively insignificant when compared with the overall crisis of Canadian federalism: an irrepressible deficit and public debt; an economic policy that is unacceptable to Quebec; inadequate job training; anaemic research and development; a costly and swollen public service, and duplication of government departments; and the growth of social and regional inequality.

In fact, we can state after the event that while the failure to ratify the Meech Lake Accord was a great disillusionment for Quebec, its adoption would, in the end, have been a great illusion for English Canada. We all know that for Quebec this accord represented an act of reparation, a precondition to the negotiation of a far-reaching decentralization that would allow the Quebec government to exercise its role as a national state. Yet there was nothing to indicate that this would be on the agenda of the coming constitutional talks if Meech Lake were adopted.

We must draw the necessary conclusions from Canada's history and political dynamics. To gain recognition of its aspirations, Quebec must proclaim its full sovereignty before negotiating any new agreement with English Canada.

Sovereignty must be declared at the conclusion of a strictly democratic process. It must therefore be decided by a referendum, a precondition to ensuring that Quebec's accession to sovereignty will have the necessary credibility to win international recognition.

Furthermore, the globalization of trade leaves little time for adaptation, and a sovereign Quebec will, in our opinion, be in a relatively stronger position to confront this challenge.

1. Consensus: a condition for development. Canada and Quebec
have achieved a high standard of living, largely through the
development of their resources. But this prosperity depends
increasingly on our international industrial competitiveness if we
are to participate in the globalization of trade.

The countries that have most successfully met this challenge are
those that have developed an internal cohesion that makes possible
the ongoing adaptation imposed by international competition. In
these countries the major social and economic agents and the
government agree to pursue both economic growth and full
employment. The government's major economic policies are then
arrived at through consensus. The social, economic and political
institutions vary from one country to another, but we know that our
capacity to benefit from the globalization of trade is directly linked
to our capacity to achieve consensus on the goals and major
policies of our society.

In Canada deep differences and the political instability they entail
make it extremely difficult to attain such consensus, and promote
doubts about the policy directions that are adopted.

In Quebec, the firm support of both major political parties for
the opening up of markets is a significant element of stability in
promoting investment. Moreover, amongst the many attempts at
concertation, the Forum pour l'emploi is particularly promising, in
our view, as a means of promoting policies of adaptation, the
necessary *quid pro quo* to our openness to global trade.

We are convinced that the effective implementation of the
necessary consensus requires a redefinition of the role of the state,
which is not a realistic expectation within the Canadian federal
framework.

2. From the state as contractor to the state as partner. Since the
Quiet Revolution the Quebec government has been particularly
active in the economic sector. Among its achievements should be
noted the nationalization of electricity and the major hydro-electric
projects; the creation of a huge pool of collective savings through
the establishment of the Quebec Pension Plan and the manager of
its funds, the Caisse de dépôt et de placements du Québec; and the
formation of many Crown corporations such as the Société générale
de financement, SIDBEC, SOQUEM, SOQUIP, SOQUIA, etc.

We should also note its financial assistance to the development
of Quebec entrepreneurs through the acquisition of holdings by the
Caisse de dépôt; tax incentives to facilitate the formation of venture
capital (Stock Savings Plan, the SPEQ, the Fonds de Solidarité des

Travailleurs du Québec (FTQ), and flow-through shares; and the deregulation of financial institutions.

Yet, despite these successes, we can say that Quebec does not have the necessary tools to confront the future, because the key to success lies in the close coordination of major economic and social policies in pursuit of clear objectives that are shared by the major social and economic partners.

The present jumble of manpower policies and programs is a virtually insurmountable handicap for businesses and individuals who are trying to adapt.

The high concentration of promotional and research and development tools at the federal level, and their unequal distribution as far as Quebec is concerned, drastically limit our ability to guarantee the long-term future of Quebec businesses and develop entrepreneurship in the leading growth sectors.

The Bank of Canada's policy of high interest rates and an overvalued dollar is completely inappropriate to the Quebec economy. The disastrous consequences will no doubt be emphasized by many of those appearing before the Commission, but we wish to point out that it is a result of the Canadian political system. On the one hand, the Ontario government acts irresponsibly toward its other Canadian partners by systematically adopting expansionary budgets while its economy is already extremely overheated. On the other hand, between 1984 and 1988 federal transfer payments grew by 8.1 percent to Ontario and by 3.5 percent to Quebec. Such patterns would never be allowed within a monetary union negotiated between sovereign states. . . .

Parti libéral du Quebec:

A Quebec free to choose

The Quebec Liberal Party did not make a formal submission to the Commission. However, in late January 1991, two months before the Commission was scheduled to report to the National Assembly, Premier Bourassa released *A Québec Free to Choose*, a 74-page report by the party's Constitutional Committee. The report is more commonly known as the Allaire Report, after the committee chairman, Jean Allaire.

The committee had been appointed in March 1990 pursuant to a resolution by the party's General Council to prepare "the political content of the second round of negotiations" after the ratification of the Meech

Lake Accord or, alternatively, "to prepare for the possible failure" of the Accord. It held two rounds of consultations with party members and leaders across the province, in the spring and fall of 1990, as well as meeting privately with non-party "experts" and other personalities. In January 1991 it met with the party's Executive Committee, and Premier Bourassa was reported to have participated extensively in the final editing of the report.

At the party convention in early March, the report was adopted with a few amendments, such as a guarantee of anglophone rights and recognition of the aboriginal peoples as "distinct nations", support of the *Canadian Charter of Rights and Freedoms*, and a call for reform of the Senate, not its abolition as originally proposed.

The following excerpts from the Allaire report follow the text of the official English version, slightly revised in light of the final French text.

The excerpts comprise part of the Introduction, the bulk of chapter 4 (A New Quebec-Canada Structure) and the Conclusion. Omitted are chapters 1 (an historical review), most of 2 (Impasse of Federalism in its Current Form), 3 (Objectives of the New Political and Economic Order), and 5 (the process). Much of the omitted material is covered in the report of the Bélanger-Campeau Commission, which was endorsed by the Quebec Liberal Party members of the Commission, or in other materials in this book.

Impasse of federalism in its current form. On the whole, Quebec and its people have been able to act and develop within the federal structure. It would be a mistake to say that federalism has not had any positive impact on Quebec. The standard of living in Quebec is among the highest in the world. Like Canada, it has developed a very generous system of health and social services. Freedom reigns in Quebec. As part of Canada, Quebec takes part in and benefits from Canada's enviable reputation among other nations in the international community. The Canadian economic sphere, in particular, offers many economic advantages.

However, a review of the history of the experience of Canadian federalism brings us face to face with an antinomy between the Canadian system's tendency toward centralization and standardization, and Quebec's ever growing determination to affirm its own autonomy and uniqueness and be fully master of its decisions and the choices that concern it. Fundamentally, that is the primary cause of the current impasse. . . .

A new Quebec-Canada structure. Under the existing federal structure, the Quebec government lacks the essential powers it needs to enable Quebec to develop fully as a distinct society, as well as the tools to allow it to secure the future of the French fact in North America. The current structure fails to reflect the realities of Quebec and Canada, and gives rise to incoherence, abuse and duplication of government efforts. It frequently encourages inaction, exacerbates the crisis in public finances, and perpetuates budgetary imbalances.

To resolve the impasse, the Quebec Liberal Party is proposing a new Quebec-Canada structure. The new arrangement involves a more flexible structure that is more in tune with Quebec's uniqueness and incorporates a stronger economic union between Quebec and Canada. This new community will allow us to manage public funds more efficiently and deliver government services more effectively. It will provide Quebec with greater control over the levers of its economic, social and cultural development, and promote greater harmony in Canada as a political whole.

The Quebec Liberal Party's proposal calls for political autonomy for Quebec through the exclusive occupation of many areas of jurisdiction and the elimination of the federal government's spending power and its residual power. In particular, all areas contributing to the development of Quebec's identity will be repatriated. Along with this initiative is a proposal for greater economic integration with Canada and a thorough redefinition of common political institutions. It implies a comprehensive reconsideration of the existing Constitution.

The new Quebec-Canada structure the Quebec Liberal Party is proposing is based on three elements: a stronger Canadian economic union, political autonomy for the Quebec state, and a reorganization of Canada's political structure.

A stronger Canadian economic union. The new economic arrangement must do more than just guarantee existing economic freedoms; it must expand them and promote their development. There is no question of reconsidering the integrity and comprehensiveness of the Canadian economic market. In fact, the Quebec Liberal Party is proposing the creation of a true common market, a market that tends toward greater integration than the current agreement between Quebec and the rest of Canada. Not only will the economic foundations of Quebec and Canada be preserved, but they will be strengthened as a result of more trade. The new arrangement will promote the reinforcement of our respective industrial and economic structures. A final objective of the initiative of the Quebec Liberal Party is an increase in our collective wealth.

In practical terms, the new arrangement between Quebec and Canada will maintain the existing monetary and customs unions. It will improve the mobility of factors of production. Canadian legislatures must refrain from imposing any kind of restriction on the free mobility of people, products and capital. As trade and markets expand to encompass the entire globe, the Canadian economic sphere must be freed from any obstacle to the mobility of productive resources.

Earlier, we pointed out that the Canadian federation, in its current form, still maintains many restrictions on trade and the mobility of these resources. There are still numerous non-tariff barriers on interprovincial trade (farm products, trucking, alcohol, government contracts, etc.). The free mobility of people, though guaranteed in the *Charter of Rights and Freedoms*, is not proof against such restrictions (non-portability of diplomas, residency clauses, etc.). An objective of a strong unified Quebec-Canada economic sphere will be to overcome such obstacles.

The Quebec Liberal Party recognizes that a genuine common market will require clear rules and dispute settlement mechanisms. We will discuss the nature and operation of these arbitration mechanisms later.*

Political autonomy for the Quebec state. Under the proposed reorganization, Quebec will move resolutely toward political autonomy. Quebec will exercise exclusive, discretionary and total authority in most areas of jurisdiction. It will eliminate the federal spending power in its areas of exclusive authority and will itself decide on how its authority is to be exercised in every sector repatriated. Quebec will also control residual powers, that is, the powers not explicitly attributed in the Constitution. This will have a significant effect on the redefinition of the distribution of responsibilities. Our proposal implies a repatriation of many powers currently exercised by the federal government and a complete reassessment of the distribution of taxation powers. In addition to fulfilling the aspirations of Quebec in terms of the development of its economy and its identity, this redefinition will make it possible to manage Canadian public finances more soundly, while reducing the current political sluggishness on major social and economic issues.

---

* There is no further discussion of this point in the document, unless it is a reference to the "community tribunal" referred to below. — Ed.

Areas of exclusive authority: Quebec. In most areas, Quebec will hold exclusive jurisdiction (see table below). Quebec will exercise full sovereignty in its areas of exclusive authority, in some areas currently shared or under exclusive federal authority and in all sectors not specifically listed in the Constitution (*i.e.*, the residual powers). In this way it will retain significant authority as part of its national economic policy: industrial policy, regional development policy, investment and research policy, etc. In the social and cultural fields, Quebec will exercise the full range of powers. This will also be the case for the environment and public security. The federal government's spending power in Quebec's areas of exclusive authority will be eliminated.

Exclusive Quebec Authority		
Social Affairs	Energy	Research and Development
Municipal Affairs	Environment	Natural Resources
Agriculture	Housing	Health
Unemployment Insurance	Industry and Commerce	Public Security
Communications	Language	Income Security
Culture	Recreation and Sports	Tourism
Regional Development	Manpower and Training	
Education	Family policy	
Shared Authority (or distributed according to authority)		
Native Affairs	Justice	Post Office and Telecommunications
Taxation and Revenue	Fisheries	Transport
Immigration	Foreign Policy	Financial Institutions
Exclusive Canadian Authority		
Defence and Territorial Security	Currency and Common Debt	Customs and Tariffs
Equalization		

These areas of jurisdiction will be exclusive with, where required, mechanisms for joint action with the corresponding bodies in the rest of Canada. Such mechanisms remain to be defined. Essentially, they will involve reciprocal agreements, agreements concerning the coordination of government action in certain strategic sectors where there is everything to be gained from a pooling of expertise, or in the definition of common standards and regulations to ensure the cohesion and smooth operation of the economic union.

Harmonized policies will therefore be required to strengthen integration. This could encompass tariffs, farm products marketing policies, corporate trade practices, portability of diplomas, environmental standards, harmonization of tax policies and even social security. These are all measures designed to consolidate economic union.

These greater powers will obviously require major fiscal rearrangements that will have to correspond to the transfers of jurisdiction called for under the new pact. The central government's tax base will be revised and its budgetary practices made subject to institutional constraints, including setting targets designed to severely limit its deficits and restrict its taxation powers.

Apart from simple historic considerations, Quebec and Canada share many common values and experiences. So its seems desirable that Quebec and Canada act in concert in areas where it is advantageous to do so. For instance, environmental standards could be harmonized. Nonetheless, the shared areas must satisfy certain criteria: functions requiring collective decisions to ensure the cohesion and efficient operation of the new economic union; functions that, when pooled, will enable services to be delivered more efficiently; and functions promoting greater economic equity. Overall, the common authorities should be as limited as possible. One of the objectives will be to reduce substantially the size of the central government.

Areas of shared authority. It will be advisable to maintain certain shared areas to optimize the economic union and respect the international character of the partners. To avoid overlaps, the areas of authority of the two orders of government will have to be clearly established. This will make it possible to prevent encroachment and incoherence.

Areas of shared authority will include: fisheries (in-shore to Quebec, off-shore to Canada); financial institutions (Quebec chartered institutions and federally chartered institutions); justice (in particular, civil law, administration of justice and the courts to Quebec, criminal law to Canada); transport (regional to Quebec, inter-regional to Canada); immigration (selection and integration to Quebec, control of health and security, and refugees to Canada). Native affairs, the post office and telecommunications will also be shared sectors. The mutual interests seem clear in each case.

As for foreign policy, Quebec and Canada will finally benefit from a concerted approach. This interdependence is self-evident considering that foreign representation must reflect the respective areas of authority of the two orders of government. On the other hand, what must not be overlooked is that Quebec will maintain the right to establish direct relations with other states and certain international organizations in areas where it exercises exclusive jurisdiction.

Finally, central institutions must be able to generate sufficient revenue to meet their responsibilities and, consequently, must have a certain taxation power.

Areas of exclusive authority: Canada. At the economic level, the continuation of a monetary and customs union is desirable. Common decision-making mechanisms will become necessary, however. This also applies to any policy or measure affecting the free mobility of productive resources (capital, products, people).

Equity towards the less affluent regions will require that some form of wealth redistribution be maintained. This redistribution will involve the establishment of a new form of equalization. Equalization must be changed to place greater emphasis on improving the conditions of production in recipient regions. The focus of the support provided will shift from maintaining public services of comparable quality to investment assistance in physical infrastructures, communications, transportation, etc.

The areas of defence, security and the coast guard are other natural areas of jurisdiction attributed to central institutions. Services thus would be delivered more efficiently in this way.

Reorganization of Canada's political structure. The Quebec-Canada structure will be based on a thorough transformation of existing institutions. The proposal assumes the abolition of the Senate, changes to the working of Parliament, the creation of a new court and a reorganization of the decision-making structure of the Bank of Canada. This new partnership will be based on the free and voluntary membership of the participating states. It will require a complete reconsideration of the Canadian Constitution.

The common political structure will be based on a Parliament elected by universal suffrage. The current Senate will be abolished. Parliament's legislative powers will be restricted to the areas of jurisdiction described above. As far as the coordinating functions are concerned, the decisions of Parliament will have to be ratified by the Quebec National Assembly and the assemblies of all the other legislatures (provincial or regional) that have adopted the same approach as Quebec. Specific targets will be set to severely limit the power of central institutions to contract debts. Institutional constraints will be imposed to curb the possibility of developing deficits at the central level.

Such a transformation of the common structures and the distribution of power will obviously require a complete recasting of the current Canadian Constitution. The Quebec Liberal Party proposes that the new pact be part of a new constitutional agreement and that it be based on free and voluntary membership of the partners. Under the new agreement, the other components of the new Canadian entity would remain free to redelegate certain powers to central institutions through administrative agreements that do not affect Quebec. Thus, regions that are unable or do not want to assume the same degree of autonomy could mitigate the drawbacks of the new order. The new agreement will include a new amending formula that will stipulate that any constitutional change will require the approval of a substantial minority of provinces representing at least 50 percent of the population of Canada, Quebec necessarily being included.

A community tribunal will also be formed to ensure compliance with the Constitution and enforcement of laws under the jurisdiction of the new central state. This tribunal will be separate from the legislative and executive authorities. It will not act as a court of appeal for Quebec courts. Decisions of Quebec superior courts will no longer be subject to appeal to the Supreme Court of Canada, but rather to a new, entirely Quebec supreme court. The make-up of the community tribunal and the appointment of the judges will reflect the proposals put forward in the Meech Lake Accord.

Finally, the institution responsible for monetary policy will be reorganized to better reflect regional realities. Delegates from each of the regions will be represented on the institution's board of directors.

The American experience has much to teach us in this regard. The Federal Reserve Bank is made up of regional representatives so that the regions have a say in determining the institution's overall policy. These decisions are put to a vote by members of the Board and the result of their deliberations is made public. This experience could be used as a model to redefine the structure of the central bank, since it ensures regional legitimacy while guaranteeing the visibility of the process.

Clearly, the monetary union will be viable only if the regions' budgetary policies are consistent. Uncoordinated and diverging policies would only work to compromise monetary stability and hence the conduct of a common monetary policy. The need for coordination is particularly important since the budget of the common authorities will be strictly limited, accounting for only a small proportion of total public spending, and will be constrained by rules such as a limitation on borrowing authority. The direction of the economic union's budgetary policy can then only be based on the coordination of the region's policies. Such coordination will affect the size and financing of national budget deficits. The decisions associated with the distribution of national public expenditures in areas of exclusive jurisdiction, as well as the fiscal measures to finance them, will be the concern of the regions alone. . . .

Conclusion. We are witness to events that will mark a turning point in international politics. On this continent, there is the Canada-U.S. free-trade treaty, an agreement that constitutes a quantum leap in the economic integration of North America. Then there is the fundamental transformation taking place in Western Europe, a transformation leading to the Europe of 1992. Are economic integration and national sovereignty incompatible? Does the committee's proposal go against this trend?

The tide of history. Eastern Europe is in the grip of radical change. Contemporary Europe has become a vast laboratory of economic, political and social experimentation. Unimaginable even a little while ago, its most immediate consequences are the emergence of nations, a reconsideration of East-West relations and the opening of markets.

In Western Europe, the countries of the European Community are building a new model of concerted political action and are achieving economic integration without compromising their national political sovereignty. They are proving that economic frontiers literally transcend political borders.

The separation of what is political from what is economic is relatively recent. It stems from the growing international move to freer trade. This phenomenon makes possible the emergence of local sovereignties. On the one hand, new nations, regardless of their size, retain access to a vast market. On the other, the redrawn political borders give rise to more uniform entities more conducive to social cohesion and management of public finances.

In the time required to settle the issue of half a dozen East European countries, achieve the unification of Germany and shift entire sections of postwar East-West dynamics, Canada, singularly, stumbles and falls over what is after all, on this scale, a modest constitutional agreement, approved on at least two occasions by 11 first ministers. We feel that is a revealing paradox.

We have entered a period in which history is accelerating, in which the rules of a new international order are being put in place.

Unquestionably, the time has come to take stock and make the right decisions.

National cohesion. A society's future wealth will depend on its ability to compete in an increasingly international economic context. National cohesion will be a major factor in the relative performance of various countries. Quebec has generally been able to fashion a broad consensus on major issues. The most recent example is the free trade debate. Quebec has proven its ability to redefine relations among government, business and labour to meet the challenges of international competition.

Since the early 1960s, Quebec has relentlessly pursued one objective: becoming a master of its own development. Five regimes, four decades, three parties, all in one direction. Over the past 30 years, Quebec has developed institutions able to contribute to economic development in a global trade context. The results are impressive: Hydro-Québec, the reform of education, the Caisse de dépôt et placement, the Société générale de financement, the Société de développement industriel, the Stock Savings Plan, deregulation of financial institutions, etc. Quebecers have succeeded in developing a unique degree of cooperation between the public and private sectors, in implementing a kind of Japanese-style cooperation between the political class, the labour movement and the business community.

Quebec society as a whole has made this transition. For instance, unions are involved in development, with the Solidarity Fund of the Fédération des travailleurs du Québec. Moreover, in the space of 10 years, entrepreneurship has blossomed in Quebec. Its universities produce more MBAs than the other nine provinces combined. The state has transformed itself in the midst of this momentum, from an entrepreneur to a catalyst. In short, there now exists a Quebec development model, along with the Japanese and German. This model is the culmination of 30 years of economic nationalism.

On the other hand, Canada is becoming a difficult country to govern, in part because of Quebec. The policy of national standards and other initiatives poorly targeted at the provinces has led the country to a perilous financial situation. The federal bureaucracy seems far removed from the reality of the country. Overlapping jurisdiction with the provinces and adversarial systems within government machinery are symptomatic of serious dysfunctions. Finally, the concept of two founding peoples and the recognition of Quebec as a distinct society have clearly been rejected by English Canada.

The lessons of history. Confederation was originally a milestone of freedom for all Canadians: one representative government, one country. For more than a century, we invested our energy in developing this country, in realizing and expanding its horizons. From the very dawn of Canadian history, from the time of Henri Bourassa and Wilfrid Laurier, we worked to give Canada its own identity, distinct from England, and to make an authentic country of this Dominion. But we also exhausted ourselves in language conflicts, legal and political conflicts, conferences and polemics that generally proved sterile, not to mention our own divisions between "federalists" and "nationalists".

In Quebec, Confederation has always been perceived as a solemn pact between two nations, a pact that could not be changed without the consent of the two parties. Circumstances have made Quebec the "national state of French-Canadians", so it is easy to imagine the frustration felt by Quebecers one morning in 1981 when they learned that their Constitution, the fundamental law of their country, would be amended without their agreement. Even more serious, an amending process was being institutionalized that would enable future amendments, again without the agreement of Quebec. Furthermore, this result contradicted a solemn promise of the Prime Minister of Canada. In a way, the Meech Lake Accord recognized the illegitimacy of a Constitution that failed to include Quebec.

Moreover, we are well aware that the cultural fabric of Canada has changed substantially. Traditional "English Canada" has become diversified through immigration and emerging regionalism. Quebec, for its part, while an open, welcoming society, is much more homogeneous and remains essentially "French" in culture.

It is in this sense that, on many occasions over several decades, we have sought, intensively and in a constructive spirit, solutions that would meet the pressing needs of Quebec and Canada. Initially, our disputes were essentially concerned with language equality. Then, as circumstances turned Quebec into the "national state of French-Canadians", Quebec increasingly had to defend its distinct nature, including the question of its status within Confederation. Ten years after the referendum, there is an urgent need to resolve economic conflicts.

Some see the failure of the Meech Lake Accord as a rejection of the French fact by English Canada. Others see it as an ill-directed protest against Bill 178, or as an illustration of the sterility of the amending formula inherited from the 1982 repatriation. As far as we are concerned, it is a fact. A fact that we must analyze in a historical perspective.

Since there is no indication that the legitimate aspirations of Quebec will change, it would be better now to follow a new, more constructive path, both for ourselves and for Canadians. That is why we advocate a new union. . . .

New Democratic Party:

A possible Canada – Phillip Edmonston

Three briefs were submitted to the Bélanger-Campeau Commission on behalf of the New Democratic Party: by Phillip Edmonston, the party's only elected MP from Quebec; by the Nouveau Parti Démocratique du Québec; and by Paul Cappon, the outgoing Associate President of the federal NDP. All three differed significantly, the major differences being between Edmonston's and the NPD-Québec's, both of which are excerpted here.

The NDP has a long history of troubled relations in Quebec. Barely two years after the founding of the federal party in 1961, the majority of its fledgling Quebec forces split to form the nationalist Parti Socialiste du Québec. The PSQ was ignored by the trade unions, won little support from the nationalist intelligentsia, and disappeared a few years later. A federalist Quebec NDP, after a brief surge in electoral support in 1965, soon ceased to have a major presence. In 1985 the party reorganized itself as an autonomous, nationalist Quebec formation maintaining tenuous links with the federal NDP. It grew quickly for a while, attaining a membership of 18,000 in 1988, many of them former PQ supporters disillusioned with that party's temporary shelving of the sovereignty option. However, with the PQ's renewed rise and the failure of the NDP in English Canada to support the Quebec party's constitutional stance, the NPD-Québec went into steep decline. In 1989 it voted to form an exclusively Quebec party wholly independent of the federal NDP. Following a vote by its Quebec council in support of sovereignty in May 1990, and its endorsement of the successful Bloc québécois candidate in a Montreal by-election in 1990, the party's federal council voted to sever its "fraternal ties" with the NPD-Québec.

Although Edmonston is the federal NDP caucus spokesman on Quebec, it is unclear to what degree his brief reflects the federal party's positions. Federal NDP leader Audrey McLaughlin, while endorsing some form of "decentralized federalism", has been staking out a position that appears to differ significantly from Edmonston's relatively sympathetic stance toward Quebec autonomy and "asymmetrical federalism".

At the party's biennial convention in Halifax in June 1991, the delegates adopted a "Canadian Constitution Resolution" calling for a "constituent assembly of Canadians to develop and recommend constitutional amendments for ratification by legislatures and the Parliament of Canada". The resolution stated that there was "only one precondition" to participation in this process: "a desire to remain within a renewed Canadian federation". The resolution lists "Quebecers' right to determine freely their future" as one of the "basic principles" guiding the NDP in the constitution debate. A section on the division of powers emphasizes the need for "effective national government" and does not propose according Quebec any increased jurisdiction.

The following excerpts from Edmonston's brief constitute the bulk of his presentation. The text follows an official English version released by Edmonston's office, slightly edited to conform to the French text presented to the Commission.

The text that follows it is excerpted from a resolution adopted by a "special policy convention" of the NPD-Québec on December 1, 1990 before being submitted to the Bélanger-Campeau Commission.

Social democrats cherish collective rights. That is why Canada's social democratic party, the NDP, has consistently voted resolutions upholding Quebec's right to self-determination since the 1940s.[*] That is why I am proud to be taking part in these hearings.

But collective rights join a list of other concerns that also need to be on any agenda that seeks to answer the question: what is Quebec's political and constitutional future? Poverty, full employment, fair taxes, the environment. . . . How will we improve the status of women in our society? How will we improve consumer protection? . . .

Our constitutional and political future is not, and must not be to build a sovereign state whose sole purpose is to provide a docile workforce and cheap raw materials to a business elite, even one that is impeccably *de vieille souche*. There is much, much more to building a civilized community than the bottom lines of Désourdy, Power Corporation or the National Bank.

---

[*] The basis of this statement is unclear. Edmonston's office, in reply to an inquiry, was unable to point to any specific document prior to 1987. The NDP was founded in 1961, as the successor to the Cooperative Commonwealth Federation (CCF). — Ed.

I am a federal Member of Parliament representing a pan-Canadian party. What Quebecers are used to hearing from spokespeople like me are warnings about the steep price Quebec would pay if it ever cut its federal links.

I don't believe that to be so.

Data compiled by University of Pennsylvania economist Robert Summers show that small industrialized nations tend to do no worse than big ones economically. Not only are growth rates similar, but per capita incomes are also equivalent. Denmark, Austria, Norway, Switzerland and Holland are examples of small nations that seem to be doing perfectly well without the security of a larger federation — in any event, until they integrate into the European Economic Community.

An independent Quebec would probably join the ranks of those smaller nations. In theory there is no reason for us not to do so. Our resource base is as good or better than that of most other countries. Our workforce is well-educated. Our economy is reasonably well-industrialized. In the last 25 years the Quebec government has forged an alliance with business that would rival the managed economies found in many social-democratic nations. This partnership has built up a base of successful Quebec companies and secures a solid foundation for a national economy.

I see two obstacles standing in the way of this political and constitutional future.

The first is the complexity of the negotiations that would be involved in bringing about an independent Quebec. How do we split up Canada's accumulated federal debt? Do we have a common currency and a common market, and if so, how do we set them up and manage them? What happens to federal property? What happens to federal public servants?

The negotiations to settle these issues would be very long and very complex; while they were going on there would be a great deal of uncertainty; and none of this is good news going into a recession.

But we shouldn't exaggerate how difficult this would be, either. At the turn of the century Norway seceded from its federal union with Sweden. There were some acrimonious negotiations at the time, but both countries survived and established new bases for cooperation.

The second obstacle standing in the way of a fully independent Quebec is psychological. [Despite a very deep disappointment and disenchantment following the rejection of the Meech Lake Accord, I believe that Quebecers are not sure that full independence is where they want to go. I would go further and suggest they are showing their customary good sense in not being sure that is where they want to go.*]

This summer, at the height of the reaction here to the rejection of Meech Lake, the Quebec City newspaper *Le Soleil* published a poll indicating Quebecers were evenly split: about a third wanted Quebec to remain a Canadian province; another third were for outright independence; and the rest were for a new economic and political association with Canada. Most other polls published since Meech was defeated broadly agree with these figures.

That is a two-thirds majority in favour of dumping the status quo. So the status quo is going to be dumped. But that could also be a two-thirds majority in favour of a new association with Canada, short of outright separation.

In an exchange early in this Commission's hearings, [Canadian Intergovernmental Affairs] Minister Rémillard asked [FTQ secretary] Fernand Daoust if he really believed that the entire Canadian house had to be levelled, and the whole structure rebuilt from the ground up. Was there not anything in the old structure, not a single room, worth preserving? Brother Laberge [the FTQ president] replied that it is hard to decide which room to keep when you've been thrown out of the house.

I want to address the issue raised in this exchange — why English Canada killed Meech Lake — in order to begin explaining why I believe that there are indeed a few rooms worth preserving in the Canadian house.

Meech Lake was defeated by Clyde Wells and Gary Filmon, two politicians who together represent 6 percent of the Canadian population. They killed a constitutional accord enacted by governments representing 94 percent of the Canadian population, and there is no question that they were able to do so because many Canadians, despite the leadership shown by most of their governments, refused to accept Quebec's identity and its need to affirm it constitutionally. . . .

But the record would not be complete if it were not put before this commission that many Canadians opposed the Meech Lake Accord for reasons that had nothing to do with Quebec. I want to put these points to you as someone who fervently supported the

---

* Bracketed words here and subsequently appear only in the official English text released by Edmonston's office. — Ed.

Accord, who campaigned on it and was elected partially in order to fight for it.

Federal spending power: As I will argue below, I was and remain in favour of a clear limitation on the federal spending power in order to ensure that Quebec is secure in its sovereignty over its own jurisdictions. However, many Canadians were uncomfortable with such limits in their own provinces. In much of Canada it has historically been the federal government that has been the engine bringing about progress through social programs, and not, as was the case in Quebec, the province.

Unbridled federal spending power does not correspond to our own needs and one way or another we are going to address it once and for all. That English Canadians don't all seek a similar solution in their own provinces does not necessarily mean they are saying "no" to Quebec.

Women's movement: Those of you who care to dwell on the 1982 constitutional process will recall that the *Canadian Charter of Rights and Freedoms* was amended late in the process to include a clause guaranteeing the absolute equality of men and women. Women in the United States fought unsuccessfully for many decades for such an "Equal Rights Amendment". Canadian feminists were rather proud to have achieved it here. Many were concerned that this section 15* of the *Charter* would become subordinate to any other principle, [including the "distinct society" clause of the Meech Lake Accord.

There was little or nothing to this objection.] Quebec has nothing to learn from English Canadian provinces about protecting the status of women. But this concern was reasonable enough for it to be addressed in the package of additions agreed to last June, and I give Canadian feminists enough credit to concede they were sincere in their concerns and not playing a trick in order to frustrate the aspirations of Quebec women and men.

The territories: Many Canadians, particularly people in the North, opposed Meech because the Accord made it impossible for the Yukon and Northwest Territories to become provinces. As the fate of Meech Lake itself proves, unanimity is a formula for failure. In Quebec we all now agree that we will never go through such a procedure again.

---

* This is obviously a reference to section 28, not section 15. — Ed.

Native people: The question of the aspirations of the North is intimately tied into another reason why some Canadians opposed Meech — the hopes and demands of Native communities.

Native people didn't and don't want to wait. They want their constitutional demands settled now, concurrently with or prior to Quebec's demands. Like Quebecers, they have been waiting a long time. That they are impatient and increasingly unsubtle in asserting their demands does not imply they reject Quebec's own aspirations as such.

Meech Lake was the culmination of the Quebec Round. We were trying to settle some basic issues regarding Quebec's role in the federation. Following its enactment, we could move on to other issues, including the concerns of Native people. I deeply regret that Native people refused to accept this. I believe they postponed rather than advanced the date of their fulfilment in helping to block the accord.

I am putting these points on the table because it is extremely important that we realize that many Canadians had excellent reasons to oppose Meech because this accord affected their own aspirations and not because they were opposed to the aspirations of Quebecers.

If you agree with me, then you cannot maintain, as [former PQ intergovernmental affairs minister Claude] Morin did in his brief to this commission, that English Canadians will inevitably reject any change to the constitutional status quo.

That governments representing 94 percent of the population endorsed Meech argues, on the contrary, that there is a great deal of willingness in Canada to allow Quebec to express its difference constitutionally.

A profound reform of the present regime, giving Quebec full autonomy over the instruments it needs to express its difference, could attract the support of a majority of Canadians and their governments — if that reform held out hope of saving the basic fabric of the country, and if that reform did not adversely affect the aspirations of Canadians in other provinces in their own eyes, as Meech Lake appeared to do.

A Canadian association. I therefore believe that it would be possible to keep some of the rooms of the Canadian house. And, in step with a majority of Quebecers, I believe that some of them are worth saving. For example:

Money, banking and tariffs. It would not be catastrophic if Quebec issued its own currency, but I see little advantage to doing so. If we pegged a Quebec *piastre* to the Canadian dollar, we would draw no new sovereignty from having it. If we didn't peg it, we might be creating a new trade barrier at a time when trade barriers are coming down. I therefore agree with Premier Bourassa that a common currency is in our best interests.

A common currency implies a common banking system. If we are to avoid the prospect of banks exploiting differences in regulation from province to province, or "country to country", we need to regulate them centrally.

In order to ensure the free exchange of goods and services, the federal government should retain its authority over tariffs and trade.

Foreign affairs. We have every reason to be proud of Canada's profile internationally. We have a seat with the Group of Seven through our federal link. Canada's role in the United Nations has been and remains an honourable and constructive one. Canada's identity as both an Atlantic and a Pacific power opens doors for us in both Europe and Asia. Quebec has its own role to play in *la Francophonie*, but with that issue amicably resolved I believe we should continue to associate ourselves with the rest of Canada in foreign affairs. However, I would add that within the embassies Quebec must be able to ensure that its economic and trade interests are being defended.

Defence. Quebecers have never been very close to the armed forces and it was therefore a pleasant surprise for us to discover, during the Oka crisis, that we have in the Canadian forces a military that is almost impeccably open to Francophones, rigorously professional, and highly competent.

The military is a highly inefficient way to spend public money: because modern armed forces are extremely capital-intensive, a dollar spent on the military produces only about a quarter the economic benefit of the same dollar spent elsewhere.

The latter point argues for keeping our spending on the military to its irreducible minimum. Since the present Canadian forces are an acceptable vehicle, associating with Canada in a common military is therefore our best option.

A role in citizenship. As I will argue shortly, Quebec requires the bulk of jurisdiction over immigration. Most intervenors agree, however, that there should be no barriers to movement of people from English-Canadian provinces to Quebec and vice versa. The simplest way to ensure there are no barriers is through a common citizenship. If we are to have common citizenship, the basic rules of the game for becoming a citizen should be the same across the country, implying a continuing federal role in citizenship.

Criminal law. The United States pays a steep price for fragmenting its criminal law among its states. Criminals who flee to neighbouring states have to be "extradited" before they face trial, contributing to the abysmally slow pace of justice in that country. Variations in penalties complicate enforcement against criminals who operate in different jurisdictions. We have avoided these problems in Canada through a unified criminal code and we should maintain it. The administration of our justice and prison system is a different matter, which I will address below.

The environment. The environment is the only jurisdiction where a good case can be made that the present federal power is insufficient.

Pollution knows no boundaries. The big stack in Sudbury is the cause of much of Quebec's acid rain. Industrial and municipal discharges from Ontario and the United States are an important source of pollution in the Ottawa and St. Lawrence rivers. Provincial jurisdiction complicates the disposal of toxic wastes because disposal sites tend not to accept waste from other jurisdictions. The resources needed to address environmental issues are very great, and we have everything to gain by pooling resources with the rest of the country to take the issue on.

I am therefore in favour of a very clearly defined, but predominant, federal role in the environment. Clear federal standards should be twinned with responsible decentralized administration.

Equalization. Contrary to the Quebec Chamber of Commerce, I am in favour of continuing this important federal program. As Quebec continues to mature economically, we will draw less and less benefit from equalization, and we should celebrate that fact. One of the benefits of a strong economy is the self-respect that comes from standing on your own feet. But in the meantime equalization assists us in maintaining the quality of our social programs. And the program will perform the same function in less well-off provinces for many years to come.

If at some point we become net contributors to equalization, what of it? Why should we be opposed to sharing with Canadians in provinces poorer than our own, in the cause of better schools, hospitals and public services?

Canada Post, Radio Canada, Canadian National, Air Canada. These federal-owned or regulated corporations provide essential services, have proven their worth, and should remain.

Census and statistics, navigation and shipping, weights and measures, patents and copyrights. There is no reason not to leave these matters with the central authority.

Some rooms we might want to eliminate. Having said all this, I believe that the present division of jurisdictions is wasteful and inefficient in a number of ways as it applies to Quebec. A more decentralized application of programs would avoid duplication, promote efficiency, save money, and allow Quebecers to tailor programs to our own needs.

Manpower training, unemployment insurance, income security. The Forum pour l'emploi has made a convincing case that the federal role in these areas should be entirely devolved to Quebec. Training is an element of education and, as such, needs to be as locally sensitive as do all other aspects of education. Federal unemployment insurance and other income security measures contribute to the multiplicity of programs, and work at cross purposes with Quebec programs.

One coherent, locally-administered income security program would do a much better job for the unemployed. One coherent, locally-administered manpower training program would do a much better job for the many thousands of Quebecers who will have to adapt to the new environment created by free trade. The Quebec ministries of Education and Post-secondary education have access to vastly greater resources to do this work than the federal government does.

Immigration. Demographic realities being what they are, Quebec will draw an increasing proportion of its population from immigration in the decades to come. It is therefore essential that Quebec control the selection and integration of immigrants. . . .

Family policy. Competing federal and provincial programs for daycare, family allowances, and other financial help for families waste money and work at cross-purposes. The entire field should be surrendered to Quebec in order to simplify its administration. The crucial role family policy plays in solving our present demographic problem goes without saying.

The justice and prison system. Our present system of multilayered federal and provincial courts and prisons shows all the familiar problems of overlapping jurisdiction: duplicated services; wasted funds; different standards and practices; work at cross-purposes. The courts, prisons and parole system should be under Quebec jurisdiction, with the exception of the Federal and Supreme Courts. . . .

The defence of Quebec's house. I am not opposed to these proposed changes being implemented across the country, but I am not opposed either to their applying to Quebec alone. The Canadian federation is already asymmetrical: Quebec collects its own taxes, manages its own pension program, and lives within its own civil code. We have not been collectively struck down by lightning bolts because of this asymmetry, and I see no reason to fear lightning bolts if we extend these precedents to other fields. . . .

What remains to be done is to ensure that this new association does not suffer in the future from "creeping recentralization". Several measures are necessary to ensure this does not happen.

Residual powers. All powers not specifically delegated to the federal government should reside with Quebec; in other words, Quebec should possess all residual powers. This would establish the principle that Quebec is sovereign in all jurisdictions except those it specifically shares with the federal government.

Limits to the federal spending power: As provided in the Meech Lake Accord, Quebec must be able to opt out of federal spending programs in areas of Quebec's own jurisdiction, with full compensation.

Supreme Court. The federal constitution should enshrine the composition of the court, establish that one-third of the Court be appointed from the Civil Law tradition, and require the federal government to select Justices for these seats from a list supplied by the government of Quebec.

The Charter of Rights. The *Canadian Charter of Rights and Freedoms* should be interpreted by the Supreme Court in light of an interpretive clause that would establish:

(1) that the government of Quebec may take appropriate measures to preserve and promote the status of Quebec as a distinct society; and

(2) that the government of Quebec has the unrestricted right to legislate on matters of language, other than as regards federal institutions and the right of official language minorities to schools as established in section 23 of the *Charter.*

A Quebec constitution. Provincial constitutions are specifically provided for in the 1982 *Constitution Act* [in section 45]. . . . Quebec should take advantage of this clause, and begin a process of popular consultation at the end of which we should give ourselves a Quebec constitution. This document would set out our institutions and enshrine our own charter of rights. . . .

For a constituent assembly – NPD-Québec

Of course Quebec is a "distinct society", and always has been. Its distinctiveness — and this should be recognized politically and juridically — is that it is founded on a people with its own language, culture and institutions, and that this people has the right, like all peoples, to self-determination, up to and including the right to constitute themselves as a nation with their own national state if that is their desire. Yet the Canadian constitution, and Canadian political and legal institutions, have never recognized this — in 1837, in 1867, in 1982 or today. And that is the issue. The Canadian federation is, from this standpoint, built on an undemocratic basis.

The Nouveau Parti Démocratique du Québec seeks a democratic solution to the national question, and thinks that trying to get Quebec to "re-enter" the Canadian federation through the negotiation of intergovernmental accords without changing this undemocratic basis can only lead to perpetuating the impasse and deepening tensions.

This is what led the NPD-Québec, as early as the summer of 1987, to express its profound disagreement with the entire process of constitutional bargaining that led to the Meech Lake Accord.

It was for this basic reason, and because the anticipated failure of the Meech Lake Accord provided final proof that Canadian federalism was unreformable under its own constitutional rules, that the National Council of the NPD-Québec voted last May in favour of sovereignty, while reaffirming the need for a uniquely Québécois constitution developed democratically by an elected constituent assembly representing all of the major components of Quebec society. . . .

This is not a new idea for Quebec. It is worth recalling the major conclusions of the *États généraux du Canada français*, which last met between March 1966 and March 1969, bringing together some 2,500 delegates from hundreds of organizations and associations. . . .

Reacting to the 1982 constitutional *coup de force* and the Canada Bill, some Quebec organizations, including the three major labour federations (the CEQ, CSN and FTQ) resurrected the idea of a grassroots process leading to the elaboration and adoption of a Quebec constitution. . . .

This is a perfectly reasonable proposal. Even now, in the wake of the most recent patchwork attempt by the federal state, we have witnessed an extraordinary mushrooming of discussions on Quebec's political and constitutional future. The major unions, farm organizations, ethno-cultural communities, anglophones, native peoples, women's organizations, employers' organizations — all of these groups and components of our society have been organizing in various ways to express their aspirations and expectations. Everyone wants to be part of this political and constitutional discussion. All the elements of a constituent assembly are rapidly being put in place. The only thing still lacking is the political will to convene it.

We are profoundly convinced that it is only at the culmination of this democratic process, this broad debate leading to a new consensus within Quebec society, and reinforced by the legitimacy and mass support flowing from it, that a Quebec government would be in a position to enter new discussions on an equal basis with the rest of Canada to determine the type of mutually advantageous relations it might wish to establish between Canada and Quebec. We think that as long as we try to skip this essential stage, the constitutional and political impasse will continue. . . .

Accordingly, the Nouveau Parti Démocratique du Québec calls on the Commission on Quebec's Political and Constitutional Future to adopt the following three proposals:

1. That the Quebec National Assembly issue a call for a referendum to convene an elected constituent assembly that would proclaim the sovereign national state of Quebec and adopt a constitution for it.

2. That, if such is the will of the Quebec people, the Quebec National Assembly undertake at the earliest opportunity the legislative process leading to the establishment of a law convening the constituent assembly of the Quebec people, defining its composition and mode of election, and ensuring the fairest possible representation of all the major components of the Quebec people.

3. That at the conclusion of the proceedings of the constituent assembly, the National Assembly sponsor a second referendum enabling the Quebec people to rule on the draft Constitution Act developed by the constituent assembly and thereby give it full democratic legitimacy.

Liberal Party of Canada (Jean Chrétien):

Independence fails the fundamental tests

"Those who reject federalism outright," said federal Liberal leader Jean Chrétien, "have the burden of proving that their alternative, that is to say, independence, will better encourage the economic, social and cultural growth of the people of Quebec."

Chrétien's 50-page written submission to the Bélanger-Campeau Commission offered a passionate defence of Canada and an extended critique of Quebec independence as costly, unstable and counter-productive for Quebec.

Quebec had benefited greatly from its participation in the Canadian confederation, he argued. The federal model gave Quebec autonomy in key jurisdictions while guaranteeing the province language rights and control over Francophone social and cultural institutions. The national tariff policy had helped industrialize Quebec. The province's citizens benefited enormously from federal equalization and transfer payments, shared cost programs and other grants.

"To depict all federal institutions as hostile and foreign to the interests of Quebec is a gross distortion of facts and of history," Chrétien said, citing federal institutions such as the CBC, the National Film Board, the Canada Council and the National Research Council. Quebec companies such as Lavalin and SNC, Chrétien argued, had taken root in Africa, the Middle East and Asia thanks to federal "financial support to buyer countries and the requirement that they 'buy Canadian'".

Quebec nationalism did not correspond to the challenges facing the province today, he suggested.

> In other parts of the world — usually those that are unstable — the resurgence of traditional nationalism is running counter to the forces of economic and political integration. The best illustration of this is the Soviet Union, which is falling apart under strong pressure from nationalisms. The same phenomenon is at work in Eastern Europe, India and several African countries, where diverse nations and ethnic groups are striving to set themselves apart.
>
> In most of these cases, the rise in nationalism has come after a period of foreign occupation, a particularly painful spell of authoritarian government, religious or ethnic conflict — or economic collapse. As in the past, nationalism presents itself as a means to free oneself from foreign oppression, to rebuild a devastated economy and to restore individual liberties. . . . For those countries that are free and better off, as in Western Europe, the fundamental challenge is not how to assert their nationalism — they did so, often to excess, in the 19th century and the first half of the 20th century — but rather how to build a pluralistic society. The challenge is how to direct nations along the path of political and economic integration.

A strong critic of Quebec nationalism, the Liberal leader was more indulgent toward Canadian nationalism.

> Canada is a country — a social model — that is very different from the United States. . . .the Canadian system is based upon a concept of the role of the state that is substantially removed from the American approach. That approach leaves individuals to fend for themselves. . . .

Canada is remarkable for many reasons: its identity, its modern symbols, its institutions, its national anthem, its flag, its constitution, its bilingualism.

In his presentation to the Commission, Chrétien allowed that some changes might be necessary in the "new Canada" he projects. He suggested reforming the Senate to make it an elected body, more representative of the regions, with a special role as protector of Francophone interests. Some form of asymmetrical federalism might be possible "in certain situations", but he was sceptical that this would be to Quebec's advantage.

Chrétien is not against recognizing Quebec as a "distinct society", so long as such recognition is subject to the federal Charter.

Provinces could be given the right to withdraw from federal programs with financial compensation, but the money must be used to achieve the corresponding "national objectives".

Quebec could be given a veto on constitutional change – like other major "regions" such as Ontario.

The excerpts that follow comprise the major part of Chrétien's critique of the independence option.

It is clear that Quebecers must decide between independence or remaining in Canada.

It is the fundamental duty of this Commission to clearly identify for Quebecers the consequences of these options.

In view of the strong consensus in favour of stability and economic development, the burden of proof is on those who advocate radical change to establish that the consequences of any such option are more advantageous and would serve the people of Quebec, now and in the long term. . . .

Independence. Proponents of the independence option argue that the achievement of independence would be relatively simple. In their view, Quebec would opt for independence and, within less than two years, negotiations would be successfully conducted with the remainder of Canada. Thus, independence would be settled and achieved within twenty-four months. In our view, such representations are illusionary.

With whom would Quebec negotiate? There is no basis in law or in fact for the assumption that the federal government has the authority or mandate to conduct such a negotiation. The Constitution of Canada does not give the federal government such power. Given the vital interest that each of the other provinces would have in such negotiations, there is no factual basis for any belief that the other provinces would simply grant the federal government an open-ended mandate to negotiate with Quebec.

Furthermore, if one assumes, only for the sake of argument, that the other provinces were prepared to let the federal government negotiate Quebec's sovereignty on their behalf, the Parliament and Government of Canada would have no power to represent or speak for the remainder of Canada, since they represent and can only represent all 10 provinces. Put another way, it would be absurd for the rest of Canada to be represented in negotiations with Quebec by the Parliament and Government of Canada — which includes popular representation of approximately 25 percent from Quebec.

Some constitutional commentators have speculated that the English-speaking provinces might themselves band together to negotiate some kind of sovereignty association with Quebec, without the government of Canada. But they have no power to negotiate the sovereignty of Quebec either, with or without association. Indeed, their powers are limited to provincial matters, however much the practice of executive federalism in the past few years may have obscured that fact.

However sovereignty were to be declared by Quebec — if this were the route Quebecers were to choose — when it happened, some formal or *ad hoc* arrangement would have to be settled upon as to who would be empowered to speak for the nine English-speaking provinces, in the negotiation of a separation agreement with Quebec. Would it be the Parliament of Canada minus the Quebec MPs and senators, who would choose a new (perhaps "national") government for the purpose? Or would a new Parliament be elected from the nine provinces, having in mind the impending Canada-Quebec negotiations? Or would it be some combination of the national and provincial legislatures that would choose the body that would negotiate the separation arrangements, to be ratified by the 10 legislative bodies? And would this all be done constitutionally, or on an *ad hoc* basis? Should the population of the nine provinces also be formally consulted to ratify the final decision?

It must be emphasized that all of the foregoing presupposes the will and decision of the reminder of Canada to stay together. Since Canada has no relevant historical precedent for this situation, there is no valid basis for knowing how the people of each of the Canadian provinces will react or whether any consensus could be achieved among the remaining provinces.

Before the remainder of Canada could begin to negotiate with Quebec, the people in the rest of Canada would have to reach agreement as to the nature, form and structure of the remainder of Canada. Could such agreement, which by definition would involve issues of constitutional structures, institutions and economic and political arrangements be reached? Reaching such agreement would be further complicated since it would depend, in part, on the nature of the arrangements made with Quebec. Thus a vicious cycle would exist. That is, to negotiate with Quebec, the rest of Canada must first reach agreement as to its political, constitutional and economic status. But for the remainder of Canada to agree on its own status, it must first know its arrangements with Quebec. Assuming the remainder of Canada could reach an internal agreement, it is clear that it would take years, not months, before meaningful negotiations could even commence.

Issues to Negotiate. All of the foregoing relates merely to some of the procedural issues that arise from the independence option. Consideration must also be given to some of the substantive issues that would require settlement in the aftermath of a decision to opt for independence.

The character and the consequences of the separation negotiations between Quebec and the new "Canada of Nine" that would be triggered by Quebec's declaration of independence are equally unknown and unpredictable. Some of the matters that would *have* to be negotiated, however, give some idea as to the complexities:

1. *Deciding how the public debt would be divided between Quebec and the rest of Canada.* Would Quebec assume its per capita share of the federal debt, approximately 25.5 percent of $320 billion, i.e. $81.8 billion? When added to the Quebec debt of $31.8 billion, Quebec would have to service a debt of approximately $113.7 billion. On a per capita basis, Quebecers would be amongst the most highly indebted people in the industrial world.

2. *Deciding how the federal assets would be divided.* How would Canada be compensated for any part of the assets and investments put in place in Quebec by the present Canada, which exceeded, on a per capita basis, those put in place in the rest of Canada? What would constitute "assets" for purposes of such a negotiation?

3. *Deciding the territory and borders of Quebec.* Would the territory of Ungava, transferred to Quebec in 1912 by the Parliament of Canada, be treated as territory, or as one of the assets which would enter into the "compensation for assets negotiations" or as a territory that should be ceded to the aboriginal peoples who largely populated it in 1912 (analogous to the land claims negotiations in the Northwest Territories)?

4. *Deciding responsibility for aboriginal people and their lands.* As we recognize that they will have a major say in that regard.

5. *The assumption by the new national government of Quebec of responsibility for the Quebec public servants who had been serving the Government of Canada.*

6. *Deciding how to deal with currency, the monetary system and the banking system.*

These are just a few of the issues that would require settlement. Dealing with these issues would be extremely difficult and it would be irresponsible to suggest that reaching agreement would be easy or quick. Again, it would take many years to resolve these matters in addition to the years required to resolve the procedural issues discussed previously.

It cannot be stated strongly enough that while Quebec and what remains of the rest of Canada are spending years consumed by difficult debate and negotiation over procedure and substance, the world will be watching and will not be standing still.

With approximately $229 billion in foreign debt, is there any conclusive argument or compelling reason to believe that the financial markets and our creditors will not be deeply concerned by the uncertainty and instability of the Canadian situation?

Another question that must be addressed is how Quebecers and Canadians would manage their affairs and get on with their daily lives and business during the prolonged period between a decision in favour of independence and ultimate settlement. This is a complete unknown.

To the extent that a clear consensus has emerged in favour of stability and economic development, the independence option with or without economic association fails the test. The burden is clearly on those who propose this option to prove that this is the best option for the people of Quebec and in the best interest of Quebec.

Turning, for the sake of argument, to the situation after independence, the question arises as to whether there is a net benefit to the people of Quebec.

One of the forces behind the current debate is concern over the future of the French language and culture. Is independence the best option to relieve the insecurity and allay the concern? Again, in posing this question and attempting to respond, the issue is not whether Quebec could survive as an independent state; the issue is whether having a totally independent nation-state called Quebec is the best option.

To the extent that the future of the French language and culture is central to the discussion, the following issues must be addressed:

1. What would happen to the one million francophones living outside Quebec? With only approximately 5.5 million francophones living in Quebec, can we afford to write off one million people? If not, what realistic option is there for them? With outright independence, the central vision of bilingualism and duality in Canada would be destroyed. There would be no further powerful justification for a commitment to the French fact outside Quebec. Any argument that they might be protected under an arrangement for economic association between Quebec and the remainder of Canada would be undercut by the fact that the arrangement, by definition, would be purely economic. Is it wise or prudent to abandon approximately 20 percent of the total francophone community?

2. Will the French language and culture be more secure without a commitment of the remainder of Canada to support the French fact in Canada? Dissenters will argue that the Canadian commitment has been and is equivocal. That is far from the truth. French is an official language of Canada. Federal government services are delivered in the official languages. The right to education in French is guaranteed in the Constitution. Over 250,000 English-speaking children are enroled in French immersion programs outside Quebec. Polls show that a majority of English-speaking Canadians recognize the equality of the two official languages and support federal bilingualism. The French language and culture have never been stronger in Quebec. Clearly serious progress has been and is being made. Is the French language and culture best served by the majority of Francophones in Canada abandoning their allies?

3. During the era of globalization, when people and communities are searching for ways to retain their identity, values, traditions and heritage, are the people of Quebec best served by renouncing the part of their history and heritage as founders and builders of Canada? Is it necessary or even logical to do so in search for security?

4. Much of the current debate is fuelled by the fact that the Quebec birthrate is one of the lowest in the western world, and immigration is insufficient. Between 1983 and 1986, Quebec suffered a net out-migration of approximately 56,000 people, of whom 53.6 percent were university graduates. Between 1966 and 1984, only approximately 235,000 people came to Quebec out of approximately 1.8 million people who immigrated to Canada. During that period, approximately 460,000 people emigrated from Quebec. Will Quebec's ability to attract and retain people be improved when Quebec is no longer part of Canada?

5. Fifty-three percent of Quebec's exports are to the rest of Canada as compared to 35 percent for Ontario. Will independence best preserve this preferred trading relationship?

6. The Canada-U.S. Free Trade Agreement has stronger support in Quebec than anywhere else in Canada because Quebecers view it as vital to their economic interests. Proponents of independence contend that Quebec would merely counter-sign all existing treaties. Is there any conclusive evidence that the other parties to such treaties would accept this without wanting to examine and deal with each case on its own merits, before establishing the framework for their future economic relationship with Quebec?

7. Is there conclusive proof that could lead one to believe that with a population of 6.7 million, Quebec would manage better in similar negotiations? Will an independent, economically weaker Quebec have the same access or make as good a deal under GATT or other trade arrangements?

8. Would an independent Quebec of 6.7 million people be more capable of protecting its inhabitants from the global forces which recognize no borders and have given rise to concerns about the future of the French language and culture?

Many more questions can be asked. The entire independence option is fraught with great uncertainty. Independence fails the fundamental tests of stability, economic development and the advancement of the best interests of the people of Quebec. It would be an adventure which would consume our energies for the better part of a generation, sapping our strength and distracting us from the urgent need to successfully deal with the urgent and enormous challenges of a rapidly emerging new world order.

It has been suggested that another option is confederalism. This is not so because independence is a prerequisite for such a regime.

Confederalism means an arrangement in which independent states retain their independent status but delegate, as the occasion arises, certain powers to a common organism. Fundamental to such an arrangement is the existence of independent states. Such an arrangement would contemplate varying degrees of relations or association in respect of certain economic and political matters. Common institutions would be established by the independent states. Persons sitting in any such common institutions would not be elected by the people but would be appointed by each independent state. The independent states delegate such matters, as they may agree from time to time, to the common institutions and they retain the power to withdraw any matter which they may have delegated.

In examining this option, this commission must consider the question of why there are no confederal entities in existence at this time. The United States, Switzerland and Germany began as confederations before they became the federations they are today. History demonstrates that confederations are fragile and unstable entities which evolve into federations. In each example we know, confederations were transformed into stable federal states.

The closest modern example resembling confederalism that may be found is the EEC. However, it must be observed immediately that the EEC, as it currently exists, is merely a transitional arrangement in a process of bringing Europe together, a process that began over 30 years ago.

Virtually every informed expert on the EEC is of the view that Europe is moving toward federalism, in a form which some suggest may be even stronger and more centralized than the Canadian model.

The European Parliament is now elected independently of the governments of the member states. The European Commission, while named by the member states, cannot have its functions changed other than by a vote of the European Parliament. The European Court of Justice has jurisdiction over matters referred by the Commission acting independently of member states. These powers are those of a supranational federalism.

The question must be asked as to why Quebecers — and, indeed, Canadians — would want to establish an arrangement along the lines of the one already being left behind by Europe? Why is Europe evolving beyond its current structures? The most likely answer appears to be that confederalism is inherently an unstable structure. This instability relates to the fact that a strong and stable economic relationship requires strong, stable and effective political structures.

The more the economic and social well-being of the individual is affected by the decision of some central structure, the more the principles of democracy require that the individual have a direct "say" in who sits on that central structure and who makes the decisions.

Furthermore, since a confederal structure contemplates that sovereign powers remain exclusively in the hands of the independent member states and there is always the right to withdraw authority from any central structure or institution, instability and uncertainty characterize the association since there is no real binding long-term commitment to the association that each of the independent states may rely upon. There is no central institution with the continuing power, authority or responsibility to ensure that the association is effective and survives.

Given the weakness and instability of the confederal option, it fails the test of ensuring the people of Quebec and Canada the stability and economic development they require. Furthermore, the best interests of Quebec and Canada are not advanced by pursuing a model which cannot stand the test of time.

But more fundamental than the foregoing is the fact that independence of each of the members is a pre-condition to confederalism. Thus, to achieve confederalism, Quebec must first achieve independence.

Although some claim there are three clear options facing Quebecers, in reality, there are only two. Those options are independence and a modern Canada.

2.

Business debates costs, benefits of sovereignty and federalism

The Commission heard from a range of business groups. Some were national (province-wide) lobbies or umbrella organizations, some of whose briefs are excerpted here. Others were locally based; the Commission received briefs from literally dozens of regional and municipal chambers of commerce, boards of trade and development agencies. Most of the latter groups focused their remarks on local issues, in particular the need for greater attention to development of regions outside the major Montreal and Quebec City urban conglomerations.

The major issues addressed by the national business groups were the advantages and disadvantages of the existing federal system, Quebec's competitive position, and the possible costs of sovereignty.

Virtually all business groups agreed that Quebec should continue to maintain close economic links with the rest of Canada, although they differed considerably on the degree of political integration this objective should entail. There was general agreement that existing barriers to trade and investment within Canada should be dismantled to enable the freest possible mobility of persons, goods, services and capital within this "economic space". Most complained of the cost of overlapping federal and provincial jurisdictions and the duplication of programs that results. Virtually all expressed alarm at the size of government debts and current deficits. There was a general consensus that the maintenance of a monetary union with the rest of Canada, while not indispensable, was desirable given the close integration of financial markets. And all business groups expressed strong support for the Free Trade Agreement with the United States as a means of increasing Quebec's international competitive standing.

Where they differed most sharply was in their respective balance sheets of Canadian federalism and the advisability of sovereignty. A major item of divergence involved complex comparisons of federal expenditures in Quebec with the amounts Quebec sends to Ottawa in taxes. As the Commission noted in its own summary of this evidence, "perceptions vary depending on one's approach." The statistical evidence was voluminous (and for that reason must be omitted here), but in the end it is doubtful that the net fiscal balance is conclusive evidence of the merits of either federalism or sovereignty. Some economists – and some federalists and sovereigntists among the business interests – argued that there was no conclusive evidence that either option was economically more sound. The non-economic considerations were more decisive, they said.

However, most business groups favoured, as a minimum, full Quebec jurisdiction over many powers now held wholly or jointly by the federal government.

Chambre de commerce du Québec:

Canadian federalism is an economic failure

The first group to appear before the Commission was the Quebec Chamber of Commerce, and its brief created a minor sensation in the media. Although declining to support a specific constitutional option, the Chamber pronounced Canadian federalism "an economic failure" and advocated a radical restructuring of the system to give Quebec exclusive jurisdiction over many powers now held by Ottawa and deprive the latter of automatic residual power. The brief was dramatic evidence of just how alienated many Quebec business people are with Canada as presently constituted.

The failure of the Meech Lake Accord is the culmination of more than a quarter century of attempts at the renewal of federalism that have failed to satisfy Quebec. It has forced Quebec to re-examine the constitutional issue in a broader perspective, and to question the nature of its association with the rest of Canada. This vision of the post-Meech situation is shared by a majority of Quebecers. It is also shared by a large proportion of business people. For example, in an IQOP poll in December 1989, 82 percent of the members of the Chambre de commerce et d'industrie du Québec métropolitain agreed that if the Meech Lake Accord failed to pass, Quebec should rethink its adherence to the Canadian federation.

However, it is important to note that the business community's uneasiness with Canadian federalism is not ideological but pragmatic: Quebec's business people are convinced that Canadian federalism is an economic failure.

This conviction is reflected in a SOM-*Les Affaires* poll conducted in April 1990 among the directors of the 500 largest industrial firms in Quebec. It revealed that the opinions favouring Quebec's independence if the Meech Lake Accord failed to pass outweighed the opinions against independence by a margin of 3 to 2. Furthermore, 85 percent of the respondents believed that the long-term impact of independence on the economic development of Quebec would be either positive (53 percent) or negligible (32 percent).

The fact that a substantial proportion of directors of Quebec's major industrial firms are willing to go that far, in spite of the economic apprehensions that independence has always raised, indicates their deep concern over the present state of federal finances and policies. This concern is also shared by business people all across the country; a resolution at the recent convention of the Canadian Chamber of Commerce warned of the "catastrophic outcome" of federal budget management. . . .

We do not wish to take a stand for the time being on the precise constitutional formula that Quebec should adopt, especially with regard to the political ties to be kept with the rest of Canada, because in so far as reinforcing the stability and growth of our economy is concerned, a number of viable options are possible. We do insist on assuring our fellow-citizens beforehand that we are participating with open-mindedness and equanimity in the incipient debate, in the hope that the end result will be a definitive and democratic choice.

Ensuring economic stability. . . . Two fundamental conditions must be met if we are to ensure the smooth running of the economy. First, Quebec must be very clear about its desire to respect the internationally accepted rules of the economic game, which are based on freedom of trade and the fulfilment of contractual agreements. Secondly, the eventual new constitutional context of Quebec must be determined in a quick and decisive manner. . . .

The first condition is to ensure the greatest possible continuity in the laws and regulations now governing Quebec's economy, both domestically and in its relations with the rest of Canada and abroad. This is the responsibility of the Quebec government.

Quebec must first and foremost protect the integrity of the Canadian common market. This means that it must categorically reject any restrictions on the free movement of individuals, goods and capital, which is now guaranteed throughout the various parts of Canada. In particular, Quebec must make it clear that its traditionally open attitude toward Anglophones and allophones, whose contribution to the building of Quebec's economy was and continues to be essential, will not change, regardless of its political future.

Quebec must also flatly reject any proposal to create new barriers to foreign financial and commercial transactions. The government must honour its commercial treaties as a member of the Canadian federation, such as the GATT and the Canada-U.S. Free Trade Agreement. It must give reassurances that it will honour all of its contractual financial agreements, whether drawn up in Canadian dollars or in foreign currency.

In addition, Quebec must convince the international community that it intends to remain active in promoting the freedom of interprovincial and international trade. It must not pass up the opportunity to show its commitment to the current trend toward a broader opening of markets, particularly in relation to interprovincial trade barriers, the Uruguay Round negotiations and U.S.-Canada-Mexico trilateral relations.

As a result of the recent orientation of its economic policy, Quebec already has a solid credibility in matters pertaining to economic freedoms, support to the private sector and the legislative and fiscal quest for competitiveness. For example, in the last decade, the trend toward deregulation of financial institutions in Canada was largely the result of Quebec's innovative influence or competition. Quebec also substantially revised the role of its impressive array of Crown corporations. Many of them have been privatized. Furthermore, the Lévesque and Bourassa governments supported both the idea and the draft of the Free Trade Agreement with the United States. Of all the regions in Canada, Quebec was the most supportive of the Free Trade Agreement. Finally, during the last decade the disparities between Quebec and Ontario in personal and corporate taxation have been substantially reduced and in some cases even reversed in Quebec's favour.

However, even if Quebec were to spend a lot of energy convincing Canada and the rest of the world that it will conform to all of the accepted rules of the economic game, this alone would not completely erase the uncertainty that burdens its political and economic future. There will always be some speculators and investors with distorted views or an extreme aversion to risk. They will refrain from investing in Quebec as long as a new constitution does not clearly guarantee the continuity of the economic environment.

The only appropriate action in this situation is to limit the duration of this uncertainty and ensure that the direction that is ultimately taken is clear and straightforward. This is the second condition that must be met in the debate. Quebec's constitutional future must be settled promptly and decisively, as the Germans did in remodelling their future less than a year after the destruction of the Berlin Wall. . . .

Rebalancing the public Finances. The imbalance in the public finances, which is particularly evident at the federal level, is one of the main sources of dissatisfaction if not frustration of our members with Canadian federalism. . . .

During the last decade Canada's central government has had the third highest rate of indebtedness of the 15 largest industrial countries. The enormous federal deficit has destabilized the Canadian economy in two ways. First, although they were not the only culprits, the federal budget deficits have contributed greatly to Canada's high interest rates. . . .

Secondly, simply to cover the interest paid on the accumulated debt, which accounts for 35 percent of its revenues, and to correct the errors of the past, the federal government is forced to increase the burden of personal and corporate taxation — thus impeding our international competitiveness — and destabilize provincial finances by unilaterally reducing its transfers to the provinces. . . .

The major problem is the government's loss of control over its expenditures on programs.

It is important that the constitutional changes proposed by Quebec help to correct the faults of the federal system that have led the central government into its current financial crisis. The objective is clear: to control the propensity of governments to spend and borrow.

One of the major causes of the rapid increase in federal spending is Parliament's general spending power under sections 91 (preamble and head 29) and 92 (head 10(c)) of the *Constitution Act, 1867.* Under these provisions, Parliament may spend in any area that is not explicitly covered by the distribution of powers in 1867, in matters of shared jurisdiction with the provinces, and even in the presumably exclusive provincial jurisdictions. The federal government has used this power many times since 1945.

The duplication of departments in both government spheres is generalized. We have two departments in education, culture, science, technology, justice, immigration, labour, manpower, revenue, industry, commerce, financial institutions, health, welfare, energy, resources, agriculture, environment, transportation, recreation, communications, urban affairs and even external affairs.

In fact, a study 12 years ago revealed that of 465 existing federal and provincial spending programs, 277 (or 60 percent) directly or indirectly overlapped.* All areas of government activity with the exception of the postal service, defence and veterans affairs, were intertwined between the two levels of government. There are plenty of examples to indicate that the situation has since worsened.

Though there is some wisdom in the notion that competition between different levels of government improves the quality of the services offered to the public, this analogy with the private sector would only be acceptable if this competition eliminated the least efficient level of administration from a given sector. But that is not what happens in the public sector where, far from eliminating the least efficient level, competition tends to generate an escalation in spending. . . .

In our view, the fundamental principle in determining the distribution of powers between Quebec and Canada must be the following: Quebec must be assigned exclusive jurisdiction over all matters of an essentially regional or local character, and of all regional or local aspects of matters that extend beyond Quebec's borders but nonetheless continue to play a role in the preservation and development of its identity.

We are aware, of course, that the clarification of jurisdictions can assume different forms, depending on the particular constitutional perspective that is chosen. For example, in a federalist perspective the distribution of powers would be revised case by case, assigning each matter or aspect of a matter as clearly as possible to one level of government only, and creating an efficient mechanism for sharing possible new areas.

If the federalist perspective is chosen, we believe that the provincial level should be assigned exclusive jurisdiction over the following matters: education and science, research and develop-

---

* Germain Julien and Marcel Proulx (under the supervision of Arthur Tremblay), *Le Chevauchement des programmes fédéraux et québécois*, École nationale d'administration publique, Quebec 1978, Table 2, p. 33.

ment, culture, justice, communications, labour, intraprovincial trade, inland navigation and transportation, coastal fishing, manpower, social security (unemployment insurance, social assistance, family allowances, old age security, etc.), regional economic development, regional environment, relations with native peoples, health, social services, urban affairs and recreation. Several matters that extend significantly beyond Quebec's frontiers should be discussed and negotiated more thoroughly with the rest of Canada: for example, defence and aerospace industry, external affairs, immigration, interprovincial trade, interprovincial navigation and transportation, deep sea fishing, the environment at large, financial institutions, postal services, the national guard and income redistribution among the provinces.

The preamble to s. 91 of the *Constitution Act, 1867* gives the federal government the residual power to make laws in relation to all matters not explicitly foreseen by the Constitution. We object to this automatism. It is seems logical to us that new jurisdictions should be granted on the basis of minimizing costs and maximizing the satisfaction of the public's preferences. The result would thus depend on the matter at hand. . . .

From a "confederalist" perspective, or in a model like that adopted by the members of the European Community, the general spending authority in all matters without exception would lie entirely with the member states (such as Quebec). The member states would then agree on explicitly delegating certain powers — and corresponding financial resources — to the Parliament of the Confederation or Community.

Whatever the system finally adopted, the priority must be a clearer sharing of responsibilities in order to minimize the ambiguity that has contributed to the current overlapping, duplication, inconsistency and wasting of resources. . . .

The structure of the new financial arrangement will obviously depend on the constitutional system that is adopted. In the event of a restructuring of the current federal system, each transfer of jurisdiction from Ottawa to Quebec should be accompanied by a corresponding transfer of taxation approximately equal in value to the federal expenditures in Quebec in that particular field. In a confederal or European system, all taxes would be levied by Quebec, which would then give Ottawa an amount proportionate to jurisdictions delegated to the new Canadian structure.

An immediate corollary of this approach is that any new constitution must put an end to the current federal-provincial transfer schemes in relation to established programs (health and higher education), public assistance (welfare) and special agreements in many other areas (manpower, regional development, etc.). A regional government that wishes to spend more in a given area will have to set up a financing plan with its own resources, rather than go begging for extra funds from the central government, which in the long run would increase its financial dependence. The principle of fiscal responsibility means, therefore, that the provinces or member states must be freed of the financial dependency on the federal government that is sustained by the present system.

We also question the present equalization payments scheme by which the less affluent provinces receive unconditional yearly transfers from Ottawa in an attempt to bring their capacity to provide public services closer to the Canadian average. This scheme was an original initiative at a time when the major social programs (health, education, income security, social services, etc.) were much less elaborate, direct grants of every kind were much more scarce, and the tax system much less progressive than it is today. We believe it is now outdated. Over the years, it has become more and more arbitrary and complex. . . .

Re-establishing monetary stability. Although the devastating impact of high interest rates and an overvalued dollar is felt all across Canada, its consequences are more serious for Quebec's economy, particularly since firms here still have the highest debt ratio in Canada.

The exorbitant interest and exchange rates resulting from federal budget and monetary policies are blatantly inconsistent with the country's trade policy, especially with regard to the Canada-U.S. Free Trade Agreement. . . .

The FTA does indeed create profit opportunities and jobs, but our monetary policy is such that these opportunities are created in the United States instead of in Canada.

The frustration felt by Quebec's business community towards the federal monetary policy is great and, we feel, entirely justified. In our opinion, in order to find a long-term solution to this problem, the following four measures must be taken: (1) preserve the Canadian monetary union; (2) stabilize the Canada-U.S. exchange rate; (3) make the Bank of Canada more representative at the decision-making level and more transparent in its decisions; and (4) fight inflation with a method that is more efficient and less damaging to the economy than chronic monetary contraction. . . .

Apart from wage and price controls, which would restrict economic freedom, the only hope of success lies in developing a spirit of cooperation and coordination [*concertation*] between the business community, the unions and the government. This spirit must be sustained by the appropriate institutions, as is the case in Germany, Japan, Scandinavia and Austria, where the economic performance is clearly superior to the average in the industrial countries. In these countries the economic partners collectively agree on acceptable annual inflation limits, which then serve as effective guidelines for wage bargaining and price increases.

Maintaining and strengthening the competitive position of Quebec and Canada would be a crucial concern in determining these guidelines, thus sparing the central bank from intervening and allowing comparatively high levels of economic growth and employment. Unlike monetary restriction, which affects all of Canada regardless of the different inflation and unemployment rates, the inflation guidelines set by social consensus could differ from one region to the next.

Establishing effective coordination and cooperation mechanisms in Quebec and in the rest of Canada will not be easy. However, we have no choice if we are to put an end to the monetary instability that is keeping our country in an almost permanent state of economic stop-and-go and job stagnation. The new constitution could, if necessary, provide for the creation of coordinating institutions and their interaction with existing institutions.

Mouvement des caisses Desjardins:

From a distinct national society
to a sovereign State of Quebec

The only major business group to advocate Quebec sovereignty was the Mouvement Desjardins, (the Desjardins Group). A unique financial institution built around a massive network of local *caisses populaires*, or credit unions, the Mouvement is Quebec's largest retail banker with 4.3 million "members" or clients, 18,300 volunteer officers and 34,000 employees in Quebec. With its holdings in life and casualty insurance subsidiaries, a brokerage firm, a trust company and a venture capital firm, it controls assets of over $44 billion.

Until recently confined to Quebec (an attempt in 1908 to obtain a federal charter was defeated in the Canadian Senate), the Mouvement Desjardins in 1989 affiliated largely Francophone *caisses populaires* in Ontario, Manitoba and Acadia (New Brunswick) and signed an agreement with the Confédération du Crédit Mutuel de France.

Its brief to the Commission shares the critique of the federalist "status quo" made by other business groups, and presents a veritable eulogy to the new class of Francophone capitalists who have emerged in recent years. While advocating "autonomy" for Quebec, largely on political and cultural grounds, it also holds out the possibility that the future State of Quebec might ultimately establish a genuine confederation with its current partners in the Canadian federation.

To prepare its brief, the Mouvement Desjardins circulated a written "consultation" to its approximately 20,000 local officers, most of them elected members of the boards of directors, credit committees and boards of supervision of each of the 1,339 local caisses. About 10,000 replied, 80% supporting Quebec's "political autonomy" as defined in this brief.

At least two major significant trends can be recognized that are of relevance to the issue we are examining: on the one hand, a certain tendency toward globalization, or at least toward internationalization; on the other hand, a tendency toward the assertion of particular national, regional, local or individual characteristics. These trends appear contradictory, but this is because they have to do largely with different realities. . . .

Exhaustion through division. In this twofold overall context of globalization of the economy and assertion of national identities, Canada seems to be wearing itself out through an endless series of misunderstandings and internal compromises rather than preparing itself for the challenges of the future.

For example, growth in manufacturing productivity has been lower in Canada than in most of the other major industrialized countries in recent years. Between 1980 and 1990, Canada fell from second to sixth rank in this regard within the Group of Seven. The Canadian Manufacturers' Association has concluded that in 10 years Canada has lost 15 percent of its competitiveness in relation to the other major industrialized countries.

The low growth in productivity is said to be due in particular to a certain technological lag, itself the result of insufficient investment in research and development.

Moreover, Canada is becoming bogged down with an enormous debt that is already mortgaging its ability to control its economy and support it during difficult times; even some international organizations are concerned about this.

Indeed, one might readily conclude that Canada does not have the structures it needs to face the challenges of the final decade of this century with efficiency and flexibility. Its federal system, which complicates decision-making through the large number and diversity of participants, handicaps its ability to adapt while depriving its components of the manoeuvrability they need in order to adjust their policies and programs to their particular situations.

In recent years, as we know, Quebec has indicated a greater alertness than most of its partners in Canada to the changes in the international situation. For example, it has modernized and relaxed the regulations governing financial institutions under its jurisdiction, and the new regulations have to some degree become a model for the rest of Canada and some other countries. Several institutions have even abandoned their federal charters to adopt the more favourable Quebec framework in order to confront international competition and the deregulation of financial activities.

In the area of free trade, Quebec was a decisive factor in the ultimate decision to move ahead. In spite of its own weaknesses, the foreseeable adjustment costs and the scope of the challenges posed by the gradual opening up of markets, Quebec understood that the evolution of the world economy left it little choice and that it was better to opt right away for competition, competitiveness and productivity, as well as creativity and audacity.

However, notwithstanding some substantial economic progress, the drop in Quebec's relative population continues to reduce its political weight within Canada as a whole and, at the same time, its ability to intervene in federal decisions and obtain policies that reflect its own needs. While the Quebec government has itself taken serious steps to bring its expenditures under control, it can only look on as the federal public debt grows, unable to intervene in any significant way in the decisions of the central government. The same situation also limits Quebec's power to act in such areas as the fight against unemployment, regional development, training of the labour force and industrial structure. Quebec is therefore penalized in some ways by its participation in Canadian federalism and loses certain powers that are essential to the full realization of its potential for development. . . .

Unacceptable status quo. The current situation appears too complex to be settled through minor adjustments. In terms of synergy and efficiency, factors whose importance cannot be ignored, the present system must take the blame for a great many jurisdictional quarrels, overlapping programs, and inconsistent priorities and policies. . . .

Where the sharing of powers is concerned, the provinces have ample motives for recrimination. For many years Quebec governments have been asking for essential powers to protect the province's specific linguistic and cultural characteristics. On the pretext that the airwaves transcend provincial boundaries, Ottawa has assumed authority over communications, and specifically telecommunications. Radio and television broadcasting fall under the supervision of pan-Canadian organizations, although they are recognized as vital means of protecting and promoting culture. In immigration, Quebec won the power to participate in the selection of potential immigrants to the province. . . .

In education, the federal government is becoming increasingly intrusive, mainly in the areas of higher and technical education, university research, second-language training and manpower training. Authority in all these fields, where the values, visions and customs of a culture are fundamental, is once again jealously guarded by Ottawa, dominated by cultural motivations that differ from ours. In manpower training, the work of the Forum sur l'emploi and the round tables pursuing that work have brought other problems to light: enormous sums are being spent, often squandered, because programs do not meet the needs of workers or businesses or correspond to regional priorities. This is a striking example of the wasted energy, money and time that often result from inefficient duplication of government efforts, divergent objectives and the inability of major national programs to meet specific regional needs.

In terms of important cultural activities, we cannot overlook the matter of representation in other countries. Quebec has fought hard to obtain agreement to a permanent Francophone presence in Canadian embassies and trade missions. Yet it is still difficult for Quebec to obtain adequate representation at various international events and to benefit fully from these foreign contacts, even in matters of provincial jurisdiction and in relations with Francophone nations.

There is also the problem of the proportion of the federal government's effort that is devoted to Quebec. In economic terms, Statistics Canada's National Accounts show that since 1960 Quebec has not been receiving its fair share of expenditures on goods and services by the Canadian government. While its gross domestic product accounted for an average of 25 percent of Canadian GDP between 1960 and 1987, Quebec received only 19.5 percent of federal goods and services expenditures. Furthermore, many analysts claim that the federal government's expenditures in the "have" provinces have greater "structuring" effects and sometimes even conflict with its own fiscal and monetary policies.

While Quebec has benefited greatly from federal expenditures linked to national social security programs, particularly between

1975 and 1985, it must be stressed that those expenditures simply support, temporarily or permanently, the purchasing power of the underprivileged. They are not nearly as productive in economic terms as commitments to research, infrastructure development or industrial expansion.

In other fields Quebec sometimes even suffers from federal economic policies. Given the province's industrial base, for example, federal monetary policy is often out of sync with Quebec economic cycles and is poorly adapted to our needs. Thus, in recent months, maintaining interest rates and the Canadian dollar at very high levels has had negative repercussions on the Quebec economy, reducing its competitiveness on international markets and negating a large part of the benefits that the Quebec economy could have enjoyed from free trade.

Many analysts maintain that the Canadian political structure has in fact fostered barriers to trade and economic development rather than sound economic structures. Because of strong regional disparities and the painful social repercussions of economic downturns, the federal government finds itself forced to intervene massively in the economy with compensatory measures, and cannot properly consider the medium and long term structural effects of such intervention.

Such practices encourage neither regional development nor the emergence of entrepreneurs. On the contrary, they tend to make political intervention in the economy a permanent and mandatory feature. Yet it is by encouraging initiative and supporting private entrepreneurship that Quebec has strengthened its economy in recent years, and not by substituting government actions for the dynamism of civil society or discouraging the organization of its living strengths.

Furthermore, the claim that it is mainly the political action of the central government that ensures Quebec's economic vitality leads to the dual conclusion that Quebec will never be able to gain genuine control over its economy and that it will be more difficult for the province to cope with the challenges of global competition. But Quebec is already an exporting region that has substantially increased the volume and quality of its foreign trade in recent years.

If there is one conclusion to be drawn from the preceding, it is that Quebec has lost at least as much as it has gained from Canadian federalism, in terms of economic structures, and thus the idea of greater autonomy should not frighten it but rather intensify its dynamism and encourage its creativity and competence.

Impasse of federalism. Since it is obvious that Canadian federalism has difficulty evolving and adapting to today's need for flexibility and efficiency, Quebec must consider alternative solutions in its economic policies.

But our reflections on that issue, as part of this Commission's research and consultation process, must also encompass other aspects of the national question, in particular the political and cultural components.

When Lord Durham came to Canada to study the causes of the dissatisfaction in the colony, he quickly saw past the shortcomings and failures of political and economic institutions to a fundamental problem: the systematic opposition of two nations and two cultures. On the one hand, the English, recent conquerors of the land, who were trying to establish their habits and customs and seize all of the lucrative trade routes; and on the other, the French, who detested their position as subjects, demanded rights and boycotted the initiatives of the conquerors.

Durham clearly saw a number of separate roots of the problem, but his whole-hearted devotion to the British Crown led him to one central conclusion: the need to assimilate the French minority (a minority in Canada, but a majority in Quebec).

Durham thought two powerful tools would suffice. The first was massive immigration of Anglo-Saxon colonists. This was attempted, but the density and solid cohesion of the Francophone community relegated the newcomers to the periphery. The British objective sharpened the Francophones' resistance and they employed their fertility to fend off the imported population. The second tool was to place Francophones in the minority through the uniting of Upper and Lower Canada, and later the creation of a wider colonial federation. In the end, Francophones would have no real authority over truly important decisions.

Finally, Durham hoped, in his very British pretentiousness of that time, that if these "ignorant" people were exposed to British institutions, in the end they would surely comprehend the superiority of those institutions and the language and culture that went with them.

Anglo-Saxon immigration, particularly with the annexation of new provinces, did of course gradually reduce the relative weight of the French-speaking population in Canada. The nature of the political institutions deprived it of any possible hope of maintaining its rights and prestige as a founding nation. From one province of two in the government of the Union, Quebec (Lower Canada) became one province of four in the 1867 federation, and later one of ten.

In such a structure, how could it be imagined that Quebec, a predominantly French province, could enjoy the slightest authority over all the basic decisions concerning its future when it was faced with nine provinces and a central government clearly dominated by a different culture? One against 10 is obviously not fair odds.

And yet the slightest demand by Quebec for special powers or arrangements under national programs, to meet the particular needs of its situation, is seen by the Anglophone majority as an unacceptable threat to the integrity and viability of Canada. Invariably, Quebec's request that its distinct character be explicitly recognized has been met with obstinate and impatient rejection.

The only conclusion that can be drawn is that, in the eyes of the Anglophone majority, there have never truly been two founding peoples of modern Canada, and that even today there is no room for a second distinct national community in Canada. But since that is what Quebec considers itself, it must find a way to endure and progress. And it cannot surrender to another people, of another culture, the supreme authority over the major choices in its political and economic life.

A distinct national community. As the traditional cradle of French language and culture in North America, Quebec today has the stature of a truly distinct national community.

Linguistically and culturally, Quebec has all the essential traits of a distinct society. Its dominant language, French, sets it clearly apart in the English-speaking sea of North America, and even from the other Canadian provinces with French-speaking citizens. The community has several distinctive cultural traits: a living and original literature, songs, theatre and cinema; its own architecture, cuisine and dress; a democratic tradition all its own; a social and community organization praised by foreign visitors; a legal tradition inherited in part from France; customs of mutual support, solidarity and trust; original cultural institutions; a religious past with its own characteristics, etc. Some specialists even speak of a "Quebec model of development", characterized by "the extensive coordination of its economy", the pivotal role of some state-owned corporations, the special vitality of the cooperative movement, and so on.

It is also a mature society. Democratically speaking, Quebec has innovated, in particular, in the financial regulation of political parties. Socially speaking, it has also made considerable headway in matters such as the status of women, consumer protection, the democratization of education and accessibility of health care, social services and many other support services to its citizens. Quebec is now a well-balanced society, capable of taking into account the various aspects of development issues, and equipped with the political, administrative and legal mechanisms needed to protect the security and freedom of its members and ensure their well-being, development and fulfilment.

With its 6.7 million inhabitants, Quebec is comparable to Switzerland (6.6 M), Austria (7.6 M), Finland (5.0 M), Denmark (5.0 M) or Sweden (8.5 M).

Today, its population is educated, dynamic and inquisitive. It shows a new concern for and increasing interest in the French language and culture, its history, its cultural traditions and heritage, its demographic and cultural survival, the protection of its resources and the conservation of its environment.

It has developed a rich and varied community life, diversified and generous social provisions, and an interesting practice of social *concertation* (economic and social forums, regional county municipalities, urban communities and professional and community networks).

Economically, the "Francophone breakthrough", though relatively recent, is vigorous and self-assured.

Since 1970 Quebec has grown at an average annual rate of 3.3 percent, a rate similar to that of the countries of the Organization for Economic Cooperation and Development. In comparative terms it would rank 11th among these countries in gross domestic product or GNP per inhabitant (US$14,716 in 1989). This is a standard of living comparable to that of the Austrians, Belgians or the Dutch, although still less than that of the Danish (US$17,062) or the Norwegians (US$18,048), whose populations and economies are rather similar to those of Quebec. . . .

Already, we have broken ground in several fields of technical expertise and engineering consultancy. For example, Quebec has made a name for itself in hydroelectricity (major dams, complex dikes and devices to protect wildlife, high-tension transmission, etc.). Hydro-Québec's experience is now acknowledged world-wide, as is that of a number of large engineering firms that have worked with it to expand their skills and develop their entrepreneurial abilities. It is stimulating to see representatives of such firms as Lavalin, Groupe SNC, Groupe LGS, Roche Groupe-conseil, ADS Associés, Dessau, Techsult, Consultants B.B.L. and others working today in many countries, exporting throughout the world the expertise developed here by our fellow citizens using our own energy and creativity.

In the manufacture of public transit equipment, Bombardier and Prévost Car have already made their mark. In telecommunications, the advanced capabilities of Bell Canada and Northern Telecom are clearly recognized. Quebec know-how is famous in biotechnology, aeronautics, aluminum production, pulp and paper, cable television, television production and computer processing services; the latter cannot be mentioned without a reference to the enviable performance of such firms as IST-Services informatiques, Groupe CGI, Groupe DMR, Systematix, Groupe LGS, Groupe Quantum, ACSI-Biorex, Groupe Sobeco and several specialized subsidiaries of major Quebec accounting and management consultant firms.

Finance and financial services is one of the sectors in which Francophones and Quebecers have made their biggest impact in recent years. The continuing advance of the Mouvement des caisses Desjardins and the National Bank of Canada has illustrated the development of Quebec financial institutions. The creation of the Caisse de dépôt et placement du Québec in 1965 marked a turning point in the takeover by Quebecers of the management of their financial assets; the purpose was to regain Quebec control over the administration of substantial pension funds previously in the hands of the Canada Pension Plan and to turn this new Quebec institution into a collective development tool in tune with our needs and priorities. The usefulness and competence of this institution have never been challenged throughout its 25-year existence. Subsequently, other specialized government institutions were added to complete the activity in specific areas: the Société générale de financement, the Société de développement industriel, the Société québécoise d'initiatives agro-alimentaires (SOQUIA), the Société québécoise d'initiative pétrolière (SOQUIP), the Régie de l'assurance-dépôts du Québec, the Société de développement coopératif, to name but a few.

As for the Mouvement des caisses Desjardins, it is proud of the wide range of services and resources it can now make available to Quebec and Quebecers. With sophisticated equipment and experts in all areas of financial services, and a vast distribution system linked up with powerful international networks, the Mouvement is now able to work effectively, not only in its traditional sphere of savings and credit but also in the area of electronic fund transfers, personal and property insurance, stock brokerage, trust and investment services, industrial and commercial loans, leasing, venture capital investment, international financial services, etc.

In addition, other financial groups are spearheading important activities with home-grown funds and resources: Groupe La Laurentienne, Industrielle-Alliance, Groupe Les Coopérants, Corporation financière Power, Groupe Mutuelle des fonctionnaires, Groupe Prêt et Revenu, Fonds de solidarité des travailleurs du Québec, etc.

To support the activities and advancement of these varied financial institutions, the Quebec government has carried out a thorough revision of the regulation of financial institutions under provincial jurisdiction. Attuned to current international trends, and designed to support the efforts at consolidation initiated by the Quebec financial network, this reform has given Quebec companies a head start over their federally-chartered competitors and provided them with the proverbial shot in the arm.

A solid experience in public and private management has evolved within all of these firms and institutions, sometimes to the amazement of our competitors. The universities are also doing their share in providing extensive training to the new generation of Quebecers in the various aspects of marketing, management, labour relations and the administration of human and financial resources. In 30 years, Quebec has made giant strides in this field. The tradition is still young, granted, but it is well on its way.

The Quebec cooperative movement is also, on the whole, highly reputed for its excellence. The Mouvement des caisses Desjardins, along with its federations of French-language caisses outside Quebec, boasts 4.7 million members, 19,700 volunteer officers, 35,760 employees and 45 billion dollars in assets. All over the globe it is attracting attention due to its activities, methods, democratic and operational organization, structures, ramifications, alliances and commitment to society, and each year several foreign delegations come to take a closer look at this cooperative network of financial services. . . .

The agricultural cooperatives, housing cooperatives, workers' cooperatives and various other categories of cooperatives also contribute strongly to the growth of the Quebec co-op movement and the consolidation of the Quebec economy. It is a vibrant, productive, well-balanced economic sector, vital to society, that has developed out of the energies, entrepreneurship, dedication and creativity of generations of Quebecers under the sole guidance of Quebec laws.

No, Quebec has not finished laying the cornerstones of its future and developing the tools it will need to assume full responsibility for that future. But it now has all it needs to take charge of the future with assurance and determination. Its primary strengths are its human resources, of course. But it also has abundant natural resources, financial resources, technical and professional know-how, and expanding experience in industry and commerce. Beyond that, it possesses a new sense of pride, dignity and confidence, a new-found assurance that is not a shivering retreat to the past but a taste for autonomy and initiative oriented toward the world outside.

The Quebec society of today is indeed able to address with attentiveness, originality and efficiency its local and regional problems, but at the same time deal with worldwide trends such as free trade and the major international issues affecting the management of development and trade, the protection of resources and the environment, the sharing of knowledge and wealth, disarmament, respect for human rights, cultural promotion, etc. . . .

Recommendations:

1. That Quebec be recognized as a truly distinct and mature national community.

2. That the decision concerning the political and constitutional future of Quebec belong to the men and women who live in Quebec, regardless of their origin, language or any other factor, by virtue of the right to self-determination recognized by the United Nations and that accordingly there is no need to submit this decision to the approval of the majority of the people forming the present Canadian federative pact.

3. That Quebec have control over its political, economic, social, legislative, administrative and fiscal mechanisms, and that, to do so, it acquire the status of an autonomous national community.

4. That, once it has become autonomous, Quebec have the capacity internationally to negotiate agreements with other sovereign nations, particularly with its neighbours.

5. That this autonomy belong to the people of Quebec who will democratically select their delegates to the government representing them.

6. That the proposed political and constitutional orientation for Quebec be defined rapidly and that the people of Quebec be fully and honestly informed of the various aspects of the question so they can actively participate in the process and calmly and confidently exercise their democratic will. ..

7. That the final decision be submitted in clear and decisive terms, by means of a referendum, to the democratic will of all Quebecers.

Explanatory note. . . . Autonomy or sovereignty means the right of a state to have the ultimate decision regarding the direction to be given to the collective action of its members in both domestic and foreign affairs.

The State of Quebec would ultimately hold all decision-making powers: *i.e.,* political, economic, social, administrative and fiscal.

The only laws effective in Quebec would be those enacted by the Quebec government, unless Quebec agreed by law to associate itself with other legislatures, for example as part of a genuine confederation.

In its quest for partners, Quebec might establish special relationships with its current partners in the Canadian federation; these relations would not necessarily be exclusive. Partnership agreements could include the free circulation of people, goods and capital, a common currency and monetary policy, defence, etc.

It might be possible to create a genuine confederation, that is, a form of political union in which member states join forces for specific purposes: for example, territorial protection, monetary and economic stability, trade, etc. In such a framework, however, the authority of the joint institutions stems from the sovereign states that created them. This means the delegation by the sovereign states of one or more specific and limited areas of jurisdiction to a central body. Aside from certain specific exceptions, decisions would require the unanimous consent of the members; conversely, this rule could be expressed in a right of veto granted to some or all of the members. This means that the central body would have no authority over the citizens; rather, each member state would have authority over its own citizens.

Association des manufacturiers canadiens:

We must regain our competitive edge

The Canadian Manufacturers Association (Quebec Division), which recently changed its name to Association des manufacturiers du Quebec, represents many of the biggest corporations in Canada, including large firms in the export sector. Its brief noted that the manufacturing sector could prosper under any form of government, and seemed to view Canada's constitutional crisis as a diversion from "major economic issues".

The CMA, deeply concerned by the erosion in the competitive capacity of Canadian manufacturers, recently released a study by its economists, who have developed a competitiveness index to compare Canada's performance with that of other members of the Group of Seven.

The overall index reveals that during the 1980s Canada's performance was the worst of the major industrialized countries, and that our competitiveness gradually deteriorated to a level that is currently about 15 percent lower than the G-6 average.

Quebec's position is currently not as bad as the rest of Canada's, for essentially the following reasons:

- Corporation taxes in Quebec are now the most competitive with those in the United States, and lower than those in the other provinces;
- Quebec has reduced its top marginal tax rate, while this rate has increased in Ontario and will increase further under the new NDP government;
- Consumer prices in Quebec are rising less rapidly than elsewhere in Canada;
- The purchasing power of low-income persons is greater in Quebec than in the other provinces;
- The average wage in Quebec is lower than in Ontario;
- Average wage increases in recent years have been lower than the national average;
- Industrial lots sell at lower prices in Quebec than in Ontario;
- The cost of housing, whether purchased or rented, is lower in Quebec than in the rest of Canada.

Consequently, the gap in competitiveness between Quebec and the other industrialized countries is about 10 percent, or 5 percent less than for Canada as a whole. . . .

Why have Canada and Quebec lost ground in comparison with the other industrialized countries? The essential cause is Canada's relative delay in lowering its tariff barriers. Unlike Canada, the United States has been in a strong position since the last world war and has never felt the need to systematically resort to such barriers to protect its economy. The Europeans understood the need for a common market as early as 1956 and have been pursuing this objective more systematically since 1968, when they realized that even the mutual abolition of tariff barriers would not give them consistent access to a single market — the United States' strong point, given the scale and vigour of its domestic market.

Canada, for its part, waited until 1976, and the Tokyo Round, before realizing that the world had indeed changed and that the quiet, reliable protectionism of yesteryear no longer corresponded to the realities of today.

It is now quite striking that the period during which we lost so much ground corresponds fairly precisely with a period in which the tensions between the federal government and Quebec were particularly acute. We won't go so far as to say that there is necessarily a cause-and-effect relationship in this, but there must be some recognition of the risk there is in letting ourselves be distracted from the major economic issues. . . .

The Choices. A survey of the available structural options can only leave us discouraged and impatient. Discouraged, because the debate is off on the wrong footing. We are trying to settle the *how*'s before dealing with the *why*'s. Change for the sake of change will lead us nowhere, and may well set us back because of the disturbances that result. It is therefore essential that we know why we are changing. An answer limited to the political aspect alone would be insufficient and unacceptable. What we must know is the kind of society in which it is proposed we develop, and what room will be given to the priorities of manufacturers which, as we have shown, have a very substantial impact on the standard of living and prosperity of the population as a whole.

Our impatience stems essentially from two factors. On the one hand, we have a lag to overcome and we have seen that this lag has gradually increased over the last 20 years or so. On the other hand, the time we spend debating our form of government distracts us from our priorities and adds to the uncertainty.

No one has yet put forward any vision of the future — in the context of today's federalism, or renewed federalism, or some Canadian economic community or some form of sovereignty-association between Quebec and the rest of Canada, or the complete independence of Quebec.

A quick look at political structures throughout the world shows that it is possible for the manufacturing sector to develop and prosper no matter what the form of government. This proves that the real issue is not the form of the relationships that Canada and Quebec will or will not want to have with each other, but rather the vision of our future they are or are not proposing to us.

In this sense, Quebec and Canadian politicians must understand that the rules of competition apply to governments as well. In an open world, the countries that display the greatest dynamism end up capturing the greatest share of investments, development, prosperity and wealth. If this reality was ultimately forceful enough to bring about the implosion of the Communist world, it is hard to see how Canada and Quebec could escape it.

Conclusion. The support of Quebec's manufacturing community to any proposal for constitutional revision of whatever scope is therefore contingent on a prior examination of the model of society it reflects.

If this model will enable Quebec manufacturers to develop their competitive capacity to a point where they can improve their position in world markets, we will support it in preference to any other model that does not offer this perspective.

To obtain our support, the partisans of the various options will have to:

• recognize the leading role of the manufacturing sector in the economy and undertake to promote its growth;

• recognize the devastating impact of the high deficit we are dragging along, and undertake to make the necessary moves to reduce it to a scale that the international community will consider more consistent with our capacities while remaining a credible industrial power;

• recognize that we will manage to maintain an enviable place in the world and regain our competitiveness only if we succeed in the transition of our natural resources industries toward know-how and high value added, and undertake to establish the monetary, financial and fiscal policies that will facilitate the investments needed to restructure our industrial base;

• recognize the importance of human resources in this transition and undertake to reform our educational system to help it respond much more rapidly and effectively to the needs of our economy;

• recognize that environmental protection and the control of existing pollution require a financial effort by the whole of society that can be obtained only if we maintain and improve our capacity to create wealth, and undertake to adopt environmental policies that do not jeopardize that capacity;

• recognize that our performance in international markets has become the main issue in the final decade of this century, and undertake to develop and encourage effective support systems for our manufacturers as well as promoting the diffusion and use of the new technologies.

In addition, the Quebec division of the Canadian Manufacturers Association believes that any process of constitutional reform in which we become involved should also strive to protect our existing achievements. There can be no question of getting involved in a process that would clearly result in an economic loss for Quebec or a weakening of our potential for wealth creation.

Among the achievements on which we should be able to continue to rely is access to the Canadian market. Our members are keen supporters of a continent-wide free-trade area, and it is just as essential, in our view, that we guarantee the existence of such a free-trade area within Canada. Indeed, there is a need to proceed with the abolition of a whole range of non-tariff barriers that still exist between the provinces.

It is incomprehensible that Canadian politicians as a class, including in this case those in Quebec, do not perceive how ridiculous it would be if a situation developed in which the restrictions on trade in goods and services between the different parts of Canada were greater than between the different parts of Canada and the United States. And, in the event that Quebec were to achieve a greater degree of political autonomy, it would still have to continue to seek greater economic integration with the rest of Canada, with the goal of being as open as possible to as many markets as possible. Logic and common sense require that we start with those who are closest to us and with whom we have the most in common. As to the appropriateness of maintaining the present monetary policy structure, we must first ask whether all regions of Canada share the same economic objectives. We must then ensure that the authority responsible for managing monetary policy is not placed in a situation, because of its unlimited power to spend and increase the national debt, to jeopardize the economic development objectives of the various regions.

Finally, let us recall that time is running against us. If we must change anything in the structure of the relationship between Canada and Quebec, it is important to do so quickly and to settle the problem for a long time to come. . . .

Quebec Economists:

Globalization modifies role of nation-state

"Economically, it cannot be rigorously demonstrated that federalism or independence is the optimal route," said the Association des économistes québécois (ASDEQ), in a brief that attracted considerable attention. "But we do think it is possible to make clear that there is less objective difference between the two counterposed situations than is frequently assumed. The economic consequences of the constitutional options probably depend less, in the final analysis, on their actual nature than on the means that may be adopted to achieve these options."

ASDEQ represents 300 professional economists in the public and private sectors. Its brief was prepared by a committee of seven members, including Claude Forget, Pierre Fortin, André Raynauld and Marie-Josée Drouin.

The growth in productivity of the Quebec economy over the last 25 years is undeniable. Annual production per employee is now 95 percent of Ontario's, compared with 85 percent in the mid-1960s. The revolution in education and the increasingly avid interest of young people in economics and business have produced a class of new, dynamic entrepreneurs that has continued to grow in number and quality in recent years. This is a good start.

But this phenomenon must not be viewed as irreversible, or our economic development taken for granted, for two reasons.

First, even within Quebec, our growth in productivity, while satisfactory in terms of *quality*, has not yet generated the growth we had anticipated in terms of *quantity* of production and employment. In 1965 Quebec lagged 8 percent behind Ontario in the employment of its population of working age. By 1980 this disparity had increased to 14 percent, and has not declined since then. In 1989 this represented an employment gap of 430,000, the equivalent of one decade of job creation in Quebec.

Among the factors that explain this unfortunate development are a fairly high wage structure, the elimination of jobs in declining industrial sectors, the English exodus from Montreal and the ongoing struggle we have had to wage against an uninterrupted succession of inflationary shocks and the ensuing persistent unemployment. It is important to keep in mind that we still have a long way to go in order to become a dynamic and prosperous region, notwithstanding the progress achieved over the last 25 years.

Secondly, it must be recalled that while we have been advancing, our competitors in Ontario and abroad have not been standing still. Thus the challenge is not to go forward, but to do so *more rapidly* than the others. And, in this regard, the game is far from won.

It is common knowledge that Canada tails other industrialized countries in international competitiveness. Of course, the Canadian dollar and interest rates are excessively high because of highly questionable macro-economic (monetary and budgetary) policies. But, even ignoring the overvalued dollar and high interest rates, we must become aware of our pronounced lag in many other aspects of competitiveness. We are slower than other countries in incorporating the most recent technological innovations into our production process. We rank among the lowest in the amount we spend on research and development. Our system of corporate and government

job training programs is the laughing stock of our competitors —
German, Swedish, American or Japanese. The financial fragility of
our firms is evident with each jolt of the economic conjuncture. Our
tax system and regulations still constitute a heavy drag on the
leading sectors of our economy. The number of our firms that are
really world-class in terms of productivity, management and strategic
planning can still be counted virtually on the fingers of one hand.
. . .

We agree with many others that the time has come, after 30 years
of interminable discussions about the constitution, to "make up our
minds" more definitively, and not let the debate drag on. This will
help to reduce the duration of the uncertainty about Quebec's
political future and thereby reduce to the minimum the damaging
consequences tn our economy.

Finally, we should take advantage of the opportunity to introduce
some elements into the new constitution that could promote our
long-term economic development. Some examples would be: (1) a
clearer demarcation between the powers of the various levels of
government, to reduce overlapping, inconsistencies and sterile
squabbles; (2) an allocation of these powers according to principles
of economic efficiency (involving considerations of diversity,
preferences and minimization of costs); (3) a limitation on the
borrowing powers of governments; and (4) a limitation on the
federal government's spending power in acknowledged areas of
provincial jurisdiction.

Destination of Shipments of Manufactured Products By Province or Region of Origin, 1984 (% of Shipments)								
Province of origin	Destination by Provinces							
	Atl. Provs.	Que.	Ont.	Prairie Provs.	B.C.	Other Provs.	Out of Can.	Total[1]
Atlantic Provs.	54.2	8.8	6.8	1.5	0.7	17.7	28.1	100.0
Quebec	4.4	52.3	17.0	3.3	1.8	26.5	21.2	100.0
Ontario	2.1	8.0	51.6	5.1	2.0	17.1	31.3	100.0
Prairie Provs.	0.6	3.8	7.3	69.4	6.0	17.7	12.9	100.0
B.C.	0.3	1.7	3.3	8.3	51.1	13.6	35.4	100.0

1. Total = Province of Destination + Other Provinces + Out of Canada.

Source: Statistics Canada, *Destination of Shipments of Manufacturers*, Cat. 31530.

Interdependence of regions: The case of manufactured goods. Within an economic and political union such as Canada's, regional interdependence is a golden rule. But this interdependence varies from one province or region to another, and it varies depending on whether we are talking about trade in goods, capital movements, the establishment of companies or population displacement. This observation can be illustrated in the case of trade in manufactured products.

The table on the previous page provides the relevant information for 1984. Reading it diagonally, one notes that a little more than one half of the sales of manufactured products occurs on the spot, within the designated regions. We can also see the importance of international exports: 35.6 percent [sic] of deliveries for British Columbia, 31.3 percent for Ontario and 21.2 percent for Quebec. About 80 percent of these exports are to the United States, which means that the U.S. market accounts for about 17 percent of Quebec's shipments. Finally, we come to interprovincial trade, which shows that the Canadian market is the most significant to Quebec, since it sells 26.5 percent of its production to the other provinces. By comparison, the Canadian market accounts for only 13 percent of British Columbia's sales, and 17 to 18 percent for other regions or provinces.

To illustrate more clearly the respective positions of the regions regarding the importance of interprovincial trade, we can compare the situations on a two by two basis, so to speak, and draw the following conclusions from the table:

Percentage of shipments from the region of origin:

1.	Atlantic provinces to Quebec	8.8%
	Quebec to the Atlantic provinces	4.4%
2.	Ontario to Quebec	8.0%
	Quebec to Ontario	17.0%
3.	Prairie provinces to Quebec	3.8%
	Quebec to Prairie provinces	3.3%
4.	British Columbia to Quebec	1.7%
	Quebec to British Columbia	1.8%
5.	Other provinces to Quebec	6.8%*
	Quebec to the other provinces	26.5%

* Percentage of the Quebec column (except for internal sales) weighted by value of shipments from each region of origin.

Generally speaking, Quebec is almost four times more dependent on the other provinces than the other provinces are on Quebec (observation number 5). This imbalance is also true of Quebec and Ontario, but to a lesser degree: 17 percent for Quebec, and 8 percent for Ontario. Bilateral trade between Quebec and more distant provinces is not very significant, but it may be noted that, without exception, the Atlantic provinces are more dependent on the Quebec market than Quebec is on them.

This analysis could be pursued for bilateral trade for each of the regions, using the table. But suffice it to note that Ontario is the most independent of the Canadian regions, selling somewhat less to the Atlantic provinces than Quebec does (relatively speaking) and somewhat more to the Western provinces. Finally, let us say that while Ontario is by far the major Canadian market for Quebec, Quebec is also the major Canadian market for Ontario, although for a much lesser percentage of its shipments, as we saw earlier. . . .

Globalization of economic relations. On July 1, 1987 the Single European Act came into force and on July 1, 1989, the Free Trade Agreement between Canada and the United States. The business media are full of references to the globalization of markets and production. There is an explosive growth in currency transactions. International trade has been growing for several years at a rate that exceeds the economic growth of the developed countries. In short, it is a time for creating large entities, for globalization. What does this mean for Canada and Quebec?

. . . Federal Europe is now a reality, with its Parliament, elected directly by universal suffrage since 1979, its budget of 55 billion ECUs, its 12,300 civil servants, its 141 offices abroad, and a wave of regulations and guidelines. Of the latter, 180 will have been enacted by the end of 1990, and 110 others are in preparation, dealing with every subject imaginable. All of them are designed to concretize the concept of a genuinely common market by December 31, 1992.

The Single Act of 1987 introduced the qualified majority vote, thereby accelerating decision-making and the pace of Europeanization. The logic of this unification has gradually extended to all matters, with further developments, in addition to the creation of the unified market, in research and development, environmental protection and fiscal and monetary policy. The impact of the proceedings and decisions of the European Commission, the European Parliament and the Council of Ministers is being gradually extended, and will soon impose conduct that, in the Canadian context, would be perceived as the height of centralization. Behind this evolution is a goal to be achieved, rather than a static vision of the respective "jurisdictions" of the Community and the member states. Clearly, the European institutions long ago outgrew the stage of mere parity "superstructures"; Brussels is now a centre of decision in its own right that is much more than the sum of the various parts.

There is not much to be gained by speculating on how far the unifying spirit now at work in Europe will go. Will there eventually be a single centralized European state? Very probably not. The sociology of Europe is opposed. There is still too much that the European Commission does not deal with for the issue to exist, and this will be the case for a long time to come. Even legislative uniformity — and this is quite complete in the areas where the numerous European guidelines apply — leaves intact the dozen "distinct societies" that constitute Europe. Underlying this develop-ment is not so much an effort at homogenization as a willingness to agree on an economic peace treaty. The Europeans are dismantling barriers created by man while proceeding to scrap the *dirigiste* [regulatory] state. That is why what is now happening in Europe is at least as much an intellectual revolution as it is a simple constitu-tional change. It is no accident that the creation of a genuine common market is accompanied by a wave of privatizations and the dismantling of national cartels. The creation of Europe marked time for years, until the Europeans were ready to turn their backs on a long tradition of interventionism and national protectionism. Only one area of resistance can be found: agricultural policy.

The European institutions, including the European Charter of Rights, the European Court of Justice, and the new freedom of movement, including for persons, create a European legal structure for individuals that is gradually taking the place of the national legal structure. The result is that the national states continue to exist, but they are less relevant. The further the Europeanization of the con-tinent, the less are frontiers able to interfere in the relations between private economic agents. Being a member of this or that state is of less significance. The emergence of major economic units does not just reproduce on a larger scale the restrictions peculiar to state structures of a more modest scope; it changes the meaning of frontiers within these units by reducing them to their simplest expression. The globalization of economic relations effects a similar transformation on a world scale, but we are not at that point yet. In terms of structures and the elimination of frontiers, the action is continental, and not beyond that.

The independence of minority and regionally focused national groups is facilitated by this development. But it should be clearly noted that it is also losing a good part of its relevance. It is not

without reason that the "Canadian" nationalists opposed the Free
Trade Agreement with the United States. The agreement makes it
less important to be a Canadian; Quebec nationalists might add that
it is also less important to no longer be one. In this respect, the
effect of the Canada-U.S. Free Trade Agreement is much more
modest than what is happening in Europe. It is harder to assume
that the Free Trade Agreement is irreversible; it is certainly more
recent and much more limited. It provides for no common institutions, not even the mandatory arbitration of trade disputes.

To sum up, in itself the trend toward globalization of economic
relationships does not have all that many implications for Canada
and Quebec. However, the emergence of continental schemes in
Europe and North America suggests a certain trivialization of the
nation state. The process is much more advanced in Europe than in
North America, where it may never experience the same development, given the inherent imbalance on our continent. It is plausible
to imagine that the emergence of continental entities will mark a
turning point in the history of humanity. It will probably not be
accompanied by the disappearance of the nation state, but it
presupposes a radical redefinition of its role. This role might
eventually be emptied of any economic content but without losing
any of its importance or its value as a way of organizing human
relations.

Conclusion. In terms of the size of its population, the educational
level of its work force, the maturity and diversification of its
economy and its social organization, Quebec has made rapid
progress throughout the 20th century. During the last 30 years its
largely French-speaking population has become fully integrated into
the contemporary international economy. As an independent state
Quebec would compare favourably under any test with a small
number of countries similarly well situated. There is simply no
question about its viability in a normal international environment.

This development has occurred here, as everywhere else, through
the development of interdependency with the entire world, and
particularly with its closest neighbours. The latter have become
more important to it, and Quebec more important to them, since its
development has paralleled that of many other regions in the
country. Quebec has no monopoly on any resources or technology
that its neighbours cannot do without. Granted, the loosening of
this interdependence would at least entail some dislocation and
additional costs. But economic life is characterized by successive
adjustments to more or less substantial dislocations, the importance

of which is determined less by their scale *per se* than by one's willingness to put up with them.

Would the Quebec economy be managed better by an independent Quebec than as a region belonging to a larger entity? There is no universal answer to this question. Interdependence applies not only to trade but to economic policies. Would we be able to isolate Quebec from world interest rates or ignore the impact of its tax system on its competitive position? Yes, perhaps, but only to a certain point, and less and less significantly as the mobility of the labour force, capital and communications facilities increased. Would the quality of its economic management be higher? How can one predict a government's acumen and political will? Greater political homogeneity might make the task easier, but the impact of some policies depends more on the critical mass of production, trade and financial flows than on the wisdom of governments.

Greater homogeneity could limit the inflation of the political market. Canada is now facing the consequences of irresponsible promises that engendered all kinds of subsidies. The growth in expectations has exceeded even the most extravagant achievements. Yet no economic community can sustain itself without some transfer payments, because economic development (which promotes interdependence and trade) is not distributed evenly throughout the whole of a given territory. Furthermore, the value of an economic and political association is not measured instantaneously but over a long period of time. Regions clearly benefit from or contribute to such transfers at varying periods. In this regard Canada is not unlike other regions or federations in which such transfers are practised. There is therefore an unfortunate naïvete in the double-entry bookkeeping that is popularly used today (and not only in Quebec) to assess the "benefits" of federalism; constitutions last longer than economic cycles.

The main significance to the work of this Commission of the globalization of the world economy, and the creation — as in Europe via the European Community — of increasingly integrated economic units, is the declining significance of states and borders. In North America an analogous movement has begun, on a much more modest scale, through the Canada-U.S. Free Trade Agreement and perhaps, tomorrow, a trilateral Canada-U.S.-Mexico accord. The internationalization of the economy means that the significance of all state structures, whatever they may be, is diminished. For example, the indicated elimination of boundaries between states within the European community, and the adoption of a declaration of human rights, makes the independence of Brittany or Alsace-

Lorraine's adherence to France rather than Germany less conse-
quential. Membership in the community in turn imposes a common
discipline on all member countries that has little in common with
the interventionist or *dirigiste* credo that has for a long time driven
the nation state. In its place is a new, somewhat egalitarian credo
according to which every country is now constrained to create a
legal and institutional environment in which all individuals and
firms, no matter what their nationality, face an essentially uniform
context that is also uniformly accessible.

The combined impact of these considerations on Quebec's choice
of political status thus tends toward zero. Granted, independence is
"possible" without entailing unacceptable economic costs, at least
in the abstract, but the actual manoeuvrability thus acquired in
order to express this independence *economically* in a destiny that
genuinely differs from the current situation likewise tends toward
zero. Therefore the role of the non-economic considerations must
— and will — be decisive.

A look at the obvious difficulty of the major countries — the
USSR, the United States, China or India — in suitably managing
their own affairs, might suggest that the complexity of reconciling
the innumerable disparities of aspirations, interests, culture,
language, etc. within each of these countries exceeds human understanding and ability except in periods when the foreign and
domestic circumstances are favourable, or when the government is
prepared to use authoritarian means to impose order and uniformity. Canada is not comparable to these giants, of course, but its
geographic size and the growing multiplicity of its avowedly
justifiable disparities may warrant some analogy.

But in these periods of doubt and scepticism, deepened of late by
the failure of the Meech Lake Accord, we must also understand
clearly the exceptional nature of the independence option and the
importance of the emotional resistance it evokes. Why? Because this
consideration may be of major importance in determining the
economic costs of this option.

One of the theories inspired by the economic aspects of the
problem, which might prove most harmful to the conduct of the
debate on the national question, is the theory of economic rationality as a reference model and basis for predicting the behavioral
patterns triggered by a clear option and firm approach in favour of
independence by Quebec. This theory might be expressed as follows: "Quebec and its Canadian partners (primarily Ontario) are
tightly bound to each other by a close economic interdependence.
If Quebecers were to express a clear preference for political inde-

pendence, this economic interdependence would necessarily lead these Canadian partners to adopt a *rational attitude* consistent with conserving their own interests and maintaining these links that guarantee both their prosperity and Quebec's."

This definition of so-called rational behaviour in a situation of interdependent choice is a crude simplification. Anyone familiar with games theory will immediately perceive its weaknesses. Games theory, incidentally, is an extension of the economic theory of maximization of utility in the absence of perfect competition.

When two or more parties find themselves in a situation in which the result of each one's strategic choices depends in part on the conduct of the others, "rationality", that is, if you wish, simple common sense connotes two entirely different meanings. This proposition, which ranks almost as a theorem, is most often illustrated by the prisoners' dilemma.

In an initial situation characterized by a lack of cooperation between the players, it can be demonstrated that it is rational and prudent for each player to assume that the others will adopt the behaviour that is most damaging to him. Indeed, since the others will necessarily make the same assumption, they will be able to minimize their losses by such defensive conduct.

In a second situation characterized by cooperation among the players, all players may improve their own situation by themselves behaving altruistically.

The essential thing, clearly, is the presence or absence of a climate of cooperation and mutual confidence at the time when the strategic choices are made.

This discussion based on games theory illustrates a proposition that has other applications in economic analysis. For example, when analyzing an adjustment in prices and employment levels, many economic analyses claim to show that the ultimate levels of inflation and unemployment are a function of the economic tools that are used. In other words, the road used to reach an objective may substantially influence the objective itself. Accordingly, we think that the task of this commission must be to define not only the goal but the means to achieve it.

The failure of the Meech Lake Accord, Quebec's abstention from federal-provincial forums, the recent inability of provinces other than Quebec to agree on the abolition of interprovincial trade barriers, and the festering resentments between the regions, all indicate that there is no predisposition to cooperate at present. On the contrary, all signs point to confrontation.

In Quebec, and particularly since June 23, 1990, we hear talk about a "relationship of forces", "the need for a clear choice", and the need to "make some major and irreversible decisions, on our own behalf, against all comers". Some even see this as essential to the mandate of this commission.

If this commission limits itself to drawing up a list of the desires and aspirations of Quebecers, without inquiring into how to translate those wishes and aspirations into reality in a context other than one of confrontation, it will have sown the seeds of a great many disappointments, and ensured that the cost of whatever option is ultimately chosen will be higher than it had to be.

No doubt Quebec can, if its people are so determined, unilaterally impose its option, but it must also be aware that this way of proceeding will simultaneously establish a cost, and in that context the cost could be high!

Conseil du Patronat du Québec:

The dangers of sovereignty

In its brief to the Commission the Conseil du Patronat du Québec (CPQ), which represents Quebec's largest employers, called for a "modern federalism" that would give increased powers to all provinces, and specifically to Quebec in such areas as immigration, manpower and family policy. The CPQ indicated it would look favourably on the adoption of a Quebec constitution that made clear distinctions between individual and collective rights and freedoms and entrenched "the right to property".

The CPQ brief strongly supported Quebec's continued membership in the Canadian federal system, to which it attributed much of the province's economic advance in recent years. In support of its views, it appended to its brief a 68-page study, *Les Enjeux économiques de la souveraineté* [Sovereignty: The economic issues], prepared for the Conseil by André Raynauld (with the collaboration of Jean-Pierre Vidal). Raynauld is a former Liberal member of the National Assembly and one-time chairman of the Economic Council of Canada.

Excerpted here are some of Raynauld's major criticisms of the sovereigntist option as it has been explained in Parti québécois literature. Not included are his discussion of regional interdependence, Quebec's productivity performance, provincial winners and losers in Canadian public finances, and the growth of Francophone ownership. His discussion of the latter topic is excerpted in chapter 7. Footnotes are omitted.

Nature of federal regime. One of the reasons for the ambiguity, if not confusion, in the debates over Quebec sovereignty is that a federal regime is already a regime of shared sovereignty. In the Canadian political system the provinces already hold exclusive and predominant powers in a large number of areas. These powers are conferred on the provinces because, in theory, people's preferences vary from one province to another. It is of the very essence of a federal regime to recognize that societies are distinct. Otherwise, we would have chosen a unitary system of government. In principle, the distribution of powers or sovereignties is made in terms of what can be called interprovincial spillovers. Powers delegated to the provinces (or for that matter to the municipalities) are those whose impact is limited to provincial territory and thus whose spillovers are negligible. This is the principle we apply to freedom: its only limit is the freedom of others.

It can then be demonstrated, as many writers do, that the people's welfare is appreciably greater where powers are decentralized and the ensuing policies are differentiated to accord with the needs and aspirations peculiar to the given population. There is no reason in principle to prevent Quebec, in a federal system such as ours, from lawfully and completely independently exercising those powers that concern the development of Quebec society and do not restrict the powers of others.

There will always be disputes as to how these powers should be applied or exercised, but these frictions or disagreements would only increase or intensify if Quebec were to repudiate the Canadian federal regime.

The second essential component of the system consists of the presence of a central government that is likewise endowed with its own powers. Following the same logic of distribution as for the provinces, the central government is responsible for all questions that extend beyond the boundaries of each province.

In a way, the central government handles the external relations of the provinces, or their foreign policy. In doing so it regulates interprovincial relations and relations with all other countries on behalf of the citizens of the whole country, and with their participation. Very often the immediate interests of the provinces conflict, and the federal government will be required to make trade-offs and temper their demands. Although often implicit or hidden, these trade-offs are countless, since any policy will necessarily have a regionally differentiated impact. Unemployment insurance is of greater benefit to Eastern Canada; agricultural subsidies to the West;

transportation to the outlying regions. The examples could be infinite.

In contrast to these federal trade-offs, there is a real question as to how an independent Quebec would settle its relations with its neighbours. For exactly the same problems would be posed. In the absence of a federal government imposing its trade-offs, Quebec could not substitute its own decisions insofar as these decisions impacted on its neighbours. So it would have to negotiate the essential agreements directly with the other provinces, collectively or separately. The power and economic strength of each party in direct negotiations would be substituted *de facto* for federal policy arbitration.

There is no question that Quebec's political power within the federal government is stronger and more extensive by far than its economic power alone. The influence Quebec now exercises over the decisions of the other provincial governments or Canadian issues outside Quebec is substantial. Independence would confer additional formal and legal powers on Quebec, but its actual, effective powers would be radically diminished.

This is the essential difference between the two options available to Quebec. The sovereigntists are convinced, on the one hand, that the federal government harms Quebec's interests and, on the other hand, that independence would allow negotiations between equals, or two on two, following the Parti québécois slogans; these negotiations, it is alleged, would extract much more significant concessions from our neighbours than is now the case. It is on these two specific statements that opinions differ. . . .

Why sovereignty? It may seem pointless to inquire about the goals of sovereignty. Parti québécois rhetoric on the matter is crystal clear: we should become sovereign in order to "flourish as a people", "to be a minority no longer", "to put an end to the waste", "so Quebec can take its place in the world" (*La souveraineté: Pourquoi? Comment?*). As to the relations to be developed with the other provinces, which obviously will determine the success or failure of the new regime, this is handled with the most remarkable discretion. First, there will be no further association of a general nature. For the Parti québécois, sovereignty association "is the name long given to its political program". An historical reminder. Then, they propose a monetary and customs union that will be abandoned without a fuss, and possibly without regret, if no agreement is reached. Finally, we find two short sentences about the intention to maintain mobility of people, goods and capital, while taking the precaution of issuing passports and erecting border posts.

Splitting up the Canadian market. In these conditions, sovereignty can only lead Quebec in one direction, toward a division, a more or less pronounced disintegration of the Canadian common market. Indeed, to the degree that you think the present national policies harm the interests of Quebec because they are the product of compromise, and Quebec is a minority, sovereignty will necessarily mean a loosening of the rules of mobility, free movement and interdependence. Back in 1980 the Parti québécois program anticipated exceptions to these rules of free movement with regard to agriculture, natural resources, work permits, and institutional investments, to name only a few examples.

There was also a foreign investment code that is quite revealing with respect to the mobility of capital. The code provides that foreign firms will be confined to certain clearly defined sectors. They will be prohibited in the so-called cultural industries or "sectors that are considered vital"; they will be admitted as co-partners with Quebec majority control in some other industries; and even in unimportant sectors they are welcome but never as 100 percent owners. Even more striking in this code is the fact that no exceptions are provided for Canadian firms outside Quebec, with which, however, we are supposed to entertain a special relationship. What would happen to non-Quebec but Canadian firms already operating in these reserved sectors? Should they sell out or shut down?

What would happen to the financial institutions, and the banks in particular? Would Canadian-owned but non-Quebec banks be considered foreign banks, as the PQ program proposed in 1980? If so, will they have to dispense with most of their branches in Quebec, since in Canadian law the limitations are quite strict in this regard? Will they be subject to the present legal limits on their overall holdings?

In the 1989 edition of the PQ program, the proposals are much vaguer than in 1980, but the inspiration and orientation are the same, and one can interpret the statements in light of either edition. In 1989, they still want "to impose certain constraints on foreign investors and financial institutions" (p. 10); we must "maintain a 'buy Quebec' policy" (p. 10), which means they would have opposed the agreement just reached on this matter. Further on it is stated that they "will shelter from foreign control" the so-called cultural firms, sensitive firms and financial institutions (p. 33). They also want to ensure "Quebec majority control" in the field of resources (p. 51). Finally, they will maintain "the quotas on imported food products" (p. 46). These are only a few examples of positions that would divide up the Canadian market, positions that are fully consistent, it must be acknowledged, with the idea that a sovereign Quebec could at last be free to serve its own interests. The insurmountable difficulty in this approach lies in assuming that our neighbours will not defend their own interests in turn, which is obviously lacking in the most elementary realism. If we wish to keep what we have and genuinely serve our interests, we should instead be looking at complementary relations, partnerships and mutual concessions.

The next subject of concern is the status of federal Crown corporations. In contrast to the preceding examples, there is no ambiguity here. The Crown corporations, and the boards and commissions, are all dismantled, since the federal government is eliminated. After dividing up the assets and debts of these corporations, which will necessarily result in new legal entities, they might in some cases put these entities back under common management, but in all cases there will be at least two shareholders instead of one. Anyone who thinks that this will maintain or strengthen Canadian economic integration is sadly mistaken.

The various cracks in the economic union illustrated by these examples would no doubt potentially weaken, slow down and set back the Quebec economy in terms of investments, production, employment and revenue. We cannot put a figure on these losses, because no one knows exactly how the new powers of a sovereign Quebec would be exercised, but they are by far the most important losses, and the most enduring. . . .

Uncertainty and risk. Investors everywhere display a normal aversion to risk, and they try to guard against it in all kinds of ways. The simplest and perhaps most widespread is to postpone investment decisions. This wait-and-see attitude affects production and employment, with resulting economic slowdown, unemployment, lost income and fewer taxes to maintain public spending programs. Many of these lost opportunities are clearly irreversible, which is why the short term can sometimes last a long time.

Faced with increased risks, one can refuse to invest, but one can also invest elsewhere. Capital movements, which occur every day between the major world capitals in anticipation of a half-point change in interest or exchange, testify to the fluidity of investment decisions and the mobility of capital. Why should it be otherwise in Quebec?

In those sectors where transfers are less costly, corporations can move as well. True, water will continue to flow under the St. Lawrence bridges, but one need only think about head offices and the services and high tech sectors, where there are few locational constraints, to attach some considerable importance to this type of reactions in the business community.

There are a number of studies and on-the-spot investigations of the head office industry . . . . We will limit ourselves here to reporting on statistical estimates that have been made on the movements of head offices. Of the 108 major firms based in Montreal in 1978, 28 left Montreal between 1978 and 1981—some 26 percent of the major firms surveyed. Using the same source (a study by Drouin, Paquin et Associés Inc., 1982), we can establish the following entry and exit record for firms of all sizes between 1979 and 1981.

	Exits	Entries	Balance
1979	282	79	- 203
1980	183	68	- 115
1981[1]	164	91	- 73
Total	629	238	- 391

[1]   First 10 months of 1981.

Political uncertainty is not the only reason for the movement of head offices. But it is noteworthy that after the referendum, in 1981, the arrivals increased and the departures decreased. Finally, let us note that, after two investigations into both head offices and particular head office activities, Reed Scowen (in September 1979) established a list of 116 firms that had relocated activities involving 8,500 jobs. The movement had therefore assumed considerable scope at that time, and, again, it suggests a largely irreversible and very costly exercise for the Quebec economy. . . .

3.

Labour, farm groups
explain support of sovereignty

Quebec's major trade union and farm organizations* often adopt common positions on political issues and have a long tradition of united action in pursuit of these political objectives. For example, in 1988 they formed a common front to campaign against the Canada-U.S. Free Trade Agreement. More recently, they have joined with the PQ, the BQ and other nationalist organizations in the Mouvement Québec, a common front to commit the Quebec government to holding a referendum on sovereignty in 1992.

A much earlier effort occurred in 1966, when the FTQ, the CSN and the Union catholique des cultivateurs (UCC, the UPA's predecessor) presented a joint brief on the Constitution to the Quebec legislative assembly. The brief rejected independence, stating that "federalism must be tried out, but under new conditions that can help it endure and accord justice to all."†

The labour and farm organizations have been major participants over the last 20 years in the Mouvement Québec Français (MFQ), a coalition of nationalist and grass-roots organizations dedicated to promoting the

---

* The Fédération des travailleurs et travailleuses du Québec (FTQ) [Quebec Federation of Labour], the Confédération des syndicats nationaux (CSN) [Confederation of National Trade Unions], the Centrale de l'Enseignement du Québec (CEQ) [Quebec education central, or teachers' union], and the Union des producteurs agricoles (UPA) [Union of farm producers, or farmers' union].

† *Mémoire conjoint de la C.S.N., de la F.T.Q. et de l'U.C.C. au Comité de la Constitution de l'Assemblée législative du Québec* (Québec, 1966), p. 18.

legislative protection and promotion of French at all levels of Quebec society.

All four organizations presented briefs to the Commission. All supported sovereignty, although each argued the case in its own way. The FTQ, for example, maintained that "constitutional status must not be confused with one's blueprint for society", and limited its discussion of social issues to those with the most direct bearing on the Constitutional division of powers, such as language, immigration and job training. The CSN and CEQ, on the other hand, argued that their support for independence was directly related to their respective conceptions of how society should be organized, which both organizations developed at considerable length in their briefs. The difference is perhaps more apparent than real, however; the FTQ was emphasizing what it perceived as a tactical need to subordinate differences over social program to the broader struggle for sovereignty, while the other centrals were attempting to explain the philosophical linkage between their social concerns and their support of sovereignty. And both the CSN and CEQ made a point of stating that they supported independence even if the social structure and policies of a sovereign Quebec did not correspond to their objectives.

All four organizations called for a referendum in 1991 to approve sovereignty. In addition, the CSN and CEQ called for the establishment of a constituent assembly to debate and approve a draft constitution for an independent Quebec, which would then be adopted in a second referendum.

Also calling for a referendum, but not for sovereignty, was another labour central, the Confédération des syndicats démocratiques (CSD). Founded in 1972 as a relatively conservative split-off from the CSN, the CSD supported a free-trade agreement with the United States. Most of the CSD's 60,000 members work in the private sector. Its brief to the Commission supported, among other things, greater "participation" of workers in management decisions, and for restoring those parts of Law 101 that have been overruled by the Supreme Court of Canada.

Fédération des travailleurs du Québec (FTQ):

Our progression toward sovereignty

With 470,000 members, the FTQ is the largest trade union centrale, or federation, in Quebec. A majority of its members belong to unions whose headquarters are elsewhere in Canada or the United States. Among these are some of the major industrial unions in Quebec. A large part of its 31-page brief was devoted to explaining the evolution of the FTQ's positions on the national question over the last 25 years, during which it has carved out a distinct position for itself within the pan-Canadian labour movement and firmly established its credentials within Quebec as a bulwark of Quebec nationalism.

———————

1. Basis of our constitutional positions. The FTQ began awakening to constitutional problems in the Sixties, when "national conscious-ness" and "social consciousness" did not sit well together. As a Quebec labour organization belonging to the Canadian trade union movement (the Canadian Labour Congress), we began negotiating for recognition of our specific character while inclining toward nationalist positions in support of improved treatment for Quebec and the French-speaking population within Confederation.

During the Seventies our conception of Quebec was asserted around our practical experiences in such matters as manpower policy and the language of work, and we began to draw up a long list of sectors in which the federal presence was unnecessary, disruptive or plainly harmful to the interests of Quebec. In many cases our positions were in advance of, or followed closely upon, the positions taken by successive Quebec governments as they sought, usually in vain, to protect Quebec's jurisdiction. This phase culminated in 1980 with the FTQ's "yes" in the referendum — a virtually unanimous decision enthusiastically adopted by more than 2,000 delegated members at a special convention convened exclusively on this issue. The vote followed four hours of continu-ous debate, and there were only 30 to 40 votes against, with about 100 abstentions. The result was particularly significant given the size and diversity of the FTQ's membership: 450,000 people, a third of whom were women, 50,000 Anglophones and allophones, and 45,000 federal employees.

We in the FTQ will always have a host of practical reasons to choose sovereignty. But now, as the debate resurfaces, between the snatches of weariness and the disillusionment of our members, there is this tranquil affirmation of a national consciousness that is no longer ashamed to flaunt itself. We want sovereignty for full employment, of course, for economic policies adapted to our industrial structure, and not Ontario's — but also, and above all, because Quebec is our only country, which we want to occupy and proclaim as our country, because it is normal for a people to have a country and Canada will always be the country of others.

Whatever the hesitations we have had in Quebec, it now seems it is Canada that is much more unsure of what it wants. The predominantly English-speaking provinces sent us a message that they did not want to recognize our special character, but they don't seem to agree on much else. . . .

There is a second reason. Over the last 25 years Quebec has changed. Not everything is perfect yet, but we can be proud of what we have managed to do in little more than a quarter century. We now have intellectual, industrial, financial and scientific elites.

We have developed unique institutions, many of our corporations operate internationally, our state apparatus and public services are modern and, overall, efficient. . . . Quebec has emerged from its industrial and cultural underdevelopment. . . .

But that's just it: having modernized, we find that maintaining the federal relationship simply curbs our energy and dampens our vitality. The *indépendantistes* of the Sixties wanted to rid Quebec of underdevelopment. Today we want to be able to develop in line with our interests without being obliged to discuss each and every one of our ideas and initiatives. What do we have to gain from Canada? Hasn't it been said enough, noted enough, that Quebec, irrespective of the conjuncture, has more unemployment than Ontario, has less research and development, suffocates from macro-economic policies designed to meet the needs of the neighbouring province? The positive changes that have occurred in Quebec in recent decades have come not from our federal link, but from our own initiatives and institutions.

But we could have done more and better if we did not always have to be content with half-measures because we lacked certain constitutional powers or had only limited powers. . . .

2. A discussion focused on the real issues. We hope that the Commission's presence and action will contribute to the quality of the constitutional debate in Quebec. But if the discussion is to deal with the real issues, there are two conditions that are indispensable, in our view.

In the first place, constitutional status must not be confused with one's blueprint for society. The FTQ will always fight for a social-democratic society, no matter what the constitutional framework. But that is not a precondition for our support of sovereignty. The FTQ believes that sovereignty is the means by which we will accede to the set of levers that will enable us to mold our society. . . .

Once sovereignty is accomplished, Quebec will still be wide open, and the political discussions will ultimately determine what a sovereign Quebec will concretely be.

Sovereignty does not by itself guarantee this or that model of political and social organization. But it does guarantee us the right to decide by ourselves; that is the essential thing, and it should encourage us, since we have nothing to be ashamed of. Quebec need not be invented from one end to another. We are a modern society, a bit behind in some respects, a bit in advance in others. Our health care and social services, our occupational health and safety, the general status of women, our efforts to integrate the disabled and visible minorities into the labour market, our labour laws, our *Charter of Human Rights*, etc. do not put us beyond the pale of western nations, far from it. If it were up to us alone in the FTQ, we would simply persevere along these lines. But everything in its time. First let us take over the political and economic levers. Then we will discuss what actions should be taken.

Secondly, we refuse to be drawn into the war of figures in which some have already got involved. A people cannot choose its constitutional status in the way you select a pension plan, on the basis of accounting statements.

A people's discussion of sovereignty must be based on a number of considerations, of which the economic dimension is only one. The economic factors must be taken into account, but they should not occupy the entire scene. This is a particular danger, in our opinion, in that, since the Eighties, in Quebec as elsewhere, persistent economic problems have led to a subordination of cultural and social issues and, in the case of the constitutional debate, the specifically national question. This trivialization of the non-economic factors undermines the quality of the discussion. . . .

3. Our progression toward sovereignty. Three major, mutually related sets of issues have prompted the FTQ to orient gradually but with increasing resolve in the direction of sovereignty: economic and employment policies, population policies, and cultural, linguistic and educational policies. In each case it is our assessment that the federal system is a source of increasing costs and inefficiency, confusion and incoherence. . . .

Economic and employment policy. Our social priority in the FTQ is the implementation of a full-employment policy; it is the central axis of our blueprint of society. Over the years we have developed a communitarian conception of full employment that is anchored in "*concertation*" practices at several levels. This conception presupposes a renewal of social relationships and a greater sophistication in the role of the state, which is now both initiator and collective leader. But, in order to develop, social concertation requires a living collectivity with a shared culture, goals, history and solidarity. Quebec society is ready to meet this challenge.

A concerted policy of full employment can only take root in a genuine country, and of course presupposes some planning and national policies that can reflect particular regional features. . . . Yet some major tools of a full-employment policy such as foreign trade and currency are an exclusive federal preserve, and Ottawa and Quebec City fight over who can levy taxes and engage in various forms of spending (employment programs, assistance to companies, income security, major projects, etc.).

Although we in the FTQ are convinced that the federal pact has never allowed the optimal development of the Quebec economy, it is in the political nature of things that the federal government would adopt measures to benefit the Ontario economy, which has always been the backbone of the Canadian economy. . . .

Occupational training is another sector in which we have as a rule been able to measure the impasse of the federal system. This is a Quebec jurisdiction in which the federal government has intervened increasingly over the years, thereby blocking the development of any coordinated policy. . . .

Population policy. Immigration is an aspect of population policy, and is thereby related to employment policy. Population policy also has to do with the protection of our cultural and linguistic specificity.

In this vital area, where the Quebec state is the only guarantor, the federal government holds sufficient power to seriously encumber Quebec's action. . . . We very much need immigration, but our manoeuvrability in selection criteria, francisation efforts, reception of immigrants, etc. is limited. In fact, even the most generous agreement with Ottawa, in terms of Quebec's demands, will always be a handicap in integrating immigrants, given the lack of autonomous existence, of sovereignty. It is *Canada* that the immigrants choose to immigrate to, as a rule; Quebec is not their choice, and there is no reason why it should be. One chooses a country, and Quebec is certainly not a country. . . .

Language policy. . . . The FTQ has always been noted for its extreme sensitivity to language issues. Part of the reason is the nature of our membership. Most of our affiliates evolved within Canadian or North American union structures in which they had to assert their Québécois character. The FTQ comprises a majority of the workers in Quebec who are employed by multinational or

Canadian-owned big businesses, in which language problems are the most acute. And almost all of the federal civil servants and most of the Crown corporation employees are members of our federation. So it is no surprise that the FTQ has been so supportive of Law 101, or that some of the events in the wake of that legislation were bitterly felt by our organization. We have deplored the gradual erosion of the *Charter of the French Language* at the hands of the Quebec assembly, the courts and, more recently, the federal official languages legislation. Quebec's linguistic situation is unique, and it needs solid language laws that can be deployed without interference and project a clear and unequivocal message in support of French as the common language, the language of work and the language of signs. . . .

Quebec-Canada relationship. For the FTQ it is inevitable that some links will exist, whatever happens between Canada and Quebec, in the form of various agreements. But we think it is important to establish that these links will have to develop from a free decision by two sovereign states. We should know from experience that relations established or maintained by constraint are not the most solid or the most productive. So it is important that Quebec make clear its intention to proclaim its sovereignty before it discusses the nature of the links to be maintained. It should also be recalled that Canada, and in particular our closest neighbours Ontario and the Maritimes, have no interest either in breaking their links with Quebec.

Some areas in which special relationships ought to exist, embodied of course in bilateral agreements, are trade, the fishing industry, the environment, rail, water and air transportation, defence and foreign policy.

Among the discussions between Ottawa and Quebec in which we feel justified in getting particularly involved are those surrounding the transfer of federal services to Quebec. Almost all of those who provide these services in Quebec, and some of those in Ottawa, are members of our affiliates. They provide services that will have to be maintained, and the cutbacks of recent years have reduced those services to a minimum. The transfer of services will of course be a part of the whole issue of assets and liabilities that will have to be discussed. The services issue is particularly touchy in that it involves working men and women and their families. We estimate that there are about 35,000 unionized federal public servants in Quebec — many professionals and none of the management and contractual workers are union members — in addition to 10,000 postal employees. When the time comes, the FTQ and the unions concerned will have to be involved in the discussions. We are concerned about both the jobs of these employees and the security of their union status.

The Quebec *Labour Code* should therefore provide that the certifications that have been granted and the collective agreements signed under federal law shall be automatically continued under Quebec legislation in respect to Quebec employees. This should not be difficult to do, since the applicable legal rules are at present, for all useful purposes, the same between the two jurisdictions. . . .

Confédération des syndicats nationaux (CSN):

A clear choice: the independence of Quebec

The 250,000-member CSN is the successor to the Catholic union centrale, the Confédération des travailleurs catholiques du Canada, or CTCC, which was founded by the Church in 1921 in part to counter the influence of the secular and international unions. During the 1960s it secularized its structures and grew rapidly with the recruitment of provincial government and social services employees in particular.

In 1980 the CSN called for a yes vote in the Referendum, and in 1987 it opposed the Meech Lake Accord on the ground that Quebec's five conditions were unclear and less than an acceptable minimum. In May 1990, the 2,000 delegates to its annual convention voted overwhelmingly in favour of "the independence of Quebec, i.e., economic, political, social and cultural independence; for an autonomous country with a State that is fully sovereign in its territory. Which means the repatriation of all the powers of a modern State in the present international context."

Excerpted below are major extracts from Parts I and III of the CSN's 107-page brief.

The rejection of the Meech Lake Accord and the numerous anti-Quebec actions in Canada during this period were interpreted by the members of the CSN and the majority of Quebecers as a slap in the face, an insult, an affront. This most recent refusal to recognize the people of Quebec as a nation made most of us realize that the cup had been overflowing for a long time.

[Newfoundland premier] Clyde Wells' fight against the Accord did not simply reflect the intransigence of the premier of a province representing 3 percent of Canada's population. It reflected the fact that, as the polls showed, the Meech Lake Accord was rejected by most of the population of English Canada. According to an Angus Reid poll in early April 1990:

> [T]he respondents said they disapproved of the Accord in significant proportions: 74% in Saskatchewan and Manitoba, 73% in British Columbia, 66% in Ontario, 65% in the Maritimes and 64% in Alberta. They objected to both the spirit of the Accord and its specific content. A Gallup poll in March 1990 showed, for example, that 53% of Canadians were opposed to treating Quebec as a "distinct society", while only 27% approved this concept. Similarly, a CBC-Globe and Mail poll confirmed that 82% of Canadians (excluding Quebec) were opposed to Quebec's having the right to adopt laws affecting the French culture and language. . . .*

From the Conquest to the Accord. This refusal to recognize the Quebec people as a nation with the right to the full exercise of its sovereignty has been manifested many times in Canada's history. Many mutually related events have occurred since 1760, although this history is not and never has been linear or straightforward.

Four years after the 1837 rebellion, the Act of Union joined Lower and Upper Canada, although this proved unsuccessful in achieving the assimilation of the Francophones intended by Lord Durham. The Canadian Confederation came into being in 1867, a birth that the people were never invited to or consulted on, nor given any opportunity to express their agreement or opposition. During the following three decades, from about 1870 to 1900, close to 500,000 poor and unemployed Quebecers emigrated in search of jobs.

In 1917, in Quebec City, a few steps from what is now the CSN building, federal troops fired on the people, a majority of whom opposed conscription. Four workers died.

In 1942, Quebec again rejected conscription. A second tragedy in the recent history of a French-speaking Quebec that, unlike the

---

* Pierre Fournier, *Autopsie du Lac Meech, la souveraineté est-elle inévitable?*, Montreal 1990, p. 109. [In Fournier's book the last sentence continues, where the CSN has placed an ellipsis: " . . . including laws that might conflict with the Charter of Rights and Freedoms." — Ed.]

English-speaking minority, had never really embraced the British realm.*

In the early 1970s Quebec experienced what has become known as the Brinks coup.† Then, with the War Measures in October, the Canadian army was sent by Ottawa with the assignment to thwart a so-called terrorist conspiracy!

In 1977, thanks to Law 101, the French language finally assumed its rightful place. It was a very temporary victory, however, and soon entire parts of this law were falling under the hammer blows of the Supreme Court of Canada.

The 1980 referendum, interpreted at the time as a defeat, proved instead to be an important stage in the evolution of Quebec's collective consciousness. This was true as well of the unilateral patriation of the Constitution in 1982 without and against Quebec.

The failure of the Meech Lake Accord made it all perfectly clear: Quebec's minimal demands were rejected. Two days later, on June 25, 60,000 Quebecers serenely affirmed, in the streets of Montreal, their confidence in the future of Quebec. Since then, poll after poll has revealed that 60 percent or more of the citizens in Quebec are favourable to sovereignty. More and more people are saying, "In 1980 I voted No, now I will vote Yes". Wider and wider layers of Quebec society are convinced they can govern themselves and want to take control of their collective future.

From "Canadiens" to "Québécois". The desire to control their own destiny runs in different ways throughout the history of the Quebec people. Quebec has evolved rapidly since the beginning of the Quiet Revolution in 1960, with its slogan *Maîtres chez nous,*

---

* In a Canada-wide plebiscite on April 27, 1942, about 80% of French-speaking Canadians voted against releasing the federal government of promises it had made to Quebecers in 1940 that it would not institute military conscription. However, in Canada as a whole the vote was 63.7% in favour of conscription, which was then implemented. See André Laurendeau, *La Crise de la conscription* (Montreal, 1962), pp. 119-20. — Ed.

† In April 1970, shortly before the Quebec provincial election in which the Parti Québécois made its first bid for power, a leading financial institution transferred securities out of its Montreal headquarters to its Toronto offices amidst extensive media coverage. The securities documents were conveyed in Brinks armoured vehicles. Many sovereigntists blamed this incident, with its clear implication that capital would flee the province in the event of independence, for the PQ's failure to elect more than a handful of MNAs. — Ed.

"Masters in Our Own House" — gaining greater autonomy and developing in all fields.

But this development is still confined within the federal yoke, which has never served the interests of Quebecers as they had hoped.

The Quebec economy has developed greatly, but agriculture is defined primarily in terms of the Prairies, and monetary and industrial policies are a function of Ontario's interests. The official unemployment rate has constantly oscillated for more than 10 years at around 10 percent, twice as high as Ontario's.

Quebec has no influence on the Supreme Court of Canada or the Bank of Canada. It must struggle continually on behalf of the language, for jurisdiction over communications and immigration, for a redistribution of the taxes paid to Ottawa, etc. Quebec's international relations are subordinate to Canadian policy. In fact, powers essential to Quebec's overall development are totally outside its control, while the distribution of some powers between the two levels of government works to Quebec's disadvantage through the resulting duplication, inconsistency, ineffectiveness and inefficiency.

Why constitute a country? You do not remain in a country because you get more out of it economically than you put in. And you do not leave a country because you get less out of it than you put in. You leave a country because you cannot, as a nation, develop fully within it. You don't leave a country and you don't constitute a country by opposition to or rejection of another country. A nation constitutes itself a country in order to secure the greatest possible mastery over its collective decisions and therefore to itself control and ensure its collective destiny and progression in the concert of nations.

The idea of a Canada including Quebec has never been anything but an illusion, a chimera, an abstract idea implanted by force, which was never really able to take shape and respond to the aspirations of the French-speaking minority. Barely 50 years ago the members of this Francophone minority, whose national home was and still is Quebec, called themselves "*Canadiens*" as opposed to "*les Anglais*". Ten or 15 years later, these "*Canadiens*" were calling themselves "*Canadien-français*" to differentiate themselves from the "*Canadien-anglais*".

For about 25 years, we French-Canadians of Quebec have been "*Québécois*". We define ourselves no longer in opposition to the dominant majority nation, but in terms of ourselves and the groups that make up our society, which encompasses — it is important to put a clear name on things — the French-speaking majority, the aboriginal nations, the Anglo-Québécois minority, and the ethno-cultural communities.

An independent Quebec must therefore spell out the individual rights of all citizens and ensure that those rights are secured. It will have to intervene in the same way with regard to the specific collective rights of each of these communities.

The people of Quebec are now invited by history to exercise this choice and to constitute a country capable of corresponding to its social, political, economic and cultural ambitions.

A democratic, collective decision. The best guarantee that the Quebec society of tomorrow will be profoundly democratic is to enable the entire population to participate fully in the decision to constitute a country and to develop a model of society that will have to be built together, collectively.

The CSN's support for Quebec independence is directly related to the kind of society it wants to build. Quebec's present powers combined with the new powers that must be recovered will help to gradually concretize this blueprint for society.

It is clear, however, that the CSN's support for independence is not conditional upon the complete acceptance of its social model by all the other existing forces in Quebec. The accession to national independence is not the end of a process but a crucial, special moment, which poses favourable conditions for achieving national demands that have been put forward for many years by the unions and mass organizations, such as the adoption of consistent policies on labour force development (including a policy of full employment, occupational training, etc.), regional economic development, language, women's equality, etc.

By bringing people closer to the centres of power, independence will pose favourable conditions for the emergence of social consensus and the reflection of the interests of the various elements of society. That is why we associate sovereignty with a model of society for the Quebec of today and tomorrow.

It is imperative, in this dynamic political approach, to take the specific needs of women into account. The national question is necessarily linked to the development of a model of society. Women have a particular interest in this, since their concerns are not satisfied in this society; a large majority of women continue to suffer intentional or systemic discrimination and domination by men — economically, politically and socially — since men occupy and continue to dominate these spheres, as is indicated by the composition of this commission. . . .

It is hard to deal with the issue of women as just one issue among others, because it is an issue that transcends them. We could make a list of indispensable steps and, using many examples, point to the petty annoyances and inertia that result from the dual jurisdictions of governments. But that is not what matters most to women. In many respects, Quebec's treatment of women has not been better than the federal government's. Quebec has often invoked federal jurisdiction to justify its own failure to act, as in the case of maternity and parental leave or childcare.

The national question also affects women in their "reproductive" capacity. We are referring here to an awakening nationalism that occasionally inspires a rise in racism and xenophobia, often expressed in the promotion of a pure nation, the nation *de vieille souche* descended from the original white settlers and based on a significant rise in Quebec's birth rate. It is only a small step from this to denying women the right to decide themselves whether they want children.

In raising this issue we are not exaggerating. There is a systematic pattern of retrograde policies like this being brought forward in conservative periods, claiming to protect so-called moral values while in fact limiting individual freedoms. An example was the recent shameful attempt by the federal government, in Bill C-43, to interfere with women's right to equality by removing their right to choice and recriminalizing abortion — a fundamental right without which there can be no equality for women within a society.

It is essential to ensure that women are, from the outset, full partners fairly represented in the various bodies working to review and revise the constitutional and political future of Quebec. Their presence will be decisive in developing a new model of society.

If they are not represented, efforts to build such a model will confront two obstacles. First we will be deprived of women's "way of seeing things", that is, proposals for social change within the specific perspective of women, a majority of the population but an oppressed and dominated majority. Secondly, if women feel that the political process and the dynamic it involves are of little or no concern to them, if they perceive, rightly or wrongly, that *plus ça change, plus c'est pareil* [the more things change, the more they stay the same], it is very unlikely that the new political option, the independence of Quebec, will be adopted by a majority in a broad consultation. Remember, women are the majority. Sovereignty will be meaningful to the degree that it helps build a better society for the entire population, who must identify with it and believe in it from the beginning of the political debate. . . .

Getting to independence. The conditions for achieving the full sovereignty of Quebec have never been as favourable as they are now. Successive polls since June 23 [1990] indicate majorities of 60 percent or more for sovereignty.

A number of economic tools originating with the Quebec state, such as the Société générale de financement (SGF) and the Caisse de dépôt et de placement, continue to contribute to the consolidation and growth of the Quebec economy. Foreign economic domination has been transformed. Today, while still fragile, a class of Quebec employers exists and is solidly established in several major sectors of the economy.

The collective capacity to develop a strong economy in the present context of globalization of economies is essential if independence is to be feasible and viable. This basis now exists, and is generally recognized on the continent. Large Quebec, Canadian and U.S. firms that speak authoritatively on economic matters, such as brokerage firms, banks and research institutes, agree: an independent Quebec is viable and can issue its own currency if it so decides.

The majority of the population — women's groups, many community organizations, students' associations, youth groups, unions — are in favour of Quebec's political sovereignty. These positions are obviously very important, since Quebec will not accede to independence unless there is a convergence of forces toward the attainment of the given objectives. What we are talking about is the relationship of forces that Quebec must build in order to confront Ottawa.

The CSN will join with all groups in society for the purpose of identifying these objectives and establishing these convergences. It is determined to do whatever is necessary to promote them in public debates and common actions.

These convergences will develop between men and women, to build a new society, founded on genuine equality between the sexes; between the Francophone majority and the aboriginal nations; between the Francophone majority, the Anglo-Quebec minority and the ethnocultural communities. Convergences, commitment and mobilization of the youth with whom and for whom Quebec's future must be elaborated and without whom any constitutional and political proposal will go astray.

This procedure of identifying convergences, promoting them and mobilizing the people concerned, is essential to establishing a broad democratic process of consultation and elaboration of the political and constitutional model for Quebec.

This grassroots participation is also the best guarantee of not only the democratic character of this collective model, but also, subsequently, the actual functioning of the new, developing Quebec society.

This is an essential element in the collective future of a sovereign Quebec. It calls for working to unify Quebecers around shared goals and thus avoiding dispersion, while being aware that divergent interests will continue to appear among the various groups that make up society. . . .

Independence necessary for Quebec's prosperity. Without entertaining any illusions, the CSN takes its stand in favour of Quebec's independence on the ground that sovereignty will bring about more favourable conditions for fulfilling many demands of the unions and mass organizations.

Quebec's becoming a sovereign state will bring the power of the people closer to the places where decisions are made. It will strengthen the people's capacity to influence those who make the decisions. It will help democracy to grow and function.

Achieving Quebec's sovereignty means collectively determining our own societal goals and achieving those goals.

In this vein, the CSN is submitting some proposals for a model of society adapted to an independent Quebec to the debate that will be held in the coming months, with the intention of developing not an ideal, utopian social program but a model of society that it thinks is realizable in the Quebec of the 1990s, and appropriate to the current North American and international context.

The CSN is publicly submitting its proposals for the independent Quebec to which its members aspire, and likewise will consider the positions advanced by other groups in society. And it does this while acknowledging that Quebec, from Day One of its independence, will not satisfy all of its demands and aspirations. In the sovereign Quebec, the CSN will continue to argue for those that are not satisfied. It will persevere in the defence and promotion of the interests of its members and allies.

Neither federalism nor neo-federalism. Establishing Quebec's sovereignty does not mean erecting a Chinese or Berlin wall around our borders. Nor is it necessary to participate in the present federal political institutions or opt for a neo-federalism in order to maintain some relations between Quebec and Canada. We will have to look at the trade treaties that Quebec will want to make with Canada, the United States, and other countries including the EEC and the countries of the Third World.

Some fields of jurisdiction may also be shared between Quebec and Canada, such as monetary policy, some communications systems and a part of defence, etc. Treaties could also establish accords for mobility of goods and persons, the sharing of embassies and consulates, environmental monitoring, etc. It will be necessary to examine the possibilities for agreement, identify the reciprocal interests and find the appropriate formulas.

There is no reason why these treaties and links cannot be developed between two sovereign countries without any abdication of sovereignty.

Referring to the European Economic Community to justify the present federal system or some form of neo-federalism is to obscure a major aspect of reality. In providing themselves with common institutions or establishing multiple links between themselves, the EEC member countries have remained fully sovereign without waiving or weakening that sovereignty. Another recent example was the Canada-U.S. Free Trade Agreement, the implementation of which has not required the establishment of a supranational government!

In the course of their respective evolution, Quebec and Canada may equip themselves with all kinds of machinery — commissions, joint committees, treaty enforcement oversight tribunals, etc. — to regulate their common relationships. But, if they are to benefit mutually, Quebec must be an independent country in which all taxes levied on its territory and all laws applying thereto shall fall within the exclusive jurisdiction of the National Assembly.

No one other than the people of Quebec shall be able to choose or decide what Quebec is to be or to do. No political institution shall be empowered to frustrate the decisions taken by the National Assembly.

For the CSN, the most important element, the most precious aspect of everything that is taking shape and being decided at this time may be summarized as follows: it is the people of Quebec and they alone who shall determine their political, constitutional, economic, social, cultural, linguistic, environmental and territorial future. They will have to be not only involved in all the discussions, but consulted and invited to declare themselves on all major decisions that involve their present and future.

Quebec's accession to sovereignty is not conditional upon Canada's agreement to proceed with these distributions of power, responsibility and jurisdiction. Quebec's future and its development are the property of its people, who must prepare to assume alone all the powers of a sovereign country.

Quebec's independence the only possible route. Since Quebec failed in its attempt to obtain the ratification of the Meech Lake Accord, which was inferior in many respects to the historical demands it had formulated for more than 30 years, a possible "Meech plus" agreement should prove illusory or unattainable. And there is not much time. Quebec's constitutional and political future must be decided both democratically and rapidly.

The CSN will no longer believe those who, once again, hold out the prospect of a strong Quebec within the Canadian confederation. Even those who are thinking in terms of some neo-federalist formula should first go the route of a declaration of Quebec independence so they can then negotiate, not as one against 10, but as equals, between Quebec and Canada.

Proposed procedure. With this in mind, the CSN proposes the following procedure:

1. That the National Assembly hold a referendum in June 1991 on a clear, concise and specific question, to be worded as follows:

Do you agree that the National Assembly should proclaim its full sovereignty over the whole of Quebec's territory, no later than June 1992?

2. That the National Assembly enact legislation creating a constituent assembly composed of representatives of the various groups that make up Quebec society; this assembly will have 12 months following the referendum to develop a draft constitution for Quebec.

3. That during the same 12-month period the National Assembly conduct negotiations with Ottawa on the transition to an independent state (division of the debts and assets, repatriation of the federal public sector, etc.) and possible agreements on economic and political power-sharing between the two countries. The National Assembly will also take steps toward the recognition of Quebec by international agencies, such as the UN, and foreign governments, including the United States.

4. That the National Assembly submit the draft constitution of Quebec for approval by referendum no later than June 1992.

This four-point procedure would mean, among other important things, that the people would decide Quebec's sovereignty, and the National Assembly would declare independence when it deemed appropriate, but at no time later than the ratification of the constitution.

Since the constitution is the fundamental law of a country, the CSN believes that it is necessary to establish a constituent assembly. This assembly, with about 100 members, should be composed of members of the government and the opposition in the National Assembly and people who accurately reflect the composition of the Quebec population: women, youth, natives, Anglo-Quebecers, the ethnocultural communities, etc. In this sense, the constituent assembly would resemble this Commission, but this time with a fair representation of groups that are part of the Quebec social fabric.

Both referendums would be held under the Quebec *Referendum Act*. Keeping in mind the 1980 experience, we emphasize that all expenditures made in Quebec during the referendum campaign must be subject to the Quebec *Election Act*, regardless of whether they originate from inside or outside of Quebec.

This procedure may be criticized for its sluggishness. However, in our view it is of prime importance, in the higher interests of Quebec and its people, that the latter be active participants throughout the procedure and be involved in all future decisions concerning such fundamental issues as the sovereignty of Quebec, its constitution, the links to be maintained with Canada and reaffirmed as a country with the other countries of North America and the world.

Not excerpted here, largely because of space limitations, is Part II of the brief, "A proposal for Quebec", which essentially sets the CSN's program on social and political issues within the context of a sovereign Quebec. Among the major points in its 11 chapters are the following:

• *Constitutional and legislative reform.* Abolition of the monarchy; a new constitution with a fixed parliamentary term of office; constitutional entrenchment of a revised Charter of Rights and Freedoms that would protect collective economic and social rights such as women's right to choice, free public and non-denominational education at all levels, free social and health services, the right to housing, the right to live and work in French, and the right to organize and bargain collectively and to strike, and would impose constitutional obligations on the state to protect the environment, establish and protect decent living and working conditions, etc.

• *Economic reform.* Repatriation of economic powers now in Ottawa's hands; abandonment of deregulation and privatization; adoption of an industrial strategy based on state support of high tech and small and medium firms; membership in GATT and support of world trade liberalization, and an economic and monetary union with English Canada, with a common currency. As for the Free Trade Agreement, "it might be desirable that an independent Quebec not commit itself to further economic integration with the United States and propose the abolition of the free-trade agreement as it affects Quebec, except for tariff reductions that have already been granted."

• *A new relationship between citizens and the state.* Electoral reform based on proportional representation, direct election of the head of state, decentralization of powers to regional authorities, and proportional representation of women in government-appointed bodies.

• *Language and culture.* Repatriation of the Quebec operations of such federal institutions as the CBC, the CRTC, the National Film Board and Telefilm Canada. French as the official language. "Full jurisdiction over language in a sovereign Quebec cannot be separated from the full exercise of our responsibilities toward the other languages. Toward the native languages and cultures, which must be protected and enhanced; toward the language of the English-speaking minority, for which a tradition of justice and openness must be maintained; for the languages and cultures brought to us by the major immigrant groupings."

• *Aboriginal peoples.* Recognition of the principle of native self-government on native lands, "within the Quebec legal framework". A framework agreement to provide for settlement of outstanding land claims.

• *Anglophone community.* A sovereign Quebec should not fall into the same trap as English Canada, which treats its French-speaking minority as "one drop among others in the great Canadian mosaic". It should recognize the right of its English-speaking minority to the maintenance of its institutions – universities, schools, media, hospitals, etc. – and ensure it has the means to develop its language and culture.

• *Ethnocultural communities and immigration.* Full control over immigration, and retention of existing admissions criteria. Much greater attention to integrating immigrants through such means as language courses and secularization of the public school system.

• *International relations.* Quebec membership in major international bodies including the UN, OECD, OAS, GATT, IMF and the World Bank; Quebec would fight to democratize the latter three. An enlarged role for foreign development assistance and *la Francophonie.*

• *Defence.* A sovereign Quebec should have its own defence policy, with spending limited to 3 percent of the overall government budget (compared with 11 percent of the federal government budget at present). Priority to protection of Quebec territory; withdrawal from NATO and NORAD "at least in their present form". Possible sharing of resources with "our partners" in North America: maintenance of air interception force based in Bagotville and radar detection installations in Northern Quebec; possible joint coastal surveillance with Canada; replacement of the army by an emergency intervention corps mandated to participate in UN peace and verification missions.

• *Manpower and labour relations.* Full Quebec jurisdiction, including over workers in what are now federal jurisdiction firms and agencies, and harmonization of the relevant provisions in repatriated areas (bankruptcy, pension plans, etc.) with Quebec labour laws.

• *Social policies.* Full patriation of federal powers and spending in health, social services, housing and education to Quebec.

Centrale de l'enseignement du Québec (CEQ):

Canadian federalism an obstacle to Quebec

The CEQ's membership of 120,000 throughout Quebec is composed primarily of teachers in public and private schools, colleges and universities; educational support staffs; and some social services workers. More than two thirds are women.

In the spring of 1990 a membership survey indicated that 74 percent of the CEQ membership favoured Quebec independence, while 19 percent were opposed. Delegates to the CEQ convention in June 1990 voted overwhelmingly to mandate the CEQ to fight for independence and the adoption of a "democratic and progressive constitution" for Quebec.

The following excerpts from the CEQ's 106-page brief focus largely on its critique of the constitutional provisions of the current federal system, one of the most comprehensive such critiques submitted to the Commission. Also of interest are the CEQ's criticism of the Meech Lake Accord. Unlike the FTQ and CSN, which simply saw the rejection of the Accord as a rejection of Quebec, the CEQ identifies some serious flaws in the Accord that in its view justified the rejection of the Accord in both Quebec and English Canada as a fundamentally undemocratic scheme.

The CEQ's was also one of the few briefs presented to the Commission that addressed the glaring social and economic inequality within Quebec society.

Other sections discussing immigration and denominational schools are excerpted later in this book. Omitted are:

• a critique of federal government economic policy for its traditional focus on income support rather than full employment through a comprehensive industrial strategy and state intervention;

• a program for democratic reform based on the creation of a secular republic elected in a two-round election process with proportional representation of parties; greater use of referenda and popular initiatives; "democratic election" of the judiciary, which would be composed equally of men and women; and a clear separation of the executive, legislative and judicial powers.

The CEQ has long been interested in the national question and has always sought to link it to a theoretical conception of democratic development, the promotion of rights and freedoms and human equality.

The 1972 CEQ convention recognized the Quebec people as a true nation and affirmed its right to self-determination. This fundamental position has been reaffirmed on a number of occasions, in particular by the special convention on the national question in 1979 and by the Conseil général at the time of the constitutional *coup de force* in 1981. In 1982 the CEQ joined in a coalition with the other trade union federations and some nationalist organizations to affirm its rejection of the new *Constitution Act,* to which Quebec has never consented. The special convention in 1979 and the Conseil général also came out clearly for recognition of the right to self-determination of the native peoples.

In 1987 the CEQ informed Premier Bourassa of its dissatisfaction with the (excessively weak) content of the terms proposed by his government for agreeing to accept the Canadian Constitution. . . .

In our opinion some of these terms were correct, but we opposed the demand for a veto on the ground that what Quebec needed was not the power to block the constitutional evolution of other governments but to be freed from the veto of others over its own constitutional and political evolution. We would have preferred that Quebec call instead for constitutional entrenchment of its right to self-determination, a demand that ought to have been treated as complementary to its recognition as a distinct society. In our opinion, increased legislative powers should have been demanded not only in immigration but in such fields as agriculture, the labour force, regional development, social affairs, communications, culture and family law. Finally, we failed to understand Quebec's silence on the problems posed by section 93 of the *Constitution Act, 1867* protecting denominational schools when an act of the National Assembly, the *Public Elementary and Secondary Education Act,* had just been overruled by the Superior Court under section 93,[*] or its silence on the linguistic problems posed by sections 133 and 23 of the *Constitution Acts* of 1867 and 1982, respectively, when the

---

[*]   These issues are discussed at length in chapter 9.

Charter of the French Language had been attacked principally on the basis of these two sections.

Meech Lake Accord. The First Ministers' Conference answered Quebec's clearly insufficient demands with a comprehensive proposal that was even more disappointing; Mr. Bourassa hastened to accept it and it was inscribed in the Meech Lake Accord. The Accord granted a veto not only to Quebec but to each of the 10 provinces over a number of constitutional amendments, including the creation of new provinces, making the constitution of provinces with a native majority in the Northwest Territories much more difficult. In immigration, it simply entrenched some powers that Quebec had been exercising *de facto* since 1977, and it reconfirmed the decisive authority of the federal Parliament in determining immigration goals and categories. No other legislative jurisdiction was provided to Quebec. The Accord allowed the Quebec government to participate in the appointment of one third of the judges of the Supreme Court, but it left intact the federal government's sole power of appointment of judges of the Superior Court and the Court of Appeal. The Accord for the first time entrenched in the Constitution the federal power to spend in areas of provincial jurisdiction; it granted the provinces the possibility of withdrawing with compensation under certain circumstances from some shared cost national programs, but it required a province exercising its right of withdrawal to comply with so-called national objectives. It granted Quebec a completely symbolic recognition as a distinct society, but it was quick to specify that this recognition had no effect on the powers and privileges of already constituted political authorities.

What the CEQ most criticized in the Meech Lake Accord, however, was the famous "linguistic duality" clause, which stated that "the existence of French-speaking Canadians . . . and English-speaking Canadians . . . constitutes a fundamental characteristic of Canada". This gave the unfortunate impression that "the existence" of citizens speaking neither French nor English could be considered not fundamental. The clause was nothing short of insulting to the native peoples, many of whom speak only their language of origin. It was also upsetting to the allophone immigrants in that it granted preferential constitutional recognition to two classes of citizens defined on the basis of individual linguistic characteristics or behaviour. . . .

The intention was to indicate that the recognition of Quebec as a distinct society referred essentially to the fact that French-speaking Canadians are more concentrated there than in the rest of Canada. A greater trivialization of the distinct character of Quebec would be hard to imagine. It constituted a justification in advance of discriminatory practices toward person who are neither Francophones nor Anglophones.

Worse still, the Accord provided that the federal government and the provinces were required to preserve the fundamental characteristics defined by the Constitution. This obligation would therefore apply to provinces with a native majority that might be created in the Northwest Territories. Which means that these new provinces would have to promote the fact that English-speaking Canadians are concentrated in Canada outside Quebec.

Is it surprising that it was the native people in the multi-ethnic province of Manitoba who gave the Meech Lake Accord the *coup de grâce*? The native peoples had excellent objective reasons to oppose the proposed constitutional amendment, but they also had some good reasons to be particularly distrustful of Premier Bourassa's attitude toward them. It should be recalled that in 1987 our premier sought to convince his counterparts in the Western provinces of the usefulness of the veto formula he was then advocating by dangling before them the prospect that they might use it to block certain demands by the First Nations.

To an organization such as ours, which is now fighting for the national independence of Quebec, this review of the contents of the Meech Lake Accord is not a matter of mere historical interest. We want the members of this Commission to know right now that we will reject any proposal to include in the Constitution of an independent Quebec any clause on linguistic duality or recognizing as fundamental the existence of one or more classes of persons. . . .

Poverty in Quebec. Quebec has made enormous economic progress over the last 30 years. Its economic structure has diversified and the services sector now holds an increasingly important position, as in other developed economies. We have also built modern financial and public sectors without which the private sector would never have experienced the growth it has.

From 1961 to 1989 real per capita GDP grew by 138 percent, while real per capita income grew by 170 percent! During the same period the volume of business investment grew by 230 percent.

However, these spectacular data obscure some realities that are a far cry from prosperity and have become encrusted in the economic and social landscape of Quebec. . . . Quebec still accounts for more than 30 percent of the unemployed and more than 30 percent of the total number of poor people officially listed in Canada, although it has only 25 percent of the active and total population. This overrepresentation is a source of concern, especially when one considers the excellent economic performance that has been registered since the 1982 recession. We have experienced a long period of growth — seven consecutive years — yet the levels of unemployment and poverty in Quebec deviate from the national average. Based on the following observations, we can go further and say that the Quebec population is growing poorer:

• More than one million people in Quebec, a third of them children, are still below the poverty line. The growing number of soup kitchens and food banks are literally overwhelmed.

• The average income of women is barely 60 percent that of men; a majority of women earn less than $15,000 a year.

• Thousands of average-income families also suffer another form of impoverishment: a decline in purchasing power through stagnating wages, the increasing cost of housing, high interest charges resulting from high interest rates, increased indebtedness, etc. . . .

• Montreal is the biggest pocket of poverty in the country. With 615,000 people under the poverty threshold, the metropolitan area has 200,000 more poor people than there are in the whole of the Atlantic provinces. . . .

• Regional disparities are worsening in Quebec, as the Conseil des affaires sociales points out in a detailed study (*Deux Québec dans un*). The population of rural regions and city centres is growing older and poorer, while the suburban areas attract the younger, better off people. . . .

For the CEQ these few observations, although only a very partial image of the social and economic situation of Quebec, indicate the fault lines that have gradually opened up over the years between economic development and social progress. They also point to the urgency of abandoning an economic policy focused primarily on economic growth irrespective of the evolution of the employment situation. And they deflate the smug optimism of those who repeat over and over that we have to create wealth before distributing it. Through constant repetition this tautology has created the impression among many people that there is a sort of automatic connection between the mechanisms of wealth creation and distribution. But a necessary condition is not always a sufficient condition. The endemic and persistent unemployment Quebec has experienced for many years, coupled with the increasing precariousness of the job market, are at the source of this breach between what is economic and what is social. . . .

A quasi-federal system that stifles Quebec. The Constitution of 1867 was not intended to meet the needs and aspirations of Quebec. It was designed primarily to protect the interests of the British Empire in North America, solidify the union of the colonies remaining faithful to the English Crown, provide a counterweight to the attractions of the American federal republic, and promote the expansion of English Canada, based mainly in Ontario, toward the West.

In Quebec the new regime was referred to as a confederation. But, contrary to what the official propaganda suggested, it was neither confederal nor even genuinely federal. Constitutional scholars describe it today as quasi-federal, i.e., intermediary between a more or less decentralized unitary regime and an authentic federal system. The fathers of the supposed Confederation wanted to make the central government a relay of the Imperial government; they wanted to give it the most important legislative powers, with a supervisory role over the activity of the provincial governments.

It is within this perspective that the following elements of the 1867 Constitution must be appreciated:

1. the appointment by the federal government of the lieutenant governors of the provinces, who had the discretionary authority to withhold assent to some provincial laws at the behest of the federal government (ss. 55 and 90);

2. the federal government's power to disallow provincial laws within one year of their assent (ss. 56 and 90);

3. the federal government's right of appeal from any act or decision of any provincial authority affecting the privileges of the Protestant or Roman Catholic minority in relation to education (s-s. 93(3));

4. the federal Parliament's authority, at the request of the federal government, to enact remedial laws in relation to the educational rights and privileges of the Roman Catholic or Protestant minorities (s-s. 93(4));

5. The exclusive power of the federal government to appoint all superior court judges (s. 96), the latter having the authority, among other things, to determine the constitutional validity of provincial laws and the legality of provincial administrative acts.

These aspects substantially reduced the federal nature of the Canadian political system, making it appear in part to be a unitary regime in which the central government delegated certain powers to regional administrations under its control and supervision.

True, the lieutenant-governor's discretionary authority not to approve legislation is now exercised only upon the advice of the premier, in accordance with constitutional convention, and it is true as well that the federal government's power of disallowance has not been used for several decades, again by apparent constitutional convention. But it is not certain that the courts could or would overrule a failure to comply with these constitutional conventions. We should recall the subtle distinction made by the Supreme Court in 1980* between constitutional legality, which the courts may uphold, and constitutional conventions, which they may acknowledge but cannot enforce.

Moreover, the federal government's power to appoint all the superior court judges remains intact. The judges of the Superior Court and Court of Appeal now assume the bulk of the monitoring and supervisory role of the provincial authorities (legislature, government and provincial courts).

The federal nature of the Canadian constitutional system is also contradicted by the federal Parliament's complete control over the existence and legal jurisdiction of the Supreme Court and the fact that this Court, all of whose judges are appointed by the federal government, is the supreme adjudicator of the division of legislative powers and supreme interpreter of the Constitution and laws, both provincial and federal.

There has been much criticism, from the standpoint of federalist theory, of the fact that all Senators are appointed by the federal government and that, accordingly, the provincial governments are unrepresented in the central institutions. In our opinion, given the original characteristics of Quebec society compared with the rest of Canada, Quebec has much less need for representation in federal government bodies, where it will always be a minority, trying to influence the content of laws and policies uniformly applicable to the whole of Canada, than it does for independent powers enabling it to enact its own laws and implement its own policies adapted to its own particular situation.

Division of powers detrimental to Quebec. The division of powers (ss. 91 to 95) clearly favours the central government which, in addition to full control over foreign policy, defence, military and naval service, navigation and shipping, aviation and air travel, broadcasting, the postal service, interprovincial and international transportation and communications, controls the most decisive levers with regard to economic development. Thus the federal Parliament has exclusive legislative authority over banks, money, currency, interest, bills of exchange, bankruptcy and insolvency and interprovincial and international trade including, probably, the enforcement of commercial treaties affecting intraprovincial trade

---

* Apparently an allusion to the Patriation Reference, *Re Constitution of Canada* (1981), 125 D.L.R.(3d) 1 — Ed.

(such as the Canada-U.S. Free Trade Agreement). It also has the unrestricted power to raise money by any mode or system of taxation. It has exclusive jurisdiction over fisheries and unemployment insurance, and predominant jurisdiction over agriculture and immigration.

With respect to the status of physical persons and their rights, the federal Parliament has exclusive legislative authority over naturalization, marriage and divorce, and the sole power to legislate especially in relation to Indians and lands reserved for the Indians as well as aliens. It has full authority over criminal law and criminal procedure, and the establishment, maintenance and management of penitentiaries. We might add that it also has exclusive legislative authority over patents of invention and discovery, copyright and weights and measures. Finally, section 91 grants it general authority to make laws for the peace, order and good government of Canada in relation to all matters not coming within the classes of subjects assigned exclusively to the legislatures of the provinces.

In addition to jurisdiction over civil rights, the administration of justice, municipal affairs, the management of public lands, health and social services institutions and education, the provincial governments are allocated general jurisdiction over matters of a merely local or private nature.

However, the fact that Quebec has so-called exclusive legislative authority in a field does not necessarily assure it the full power it needs in that field.

Indeed, it is necessary to read the list of so-called exclusive provincial powers side by side with the list of federal powers. Some fields of jurisdiction overlap, in which case the federal power will as a rule prevail. For example, the provincial authority over civil rights is limited by the powers specifically allocated to the federal parliament allowing it to intervene in this area (trade, bills of exchange, bankruptcy and insolvency, marriage and divorce).

Quebec's repatriation of full and exclusive jurisdiction over family law, which was discussed and virtually adopted in 1980, would have enabled it to correct some inconsistencies resulting from the fact that, for example, Quebec has general jurisdiction over the civil law and in particular the solemnization of marriage while the federal government has jurisdiction over the substance of marriage and divorce. The National Assembly had adopted a division of the *Civil Code* dealing with marriage and divorce, which was to come into force once this repatriation was completed. But since this never happened, an entire division of the *Civil Code* of Quebec remains inoperative.

Federal jurisdiction over criminal law allows the central government to intervene in a host of areas through characterizing particular acts as criminal. Thus, by criminalizing abortion it intrudes on the orientation of our civil law and on the nature of the services that might legally be dispensed in our health establishments.

Constitutional obstacles to the exercise of Quebec powers. In theory Quebec has exclusive jurisdiction over the administration of justice, under head 14 of s. 92 of the *Constitution Act, 1867*, "the constitution, maintenance and organization of provincial courts, both of civil and of criminal jurisdiction, and including procedure in civil matters in those courts". However, since the appointment of superior court judges is explicitly assigned to the federal government, Quebec does not have the power to reduce the jurisdiction of these superior courts and therefore is not fully competent to create new courts and freely define their powers.

Furthermore, s. 133 determines the use of the French and English languages in court proceedings. Quebec has no power to modify the provisions of this section, which grants judges the discretion to publish their judgments in French or English, according to their preference, and accords the same freedom of choice to any individual or corporation appearing before the courts, as well as to anyone commencing proceedings, without the need to take account of the preference of other parties. Thus it is impossible to guarantee the right to a trial in French and a judgment in French in Quebec today, just as it is impossible to guarantee the right to a trial in a native language or any other particular language. Chapter III of the *Charter of the French Language* was ruled unconstitutional on this ground.

In theory Quebec has exclusive jurisdiction in education. But section 93 obliges it to protect the denominational schools privileges that Catholics and Protestants had in 1867. The courts have interpreted this obligation more or less broadly depending on the period, adding uncertainty and undermining Quebec's supposed exclusive jurisdiction. As well, s. 23 of the *Constitution Act, 1982* imposes criteria for the right to an English education in Quebec. These criteria, as we know, are different from those established by Quebec's Law 101 in 1977. Neither s. 93 of 1867 nor s. 23 of 1982 can be amended without the agreement of the federal Parliament and probably (depending on the applicable amending formula) the legislatures of at least six of the nine English provinces. Thus, despite the fiction that the Quebec legislature has exclusive jurisdiction over education in Quebec, such is not the case.

The 1867 Constitution granted taxation powers to both the federal government and the provinces. In the former case, s. 91, head 3 refers to "the raising of money *by any mode or system of taxation*". In the case of the provinces, s. 92 refers to "*direct* taxation within the province in order to the raising of a revenue *for provincial purposes*". The inequality is obvious. Not only is the federal government not limited as to the form of taxation, it is not limited as to the place of collection (in Canada or abroad) or the reasons for the taxation. The province, however, is limited to the field of direct taxes, can tax only within the province, and only to finance operations within provincial jurisdiction. Grafted onto these constitutional provisions is the doctrine of the federal power to spend even in areas of exclusive provincial jurisdiction. Meech Lake would have definitively entrenched this doctrine. But even without this entrenchment, it must be noted that the courts appear to have swallowed the spending power doctrine. It effectively authorizes the federal government to intervene in any field and legislate indirectly by submitting to its own criteria the attribution of grants, subsidies and allocations in the programs it is promoting on behalf of "national objectives" that it defines. Under this doctrine the exclusive nature of the legislative powers of the Quebec legislature may well be nothing but a fiction.

In the distribution of legislative powers between the Canadian federal parliament and the Quebec legislature, the latter has been handed the short end of the stick. Most federalists acknowledge that Quebec does not have the powers it needs to promote our national interests effectively and coherently. That is why, for at least a half a century, all of the successive governments in Quebec City have demanded a substantial increase in Quebec's legislative powers. (The Bourassa government's demands during the negotiating round that led to the Meech Lake Accord were an exception to this rule; but since the Accord failed and resulted in a new redefinition of Quebec's demands, we can say that, generally speaking, the tradition was not irremediably broken.)

The Canadian constitution is unreformable. But the time has come to acknowledge the obvious impossibility of obtaining satisfaction within the framework of the Canadian constitutional system, even on the most moderate demands of the Quebec federalists. There are many, cumulative reasons for this. In the first place, Quebec's needs are not necessarily shared by the other provinces, which constitute a common social and cultural entity with the same language, system of law and civil institutions. On the one hand, the federal government refuses to concede jurisdiction to a single province when a majority of provinces do not want such powers. On the other hand, the other provinces refuse to allow any special status to Quebec by contributing their constitutional assent. Thus in 1980, the federal government withdrew its offer of jurisdiction over marriage and divorce because the English provinces were uninterested; Quebec was isolated, since neither the federal government nor the other provinces would agree to a transfer of jurisdiction to Quebec alone.

The amending procedure, previously uncertain, is now clear and it is extremely rigid. Any amendment affecting the division of powers must receive the approval of the federal Parliament and the legislatures of at least seven provinces that have, in the aggregate, at least 50 percent of the population of all the provinces. Parliament therefore has an absolute veto over any amendment and the English provinces must agree among themselves by a two-thirds majority, while there is no absolute requirement for Quebec's consent.

If it appears almost excluded that Quebec could gain any new powers, is it at least guaranteed the powers it already has? Theoretically, it has the authority to withdraw from any constitutional amendment affecting the distribution of powers. But the federal government's invasion of provincial jurisdictions does not always need an explicit amendment. The federal government has other, effective instruments at its disposal. The powers it already has allow it to intervene in a host of fields that from any other standpoint would appear to fall within provincial jurisdiction. Where there is a conflict of laws based on defined jurisdictions, the federal law will prevail. Other intrusions are justified by the "national dimensions" or "emergency" theories. Any dispute will be decided by the courts, all of whose judges are appointed by the federal government.

Three major events in the last half-century have significantly reinforced the federal position on the possible invasion of provincial jurisdiction: (1) the abolition in 1949 of appeals to the Privy Council, making the Supreme Court of Canada the final arbiter in constitutional matters; (2) the *Constitution Act, 1982*, which reinforced the courts' power of intervention in constitutional debates; (3) the Canada-U.S. Free Trade Agreement, which came into force in 1989. The effects of the first two events are generally well known, those of the third much less so. Many constitutional experts believe that the Free Trade Agreement opens the door to an almost complete [federal] takeover of commercial law and greater federal intrusion in the law of professions, occupational training and manpower policy (s. 6 of the *Constitution Act, 1982* had already limited provincial powers in this regard).

There are virtually no guarantees for Quebec as long as it remains subject to the infernal machinery of the constitutional regime that now governs us. We think it is time to get out.

Union des producteurs agricoles (UPA):

Canadian federalism has had its day

Under Quebec law the UPA represents all 48,000 agricultural producers in the province. Affiliated to it as well is the Fédération des producteurs de bois, which represents 120,000 private woodlot owners, 35,000 of whom are also farmers.

The UPA's affiliated federations and unions administer more than 20 joint marketing plans affecting 90 percent of its members.

Excerpted here is the UPA's critique of agricultural policy and structures under the existing federal system, and its view of the economic relations a sovereign Quebec should seek to establish with Canada and other countries.

At the UPA's annual convention in December 1990, 99.2 percent of the delegates voted in favour of Quebec sovereignty. An internal survey released a few weeks earlier by the UPA indicated that 72 percent of its members (and 40 percent of its Anglophone members) were sympathetic to sovereignty.

However, the Quebec Farmers' Association, a voluntary association of English-speaking farm families, presented a brief to the Commission opposing sovereignty primarily on the ground that it would jeopardize Quebec's current favourable position under the supply management system for milk and poultry production.

Economic policy and equalization. Quebec's political history, from Confederation to today, is one of interminable battles to exact the powers it needs to develop fully. It is also a history of direct intrusion into jurisdictions we thought Quebec had already acquired, a history of duplicated structures, overlapping policies and a multitude of federal-provincial quarrels to enforce respect for the peculiarities, policies and democratic choices of Quebec. And it is a history — a very sad one, moreover — of continual struggles to ensure that federal funds are fairly distributed in Quebec.

The Quebec agricultural sector can claim all of these aspects of Quebec's history under federalism. Two departments of agriculture operate in Quebec, with two farm income stabilization systems, two federal-provincial levels of involvement in joint collective marketing plans, and two levels of intervention in research and farm credit.

This dual structure is explained by four factors:
- constitutional jurisdictions that are unclearly distributed;
- a Canadian agricultural policy based on the needs of Western Canada;
- non-compliance with the democratic decisions of Quebec producers and our particular needs in agricultural development; and
- the great unjustness to Quebec in federal transfer payments.

Under the Canadian Constitution (s. 95), agriculture is a jurisdiction that is shared between two levels of government, but with federal predominance where federal and provincial laws conflict. The respective jurisdictions, somewhat unclear from the beginning, have become entangled under other constitutional provisions. Health standards and meat inspection are two examples of the mess that can result with two governments intervening.

This imprecise sharing of constitutional powers has resulted in frictions and repeated attempts by Ottawa to meddle in provincial policies. It has also resulted in decades of long and costly legal spats related to the lack of clarity in the Constitution. No doubt the most eloquent example is the joint marketing plans. In Quebec everyone will recall the famous egg war, which lasted for about 20 years.

Since the beginning, Canadian farm policy has been designed mainly to aid Western grain producers and has poorly served the interests of Quebec farmers. We have had to develop our own programs adapted to the Quebec situation to mitigate the deficiencies in these policies and the unfairness to Quebec of federal transfer payments.

Despite the unsuitability of Canadian agricultural policies, the federal government has constantly sought to deny us the right to have our own programs designed in accordance with our needs and the goals we have set for ourselves in Quebec over the last 25 years. A quite recent illustration of this is stabilization insurance. When the federal policies were being overhauled we had to fight hard to allow the use of a cost of production formula, based on our own 1975 program in Quebec, that is unique in Canada.

Federal obstinacy was seen again in the international GATT negotiations. We had to spend a lot of energy in Ottawa, and even in Geneva, convincing our Canadian representatives in this international forum of the legitimacy of agricultural policies that are beneficial to Quebec, such as Canada's milk and poultry supply management programs (these two sectors account for 50 percent of

Quebec farm revenues), Quebec's income stabilization insurance, the Quebec farm credit program, and crop insurance.

Once again we found, as we had so many times in the past, such as during the revision of the Crow's Nest freight rates in 1982, that the whole political community in Quebec had to be mobilized in order for us to get a hearing, to be understood and change the direction of Canada's policy.

History being what it is, Quebec is not at the GATT bargaining table in Geneva to defend its own interests, nor will it be there if the constitutional status quo is maintained. Quebec is not there to expend the energy it must in order to build an eighth agreement that will be to its advantage. It must waste its energy instead convincing a central government that is more sensitive to the concerns of the Western grain growers than it is to those of Quebec. And, to defend us in Geneva, we have to rely on people who, less than two months ago, did not believe in the originality of Quebec programs or the merits of the farm policies being implemented in Quebec.

There is no further need to demonstrate the iniquity of federal agricultural transfer payments to Quebec. A joint document by the UPA, the Coopérative fédérée, and the Quebec government in May 1988 states: "Since 1980-81, this iniquity has increased and the cumulative balance sheet of federal intervention, compared with the importance of Quebec agriculture, is negative."[*]

The fact is, Quebec agriculture accounts for 16 percent of Canadian farm revenues, but receives only 6.4 percent of federal expenditures. The Western provinces, on the other hand, rake in 60 percent of federal farm spending. Saskatchewan alone, which accounts for 18 percent of Canadian farm revenues, receives 31 percent of the federal funding.

Understandably, grain production has for several years been in a serious crisis related to the chaos in international markets. But our red meat producers are suffering, too, through the transfer effect of the depression in grain prices on livestock production. With the exception of the tripartite federal stabilization program in the Quebec pork producing sector, and several other recent transfers that have increased Quebec's share of federal spending to 6.4 percent from 5.5 percent over the last two years, Ottawa is not helping to support red meat production in Quebec.

---

[*] *Les interventions fédérales, une question d'équité,* a joint publication of the Quebec Ministère de l'Agriculture, the UPA and the CFQ.

Furthermore, how can we explain the fact that average payments have been almost $20 per ton of grain lower in Quebec, on average, since 1988? Yet these are the same grains and the same low prices in both East and West.

In reality, the only structured federal policy that has benefited Quebec, and one that we cherish, is the production quota supply management policy. And in terms of the federal funds distributed to the dairy sector to support domestic consumption, it could not be fairer.

The federal government is paying $6.03 per hectolitre in subsidies to support domestic consumption of dairy products, regardless of where the dairy producers are located. Unfortunately, this subsidy will be gradually but substantially reduced under the Canadian proposals at the GATT talks. And with it will disappear the only example of equity in the distribution of federal funds to Quebec.

As in other sectors, Quebec has for years been trying to obtain its fair share of federal agricultural funding and to invest these funds in terms of its own priorities, policies and programs. We have been trying to continue developing Quebec agriculture with this funding, which is based on the four pillars of our agricultural system: supply management, income stabilization, farm credit and crop insurance. Every time, this has meant wasting energy in usually fruitless fights to enforce our point of view.

Through the taxes and charges they pay to Ottawa, Quebec taxpayers are subsidizing a department that is not producing the returns it should. Each year they see several hundred million dollars in funds go up in smoke, when in normal conditions this money would be used to create or at least maintain jobs in the food and agricultural sector in Quebec, a sector that accounts for 11 percent of total employment in Quebec, let us remember.

Since Quebec agriculture gets only 40 percent of what it would normally and lawfully get, given its weight in Canadian agriculture, we dare say that Quebec taxpayers, who are responsible for 23 percent of the country's tax revenues, are annually paying $700 million too much. This money is being invested in agriculture elsewhere in Canada.

This net fiscal contribution by Quebecers largely goes to support Western agriculture, and in particular to support the agricultural diversification and food processing goals that the grain-producing provinces have been pursuing for several years. In other words, Quebec is massively subsidizing, through its taxes and charges, its competitors in livestock production.

The story of federal-provincial relations in agriculture is pretty much the general story of federal-provincial relations in all sectors, and in particular in those that are crucial to Quebec, such as research and development, transportation, manpower training, federal purchases of goods and services, in short, whatever helps to build the economic structure of Quebec.

But it might be alleged that, overall, Quebec gets more from Ottawa than it pays in taxes and duties.

Without engaging in polemics in this regard, we think it is appropriate to take a closer look at three issues:

• the cost to Quebec of the duplication of structures and programs;

• the nature of federal spending in Quebec; and

• the relation between federal transfer payments and the federal government's monetary policy.

The most recent study available on the cost to Quebec of the duplication of federal-provincial structures dates back to 1978.[*] The authors identified no fewer than 221 federal programs and 244 Quebec programs that overlapped. Overall, excluding from the total all instances in which the federal government assisted the Quebec government in implementing a joint program, 49 percent of the Quebec programs resulted in duplication of government services provided by federal programs. The authors found generalized overlapping in all areas of government action except the post office, national defence and veterans' relief.

And this situation has not changed, observers say. The programs and structures have continued to develop, with the federal administration growing and Quebec footing the bill for the operation of a dual structure.

This probably means that hundreds of millions, if not billions, of dollars are being squandered in payments by Quebecers to the federal government — hundreds of millions of dollars that could be recovered and put to productive use by Quebec and for Quebec.

A revealing example is meat inspection. According to the study we mentioned earlier, Ottawa annually invests some $250 million in this field, which is fully and similarly covered by the Quebec government. Quebec spends about $60 million a year funding this program, a "pure" duplication. How many similar cases could we find in a detailed study of the cost of overlapping to Quebec?

---

[*] Julien and Proulx, *op. cit.*, cited *supra*, p. 86.

So when we draw a balance sheet of federal tax revenues from Quebec and federal spending in our province, we should not lose sight of the fact that this duplication cost is a part of the "net gain" from federalism.

Thus we find it rather hard to conclude that federalism has benefited Quebec on the rough basis of a comparison of two columns of figures, as a recent study commissioned by the Conseil du patronat du Québec does, without inquiring as to what those figures mean.

Similarly, in connection with the public accounts, we note that Quebec certainly has its share, or a major share, of federal transfers under unemployment insurance (a simple transfer, but a dual structure) and social assistance. But federal expenditures on the economic structure, the genuinely productive investments that create jobs and productive and competitive capacity, are not being made in Quebec.

Research and development expenditures are significant in this regard. During the last three years more than 50 percent of federal spending on this item (an average of $1.2 billion) was done in Ontario, compared with less than 20 percent in Quebec.

Likewise, we are inclined to relate the significance of public assistance in federal transfer payments to both Quebec's economic situation and the federal government's monetary policy, which acts to the detriment of Quebec's economy. In our view, two issues are posed:

• isn't the size of these items explained by the need to correct the painful effects of federal policy, especially the excessive interest rates?

• and, if that is the case, is fiscal federalism as beneficial to Quebec as is claimed?

Monetary policy. We are not competent to calculate the negative effects of excessively high interest rates and an artificially swollen exchange rate on investments, Quebec exports, jobs — in short, the proper functioning of the Quebec economy. We will simply point to the following facts:

• Each 1-point increase in interest rates adds close to 2 billion dollars to the federal deficit in the first year and 3.5 billion dollars in the fourth year.* Quebecers pay 23 percent of this, or more than $460 million in the first year and more than $800 million in the fourth. There is general agreement that Canadian interest rates have

---

* Figures from last federal budget.

been 2 to 3 points higher than they should be for a year, owing to the Bank of Canada's inflation phobia.

• According to the Association des industries forestières du Québec, for each 1-cent increase in the value of the Canadian dollar, Quebec pulp and paper exports decrease by $50 million dollars annually.* Experts across Canada say the Canadian dollar is overvalued by at least 5 cents in relation to the U.S. dollar. That means $250 million that the Quebec forest industry is losing annually. How many Quebec jobs are being sacrificed in this prime sector of our economy because of the federal government's poor monetary management?

• This monetary policy has a harsh effect on agriculture. Given the financial structure of our farms, we estimated when the last Wilson budget came down that we would lose between $1,135 and $8,690 per farm, depending on the sector, each time interest rates increased by one and a half points. These losses would indicate that Quebec farmers are staving off mass bankruptcy by living off a part of their provision for depreciation.

In our opinion, "net" federal transfers provide only partial, book-keeping and non-structuring compensation that is to a large degree designed simply to lessen the effects of federal decisions that harm Quebec's economy. . . .

Economic and monetary union: a reality, a necessity. In redefining Quebec's political and constitutional status, crucial importance must be given to the economic union between Quebec and Canada; similarly, Quebec's participation in the various international agreements, particularly the GATT, must be considered essential.

The economic links created within Canada are a reality that Quebec cannot ignore, just as it would be very hard for the Canadian provinces to scoff at these economic links, which make them dependent on the Quebec market.

Overall, Quebec ships 26 percent of its manufactured products to other Canadian provinces. Shipments to Ontario alone were estimated at $12.6 billion in 1989. But Quebec also provides a $13 billion market for Ontario manufacturing shipments.

The latest available figures on food shipments indicated that in 1984 the sales of Quebec firms in Ontario totalled $1 billion, while the corresponding Ontario sales in Quebec were $1.5 billion, a $500 million advantage for Ontario.

---

* *Les Affaires*, 29 September 1990.

We do not have precise figures for Quebec's trade with the Prairie provinces. However, we estimate that 90 percent of Quebec's supplies of wheat for human consumption come from the Prairie provinces and Ontario — an $82 million market for these provinces.

Similarly, 93 percent of Quebec's beef supplies come from Alberta. In 1989 the Quebec market represented sales of $750 million for Alberta (and to a lesser degree, Ontario).

Thus, there are mutual interests in maintaining an economic union within the Canadian economic space.

In this regard, incidentally, an important point should be noted concerning the existing links between Quebec and the rest of Canada in terms of national marketing of farm products and the interprovincial distribution of production quotas in the poultry and dairy sectors. In any negotiation of economic union with Canada, the maintenance of this distribution of production and of import controls under Article XI of the GATT should be treated as the top priority.

In particular, Quebec dairy producers are now allocated 48 percent of Canada's industrial milk production. A solid Quebec milk transformation industry dependent on shipments of dairy products to markets in the various Canadian provinces has developed around this division of the Canadian quota. Obviously, our quotas will always face some danger of being challenged. Already, outrageous pressure is being exerted by the other provinces to reduce Quebec's share of the national quotas. But the current risks of a loss of quotas are lessened, albeit not eliminated, by East-West interdependence and the existence of international trade arrangements.

This last point suggests a final recommendation to the Commission members regarding economic union. It is clear to us that a Quebec that claims status as a nation must be a signatory of the GATT.

Furthermore, since more than 15 percent of Quebec's national production of commodities (excluding services) is shipped to international markets, it would be inappropriate not to agree on assuming "Most Favoured Nation" status with the 105 contracting parties of the GATT.

Similarly, we support the negotiation of a monetary union with the rest of Canada. However, Quebec will have to negotiate advantageous terms with respect to the exchange rate and the establishment of interest rates. . . .

4.

Women in the distinct society

The Bélanger-Campeau Commission was widely criticized for its failure to include representatives of significant sectors of Quebec society among its members. Particularly striking was the lack of women: only eight of the 36 commissioners, and only one of the nine commission members on the steering committee, were women.

The Commission report itself devoted a mere two paragraphs in its 90 pages to the particular constitutional and political issues expressed in briefs presented to it by women's groups. One paragraph observed that the value placed on women's equality in Quebec society is a feature of its distinctive character. The other acknowledged that the time had come for the existing equality in principle between the sexes to be reflected in practice – for example, through increasing women's representation in Quebec's political institutions. However, the Commission made no specific recommendations as to how this might be done.

As for the presentations to the Commission, "far too many briefs – excepting those presented by women's groups – simply did not deal with women's issues at all," wrote union leader Lorraine Pagé, a member of the Commission.* "Obviously, we did not expect the Conseil du patronat to deal at length with the status of women. But what a disappointment to read or hear nothing – or so little – about immigrant women in the presentations by the cultural communities; what a gap there was in the excessive silence of the First Nations on the situation of native women. And even when some briefs . . . dealt extensively with the issue, all the attention was on other aspects."

Of the briefs by women's groups, the two excerpted in the following pages are of particular interest for their detailed statements of the alienation Quebec feminists experience within the existing federal system,

---

* "Les femmes dans le Québec de demain", *Le Devoir*, March 7, 1991.

and the proposals they advance to ensure women's equality in the Quebec of the future.

The Fédération des femmes du Québec (FFQ, or Quebec women's federation), which describes itself as "democratic and nonpartisan", is an umbrella organization for 115 associations with about 100,000 members in all walks of life. Formed in 1966, it is comparable in size and representativeness to the National Action Committee on the Status of Women in English Canada.

The Conseil du statut de la femme (CSF, or Status of women council) is a consultative and research body created in 1973 to advise the Quebec government on issues of concern to women. Roughly analogous to the federal government's Canadian Advisory Council on the Status of Women, it is composed of 10 members appointed by the government on the recommendation of their respective constituencies: four from women's groups, and two each from the university, business and trade union milieus.

The FFQ brief, presented on behalf of its Board of Directors, came out clearly in support of Quebec sovereignty. The CSF refrained from making any recommendation on Quebec's political status, on the ground that this was not within its mandate. Both briefs were strongly critical of the lack of women on the Commission. And both addressed the substantive issues that divided Quebec women's organizations from their counterparts in English Canada during the debates over the Meech Lake Accord and the meaning of the "distinct society" clause.

Fédération des femmes du Québec:

Women need the greatest possible political autonomy for Quebec

Sovereignty the substantive issue. Beyond Quebec's constitutional status, it is the social and political proposals that interest us. In our view, it is impossible to elaborate a political plan without a social plan, and the latter must have a feminist content.

We believe that the possibility of achieving significant changes in the social and political fabric of Quebec will be proportional to the degree of autonomy Quebec obtains. And we believe that greater manoeuvrability for Quebec will promote the development of a feminist model of society, provided that women are closely associated with all phases in the development of this model. To define and implement a plan for society, we need a framework that we can be part of.

With this in mind, and although we are fully aware that political autonomy is not the only condition for such changes, we think that women as a social group have an interest in choosing the greatest possible political autonomy for Quebec.

On the substantive issue, the FFQ's provincial Board of Directors has made its choice, for sovereignty. Here is why.

Under the Canadian constitution, Quebec cannot implement a model of society that corresponds to its aspirations.

This is what the FFQ has found over the years in the course of our work on various issues of concern to women. The positions we have taken on issues such as the provincial repatriation of marriage and divorce (1980), pension reform (1983), occupational training (1987) and abortion (1990) illustrate clearly not only the difficulty but the limitations for Quebec women in also being Canadians. . . .

(a) The division of powers between the two levels of government. Under the present confederal regime, the division of powers between Ottawa and Quebec City is a source of policy incoherence, and Quebec women pay the cost.

For example, in 1980 only the Quebec women supported the proposed transfer of jurisdiction over marriage and divorce from the federal government to the provinces. The FFQ, as a participant in the discussions, thought it inconceivable that marriage and divorce, which are part of family law, should be under federal jurisdiction when family law as a whole (including matrimonial regimes) was under provincial jurisdiction. In 1980 family law underwent a significant reform in Quebec. As part of this reform the Quebec government was prepared to adopt its own divorce legislation, which would recognize no-fault divorce, for example. The FFQ members wanted Quebec to have overall control of family law. But the proposal was rejected by the women from the other provinces and the transfer in jurisdiction never took place.

With regard to pension reform, in 1983 the FFQ was advocating that women who left the labour market to look after young children or disabled persons be allowed to participate in the plan. We have always felt that Quebec's refusal to commit itself to this reform was related to its inability to obtain guarantees that it would recover the sums that the federal government would save through a decrease in the number of women in Quebec who receive the guaranteed income supplement. . . .

Another issue . . . was occupational training. Less prepared than men for the requirements of the job market, and concentrated in low-paying job ghettos, women are extremely dependent on training programs for access to non-traditional trades, occupational categories facing labour shortages, or expanding sectors of the economy. Women have special needs in occupational training. But training programs are funded and defined by Ottawa, which sets the priorities, while the programs are implemented by Quebec. As a result they are not necessarily responsive to the needs of Quebec women.

Another case that directly affects women is that of maternity leaves. These are covered by Ottawa under the unemployment insurance program, preventing Quebec from developing a more coherent family policy.

This list is not exhaustive. We have mentioned only a few of the issues that have been addressed by the FFQ in previous briefs. It is our analysis that the source of the incoherence is not only the division of jurisdictions between the two levels of government but the competition between them. If neither the federal nor the provincial government wishes to intervene in a matter they toss the ball back and forth and slough responsibility off on each other. And if either or both decide to intervene, they compete instead of being complementary. This situation is of course attributable to the lack of clarity in the *British North America Act* of 1867, which, in sections 91 and 92 on the division of powers, left unanswered a number of points that have been the subject of disputes throughout the twentieth century. But, since Quebec's interpretation of the Act has always differed from that of the other provinces and Quebec is always seeking new powers, the competition between Ottawa and Quebec is particularly intense. We conclude that, as long as we have two governments competing with each other, it will be very difficult to define coherent orientations and work together.

Why, then, retain some powers in Quebec? Because of the distinct character of Quebec society.

(b) *The distinctiveness of Quebec society.* The FFQ has learned from its experience with Canadian and Quebec women's groups over the last 10 years or so that Quebec women, unlike their Canadian sisters, have greater confidence in their provincial government than they do in the federal government. For example, the discussions around the Meech Lake Accord in 1987 revealed that women in the other provinces look to the federal government to maintain social programs, while this is not the case in Quebec. It is not that Quebec women think the provincial government is necessarily better than the federal one, but because they feel that this is where they can intervene most effectively, where they can most easily present their demands with the greatest possibility of influencing decisions. . . .

By focusing on the provincial level, we have achieved substantial progress in the status of women, and this is not unrelated to the distinctive character of Quebec, as the FFQ emphasized in its testimony before the Joint Committee of the Senate and House of Commons on the 1987 constitutional agreement. That is why we did not dismiss the agreement, in contrast to many Canadian women's groups, which thought the concept of a distinct society was a threat to women's rights.

In 1980, in the debate over repatriating jurisdiction over divorce, the Quebec women also took a distinct position. The FFQ, unlike the women from the other provinces, favoured the proposal in the belief that a provincial law would be more likely to satisfy the interests of Quebec women, since divorce is related to things that are private, to one's way of thinking, to culture. Laws should reflect the social principles of a community. The FFQ thought that a divorce act developed on the basis of Canadian values would not correspond to the particular needs of Quebec women.

Another issue on which the FFQ has taken a position, and on which it has observed Quebec's distinct character, is abortion. The way this issue has been dealt with in Quebec reflects a greater open-mindedness than in the other provinces. After Dr. Morgentaler's acquittal our justice system refused for years to get involved in futile prosecutions and tolerated the abortions that were being performed in the CLSCs, the local community health clinics, without recourse to the therapeutic abortion committees required by law. Through-out this period Quebec has stood out among the provinces in its recognition of women's right to control their own bodies.

What distinguishes Quebec from the other provinces, in addition to language, is its culture. Here too, we have found, Quebec women and men have clashed with Canadians from other provinces. This is why we ask ourselves: can we continue to be effective, to live together and build a common future when we do not even manage to establish a consensus on basic issues?

To develop and implement a coherent plan corresponding to Quebec's distinctiveness, Quebec needs particular powers. Because of its distinct culture, Quebec must retain certain powers if it is to avoid assimilation. Since the Quiet Revolution Quebec has been trying to establish and protect its jurisdiction on a case-by-case basis. Under constant siege from Ottawa, and with its own functions, role and powers in jeopardy, Quebec has had a reactive policy, not an active one. Competing with the federal government's greater spending power, Quebec reacts to the latter's initiatives and spends its time negotiating with it, without being able to act freely and autonomously.

We feminists understand the importance of autonomy and identity, concepts that have always been at the heart of our struggle. We have refused to dissolve our identity as women into that of our fathers and husbands; and today we refuse to dissolve our Quebec identity into the Canadian identity. We know the price of autonomy, but also its value.

Our feminism is expressed collectively; it is part of a specific cultural reality, that of Quebec, and it is not independent of the social and political context. For example, let us recall that the birth of neo-feminism in Quebec in the early 1970s was closely related to the goal of national liberation. Feminist groups situated the struggle of women within the struggle for national liberation, as was illustrated by the slogan "No women's liberation without the liberation of Quebec. No Quebec liberation without the liberation of women." Then, as today, it was not feminism that was exclusive to Quebec women, but the context in which it was developing.

So if we want a feminist plan for society to develop and take shape in Quebec, a plan for women and men alike, defined on a parity basis by both sexes, a coherent plan that corresponds to the needs and aspirations of Quebec women and men, Quebec must be in charge of the major tools and programs it needs in order to develop and flourish. Yet the problems it has encountered in negotiating the repatriation of powers in such fields as manpower, job training, economic development, immigration and taxation prove beyond a doubt that it is impossible to negotiate on an equal footing with the Canadian government within the present framework. It is necessary to create a new relationship of forces. And only political sovereignty can secure this. . . .

Organizing sovereignty. Since it is the overall future of Quebec that interests us, we think that the changes in Quebec should not be limited to a fundamental modification of the relationship between Quebec and Canada, but should be situated within an overall plan for society. What we need to collectively redefine is not only our relationships with Canada but what this new country of Quebec will be. It is social relationships as a whole that must be re-envisaged.

To ensure a feminist content in this plan for society, we will now propose some parameters that can help in designing — at a later stage, following a collective thinking process — a model political and constitutional status for Quebec.

1. The proposed constitution. In our opinion, the constitution of a country should reflect the fundamental values of the society, those values that are the product of a national consensus and require protection. This necessarily means, we think, establishing particular orientations at this stage.

A constitutional proposal should include, in addition to the declaration of independence or sovereignty:

• Entrenchment of the Quebec *Charter of Human Rights and Freedoms*, with particular sections devoted to:

- *general rights of all citizens, male and female:* the right to a job, health, housing, education, a healthy environment, income security and physical security;

- *specific rights of women:* formal recognition of equality between men and women; the right to control one's maternity;

- *children's rights:* in accordance with the provisions of the United Nations *Convention on the Rights of Children*;

• Recognition of the aboriginal rights of the First Nations, as defined in the *Canadian Charter of Rights and Freedoms.*

The economic and commercial relations to be established with Canada and other countries should by no means be incorporated in the Constitution, but should be confined to conjunctural agreements.

The new constitution should be elaborated by a constituent assembly elected by universal suffrage and composed equally of men and women.

The proposed constitution should be submitted to the entire population for ratification. It will be the property of the citizens of Quebec, and should not be the subject of any negotiations with other countries, including Canada.

2. Organization of the new State of Quebec. Parallel to inscribing fundamental values in the constitution, the Quebec state will have to make these values meaningful in political, legal and economic terms. . . .

• *Genuine regional development.* Once sovereign and freed from Ottawa's rivalry, Quebec will no longer fear regional decentralization, which under Confederation undermines its powers. With increased powers and autonomy, a new distribution of authority will be necessary between the central Quebec government and decentralized municipal and regional structures. . . . These new relationships should be based on recognition of the right of the regions to be

involved in the definition and implementation of their development.
. . .

For a renewed welfare state. Such decentralization is indispensable to the development and expansion of a welfare state of a new type. Women have traditionally been responsible for caring for children, the elderly, the disabled and the sick, yet have not enjoyed financial equality with men commensurate with these responsibilities in an economic and fiscal system that recognizes only salaried labour. Women need state intervention to support them in their role as providers of care and help to overcome the inequalities related to their traditional responsibilities.

This is particularly so for immigrant women. . . .

Quebec has an acute problem of poverty, and the future State of Quebec will have to tackle this as a priority. A new distribution of wealth is needed between the regions in Quebec, between the neighbourhoods in the urban centres, between the ethnic groups that make up our population, and between men and women. The sad reality is that women make up the vast majority of the poor — those on welfare or low incomes, the elderly or single parents. Among the measures needed to secure a fair distribution of wealth are . . . the development of access to equality programs, job training and a policy of full employment. . . .

We are convinced that economic development and social development are closely linked, and that economic development must be defined in terms of social development, and not the contrary as is too often the case today. . . .

Conseil du statut de la femme:

Women in Quebec and English Canada – Two different conceptions of the state

1. Impact on women of overlapping government jurisdictions and activities.

Labour. The labour force profile has changed dramatically over the last few decades. Once marginal, the presence of women on the labour market is now an irreversible phenomenon. But while women constitute 43 percent of the Quebec workforce, their situation still differs from that of men: concentrated in the service sector, women employed full time in 1988 earned only 66 percent of what men earned.

Governments have developed a number of measures to cope with these changes, among them employment equity and equal access programs. The Council notes that the Quebec and Canadian governments have adopted different philosophies with regard to these goals, leading to significant disadvantages for employers. And the inconsistency collectively impedes women in their quest for greater social justice.

Reconciling motherhood with paid employment continues to be a challenge for women. This is the area in which, in our view, the distribution of powers between the two levels of government has the most direct impact. We have examined in particular the issues of parental leave and the protective reassignment or cessation of work of pregnant or nursing employees.

Parental leave. In Quebec most women employees have the right to maternity leave under a Quebec law, the *Labour Standards Act.* However, income compensation during the leave is granted primarily under the federal *Unemployment Insurance Act.* This produces a number of discrepancies.

• Income replacement during maternity leave is less than what is provided by other Quebec social assistance schemes. Unemployment insurance, which replaces income during maternity, pays taxable benefits equal to 60 percent of gross pay, with an insurable maximum pay of $33,280 in 1990. Quebec social assistance schemes, however, pay much higher benefits to victims of occupational accidents and diseases or vehicle accidents: 90 percent of net income with an insurable maximum pay of $40,000 in 1990. So it is more advantageous to have a highway accident than to give birth to a child.

• For a number of years the unemployment insurance program allowed 15 weeks of benefits after a two-week waiting period, while the *Labour Standards Act* provided a maternity leave of 18 weeks.

It would appear that unemployment insurance, with its inconsistencies in waiting periods and limitation of coverage to employees, is an inappropriate tool for income replacement during maternity, and that the shared jurisdiction between Quebec and the federal government creates a complex system entailing additional costs and discrepancies, and preventing Quebec, to some degree, from adopting a consistent integrated policy of parental leave that would allow income replacement during the mother's maternity leave or both parents' parental leave.

Protective reassignment of pregnant or nursing workers. The *Occupational Health and Safety Act* allows most women workers to resort to protective reassignment when the circumstances so require. However, a section of the female workforce — Quebec employees of the federal government and businesses under federal jurisdiction — which we estimate at about 120,000 (or 8.5 percent of all working women), are excluded from this protection.

This is because labour conditions and labour relations in some sectors such as interprovincial and international transport, the banks and communications, are under the exclusive jurisdiction of the federal Parliament. . . .

The part of the *Canada Labour Code* dealing with occupational health and safety in businesses under federal jurisdiction has no specific provision protecting maternity in the workplace, and is based on different principles than the Quebec act. The effect of this division of powers is to create two categories of working women, those who can benefit from the protective reassignment provisions and those who cannot. A Quebec policy of parental leaves would likewise fall victim to this dichotomy, and women working in firms under federal jurisdiction would be unable to benefit under it.

Family law. Jurisdiction in family law is shared between the federal Parliament and Quebec's National Assembly. Parliament has jurisdiction over marriage and divorce. Under its marriage jurisdiction it can adopt laws concerning the capacity of the parties, for example with respect to age or degree of consanguinity. Under its divorce powers Parliament has adopted legislation governing the grounds for divorce and ancillary provisions related to alimony and custody of children.

The National Assembly has the power to make laws concerning the solemnization of marriage. It may also, pursuant to its general jurisdiction over property and civil rights, legislate in the area of matrimonial regimes, estates, adoption, the effects of marriage and separation as to bed and board and its effects on support and the custody of children.

In short, Quebec women marry under provincial rules governing the solemnization of marriage. They separate under rules established in the Quebec *Civil Code* (grounds, support, custody). But they divorce under federal rules (grounds, support, custody). Moreover, in the case of separation and divorce, provincial rules provide for a distribution of the family estate and the possibility of applying for compensatory benefits.

More specifically, the current division of powers prevents the implementation of some provisions in the *Civil Code* concerning, among other things, the age of marriage and the spouses' ability to request a divorce without having to explain why if they submit a draft agreement settling the consequences of their divorce.

In addition, art. 638 of the *Civil Code*, which generally provides that support payments are adjusted to the cost of living on January 1 each year by operation of law, applies to separation but may not apply to divorce, according to some case law (now on appeal). Quebec women who divorce, as opposed to those who separate, must therefore ask the court to index their support payments.

This splitting up of family law unnecessarily complicates women's lives, prevents Quebec from implementing the final section of its family law reform, and will probably produce some inconsistencies.

Income security. This is of definite importance to Quebec women, whose average income in 1988 was only $13,560 as opposed to $24,298 for men. In 1990 more than 200,000 adult women, mainly single women and single-parent family heads, were receiving social assistance benefits in Quebec. They represented 55 percent of adult recipients.

Single women aged 65 and over likewise suffer from inadequate resources. Women are employed for shorter periods than men and have fewer payments into the Quebec Pension Plan. In 1986, for example, only 54.1 percent of women, compared with 82.6 percent of men, were recorded as making contributions to the plan. And because of their relative absence from the labour market in the past, only 33.6 percent of women 65 and over received a QPP pension in 1988, as opposed to 85 percent of men. Furthermore, the average pension payment allocated to elderly female contributors was only 58.3 percent of the payments to retired males, as a result of women's lower earnings and shorter employment records. Income security is therefore an issue of prime concern to women.

At present the two governments operate largely parallel income security programs. Here is what we have found with respect to family allowances, social assistance and old-age security.

Funding for child support. This includes not only family allowances but also tax credits and deductions, allowances for young children and birth allowances allocated by both levels of government or either one. Although the first major attempt to assist families was the establishment of the family allowance program by the federal government in 1945, it must be noted that the government is today tending to reduce its assistance because of its budget problems and a relatively reassuring demographic situation in [English] Canada. At the same time Quebec is attempting, under its family policy, to increase its assistance. Two governments, two orientations. Structurally, the presence of two levels of government in this field produces a multiplicity of programs, increased costs and an extremely complex system for both women and men.

Social assistance. Under the *Income Security Act*, Quebec grants last-resort assistance to persons with little or no income. Through the *Canada Assistance Act* the federal government repays 50 percent of a province's expenditures on such a program, provided it meets the criteria in the Act. This latter requirement restricts a province's flexibility in defining policies adapted to the particular situation of its population, although needs may vary from one province to another.

Old-age income security. A range of competing programs designed to provide financial security at retirement are now being operated by the two levels of government: the old-age security pension, guaranteed income supplement, Quebec Pension Plan, tax shelter incentives through group plans or registered retirement savings plans, age amount tax credit, etc. These programs are designed to provide income at retirement, reduce the tax liability of retirement income, or encourage social or individual planning for retirement during one's active life. However, the large number of programs or provisions makes adjustments hazardous. For example, if Quebec were to decide to enrich benefits under its public pension plan, equity would require that it obtain financial compensation from the federal government equal to what the latter saved through reduced costs for its guaranteed income supplement program in Quebec. In this context, in which both levels of government are administering programs, how is it possible to erect a genuine retirement security policy?

The federal government entered the field of income security in a time of economic growth, when the federal government had fairly significant room to manoeuvre financially. The government's current budget situation, however, suggests that harder times lie ahead, as indicated by its disengagement in the field of unemployment insurance. Moreover, there are obvious disadvantages in these interventions, such as the multiplicity of provisions, increased costs and complexity, and the difficulty in achieving an integrated and coherent income security policy.

Federal government spending power. The federal government's spending power is generally defined as Parliament's power to pay certain sums to individuals, organizations or governments for purposes for which the federal Parliament does not necessarily have authority to legislate. The Quebec government has always had reservations with regard to the exercise of this power, regardless of which party formed the government. One can understand why by studying, for example, the situation in the field of childcare services.

The two levels of government provide such services in different ways: the federal, through tax deductions for costs incurred by employed parents, and the provincial, through funding the start-up and operations of childcare services and the low-income parents using them.

The allowance by both governments of a childcare tax deduction forces parents to make two claims based on attribution rules that are not necessarily similar, which adds to the complexity of the returns and can mean that parents are not getting the maximum tax reduction they are entitled to.

The federal government helped get childcare services started through its Local Initiatives Projects (LIP) job-creation program. However, when this type of program ended, those who had established the first community daycare centres turned to Quebec City for funding. In 1974 the "Bacon plan" was established, followed by the adoption in 1979 of the *Childcare Services Act.*

The federal government was then theoretically contributing 50 percent of the funding through the *Canada Assistance Act.* In reality, however, it covered only 30 percent of the actual expenses because guidelines in the Act blocked the reimbursement of some expenditures (funding of low-income parents whose children attended a private or school childcare centre, etc.).

In December 1987 the federal government unveiled its childcare policy. Although generally favourable to the federal government initiative because it would provide it with new funding, Quebec expressed some reservations, noting in particular that the planning and establishment of priorities in this area fell within its exclusive jurisdiction and that the federal contribution should be stable and predictable. It will be recalled, however, that the federal government did not proceed with its policy. At the time the federal project was abandoned, Quebec was in the process of adopting a new policy on funding childcare services, and had to renege on some of its commitments.

It will be seen, then, that the acceptance of federal government funds entails constraints that may signify an intrusion by the federal government in a provincial area of jurisdiction. Nor is Quebec sheltered from a subsequent disengagement by the federal government, which could at some point jeopardize the continuity of services. Nor is it certain that the money will be allocated to Quebec priorities, since Ottawa's concern is primarily to establish a national policy (for example, the federal government wants to allocate part of the new resources to tax assistance). Given the size of the country and the diversity of situations, it is probably harder for Quebec parents to get their priorities to come first federally than it is in Quebec.

Abortion. Quebec has for many years ensured accessibility to abortion services through family planning clinics and reimbursement of related fees by the health insurance plan, the Régie de l'assurance-maladie. This accessibility reflects social acceptance of the interruption of pregnancy as a medical act with due respect to a woman's choice and her physical integrity.

Lacking jurisdiction to control such medical practices, the federal government has sponsored legislation to put abortion in the *Criminal Code*, thereby transforming a medical act into a crime. In a way, this is a misappropriation of jurisdiction, since abortion is an issue that in our view should be dealt with as a health matter under provincial jurisdiction. This legislative intervention is a clear setback for women, an attack on the fundamental principle of reproductive autonomy and one's physical integrity, and could have an impact on accessibility to services in the Quebec health system.

Immigration. This is an area of concurrent jurisdiction, with federal paramountcy, in which the Quebec government has for some years been demanding constitutional amendments. Needless to say, it is an area of substantial significance to Quebec, given its demographic situation and in particular the distinct Francophone character of Quebec society. The Council has taken a particularly close look at the access of immigrant women to language training.

Under the *Act respecting the Ministère des Communautés culturelles et de l'Immigration*, the Quebec government must ensure that people settling in Quebec acquire a knowledge of the French language either before or immediately after their arrival in Quebec.

Immigrant women must speak French to escape from the job ghettos, put an end to their isolation, and integrate into Quebec society. In 1986, according to data of the Quebec immigration department, 90,645 women aged 15 or over who were born outside Canada and resided permanently in Quebec were unable to conduct a conversation in French. About 68 percent of the women who arrived in 1987 (6,553 women) and 70 percent of those arriving in 1988 (6,793 women) were in this situation.

Generally speaking, both governments are involved in language training, and they carry out a range of programs, both full- and part-time. The eligibility criteria and allowances vary depending on the immigrant's status and whether or not she has declared her intention to enter the job market. In 1988-89, a total of 2,898 out of the 6,793, or 43 percent, of the women who did not speak French when they arrived in 1988, took French courses.

In view of the continuing predominant role of the family in the socialization of children, the limited access to language training of immigrant women who are raising children and do not intend to work outside the home represents a significant structural barrier to their integration into Quebec society and delays the integration of their children. Furthermore, it is possible that many prospective immigrant women are unaware that two incomes are generally needed to support a family in Quebec, and so they do not declare any intention to work. Even if they do not want to work outside the home when they arrive, many immigrant women will probably have to join the workforce without having been able to take advantage of the French courses designed for prospective or present employees.

Finally, some immigrant women who have not had prior training in French are already on the labour market and are confronted with the double workday, which further limits their access to such courses. A policy of integrating immigrant women should take into account their particular situation and the decisive role they play in the integration of their family members into Quebec society. . . .

2. Constitutional guarantee of women's rights.

The Canadian Charter. . . . A study of the initial experience with the equality rights provisions by the Canadian Advisory Council on the Status of Women,* published in 1989, included a compilation of the judgments involving section 15 since it came into force on April 17, 1985. Surprisingly, most of the 591 cases that had been tried involved not minority groups or victims of discrimination, but commercial or criminal cases such as drunk driving, the regulation of landing rights, or soft drink containers. Forty-four of the judgments actually dealt with sexual equality. But in three out of four it was a man who claimed sex discrimination, sometimes mounting a successful attack on laws or programs designed to improve the situation of women, such as social assistance benefits for single mothers in a Nova Scotia law, or the protection given to sexual assault victims in the *Criminal Code*.

In addition to this disappointing statistical profile, the authors report, there is a problem in the very concept of equality that is adopted in these initial judgments: a narrow, formal conception of equality that in some respects recalls the treatment that prevailed under the *Canadian Bill of Rights*. Yet section 15 had been drafted,

---

*   Gwen Brodsky and Shelagh Day, *Canadian Charter Equality Rights for Women: One Step Forward or Two Steps Back?*, CACSW, Ottawa, 1989.

under pressure from Canadian women's groups, precisely to avoid the traps in the previous legislation.

Notwithstanding these difficult beginnings, there is still some hope. In *Andrews*, its first judgment on section 15, the Supreme Court of Canada corrected this tendency by analogizing with a broader concept of discrimination that has developed, for example, under the various provincial and federal human rights codes. In a second judgment, *Turpin*, it explained that a legislative distinction is not necessarily an infringement of the right to equality and recognized that it is mainly underprivileged groups that suffer discrimination. Furthermore, in relation to abortion, the *Morgentaler* judgment, based on the right to security of the person rather than the right to equality, and the *Daigle* case, showed that women's interests could be taken into account by the Supreme Court within a framework other than that of section 15.

The Quebec Charter. The Quebec *Charter of Human Rights and Freedoms* also recognizes a comprehensive right to equality; it provides protection against discrimination in particular activities designated by the Act. It covers not only state action but private relationships. It offers a range of remedies, including a complaint to the Commission des droits de la personne and, in the near future, a specialized tribunal. Under a 1983 amendment, the Charter prevails over any contrary legislation unless otherwise specifically provided. Moreover, its quasi-constitutional character or the "very special" nature of human rights legislation has been recognized by a number of judgments of the Supreme Court of Canada. We might mention as well that the Quebec Charter, unlike the Canadian one, includes a chapter on economic and social rights. Although the courts would have some difficulty enforcing these rights, they constitute a moral commitment to certain social justice values.

On the basis of some provincial charters and the *Canadian Human Rights Act*, the courts have adopted a concept of discrimination that includes non-intentional or systemic discrimination,* and which can be used to demand measures to counter the harm done to women, at least in the area of employment. The same concept applies in the case of the Quebec Charter.

---

* In *Action Travail des Femmes v. Canadian National Railways*, [1987] 1 S.C.R. 1114, for example, the Supreme Court approved quotas set by a Quebec human rights tribunal for hiring women in blue-collar jobs at CN.

Women have made considerable use of the Quebec Charter. Between 1976 and 1987, 30 percent of the 8,500 investigation files opened by the Commission involved alleged sex discrimination. With few exceptions these complaints were originated by women. This percentage does not include other complaints lodged by women under other grounds of discrimination, or other actions by the Commission in the areas of equal access, wage equity, education and public awareness programs.

A few observations. The record of the Canadian Charter in terms of concrete results for women has been slim so far. The experience of these first years tends to confirm the reservations expressed in Quebec at the time of its enactment (see, for example, this Council's brief on the federal government's draft resolution on the Constitution, 1980). Access is difficult if not impossible for most women; judicial interpretations are often ill-adapted to the concept of equality; and women's demands are judicialized at the expense of other forms of action. In any event it seems clear that to this point the Canadian Charter has not been the instrument of social and economic reform that many feminist groups in English Canada had hoped.

With the Quebec Charter, the concrete results for women are more immediate, mainly because — like other human rights legislation — one of its major objects is to apply to the private sector, i.e., to the daily, concrete situations of inequality likely to occur most frequently. Here the interpretation of the notion of discrimination is fairly favourable to women and it is possible to enforce the rights in the Charter through a relatively simple administrative procedure.

Of course women have had and still have criticisms of the Quebec Charter and the operation of the Commission des droits de la personne: delays in dealing with investigations, the negative balance sheet of the impact of section 19 which establishes the principle of wage equity, a conflict between the investigation and mediation roles, etc. However, the Commission has taken these criticisms into account and on several occasions the legislature has made corrections, such as in 1989 with the creation of a Tribunal des droits de la personne.

Over and above the deficiencies that can be found in each of these legal instruments, it is indisputable that granting constitutional protection to human rights and freedoms, including the right to equality, gives some permanence to these rights and shelters them from government interference. Entrenching rights gives them a formal and symbolic character and helps to establish them as fundamental values of our society.

Two different conceptions of the state. Each of the Charters has its own distinct philosophy and is inspired by a different concept of the state. At the heart of the discussion around the Meech Lake Accord was the articulation of the relationship between rights and the state — the relationship between individual rights and a society's right to protect and promote its distinct character. A much-debated aspect was the relationship between women's rights and the status of distinct society demanded by Quebec. . . .

Most feminist groups in English Canada were strongly opposed to some aspects of the Accord, in the belief that the distinct society clause endangered women's equality rights. On the other hand, women in Quebec, as the Fédération des femmes du Québec put it, saw no explicit or potential risk in the concept. The briefs to the Joint Committee on the Constitutional Accord of 1987* testified on the contrary to the confidence Quebec women had in their legal tools, and especially their social strength, which they thought was substantial enough to overcome possible injustices by a Quebec government within the framework of a distinct society. They pointed to the progress achieved in terms of women's status in Quebec over the last 20 years, saying that a tradition of equality had developed and was one of the things that characterized the distinct society; they relied as well on the set of legal tools and programs the Quebec government had armed itself with in order to make equality a substantive reality.

Quebec native women also participated in this debate, from a somewhat different perspective. The Association des femmes autochtones du Québec said they did not fear any threat to their rights as women in the Quebec provincial context. However, as native peoples, they had collective aspirations that they shared with natives in the rest of Canada.

Generally speaking, in the wake of the polarization of the constitutional debate it is only the differences between women in Canada that are remembered. Although these differences exist, it is important to draw attention to one major feature: for Quebec women, native women and women in the other provinces, *the right to equality between men and women is considered a fundamental*

---

* Barbara Roberts, *Smooth Sailing or Storm Warning? Canadian and Québec Women's Groups and the Meech Lake Accord,* Canadian Research Institute for the Advancement of Women (CRIAW), 1989.

right. The differences lie not in a different conception of the relative location of this equality since, no matter what one's political position, there is a consensus on the need to guarantee non-discrimination on the basis of sex and the affirmation of equality between men and women. The differences are over the appropriate instruments and institutions in a given society to secure this equality as effectively as possible in terms of the historical, social and cultural situations in which women live.

Thus, during the discussions, the difference between Quebec women and the women in the other provinces had to do with their relationship to the state. For the latter women, the provincial government is often the one that must be distrusted. They are more likely to look to the federal government and use national strategies such as the Charter. For Quebec women, the primary government that concerns them is the one in Quebec, which is also the one they most seek to influence and expect the most from. They give great weight to affirmative action by their government to improve their social and economic rights. As Barbara Roberts pointed out in her analysis of the positions of the feminist groups in Quebec and Canada on the Meech Lake Accord [see footnote, previous page]: "In a sense, then, they stand on different shorelines, looking out over the same lake, interpreting what they see in the light of the conditions they observe on their own beaches.". . .

The abstract affirmation in a legal instrument of the principle of equality between men and women is at most only a safety net. In English Canada they have begun to think more critically about this issue and to adopt a more balanced approach toward the usefulness of a charter as a means of obtaining concrete rights for women.* The same thing is happening in Quebec, where the principle of equal salary or wages for equivalent work, as established in the Quebec Charter, is apparently insufficient to secure actual wage equality between men and women. In fact, these experiences clearly demonstrate the irreplaceable role of the state, which cannot completely abandon its responsibilities to the judiciary.

Quebec women have had a privileged relationship with the Quebec state over the last 20 years; they have addressed to it demands for reforms, laws, programs and policies that could ensure them an equal place in Quebec society. The state must continue to

---

* See, for example, Lise Gotell, *The Canadian Women's Movement, Equality Rights and the Charter*, CRIAW, 1990.

play a role in the future in advancing their rights, concretely and effectively, in the many fields of concern to women.

3. Representation of women within institutions

The political institutions and their underlying culture were forged by a male elite and developed long before women obtained political rights. They were formed in periods in which so-called public affairs ruled out any concern with individual welfare; such issues were reserved to the private domain, which was in some ways a female preserve. This cleavage between private and public also reflected the sexual division of labour that was accentuated by industrialization.

The political field is now substantially wider, particularly with the advent of the welfare state and the extension of democratic rights, and what were once considered strictly private or family matters are now in the public domain. As part of this process, and concurrently with gaining political rights, women have managed to elevate some of their concerns from the private sphere to the rank of political issues. Yet they are worried by a trend of thinking that would encourage the state to withdraw from the social domain. Such a retreat would be incompatible with the contemporary situation, in which the wider role of the state is intrinsically linked to changes in the role of families and the breakdown in traditional private support systems.

Obviously, women's interests are not limited to social issues; all public affairs are of concern to them and they must participate in decisions affecting society as a whole so that women's reality is reflected in discourse, decisions and policies. However, notwithstanding the political force they represent, women still have little power and continue to be underrepresented in political institutions.

Representation is still weak. Although women obtained the right to vote and run for office in provincial elections in 1940, no woman was elected to the Quebec Legislative Assembly until 1961. At the federal level they had to wait even longer; given the right to vote and stand as candidates in 1918, Quebec women were not elected to the House of Commons until 1972. In both parliaments, their number increased very slowly during the 1970s, although in the 1980s some progress has been made in both the absolute and relative number of successful women candidates in general elections.

However, the 1989 general election in Quebec indicated a slowing of this trend. Was it a conjunctural phenomenon or the so-called "glass ceiling" effect, that invisible barrier that appears in organizations in which women hold about 20 percent of the positions traditionally reserved to men? Is this phenomenon, previously identified as a barrier in the better jobs, now manifesting itself in politics? This is of particular concern to us in that it occurs at a time when women are about to attain the threshold of a "critical mass", i.e., the number that would enable them as a group to initiate some change.

At present, women occupy only 23 (or 18.4 percent) of the seats in the Quebec National Assembly, and 13 (17.3 percent) of the 75 Quebec seats in the House of Commons. In the Senate, the three female senators represent only 12 percent of the Quebec delegation, despite an impressive number of appointments to the Senate in recent years.

A number of factors still prevent women from taking their rightful place politically. Indeed, although some important progress has been made in removing sexist stereotypes in the process of socialization of both boys and girls, women continue to have a different personal and collective experience from that of men.

However, the progress achieved in terms of socialization has not been fully reflected in practical terms. While women have moved into the public arena through their presence in the labour force and their growing participation in political life, they have not been relieved of their family responsibilities to the same degree, despite the trend toward greater sharing of tasks within the family. These responsibilities prevent or delay the involvement in public life of many women with the requisite ability and interest. At a certain level political action seems incompatible with a satisfactory family life, especially for members of legislative assemblies and governments.

Structural changes needed. In addition to these cultural and social obstacles, which can be surmounted only through changes in the mental attitudes and conduct of both men and women, there are structural barriers. Some are related to the organization and burden of work within the political institutions; others are often associated with relatively procedural issues having to do with representation, for example.

Are there procedures to ensure equitable representation of women in elected political bodies? It is generally thought that voting procedure may have an impact on the composition of an assembly. Some people place a lot of hope in proportional voting; others, seeing genuinely systemic discrimination, demand quotas as a remedy while still others rely instead on adaptations to the first-past-the-post system.

Each of the possible formulas has advantages and disadvantages that would have to be analyzed very closely. It should, however, be recalled that any change in the voting procedure would be a significant political change that might affect not only the composition and functioning of institutions but the political culture of the population as well. Voting procedure is not an agent of social change, and it cannot, therefore, ensure equitable representation of women without the collaboration of the political parties and the increased participation of women themselves.

Parties, on the other hand, are the mandatory vehicles for access to legislative assemblies and, increasingly, to the major city councils. It is up to them to determine who will run. In doing so, they must try to ensure fair representation of the various components of society through eliminating barriers that might impede some groups.

The small number of women candidates has often been attributed to the conservatism and caution of the political parties. However, the results of elections over the last 10 years have shown that the parties' fears are now unfounded, since today the success rate of women is similar to that of men. Knowing that voters no longer make any distinction between candidates on the basis of sex, the parties should establish compensatory measures to attain a balance in their male-female representation.

And the parties should examine their structures, practices and habits so as to identify the potential hurdles facing women candidates. They may find it necessary to establish structures to facilitate the participation of women who show the requisite interest and ability to represent the party, and provide them with ongoing support.

5.

Quebec's First Nations state their case

Any change in Quebec's constitutional status must take into account native peoples' demands for recognition of their aboriginal and treaty rights, and more generally their right to self-determination. Native peoples have outstanding claims of sovereignty over very large parts of Quebec. The potential of these claims to conflict with Quebec's own political and constitutional aspirations was underscored in June 1990 when Canadian native leaders played a key role in defeating the Meech Lake Accord on the grounds, among others, that the Accord's recognition of Quebec as a "distinct society" was not accompanied by corresponding constitutional recognition of the distinct character of the aboriginal peoples.

Many briefs to the Commission addressed the issue of native rights, and the Commission heard directly from almost a dozen native organizations.

Native sovereignty claims have a strong legal foundation. The aboriginal peoples were sovereign societies before the arrival of the Europeans in North America. They never surrendered that sovereignty, and it is becoming apparent that no statute — French, British or Canadian — has ever extinguished it. In fact, immediately after the British Conquest of French North America, the *Royal Proclamation of 1763* reserved much of the land outside the immediate bounds of the colonial settlements for the use of "the several Nations or Tribes of Indians . . . as their Hunting Grounds" unless such lands were "ceded to or purchased by" the Crown.

The *Constitution Act, 1867* gave the federal government exclusive jurisdiction over "Indians, and Lands reserved for the Indians". Subsequent legislation in 1898 and 1912 extending Quebec's boundaries to their present limits instructed the province to "recognize the rights of the Indian inhabitants . . . to the same extent" as the federal government. Quite apart from issues of territorial sovereignty, negotiations of native claims implicate Quebec because they cover resource development rights and transfers of services in such areas as education, health and municipal affairs that are currently under Quebec's jurisdiction.

It is now widely acknowledged that all levels of government have been scandalously derelict in their obligations toward the native peoples. Yet, as recently as the 1960s, no level of government was prepared to recognize aboriginal claims as having any legal status. Furthermore, liberal white society generally perceived the solution to the "native question" within a perspective of ending special treatment for aboriginal peoples. The 1969 federal "White Paper" on Indian Policy asserted that "aboriginal claims to land . . . are so general and undefined that it is not realistic to think of them as specific claims capable of remedy except through a policy and program that will end injustice to the Indians as members of the Canadian community."

Native activists' first victories in reversing this pattern of official neglect and hostility were achieved in the courts, in particular in a number of landmark decisions by the Supreme Court during the 1970s. In 1982, as a result of intense native lobbying, the new *Constitution Act* explicitly immunized "aboriginal, treaty or other rights or freedoms that pertain to the aboriginal peoples of Canada" from possible attack under the individual rights oriented *Charter of Rights and Freedoms*. The 1982 Act also "recognized and affirmed" existing aboriginal and treaty rights, and provided that within one year a constitutional conference of First Ministers would meet, with the participation of native representatives, to discuss "constitutional matters that directly affect the aboriginal peoples of Canada, including the identification and definition of the rights of those peoples to be included in the Constitution of Canada."

Successive First Ministers' conferences between 1984 and 1987 ended in stalemate. Quebec was boycotting federal-provincial meetings during much of this period to protest the unilateral patriation and amendment of the Constitution without its consent, and did not attend the initial conferences.

However, in 1983 the Quebec Cabinet adopted a 15-point statement of principles that for the first time explicitly recognized the existence in Quebec of aboriginal "nations" and their right "to own and control the lands that are attributed to them", while specifying that such rights "are to be exercised by them as part of the Québec community and hence could not imply rights of sovereignty that could affect the territorial integrity of Québec". And in 1985 the National Assembly adopted (with the Liberal opposition voting against) a resolution recognizing the existence in Quebec of 10 nations: the Abenaki, Algonquin, Attikamek, Cree, Huron, Micmac, Mohawk, Montagnais, Naskapi and Inuit. (In 1987 the Malecites were added to the list.) The native population in Quebec is approximately 60,000, of whom 6,000 are Inuit.

The resolution urged the government to pursue negotiations with these aboriginal nations and to sign agreements with those that so wished

guaranteeing
- the right to self-government within Quebec,
- the right to their own language, culture and traditions,
- the right to own and control land,
- the right to hunt, fish, trap, harvest and participate in wildlife management, and
- the right to participate in, and benefit from, the economic development of Quebec,

"so as to enable them to develop as distinct nations having their own identity and exercising their rights within Quebec".

The 1985 resolution also urged the establishment of a permanent parliamentary forum to enable the aboriginal peoples to express their rights, needs and aspirations. This forum was never created.

The first, and so far the only substantial native land claim to be successfully negotiated was the *James Bay and Northern Quebec Agreement* of 1975 between Canada, Quebec, the Cree and the Inuit. Although similar in some respects to the treaties concluded a century ago between Canada and the prairie Indian peoples, the James Bay Agreement is contractual in nature and most of its provisions have been ratified in federal and provincial legislation. In 1991 the Federal Court held that the Agreement has the force of a federal law.

The Agreement came in the wake of a court injunction obtained by the native people that temporarily halted construction of the James Bay Hydroelectric Project. This Quebec project involved the damming and diversion of several major rivers flowing into James Bay and the flooding of several thousands of acres of land, threatening the livelihood of many native people in northern Quebec still engaged in the traditional hunting economy. Under the Agreement, the Cree and Inuit in the affected area surrendered their aboriginal title to these lands (including the right to royalties from natural resource development) in return for monetary compensation, recognition of their hunting, fishing and trapping rights and ownership in certain lands, and local self-government over school boards and the provision of health services. The implementation of the Agreement under a complex over-arching administrative structure has been marked by constant jurisdictional disputes between Quebec and Ottawa and native complaints of failure by both levels of government to fulfil their commitments under the Agreement.[*]

---

[*] For an overview of these issues, see Wendy Moss, "The Implementation of the James Bay and Northern Quebec Agreement", in Bradford Morse (ed.), *Aboriginal Peoples and the Law: Indian, Metis and Inuit Rights in Canada* (Ottawa, 1989), pp. 684-94.

In 1978 the Naskapis in the Schefferville region signed the *North-East Quebec Agreement*, which was similar to the James Bay Agreement.

The various native claims in Quebec today are of three types: comprehensive land claims (outstanding claims by natives who have never signed a treaty), specific land claims (for the enforcement of existing treaty rights) and demands for governmental autonomy.[†]

In the far North, the **Inuit** and other residents of Nunavik are claiming a form of autonomy and recognition of their own constitution in this territory. As their brief excerpted below explains, this constitution would establish an autonomous "non-ethnic" government enjoying certain legislative, executive and judicial powers by delegation from the provincial and federal governments.

The James Bay **Cree**, as part of their ongoing campaign against the Grande Baleine hydroelectric development project (the new phase of Hydro-Québec's multi-billion dollar northern development scheme), have taken court action to have the James Bay Agreement nullified on the grounds, among others, that neither government has fulfilled its obligations under the Agreement.

Both the Inuit and the Crees in Northern Quebec have aboriginal land claims in the James Bay and Hudson Bay regions, including lands now part of the Northwest Territories that have never been the subject of any treaty or agreement. In addition, two native groups outside Quebec claim aboriginal rights in Northern Quebec. The **Belcher Islands Inuit** in the Northwest Territories claim rights on the coast of Hudson Bay. They are now discussing with the Northern Quebec Inuit in order to determine the limits of their respective territorial claims. The **Labrador Innu** have claims south of Ungava Bay that overlap with those of the Montagnais and Naskapis.

To the south of the lands covered by the *James Bay and Northern Quebec Agreement*, the **Attikameks** and **Montagnais** have never signed a treaty with either Ottawa or Quebec. However, in 1988 they signed a framework agreement with both governments listing the items to be negotiated and setting deadlines. The excerpt from the Attikamek-Montagnais brief presents their explanation for the current stalemate in these negotiations.

The **Algonquins** have likewise never signed a treaty or extinguished their aboriginal title in their lands. In 1989 they filed a comprehensive land claim covering 200,000 km². The federal government has not yet accepted this

---

† The following discussion of existing claims is largely based on information in a brief presented to the Commission by David Cliche, an environmental and northern affairs consultant.

claim. Algonquin Chief Richard Kistabish has recently come out in favour of Quebec sovereignty and demanded that the native peoples be made partners in Quebec's accession to sovereignty.

The **Hurons** and **Abenakis**, who fled to Quebec from the English colonies further south in the 17th century, have not yet filed a comprehensive land claim on their territory in the south of the province.

The Gaspé **Micmacs** have never signed a treaty and could therefore claim unextinguished aboriginal rights in that territory. Following confrontations with the Quebec government over salmon fishing in 1983, they signed a development protocol with Quebec.

Finally, the **Mohawks** have filed comprehensive land claims with the federal government on two occasions, in 1975 and 1986. These were rejected largely on the grounds that the land in question was within the territory covered by the *Royal Proclamation of 1763*. However, as a result of the recent Mohawk blockades at Oka and Kahnawake, the Quebec and federal governments have agreed to discuss their land claims. The current claims include a comprehensive claim covering their aboriginal rights over the major part of Southwestern Quebec (including the Island of Montreal) and specific claims concerning the enlargement of their existing reserve.

The negotiations over the Mohawks' specific land claims, which began in 1979, have been complicated by the fact that both Ottawa and Quebec will negotiate only with the Band Council, the native government established under the *Indian Act*, and not with the Longhouse, the traditional Mohawk government which has continued to exist over the years and has gained credibility from the Band Council's inability to settle the outstanding land claims. The Warriors, who helped lead the confrontations in the summer of 1990, are the armed wing of the Longhouse.

Quebec has been negotiating with the Mohawks since the early 1980s with regard to the eventual takeover by the natives of health and education services and the administration of justice within their territories.

As the above record indicates, official Quebec's attitude toward the demands of its native peoples is ambiguous, at best. This ambiguity was reflected in the debates around the establishment and proceedings of the Bélanger-Campeau Commission. Both major parties in the National Assembly resisted widespread demands that at least one of the Commission members be a representative of the aboriginal peoples. The Commission itself turned down a government proposal that it hold a separate forum on native issues similar to the youth forum it did hold, although the Commission undertook to hear from all native groups that filed a brief with it. The Commission report barely mentioned native concerns, however, except to mention the urgency of negotiations to "realize aboriginal self-government" and deal with native concerns without "waiting for a final answer to the question of the political and constitutional future of Quebec". It also called for the adoption of a process for settling existing disputes in consultation with the aboriginal peoples, without indicating how this might be done.

Yet native groups presented the Commissioners with a wealth of materials documenting their concerns and demands. Most groups refrained from advocating any particular constitutional option for Quebec vis-à-vis Canada, saying this was a matter for the majority of Quebecers to determine. Their contributions focused instead on their interpretations of their own right to autonomy or sovereignty and the need to resolve these issues irrespective of the constitutional framework Quebec ultimately adopts.

The following selections provide a flavour of their submissions. And the final brief selected, by the Parti québécois, is an interesting illustration of how one major non-native institution in Quebec is grappling with the challenge posed by the native peoples' claims.

Assembly of First Nations:

We have never surrendered our sovereignty

This is the major part of the brief presented by Konrad Sioui, regional chief for Quebec and Labrador and a vice-chief of the Assembly of First Nations, the organization representing registered status Indians across Canada.

Some of our nations . . . have presented briefs before this Commission. Others decided not to do so for internal reasons that concern them alone. The Cree Nation, for instance, decided to hold its own commission of inquiry within its nation, among its members. . . .

Some of our First Nations signed treaties with the Crown and therefore have certain rights arising from these treaties. We all have aboriginal rights as native peoples. In Canada, we include 50 distinct nations, 11 of which are established in Quebec and Labrador. This means that there are over 50 distinct languages spoken by the members of our nations. In addition, given the circumstances, many of us speak English and share English customs. Here in Quebec, of course, the majority of natives speak French and share French customs. But we are first and foremost citizens of our First Nations, regardless of whatever else we may be.

The Inuit of Quebec, the James Bay Cree and the Naskapi of Northeastern Quebec occupy land, under treaties, which accounts for approximately one-half of the land mass of Quebec. The Montagnais, Attikameks, Algonquins, Micmacs, Mohawks, Abénakis, Malécites and my own people, the Huron-Wendat Nation, have aboriginal titles to about one-third of the balance and we also occupy many areas designated as reserves under the Canadian *Indian Act*. The Canadian Constitution recognizes and affirms our existing aboriginal and treaty rights, and we can exercise these rights in this province. . . .

According to Bill 90, your duties include examining and analyzing the political and constitutional status of Quebec and making recommendations thereon. If you don't mind, I would like to say right at the outset that the first part is easy. Quebec is a province or a constituent component, politically and constitutionally, of the Canadian confederation. Constitutionally speaking, Quebec is equal to the nine other provinces. Like all the other provinces, Quebec has the right, for instance, to use provisions in the *Charter of Rights and Freedoms*, which came into force in 1982 when the revamped Canadian Constitution was proclaimed. And, constitutionally, Quebec exercised its right to use the "notwithstanding" clause of this Charter. Like all the other provinces, Quebec also has the right, to take another example, to appeal cases to the highest court, the Supreme Court of Canada. And Quebec has availed itself of this right, as I know personally because Quebec appealed the *Sioui* case concerning the Hannenorak Treaty of 1760 with the Huron with the Huron-Wendats, and the Sioui involved were my brothers and I.

So, what I am saying is that Quebec's political and constitutional status is the same as that of the other provinces, in keeping with the power described in section 92 of the Canadian *Constitution Act, 1867*. And Quebec is a dynamic, strong player in the Canadian Constitution game — correctly invoking its right to turn the Constitution to its advantage and to seek the reform of constitutionally recognized Canadian institutions.

Quebec has not abandoned its Canadian constitutional sovereignty. And no one has objected to Quebec's exercising its authority as a sovereign power within the Canadian Confederation.

You are just as familiar as I am, Messrs. Co-chairmen, with the events of last summer, when Quebec used its statutory right under the federal *National Defence Act* to call on the Canadian Armed Forces to assist Quebec's civil authorities at Kanesatake and

Kahnawake, when the federal fiduciary authority failed to act. No other government opposed Quebec's right to do this. Quebec therefore took action.

Right to self-government. Now that I think I have helped you with the first part of your task, there are some problems with the second part: making recommendations with regard to Quebec's political and constitutional status. Messrs. Co-chairmen, it is not my job as a spokesman for the First Nations to say whether Quebec should change its status or how it should be changed. This is an issue that concerns Quebec and its other partners in Canada — the provinces and the federal government.

My duty on behalf of the First Nations is, as far as possible, to ensure that there are no provisions that would compromise *our* rights, interests or goals. It is also not my duty to enter into a debate with anyone who advocates a unilateral declaration of independence by Quebec, which would definitely be illegal under Canadian law by the way, as well as under international law. You are well aware that the Canadian Constitution does not contain any provisions that allow provinces to separate from Confederation and international law prohibits secession without the consent of the existing nation state.

Now, I would like to return to the question of the political and constitutional status of the First Nations of Canada that live in what we now call the Province of Quebec, and also to the question of *our* rights, interests and goals which, as I mentioned earlier, must not be compromised by any decision made by Quebec.

Messrs. Co-chairmen, there is an assertion in the preamble to Bill 90, which establishes your Commission; the first assertion, in fact, is that Quebecers have the right to self-determination. You should know that the Assembly of First Nations has never intended in its resolutions to deny the Quebec people their legitimate right to politically and constitutionally define themselves. I would like to point out, however, that the only peoples mentioned in the Canadian Constitution and recognized as such are native peoples, including the Indians of the First Nations. When we have asked for this freedom or right, though, as Quebec is doing, it has been denied us by the federal government and the provinces, including Quebec. They are afraid that if native peoples exercise their right to self-determination and opt for full or absolute sovereignty, Canada will be dismembered and its territory reduced, and this is prohibited by international law.

Our critics fail to admit that for five years, during the First Ministers' conferences on aboriginal issues, we tried to negotiate our own path *within* the Canadian Confederation, *within* the Canadian Constitution, rather than *outside* it. We have absolutely no intention of breaking up the country. What we want is the recognition and protection of our internal sovereignty by the Canadian Constitution, in the same way that the internal sovereignty of Quebec or any other province is recognized and protected. Four years ago my colleague Chief Joe Mathias of the Squamish Nation in what is now called British Columbia explained at a meeting of the First Ministers what we mean when we introduce the general idea of sovereignty. . . .

"Our intention", he said, "is not to enshrine Indian sovereignty in the Constitution in such a way that aboriginal peoples are placed above federal and provincial sovereignty. . . . What we want . . . is a balance. We don't want aboriginal sovereignty over Canada or federal-provincial power over us, but rather a balance, with a level of federal-provincial government and an aboriginal government enshrined in the highest law of the land."

Messrs. Co-chairmen, you must wonder why the First Nations want their sovereignty protected. What do we want constitutionalized? Let's go back to Chief Mathias and the way he explained this on behalf of the Assembly:

"[The First Nations] exist, we survive, we have our own cultures, we have our own languages, our own religions, and so on. Before colonization by the Europeans, we had the land. We exercised our jurisdiction over this land. When the Europeans landed here, they didn't see 560 Indian bands confined to aboriginal or traditional tracts of land. They saw aboriginal peoples, the First Nations, exercising their jurisdiction over this land."

This is the initial sovereignty, Messrs. Co-chairmen, that we never surrendered. The Europeans did not "discover" our land; they did not settle on uninhabited land. These lands were already inhabited. Nor were we conquered by the French or English during territorial wars. The First Nations of Quebec did not surrender any land to the French or anyone else.

Messrs. Co-chairmen, it is an undeniable fact that the French had no title to the traditional lands of the native peoples that could be transferred to the English after the Battle of the Plains of Abraham.

I make no apology for indulging in this short history lesson because I think it is very, very important for Quebecers to realize that the native peoples never legally surrendered or lost their title or jurisdiction over their aboriginal lands. School children are told that France relinquished Canada to Great Britain in the Treaty of Paris of 1763 and that, with the exception of Saint-Pierre and

Miquelon, all of the *terra firma* of North America east of the Mississippi then came under the control of the British. What French territory? You can't surrender something that you don't even have and France had no legal title! And if it had, later in that same year, 1763, the British sovereign recognized our nationality and our internal sovereignty as First Nations in a royal proclamation. In the *Sioui* case I mentioned earlier, the Supreme Court of Canada unequivocally declared this year [1990] that the First Nations were recognized as independent nations by the French and English crowns — and we have never surrendered our nationality of our own free will.

The *Quebec Act* of 1774, which is recognized today as the basis for the freedom of Quebecers within Canada, did not annul the *Royal Proclamation of 1763*. The rights and freedoms stipulated in that proclamation were preserved specifically as a part of the supreme law of Canada by section 25 of the Canadian *Constitution Act, 1982*, and they still exist, to an even greater extent than the *Quebec Act* of 1774.

Yes, I am completely familiar with the seigniorial system and land titles that the French established here in Quebec, but, as I have just mentioned, these First Nation territories were not uninhabited and they were not "discovered". Since our peoples were not conquered and we did not transfer our land by treaties, the seigniorial system had no legal basis.

Messrs. Co-chairmen, I repeat that the internal sovereignty and jurisdiction of the First Nations, including our right to self-government within Canada, remain intact, despite the existence of all the provinces, Quebec included. Therefore, if the Quebec government planned to separate from the rest of Canada, or even if the rest of Canada gave their consent to such a separation, very serious consideration would have to be given to the rights of the First Nations, including our title to traditional lands.

In fact, Gentlemen, we will also need to discuss how to implement the provisions in our treaties with the Crown in right of Canada. . . .

If Quebec needs to be described as a distinct society to do it justice, then isn't it essential to describe the First Nations in the same way? If French culture needs to be forcefully preserved in the Constitution, why is this not vital for our cultures? How can Francophones and Anglophones be considered the two founding peoples of this country when it was inhabited by native peoples at least 70 centuries before Julius Caesar conquered the forebears of the French and the English?

Meech Lake Accord. Messrs. Co-chairmen, if you don't mind, I would like to explain at this point why we were opposed to the signing of the 1987 constitutional agreement, the Meech Lake Accord. It was not because we like Quebecers any less, but because we like native peoples more. It is very important to understand that between 1987 and 1990, our sole aim was to make concrete amendments to the agreement and not to kill it. We were never in a position to make any changes at all. We never said "no" to Quebec. Without amendments, as it stood, this agreement would have constitutionalized a false view of history, complicated the present and distorted the future.

Although the legitimate concerns of Quebec need to be met, our legitimate concerns must also be satisfied. Although Quebec has been waiting for justice since 1763, we have been waiting for it too. As far as Quebec is concerned, at least the French *Civil Code* and the Roman Catholic religion were reinstated by the *Quebec Act* of 1774. At least the sovereignty of Quebec associated with the sovereignty of the other provinces was adjusted in the Canadian constitutional agreement of 1867. But in our case, the laws and traditional religions of the First Nations were suppressed and the exercise of our sovereignty denied by the British and Canadian governments. We can therefore sympathize with your situation and your aspirations more than anyone else, but if justice is to be doled out, native peoples must be at the top of the list.

You know, the late Premier Lévesque suggested that if we helped Quebec, Quebec would help us in return. We answered that the opposite should be the case. As soon as the Meech Lake Accord was drafted in 1987, a great deal of pressure was put on native peoples so that they would support this arrangement, and all kinds of promises were made. But when all was said and done, there were no firm guarantees that we would have been significantly involved in talks on the so-called Canada clause or that we would be recognized as distinct societies. And there would not have been any specific provisions recognizing our existence as a fundamental characteristic of Canada.

Messrs. Chairmen, I would like to tell you and the other members of this commission, as well as all Quebecers, that the native peoples strongly urge you to seriously consider remaining within Canada. Let's avoid the tactical error of concluding a deal behind closed doors. And let's sit down together with all the real components of Canada, and work towards integrating our collective interests, under a confederal or federal national council, for example, resuming the discussions as if Canada simply didn't exist any more. Let's create it together: the Quebec people and native peoples will be given leading roles, you can count on that.

Otherwise, we reserve the right to hold our own referendum in which all the citizens of the First Nations in Quebec and Labrador and in Canada will choose the kind of political and constitutional alliance that they would like to continue to belong to of their own free will.

Attikamek-Montagnais Council:

For an equal relationship between our peoples

The Council represents the nine Montagnais communities (pop. 11,000) and three Attikamek communities (pop. 4,000). As explained in the editor's introduction to this chapter, the Council is currently involved in land claims negotiations with the federal and Quebec governments. "At the heart of these negotiations", they said in their brief to the Commission, "is the recognition of [our] *projet de société*," that is, a model of a society still based largely on the traditional hunting economy. That is the focus of these excerpts from their brief. Omitted here is a lengthy description of the Attikamek and Montagnais peoples' experience fighting low-altitude military flights over their land by NATO forces. Although NATO has now abandoned plans to build a tactical fighter training base in Labrador, such flights will continue under an agreement between the defence ministers of several NATO countries, including Canada. Attempts by the Naskapi, Montagnais and Innu peoples to obtain an injunction prohibiting these flights have been unsuccessful.

What will happen if Quebec chooses its own constitutional future? What will become of the obligation to the native peoples now imposed on it by the Canadian constitution? What will become of the particular role of the Crown in right of Canada toward the native peoples or nations residing in Quebec? And what will become of the comprehensive land claims negotiations, for example, that Quebec has already undertaken with some native peoples and the Government of Canada? Will Quebec agree to recognize the right to governmental autonomy that the aboriginal nations have claimed for years? What will be the attitude of this Quebec, endowed with a new constitutional status, toward the right of self-determination that also belongs to the native peoples living within the boundaries of

Quebec? What links will the native peoples be able to maintain among themselves, irrespective of Quebec's new constitutional status? What will be Quebec's international role in the discussions on the proposed Universal Declaration of the Rights of Native Peoples?

It is certainly clear to us in the Attikamek-Montagnais Council that the Quebec government's intentions in this regard will have immediate repercussions on our own model of society, which is designed to secure the continued existence of our special relationship to our aboriginal lands and to protect our culture in a contemporary context. We know we must change, although so far we have preferred to confront our deep ambitions rather than dwell on our recent past with the many injustices and inequities that have been committed against us. And we are still willing to apply this dynamic and open approach to the governments and peoples with whom we are attempting to reach mutually satisfactory agreements. But if we were forced to conclude that the government of Quebec, for example, did not intend to respect our rights, satisfy our needs or share our ambitions, we would then be confronted with the unavoidable necessity of reconsidering our strategies and alliances. While to this point we have consistently given the benefit of the doubt to this government, representing as we do a minority whose existence is still threatened in North America, we now think we are justified in demanding some concrete indications of solidarity on its part. . . .

At the heart of our negotiations with the Canadian and Quebec governments is the recognition of our model of society.

We think it is appropriate to make a distinction here between the content of this model of society and the methods used to create awareness and an acknowledgement of it among governments and the population as a whole.

A. *Our model of society.* Obviously there are many ways to express this model. Our challenge is to find the words, the expressions, the concepts that can accurately reflect the model of society of the people we must represent while remaining comprehensible to government functionaries.

This is no mean challenge. And, we must confess, the exercise has remained a parlous one, no doubt because of the discrepancy between the concepts generally used by the native peoples and those used by the technicians, civil servants and lawyers of the government ministries. For example, our Montagnais hunters will sometimes be amazed at the attempts that are made to specify in a land claims agreement that their rights in their aboriginal territory are indeed full ownership, thinking that these lands have always belonged to them. But the legal reality is quite different; to government legal counsel, the native people have at most a usufructuary right in these lands. This puts an organization like ours in an extremely uncomfortable position. Caught betwixt and between, it must try to get more out of the governments while some of its own principals have the impression it is selling off their territory.

Having said that, it seems to us that the underlying model of society of the Attikamek and Montagnais is clear and easy to understand. No matter how expressed, this conception does exist in native society, and has existed for a long time, if not since time immemorial. And in our opinion, it is essentially based on two major concepts: the relationship to an aboriginal land, and the persistence of a particular culture.

The Attikamek and Montagnais — hunters and non-hunters alike — have always had a special relationship to the land and its resources. It is a part of our history, our legends, our identity. It is a source of well-being. But unfortunately it is terribly threatened by the various development projects, in particular hydro-electric projects, the various land development schemes and the low-altitude flights by military planes. . . .

But our attitude toward our struggle to protect our lands from low-level flights or any other attack on our aboriginal rights is in keeping with our desire to guarantee the persistence of our particular culture, no matter what the cost.

This culture is original, unique and still very much alive. Obviously, it is linked to language, both the Attikamek language and the Montagnais language. It is also linked to the kinship structure that is still extant among the Attikamek and Montagnais, which allows a very broad extension of the family and ensures an extremely intense community life both in the hunting lands and between individuals within the communities. This culture is expressed, in part, in a different way of envisaging life, time, school, work, the roles of children and seniors. But this culture has likewise been threatened since our people began participating in a society that demands their integration without taking the trouble to know or develop this culture.

In our opinion, our model of society is based on some specific objectives: on the one hand, to secure the continued existence of the relationship with the aboriginal land and culture of the Attikamek and Montagnais, and, on the other hand, to enable them to flourish in a contemporary context.

B. Methods used to create awareness and recognition of this model of society. . . . Because of the existence of the aboriginal rights of the Attikamek and Montagnais, governments have agreed to negotiate with them and, whatever Quebec's constitutional status, it will be necessary to ensure that these negotiations can continue in full justice and equity. For us, the purpose of these negotiations is essentially to restore to us our due place within the dominant society, be it called Quebec or Canadian. Our goals in these negotiations may be summed up in two major ideas. In the first place, rights issuing from territorial treaties, our political institutions, our hunting, fishing and trapping activities, our economic levers based on access to all of our natural resources, our social security based on a guaranteed minimum income, and our cultural affirmation. And secondly, the possibility of flexibly construing, amending and even improving the agreement or understanding that will be reached with the governments, because it is impossible at this point to anticipate everything.

Unfortunately, all too often in these negotiations the governments take refuge in a legalistic and petty logic. Here are a few examples. Under the pretext that the lands of the Attikamek and Montagnais have suffered greater encroachments than those of the native peoples living further north, we are offered ludicrously small land areas in which to own or simply exercise individual hunting, fishing and trapping rights. The governments are trying to focus the negotiations on the concept of the actual needs of the Attikamek and Montagnais rather than agree to think in terms of governmental autonomy peculiar to the aboriginal nations, an autonomy we can exercise not only now but in the future. Claiming a need for certainty, the governments are violently opposed to any notion of a dynamic agreement that could progress over time. They are distrustful of any flexible mechanism for interpreting the agreement in future, such as procedures for mediation, conciliation or arbitration. . . .

Makivik Corporation and
Nunavik Constitutional Committee:

For a single non-ethnic government in Inuit territory

The overwhelming majority of the population of Nunavik, the vast region north of the 55th parallel, is Inuit. However, Nunavik (formerly known to whites as Nouveau Québec) also includes all permanent residents of the region. It is administered by the Kativik Regional Government, an institution established pursuant to the James Bay Agreement.

Makivik Corporation, likewise created under the Agreement, is a development corporation collectively owned by the Inuit of Quebec that administers the compensation monies from the Agreement. It owns a number of companies, including a couple of local airlines, and invests in local industries such as a shrimp fishery. Mativik Corporation also represents the Inuit of Quebec in such bodies as Inuit Tapirisat of Canada and the Inuit Circumpolar Conference.

The Nunavik Constitutional Committee was created in regional elections in April 1989. Its six members have developed proposals for a constitution and new structures to provide for greater self-government for Nunavik.

Not all Inuit in Quebec agree with this perspective. Three of the 14 Inuit communities have largely boycotted the institutions established under the James Bay Agreement, and refused their share of the compensation monies. They say they never granted the Northern Quebec Inuit Association (the predecessor of Makivik) the right to cede title to their land.

The following is the bulk of the brief presented to the Commission in English on December 18 by a delegation headed by Senator Charlie Watt, an elected Inuit leader who negotiated the original James Bay Agreement.

Nunavik and Quebec. An unprecedented event took place with the signing of the *James Bay and Northern Quebec Agreement*. It went largely unnoticed and unreported amidst all the hoopla over the compensation monies being paid to the Cree and Inuit. However, we wish to highlight it here: for the first time in the history of Canada, a group of aboriginal peoples, having been offered a real choice, opted to have their lands and institutions come under provincial jurisdiction.

During the negotiations leading up to the *James Bay and Northern Quebec Agreement*, the Inuit were given the option of living on reserves coming under federal jurisdiction. Many people assumed that this would be the natural choice of Inuit. However, Inuit opted for Quebec jurisdiction, a decision which initially caught both federal and Quebec Governments by surprise.

Not only did Inuit opt to come under provincial jurisdiction, they also chose to have their territory and communities serviced and administered by non-ethnic bodies. In other words, the Kativik Regional Government, the Kativik School Board, the hospitals, and the municipalities of Nunavik are all public institutions which service the needs of Inuit and non-Inuit citizens. Moreover, all Nunavik residents are eligible to vote and run in any elections relating to these public institutions.

The non-ethnic nature of Nunavik's institutions means that Inuit communities are open to all Quebecers. Although most of the land in these communities may be privately owned by the Inuit, Inuit and non-Inuit have the same right to use public facilities as they would in any other Quebec municipality.

Inuit were well aware that by opting for provincial jurisdiction and public institutions, they were in fact becoming full-fledged citizens of Quebec. Although this means they are entitled to the same rights and privileges accorded to all other citizens, it also means that they have assumed the same responsibilities. In particular, it means that Inuit are full taxpayers and proud to be so.

These decisions indicate a pattern whereby the Inuit consciously tied their future to that of Quebec. Instead of proceeding with the status quo by coming under federal jurisdiction, they took a leap of faith. They clearly placed their hopes, fortunes, and their survival as a people within the Quebec domain.

This was not a decision which the Inuit took lightly. Provincial jurisdiction was unknown territory. The Inuit knew there were risks, and for a while, it looked as if they made the wrong choice. This occurred shortly after the signing of the *James Bay and Northern Quebec Agreement*. At the time the Quebec Government was badly prepared to assume all of its obligations under the Agreement. It was also unaccustomed to dealing with the Inuit on such a comprehensive basis and the relation between the two groups was strained for a time.

In recent years the situation has changed for the better, and both sides now view the Agreement as a workable and beneficial tool. Inuit are now in control of a variety of regional institutions, and they have seen dramatic and costly improvements in their housing, medical services, and community infrastructures. On the other hand, the use of non-ethnic institutions under the Agreement meant that

Quebec could finally extend its administration, its governmental structures, and services to all of its citizens throughout the entire province.

Despite the many improvements brought about by the Agreement, Inuit are still facing enormous difficulties in a number of areas. Inuit society is plagued by numerous social ills, many of which can be traced to substandard education and dismal employment prospects. Furthermore, both the Quebec Government and Inuit have acknowledged that Nunavik still lacks some overall self-government powers and structures.

Recent efforts to promote self-government. Effective self-government arrangements for Nunavik have long been a dream of the Inuit of Quebec. It was the motivating force behind the creation of Makivik's predecessor, the Northern Quebec Inuit Association. Needless to say, it was also one of the underlying objectives in the negotiations leading to the *James Bay and Northern Quebec Agreement.*

Throughout the negotiations the Inuit placed a top priority on obtaining greater self-government powers for their region. The result was reflected in the final Agreement. It provides for a variety of autonomous bodies with some real decision-making powers. These include the Makivik Corporation and, as mentioned before, numerous public institutions. Together these bodies have, in varying degrees, the power to deal with such important matters as education, housing, health care, economic development, and various local and regional services.

These institutions democratized the region's decision-making process and they clearly placed the Inuit in control of administrative bodies which were previously the exclusive domain of federal or Quebec bureaucrats. Despite these accomplishments, it soon became evident that Nunavik was lacking overall powers and structure required for effective self-government. It has become obvious that the region's decision-making powers are fragmented — they are divided up among autonomous organizations which often work independently of each other.

Inuit want self-government arrangements in Nunavik which they can rely on to set their priorities, determine their future, and ensure the survival and growth of their culture and society. Thus, only a few short years after the signing of the *James Bay and Northern Quebec Agreement,* Inuit were again calling for effective self-government powers and structure for Nunavik.

Their call was heard by Premier René Lévesque in 1983. He invited the Inuit of Nunavik to develop and submit proposals for new self-government arrangements for their region.

It was an offer that was quickly accepted by the Inuit. It set in motion a long and sometimes difficult task that is still on-going. In 1987 a referendum was held in the region which decided that the constitution for a proposed Nunavik Government would be drafted by a Working Group composed of elected members. It was also decided that the Working Group would be financed through a voluntary tax. It was the results of this referendum that led to the April 10, 1989 election of the Nunavik Constitutional Committee. Both the referendum and elections were organized with the assistance of Quebec's Chief Electoral Officer.

The voluntary tax has also been implemented and has succeeded in raising close to $50,000 in a region that can only be described as less than affluent.

The Nunavik Constitutional Committee has proceeded with its work by carrying out extensive consultations with the people of Nunavik. It has endeavoured to keep various Quebec ministers and officials informed of its progress.

The Committee has completed its first draft of a constitution for a Nunavik Government. It proposes the creation of a single non-ethnic government for Nunavik. This government would come under Quebec jurisdiction and would function with powers delegated by the Quebec National Assembly.

The first formal discussions with Quebec on the Committee's proposals were to begin in the spring of 1990. However, these discussions were put on hold due to circumstances that were beyond the control of ourselves or the Government of Quebec. We expect these discussions will begin shortly.

New arrangements. Quebec is now undergoing a process to determine its political and constitutional future. We can safely conclude that this process also entails the rejection of Quebec's current political and constitutional place in Canada. In other words, the process itself is a rejection of the status quo.

Inevitably some will argue that this process actually undermines the existence of Canada as a viable country. This may turn out to be the case if people try to hang on to the status quo at any cost. In reality, the viability of Canada as a country can only be enhanced by abandoning the status quo and accommodating the necessary changes.

Having disowned the status quo, where do we go from here? It is obvious that Quebec will insist on all that it needs to secure its future and control its destiny. This is perfectly understandable. However, once it has attained its objectives, Quebec should take steps to maintain strong links with the rest of Canada wherever possible. A Quebec that is secure in its future would probably find such links to be both rewarding and useful.

We also believe that it is important for Quebec to be honest with itself about who is entitled to be a full participant in any decisions concerning its political and constitutional future. Over the years Quebec has sought to have the Inuit identify themselves as full-fledged Quebecers, and the Inuit have responded with a series of critical decisions by which they tied their future to that of Quebec. As a result, the existence of the Inuit and Nunavik as an integral part of Quebec can no longer be denied simply because it may complicate Quebec's view of itself.

It is time for Quebec to demonstrate its commitment to the Inuit by making them a full partner in various processes to determine Quebec's future. Input through consultations and public hearings will not be enough. Inuit and the people of Nunavik must be involved in the mechanics of developing new arrangements for Quebec where these arrangements will directly affect the North. Ultimately, the legitimacy of such arrangements may well be measured by the extent to which the Inuit Nunavik were involved in the relevant decisions.

There are numerous examples of where our involvement will be essential. We know that in the coming years Quebec will be preoccupied with working out the details of whatever relationship might be put in place between *southern* Quebec and *southern* Canada. Unfortunately, this means that the need to work out the details of the relationship between *northern* Quebec and *northern* Canada may be ignored.

Some Commissioners may be aware that the Inuit of Quebec have been solidifying their ties with fellow Inuit in the rest of Canada, Greenland, Alaska, and even the USSR. This is especially important in relation to the Northwest Territories and Labrador where Nunavik Inuit have many relatives and close friends. Thus, a new arrangement for Quebec based solely on a South-South relationship between itself and the rest of Canada will be incomplete. Any proposals for Quebec's political and constitutional future will have to address the North-North relationship between Nunavik and the Northwest Territories and Labrador. This will require the direct participation of the Inuit of Nunavik.

The options Quebec chooses for its future may well raise other concerns for the Inuit of Nunavik. Depending on how Quebec proceeds, Inuit will want to know what will happen to the rights and guarantees that they fought so hard to have entrenched in the Canadian Constitution. Likewise, they will ask what will be happening to the federal government's obligations to the Inuit under section 91(24) of the *Constitution Act, 1867*.

We raise these concerns not to be obstructionists, but because they are important to us. It is possible that many of our questions will be easily answered. However, dealing with some of our concerns may prove to be a complicated undertaking. Whatever the case, any new arrangement for Quebec will have to address our issues to the same extent that it will have to deal with concerns of Quebecers in general. Again, we believe that such an undertaking will only be possible with the direct participation of the people of Nunavik.

Economic considerations. A number of Quebec leaders have made it clear that any proposals for Quebec's political and constitutional future will have to be assessed in terms of its economic viability. They obviously believe that it would be pointless to pursue any new arrangements if they fail to provide Quebec with the economic resources necessary to promote its interests and control its destiny.

We are already witnessing the inevitable debate over whether Quebec would be better off under Canadian federalism or some other arrangement. We can be fairly sure that this debate will not provide any crystal clear answers either way. Without such a clear cut answer, there will be a degree of economic risk in any decision by Quebec to move away from the Canadian status quo.

Many Quebecers are likely to accept such a calculated risk once Quebec's choices for its future are made clear. And why not? Quebec's impressive economic performance of recent years indicates that it should be able to withstand any economic disruptions that might result from a change in its political status.

Unfortunately, the situation is far different in Nunavik. Constant recession is probably the best way to describe the state of our economy.

It is true that most people have come to accept poor economic statistics from the outlying regions. However, from the perspective of those who suffer its consequences, these statistics are unacceptable because they make too many victims. We can no longer tolerate alcohol and drug abuse, a high rate of juvenile delinquency, violent deaths, chronic unemployment and large welfare rolls. We can no longer accept that our youth be doomed to a lifetime of unemployment.

On top of all this, the people of Nunavik must endure what is probably the highest cost of living of any region in Quebec. The costs are often two to three times higher than in southern Quebec. Last spring Makivik conducted a survey comparing Southern food prices to the average prices in three Nunavik communities. We found that milk which cost $1.02 in the South is priced at $2.22 in the North. A 99 cent bag of carrots cost $2.54 in our communities. Nunavik residents will often pay $8.00 for potatoes that would sell for $1.99 in Montreal. And the list goes on and on.

The under-developed state of our economy also dampens our hopes for effective self-government arrangements for Nunavik. We know that it will be close to impossible to sustain a strong Nunavik government without a solid economic base and resulting tax base.

There is some good news on the horizon. Like elsewhere in Quebec, a sense of entrepreneurship is taking root among some of our people. A number of small businesses are being established in Nunavik's larger centres which cater to the tourist industry or the service sector. They are beginning to produce some jobs, although there are too few to have any significant impact on the region's economic statistics. These small businesses could probably create many more new jobs if Nunavik was able to support a substantially higher level of economic activity. This is unlikely to happen until the people of Nunavik become true partners with Quebec in the development of the region's resources.

To summarize, we want to emphasize that Nunavik's limited economy has no leeway in which to absorb the negative effects of any economic disruption brought on by the political uncertainty surrounding Quebec's future. We therefore believe that the Quebec government should protect Nunavik from this possibility by taking immediate steps to foster economic growth in our region. Like many other Quebecers, the people of Nunavik will ultimately have to assess options for Quebec's future in terms of the region's economic development prospects. . . .

Parti québécois:

A new social contract with native peoples

In the wake of the Mohawk standoff at Oka and Kahnawake in the summer of 1990, the Parti québécois established a task force on native issues to prepare proposals for the party's program. Headed by David Cliche, a former federal government administrator of the James Bay Agreement, the task force also included PQ MNA Denis Perron and native representatives Joe Norton and Andrew Delisle (Mohawks), Max Gros

Louis (Hurons), Bernard Cleary (Montagnais), Richard Kistabish (Algonquins), Simeonie Nalukturuk (Inuit) and Rita Dagenais (Micmac).

As Cliche told the Commission in a separate presentation, the PQ is concerned that native people be reassured that Quebec sovereignty, the party's objective, does not threaten their rights, and that successful negotiations between a PQ government and the native peoples result in agreements that will avoid a potential challenge to Quebec sovereignty by the federal government on the pretext of defending native rights.

The task force proposal calling for a "new social contract between the Quebec nation and all native nations" was endorsed by the PQ National Council and by a large majority at the Parti québécois convention in January 1991. The resolution as adopted is published below, minus its preamble. Among other things, the policy proposes that native governments have the power to levy their own taxes and that native nations be represented in the National Assembly.

---

1. Governments of native nations. The Constitution of a sovereign Quebec shall establish the right of the native nations to their own responsible governments, empowered, albeit gradually for some, to govern the lands they now possess or occupy such as the Indian reserves, native settlements, Category 1 lands [under the James Bay settlement], as well as such territories as may be ceded back to them following negotiations with the Quebec government. In such negotiated agreements between the parties, Quebec and the native nations may at any time agree to modify the boundaries of these lands in order to promote the development of both the native and Quebec communities.

The Quebec Constitution shall also recognize the choice of any native nations that so desire to participate fully in other forms of government that are established within Quebec.

The Quebec government will sign evolutionary agreements with native nations wishing to establish their own governments. These agreements will determine the powers allocated to these governments, such as their definition of citizenship code, taxation systems, education, native language and culture, health, environmental and resources management, economic development and public works, etc. These agreements shall also establish which powers shall be shared as well as any measures required for good neighbourliness. The statutes of Quebec shall be amended as needed for the implementation of these agreements.

Under these agreements, the financing of native governments may be secured, in part, from the following sources:

- native governments shall levy taxes, including income tax;
- within the framework of the territorial co-management agreements described below, the native governments may derive some revenues;
- based on methods to be determined, the Quebec government shall participate in the funding of native governments, taking into consideration the native peoples' ability to pay, the need to reduce social and economic disparities, and the desire to provide native communities with living conditions conducive to their participation in the development of Quebec.

The ultimate aim of the native governments shall be the full assumption of their financial responsibilities.

In order to protect the negotiation and implementation process in relation to these agreements, a Parti québécois government shall establish an ombudsman procedure to deal with native claims and issues.

2. Partners in Quebec's development. A Parti québécois government shall apply a sustainable development policy, which means that environmental issues will be given equal importance with economic issues in decision-making. Such a policy will promote the integrated management of territorial development in accordance with agreements reached with the native peoples. The Parti québécois government shall take the "green turn" long-awaited by Quebecers. Chapter 3 of our program describes this policy.

A Parti québécois government shall recognize that native people in Quebec have a special relationship with the land, and that they exercise their traditional hunting, fishing and trapping activities over large territorial expanses that are also used by others. The often excessive use of resources (such as clear-cutting of our forests, thoughtless hydroelectric and mining developments, and overkilling of animal species) together with poor communications between the different users of the same lands, generate regional conflicts and environmental degradation. It is therefore necessary to involve the native nations, through procedures to be determined, in the development and management of the lands on which they conduct their traditional activities.

A Parti québécois government shall therefore propose agreements to the native nations delineating those territories over which each nation shall have the right to exercise its traditional activities. These agreements shall also establish procedures for the joint development and management of these territories so they concurrently support the natives' traditional activities and the sustainable development of natural resources. Under such agreements the native governments may receive a share of the revenues or royalties that the Quebec government shall derive from resource development in these territories. The natives will thus become our partners in development.

3. Transition. Within the perspective of the native nations becoming partners in Quebec's development, and within the framework of the electoral reform contemplated in chapter 1.B of our program, the Parti québécois government shall determine with the native nations their appropriate representation in the National Assembly of Quebec, in accordance with schedules and procedures to be specified.

The Parti québécois government shall give priority to the conclusion of agreements, the major features of which are described above, defining the powers of each government. These agreements shall be concluded without extinguishing aboriginal rights, and shall be reassessed in light of decisions of the Quebec courts and any amendments to the Quebec Constitution.

The Parti québécois government shall honour all existing treaties and the vested rights of the native nations until such time as they are replaced by new agreements between the Quebec government and the native nations.

6.

Anglophones seek their place

One of the clearest indications of the profound changes in Quebec over the last quarter century is the changed perception that the province's native English-speaking population has of itself. Many, if not most, English Quebecers now see themselves as a distinct minority community within Quebec, rather than simply an extension of an English-Canadian majority in a wider political framework. They are the only English-speaking linguistic minority in North America.

But if a definable Anglophone *community* is now emerging, as groups like Alliance Quebec argue, it is by no means united in its approach to the changes and trends in Quebec society.

The Commission heard from many Anglophone organizations and individuals, and received briefs presenting a wide variety of views. They ranged from an Anglican canon in the Eastern Townships who wanted a cross-Canada referendum to determine which official language should be enforced throughout the country, including in Quebec, to an *Association des anglophones dans un Québec independant*. Several groups, particularly those representing young Anglophones, articulated their support for Quebec's right to self-determination.

Excerpted here are briefs from two of the most representative Anglophone organizations, Alliance Quebec and the Equality Party.

Alliance Quebec was founded in 1982. It is heavily funded by the federal government pursuant to the *Official Languages Act*, receiving more than one million dollars a year from that source. It has been a prime instigator of much of the litigation successfully challenging various parts of Quebec's language legislation, Law 101.

To prepare its brief, Alliance Quebec sponsored "community round tables" throughout the province. It reports that these consultations attracted the participation of more than 2,500 individuals and 240 groups. Appended to the Alliance Quebec brief were 102 pages of short one- or two-sentence excerpts (in both English and French) from the comments made at these round table meetings, organized under various headings designed to demonstrate the "perceptions" and "concerns" of Quebec Anglophones. These are summarized in the brief, with the explicit qualification that "We are not here today to discuss whether these perceptions are founded or unfounded."

Notwithstanding its opposition to much of Quebec's language legislation, Alliance Quebec has astutely avoided casting itself in the role of a defender of status quo federalism. Its president Robert Keaton was quick to indicate agreement with the general thrust of the Allaire Report: "It is not a bluff. It is a warning to English Canada. . . . Canada has to get moving and take Quebec's demands seriously."

"It puts us on the Canada route rather than the fast track of separatism."*

The Equality Party, on the other hand, has positioned itself as a more aggressive, even belligerent mouthpiece for a significant layer of Anglophones who are frustrated with their new-found sense of minority status. Founded just before the 1989 Quebec election, it elected four MNAs in predominantly Anglophone ridings in the Montreal area. As a recognized party in the National Assembly, it had one representative on the Bélanger-Campeau Commission, and party leader Robert Libman attended the hearings as an *ex officio* participant with voice but not vote.

The Equality Party grew out of massive Anglophone disaffection with the Quebec Liberal Party over Bill 178, which re-enacted the prohibition on English outdoor commercial signs and advertising in the wake of the Supreme Court judgment overruling such provisions in Law 101. Its brief attacks the federal government for failing to use its formal power of disallowance to overrule Bill 178 and at least parts of Law 101.[†] Indeed, it is hard to see what would remain of Law 101 if the Equality Party's conceptions were to prevail. Its brief attacked labour union demands for French as the language of work, a reference to the francization of firms under Law 101. It called for parents' freedom of choice of the language of education of their children. And it violently opposes any attempt to circumscribe the use of English on commercial signs in Quebec. (Alliance Quebec opposed Bill 178, too, but is not opposed to mandatory French predominance on commercial signs.)

---

* "Alliance Québec appuie le rapport Allaire et le Parti égalité s'y oppose", *Le Devoir*, 30 January 1991, p. A-3.

† The Equality Party position on Law 101 is unclear. Its brief, as excerpted here, calls for both its abolition and the elimination of "certain sections" of the law. Questioning in the Commission hearings failed to clarify the party's position.

It is the signs issue that underlies much of the Equality Party's vehement opposition to the "notwithstanding clause" in the *Canadian Charter of Rights and Freedoms*. A little background may be necessary on this point. Law 101 required (in s. 58) that "signs and posters and commercial advertising" should be solely in French, subject to certain exceptions (advertising in non-French news media; messages of a religious, political, ideological or humanitarian nature; signs and posters respecting the cultural activities of a particular ethnic group; and signs inside firms employing four employees or less). When Anglophone businesses challenged this provision, they relied in part on s. 2 of the Charter guaranteeing freedom of expression.

The Supreme Court ruled the signs provision invalid, not under s. 2 but under a provision of the Quebec *Charter of Human Rights and Freedoms*. But at the same time the Court, in answer to a request by the Quebec government, upheld the constitutionality of s. 33 in the Canadian Charter, the "notwithstanding" or legislative override clause.* This provision states that Parliament or a provincial legislature may expressly provide that legislation shall operate notwithstanding s. 2 (freedom of expression, conscience, assembly, etc.) or ss. 7 to 15 (due process and equality rights) of the Charter. Any such derogation must be renewed within five years. The notwithstanding clause does not affect voting and election rights, mobility rights, or language rights in the Charter.

Section 33 was inserted in the Charter in 1981 at the insistence of the Western premiers, and has been used by Saskatchewan to exempt anti-strike legislation, and by Quebec in the case of Bill 178, which invoked the clause to immunize its provisions from Charter review.†

The notwithstanding clause was inserted in the Charter as a protection

---

* *Attorney General of Quebec v. La Chaussure Brown's et al.*, [1988] 2 S.C.R. 712.

† Indeed, in 1982, soon after the Charter came into force, the National Assembly enacted a general provision pursuant to s. 33 that all existing Quebec legislation should operate notwithstanding the Charter provisions in question. Furthermore, all subsequent legislation adopted under the Parti Québécois government included a similar clause. The Liberal government elected in 1985 declined to continue this practice, which had been a conspicuous manifestation of Quebec's hostility to the 1982 Constitution. The general provision lapsed under s. 33 on June 23, 1987, the day the National Assembly adopted the Meech Lake Accord and set the three-year clock ticking on ratification of the Accord.

of the limited supremacy of elected legislatures over the judiciary.* In some ways Quebec Anglophones' opposition to the clause has become a metaphor for their resistance to the Francophone majority's right to impose its own policy in the field of language, so vital to the self-definition of each ethnic group.

Bill 178 was also criticized by many Francophones in Quebec, but for opposite reasons: many felt that Bourassa was not going far enough in defending the PQ language law when the new legislation allowed the limited use of English or other languages on *inside* signs as long as French was predominant. The signs legislation has become a flag for both sides in the language battles, and intelligent discourse on the matter has become difficult. For example, when Charles Taylor, a newly-appointed member of the Conseil de la langue française, which administers Quebec's language laws, voiced the opinion (in May 1991) that the signs provisions should be eliminated, he was met with an outburst of indignation from the Francophone media and the PQ Opposition; yet, statements to the same effect by Bloc québécois leader Lucien Bouchard a few days earlier attracted no such criticism. It is hard to avoid the conclusion that Taylor's remarks were particularly objectionable simply because he is Anglophone, albeit fluently bilingual.

To some degree, as well, the conflict over language of signs reflects a confusion between individual rights and collective rights. As a minority, Quebec Anglophones present their concerns in terms of the former, while often ignoring the real need for the Francophones, a minority in a wider context, to take collective action to defend their language and culture.

A related problem is the confusion between the personal and the public: many Anglophone leaders tend to counterpose bilingualism – an individual's knowledge of both languages – to the public policy of preferring French as the sole official language in Quebec. Yet the two are quite different; while it is generally acknowledged that knowing more than one language is a personal asset, it does not follow that a minority language should have official status, let alone equal status, as a language of the state. In some ways the equation of personal bilingualism with official bilingualism mirrors the error of the English-Canadian francophobes who

---

* For the historical background, see Robert Sheppard and Michael Valpy, *The National Deal: The Fight for a Canadian Constitution* (Toronto, 1982), pp. 148-50; for an excellent critical legal discussion of the provision (and, indeed, of the entire Charter), see Michael Mandel, *The Charter of Rights and the Legalization of Politics in Canada*, (Toronto, 1989), pp. 75-81.

protest that the federal official languages policy is "shoving French down our throats".

Other aspects of the Equality Party brief are unclear, as well. The party claims to favour language-based school boards, but under questioning at the Commission hearing its representatives were unable to explain whether these should replace the current guarantees of denominational schools.

The party also displayed a rather selective bias in its approach to minority rights, saying the Quebec government had broken a social contract by imposing certain language laws, but that the federal government had merely "been remiss in supporting the claims" of Francophones outside Quebec and of native communities. Moreover, it inveighed at length against anti-Anglophone bias in Quebec's French-language media while ignoring at least equally prevalent anti-Francophone bias in the English-language media.

An ominous note, as well, was the party's reference to the danger of Quebec "partition" in the event of sovereignty. Again, the exchanges before the Commission failed to clarify what it had in mind.

The following selections follow the official English versions released by these organizations.

Alliance Quebec:

A place for all Quebecers

The 800,000 members of Quebec's English-speaking community represent a tremendous diversity of cultural, racial, economic and educational backgrounds. There cannot be a profile painted of a "typical English-speaking Quebecer"; such a creature does not exist. Nevertheless, the results of Alliance Quebec's consultations suggest that this very diverse community has come together on a number of key concerns.

The concern most often expressed and with, perhaps, the most emotion, is for the place of our community in the future of Quebec. The level of disquiet expressed by English-speaking Quebecers about their place in Quebec is striking; a sense that we are not accepted as full and legitimate members in this society — that the commitment, contribution and potential we have demonstrated are not recognized or appreciated.

Participants in our consultations suggest that the consequences of this problem are pervasive. They touch on everything from the rejection of our community's right to include English on commercial signs to the perception in our community that our young people cannot compete for gainful employment on an equal footing. They also include an often-noted belief that our community's successful efforts to master French have been ignored, and a certain resentment that our recognition of a changing Quebec has gone unappreciated.

We are not here today to discuss whether these perceptions are founded or unfounded. We are not here to question the ability nor the will of Quebecers to live together.

We are here to underline the existence of these deeply-felt perceptions and to put forth our community's vision for a stronger Quebec within Canada. We are here to underline that our perceptions, our vision must be recognized and addressed by the members of this Commission, and by all of Quebec society.

Ensuring our institutions. English-speaking Quebecers want solid guarantees that the institutions which have served and shaped our community will continue to do so. We insist that our access to these institutions must in no way be limited. These institutions — schools, universities, hospitals, social service centres and cultural organizations — represent the core of a community, and the best assurance of a secure future.

Demographics already suggest that this future is in some doubt.

Census data reveal a dramatic decline in Quebec's English-speaking population between 1971 and 1986. The proportion of senior citizens in the English-speaking community is growing rapidly and a disproportionate percentage of the decline is comprised of young people. We continue to experience a net loss in population.

The birthrate in our community is even lower than that of Quebec as a whole, which is among the lowest in the industrialized world. These factors are even more accentuated in English-speaking communities outside of metropolitan Montreal.

In 1975 there were 232,444 students enroled in English schools in Quebec. By 1986 that figure had dropped by 50%. Today, there are less than 100,000 students in English schools across the province.

Our community feels vulnerable because it is vulnerable. We have amply demonstrated the ability to adapt to a changing Quebec. Nevertheless, we need the formal recognition that our schools, hospitals and all the institutions which have defined our long history, will have a long future as well.

It is recognized that institutions, unlike fundamental rights, can and should change through time, but mechanisms must be found to provide the community with solid assurances that a basic infrastructure of institutions will be supported and sustained.

The English-speaking community has identified several areas in which it wishes to be guaranteed a measurable level of service in the English language. Health and social services, education and access to justice are noted as absolute priorities. Even though guarantees in some fashion do exist in each of these areas of service, our sense of vulnerability stems from a belief that the government does not act on our needs with the vigour and commitment required to inspire confidence and trust.

The question of institutions and service delivery relates to another issue of concern to our community. The disproportionately low representation of English-speaking Quebecers in the Public Service has an indirect impact on service delivery. As many participants in our consultations noted, equitable participation for our community would provide one of the best guarantees of government responsiveness to the particular concerns of English-speaking Quebecers. . . .

Promotion of the French language. About 60% of Quebec's English-speaking community is now bilingual. That figure stood at about 35% in 1971. Eighty-five percent of the students in English schools receive more French second-language instruction than is actually required by the Quebec Ministry of Education. Almost half (49%) of English-speaking Quebecers believe that they have a *personal* role to play in the promotion of the French language in Quebec.

There should no longer be any doubt: English-speaking Quebecers believe that they must make every effort to become bilingual. We are acting upon that belief. In part, this is a recognition that fluency in French is essential for full social, economic and political participation in this society. The conviction runs deeper, however. It is an expression of our commitment to Quebec, and of our participation in the distinctiveness of Quebec. . . .

The predominance of French is acknowledged. It must be noted, however, that deep resentment remains towards the prohibition of languages other than French on commercial signs, contained in Bill 178. Alliance Quebec has always acknowledged the appropriateness of having French predominate on commercial signs. In fact, we outlined such a solution before Quebec Superior Court and up to the Supreme Court. Our argument was then and remains today that merchants must have the option of using other languages in addition to French. The government of Quebec responded with Bill

178. It remains a symbol of a fundamental difference of perception between our community and those who support this legislation.

This is not a "zero-sum" game. The public expression of our language cannot be viewed simplistically — as it is by some — as subtracting from the strength and visibility of French. It doesn't work that way. The promotion of French is a goal our community can and does support. English-speaking Quebec is, and will continue to be, a strong partner in a predominantly French Quebec. It has resisted and will continue to resist any initiative suggesting an *exclusively* French Quebec. . . .

Towards renewal. The more than 240 round-table reports we received from our consultations included a few which called for status quo federalism, and a few that supported the idea of an independent Quebec. The vast majority of groups concluded, however, that the current federal system is not working in the best interests of all Canadians, that changes are necessary and desirable. The vast majority concluded that these changes must occur within a federal framework. . . .

At this time, we believe it would be unproductive to indulge in the assignment of specific fields of authority to one level of government or the other. It is the principles that *underline* that authority which must be established. These principles will then provide the framework for the detailed discussions which will follow.

We believe that the creation of a new relationship should be based upon the following:

1. Canada must provide for the economic well-being of all citizens through a strong macroeconomy which can withstand the potentially disruptive impact of a highly competitive world. Within this responsibility, Canada must assume its role in the promotion of the Quebec identity.

2. All governments within Canada have the responsibility to protect and promote minority rights, within their jurisdictions.

3. In its legitimate promotion of the predominance of the French language and culture, Quebec must recognize the requirements of a pluralistic society of many backgrounds.

One of the Commission's greatest concerns must be to consider the process by which Quebec will negotiate any new relationship with the rest of Canada. Quebecers should not underestimate the willingness of other parts of Canada to seek change. Canadians are coming to understand that the constitutional context is changing and people in other regions of Canada are expressing dissatisfaction with the present state of federalism. There have been public processes for constitutional review initiated by other provinces and by the federal government. There is public discussion of an economic union amongst the Atlantic provinces. And across the country there has been widespread rejection of the old ways of dealing with constitutional matters. . . .

Equality Party:

Quebec has violated a social contract

The Notwithstanding Clause. There is a fundamental difference between a government elected democratically by the majority of the citizens on the one hand, and the *Charter of Rights and Freedoms* on the other hand.

A government which has been elected by the majority of citizens enacts and applies laws. All voting is by majority and this is perfectly legitimate.

The *Charter of Rights and Freedoms* is different in that it provides a check against the tyranny of the majority. The Charter expresses universal principles to guarantee the civil rights and fundamental freedoms of each citizen. Such rights and freedoms are inalienable whatever the desire of the governments or the mood of the majority of the citizens. The rights and freedoms described in the Charter are individual and universal. They apply to each and every one, and they transcend language and culture.

However, because of the existence of the notwithstanding clause, which may be used to bypass the Charter, fundamental freedoms are at the mercy of the Government and this is the same as saying that we do not have a *Charter of Rights and Freedoms.*

The only goal and effect of the Notwithstanding Clause is to enable a Government to wrongly suspend the fundamental rights of its citizens, and in particular to suspend the freedoms of opinion, expression, religion and association. The Notwithstanding Clause has no other aim, no other effect, no other justification.

Today, therefore, in Quebec as well as throughout the rest of Canada, we virtually have no *Charter of Rights and Freedoms* and our fundamental rights are at the mercy of the politicians. This is a dangerous situation, which must be corrected as soon as possible. We will recommend that the Notwithstanding Clause be abolished without any further ado.

Violation of the social contract of Confederation. The debates which took place at the time of Confederation were very clear. Quebec was created with the following promises:

• The French-speaking leaders promised the English community, which was going to become a minority in Quebec, that their rights would be respected.

• The Federal Government promised to veto or disallow any Quebec legislation which would suspend the individual or historic rights of the English-speaking minority.

The Quebec Government has broken this social contract by imposing language laws which contain discriminatory sections — Bills 22, 101 and 178.

The Federal Government has broken this social contract by failing to veto these laws which suspended individual rights and historic rights.

The Federal Government has long been remiss is supporting the claims of French-speaking people outside Quebec and of the native communities. . . .

Quebec public servants. In Quebec, the public service is for all intents and purposes a monopoly held by a single ethnic group and, despite many promises, the situation does not seem to be getting better.

To this day, very few Quebec civil servants have been members of minority communities representing approximately 18% of the Quebec population.

Out of 54,000 civil servants, only 2% are from minority communities.

With regard to English-speaking Quebecers, the situation is even worse:

• Total: Only 396 (out of 54,000), i.e. 0.75%
• In Montreal: Only 87 (out of 10,791)
• In the Eastern Townships: Only 5 (out of 1,108)

Out of 4,300 members, the Quebec police force has only one member of the visible minorities. In comparison, the Ontario police force has 78 natives and 69 Asians, Africans, and Latin Americans, i.e. 3.2%. In Texas, 23% of the State police force is from the minority communities.

The situation is just as alarming for the minorities, and particularity for the visible minorities with regard to municipal employees (including policemen and firemen).

The Government has no valid excuse not to hire employees of various origins. It is essential that members of Quebec minority communities be part of the civil service for the following reasons:

- Well-paid jobs, good working conditions and good security
- Factor of social change
- Natural means for social and political promotion
- Factor of integration into society

By being represented at all levels of the civil service, the minority communities can feel that they are part of the Quebec community.

Moreover, since all citizens are taxpayers, the minority communities should have proportional representation. If they are not given their fair share of the public service jobs, they are financially deprived of what is due to them.

Respect of minorities in Quebec and throughout Canada. When, a few months ago, the Municipal Council of Sault Ste. Marie, Ontario, declared their city to be unilingual English, it was encouraging to see that there was in Quebec, as in the rest of Canada, a consensus against intolerance, against unwarranted hostility, against a lack of respect for minorities, and against reactionary language laws.

We salute all the politicians — whether French or English — who stated their support for the French-speaking people in Sault Ste. Marie. And we salute all the newspaper people and columnists who clearly showed for several days that they too were allergic to intolerance and bigotry.

We salute, in particular, those who sharply criticized APEC, an organization whose motto is, English Only, and who [sic] absolutely refuses to accept institutionalized bilingualism.

Quebecers have problems similar to those of Ontario people.

- Bill 101 states, among other things, that all Quebec municipalities are unilingual French (except those whose population is at least 50% English-speaking)
- Bill 178, notwithstanding the *Charter of Rights and Freedoms*, bans outdoor signs in a language other than French everywhere in Quebec.

As objective analysis of what is happening in Ontario and in Quebec leads us to conclude that there is intolerance almost everywhere, in Quebec as in the rest of Canada, that the rights of minorities are not respected, and that an effort must be made to improve the situation.

It clearly appears that the vicious circle of the language crisis is taking the magnitude of a religious schism. APEC in Ontario, and the PQ, MNQ, MQF, and SSJB in Quebec have in common the same refusal to recognize the identity of other communities. One wants everything to be done in English while the others want everything to be done in French, without taking into account the aspirations of their respective minorities.

The reasons which led the Municipal Council of Sault Ste. Marie to declare the City unilingual English are the same as those that led the Quebec Government to declare the province unilingual French — the intolerance of a majority toward its minority.

French-speaking people outside Quebec should be accepted with more generosity by their majority fellow citizens. They should enjoy more social, educational and other services in French as soon as possible, and they should have more control over their institutions.

By the same token, Bills 101 and 178, which go against modern democratic values, should be abolished as soon as possible. How is it possible to have Canadians outside Quebec agree to give French a status equal to English in the presence of Quebec laws which restrict use of English? . . .

We believe that the elimination of such major irritants as Bill 178 and certain sections of Bill 101 would very much facilitate the development of French throughout Canada, would contribute to the cultural advancement of the French communities outside Quebec, and would greatly help such organizations as Canadian Parents for French, which want to spread the teaching of French as well as English throughout Canada. . . .

Separation: Is it possible legally without breaking up Quebec? To our knowledge, there is no mechanism in the Canadian Constitution to allow for the separation of one province. The only legal and democratic possibility is to use the amending formula which is included in the Constitution, i.e., at best, to obtain the consent of seven provinces representing at least 50% of the population of Canada or, at worst, obtaining the unanimous consent of the provinces.

Since Quebec has benefited from federalism during the last few years by receiving billions of dollars, we run the risk of being asked to repay the excess amounts received, as well as our share of the deficit, etc., if ever we ask for separation. There are many people who will feel that it is not fair that Quebec be part of Canada only as long as it is sufficiently profitable.

We believe that it is highly improbable that consent to sovereignty will be granted without laborious and complex negotiations with the Federal Government and the other provinces. This could quite possibly lead to demands for a partitioning of Quebec.

A summary analysis shows at least two possibilities of partitioning Quebec.

(1) Many Quebecers who are attached to Canada will argue that if Canada can be split, so can Quebec. They will demand a new

political entity which would respect the fundamental rights of all citizens and would keep French and English as official languages.

(2) The aborigines would claim independent territories which they would probably obtain. Such territories could be extensive, particularly in Quebec's Far North.

These risks are possible because Quebec includes many communities which live together in the same province. If there was to be separation, and unless all the various Quebec communities express their agreement for such a separation, there would unquestionably be partitioning within Quebec. The proponents of Quebec independence are therefore, whether they realize it or not, fomenting a possible partitioning of Quebec.

As Quebecers strongly attached to Quebec — the whole of Quebec — we prefer a strong united Quebec within a united Canada.

Our position on this is very clear. We are opposed to the partitioning of Canada and to the partitioning of Quebec. . . .

Guarantee the liberty of choice. Many studies have shown the learning and knowledge of two languages were beneficial for the development of children. By the same token, we firmly believe in the equality of rights whenever possible. We recommend the following:

The Constitution should guarantee all parents in Quebec the right to select one of the two official languages of Canada as the principal language of education for their children, so that the unacceptable practice of recognizing for some what is refused to others may cease. . . .

7.

Status of French and Francophones in Quebec — Progress and perils

The following article by André Raynauld describes the remarkable progress achieved by French-speaking Quebecers over the last three decades in overcoming their inferior economic and social status within Canada and Quebec. Raynauld was one of the first to document the subordinate position of Francophones, in studies for the Laurendeau-Dunton royal commission in the 1960s. His essay is a chapter in a larger study by Prof. Raynauld appended to the brief submitted to the Bélanger-Campeau Commission by the Conseil du Patronat, another part of which was excerpted in chapter 2. The study was commissioned by the Conseil, and is excerpted with permission.

The progress of Francophones[*]

By André Raynauld

The underlying political issues, for all Quebecers, involve the French language and culture and the socio-economic status of Francophones in Quebec.

Yet it is precisely on these fundamental issues that progress has

---

[*] This essay is taken in part from André Raynauld, "The Advancement of the French Language in Canada", in Association for Canadian Studies, *Demolinguistic Trends and the Evolution of Canadian Institutions*, Montreal 1989, pp. 93-104. — Author's note.

been the most rapid, and even spectacular, over the last 30 years. This recent history demonstrates beyond the shadow of a doubt that Canadian federalism has not been an obstacle to the advancement of French and the affirmation of Francophones. Accordingly, one can argue that full sovereignty has not been needed to protect and promote what we rightly consider the essential features of our collective life.

Advancement of French. Demographers tell us that the survival and status of a language depends on the number, population density and status of those who use it. Before getting into the details of our successes, we should take a look at each of these conditions.

Obsessed as we are with percentages, such as those showing Quebec's relative decline in population, we fail to realize that the number of Francophones in Canada has increased steadily. Of the 3.5 million people in Canada in 1871, barely a million were of French extraction. In 1986, the census revealed that 6.4 million Canadians claimed French as their mother tongue, and 6 million considered French their usual language. Further, as a result of the spectacular growth of bilingualism among Anglophones, the number of Canadians who could speak French in 1986 was over 8 million, which represents an increase from 29.9 percent of the population in 1931 to 32 percent in 1986. Anyone who noted this long-term trend for the first time would have some difficulty understanding why there is such widespread concern among Quebecers about the future of the French language.

If the French-speaking population were dispersed over the entire continent, one would have to admit that it was threatened; hence the notion that concentration or density over a given area is a determining factor in the vitality of a language. The demographers demonstrate convincingly that Quebec is clearly becoming more Francophone than ever. The proportion of Quebecers whose mother tongue is French rose from 79.7 percent in 1931 to 82.8 percent in 1986. What we consider even more important is the proportion of Quebec's population who can speak French: 93.5 percent in 1986 compared with 85 percent in 1931. On the other hand, the proportion of unilingual Anglophones dropped from 13.8 percent in 1931 to 5.7 percent in 1986. There can be no doubt that French is the common language of Quebec. If we carry the analysis further, we find a growing geographical concentration of Francophones and Anglophones in Canada, which is expressed in Quebec by greater linguistic homogeneity than ever before.

To the degree that the density of the French-speaking population is a decisive factor in the survival of the language, it can no doubt

Table 1. Average employment income for men and women in Quebec in 1970 and 1980

Language groups	Men 1970 $	Men 1970 RRC	Men 1980 $	Men 1980 RRC	Women 1970 $	Women 1970 RRC	Women 1980 $	Women 1980 RRC
Unilingual Anglophones	8,171	1.59	17,635	1.22	3,835	1.24	10,271	1.17
Bilingual Anglophones	8,938	1.74	19,562	1.36	3,956	1.28	10,759	1.22
Unilingual Francophones	5,136	—	14,408	—	3,097	—	8,801	—
Bilingual Francophones	7,363	1.43	19,547	1.36	3,842	1.24	11,195	1.27
English-speaking allophones	6,462	1.26	15,637	1.09	3,329	1.07	9,753	1.11
French-speaking allophones	5,430	1.06	13,287	0.92	3,241	1.05	8,191	0.93
Bilingual allophones	7,481	1.46	17,946	1.25	3,881	1.25	10,868	1.23
Other allophones	4,229	0.82	10,003	0.69	2,343	0.76	7,539	0.86

RRC: Ratio to reference category (unilingual Francophone). For example, 1970 earnings of unilingual Anglophones were 59% higher than those of unilingual Francophones.

Source: Vaillancourt, F., *Langue et disparités de statut économique au Québec, 1970-1980.* Quebec: Conseil de la langue française, p. 87.

be argued that French is less threatened today than it was in the past. Despite the remaining irritants, which should be overcome with a little goodwill on both sides, federalism is not a threat to the expanded use of French in Quebec.

Advancement of Francophones. Socio-economic status is another factor determining the status of a language. This status can be measured in several ways, but whatever criteria are used, the advancement of Francophones in Quebec has been remarkable in all respects. The "backwardness" of French Canadians that was the favourite theme of social studies for several decades is a thing of the past. It has been eradicated over the last 25 years through better education, mobility, access to management positions, notably in the federal public service, and much greater involvement in the business world.

Let us look first at income disparity. In the Greater Montreal area, the discrepancy in employment income between French-mother-tongue and English-mother-tongue male employees went from 51 percent in favour of Anglophones in 1960 to 33 percent in 1970 and 14 percent in 1980 (Boulet and Lavallée 1983). The discrepancy between bilingual Francophones and bilingual Anglophones was 36 percent in favour of Anglophones in 1960, 22 percent in 1970, and 2.6 percent in 1980. In Quebec as a whole, average employment income in 1980 was the same for bilingual Anglophone and Francophone males (Table 1). Bilingual Francophone women even earned slightly more than their bilingual Anglophone counterparts. Unilingual Anglophones earned less than bilinguals of both language groups and sexes, but more than unilingual Francophones.

Anyone who is moderately familiar with this type of analysis will immediately recognize that an individual's income depends on such factors as age, education, experience and occupation. What is interesting about these studies is that we can standardize the characteristics of the two linguistic groups and measure the impact on the average income of each. For example, we just saw that in Quebec in 1980, unilingual Francophones earned less than unilingual Anglophones. However, if the attributes of each group are taken into account, the net effect of language is quite different from what the gross averages seem to suggest, as we see in Table 2. On a net basis, a bilingual Francophone earns 5 percent more than a unilingual Francophone. This means that, all things being equal, it is in the best interest of Francophones to learn English. But this incentive to bilingualism has become marginal and has decreased considerably since 1960. More remarkable by far is the fact that

Table 2. Effects of basic individual attributes on employment income for men and women in Quebec, 1970 and 1980, percentages

	Men		Women	
Factors	1970	1980	1970	1980
Linguistic factors (reference: unilingual Francophones)				
Unilingual Anglophones	10.11	-7.16	0	-4.60
Bilingual Anglophones	16.99	0	0	0
Bilingual Francophones	12.61	5.11	9.73	7.50
English-speaking allophones	0	-16.27	0	0
French-speaking allophones	0	-20.03	22.82	0
Bilingual allophones	6,025	-6.41	11.10	0
Other allophones	-17.64	-45.11	0	0
Standardization factors				
Education (reference: primary 1-4 years)				
Primary (5-8 years)	5.87	-13.25	0	-11.48
Secondary (9-10 years)	19.98	-6.44	0	0
Secondary (11-13 years)	35.61	13.46	35.06	22.71
University (1-2 years)	68.34	25.82	73.66	58.08
University (3-4 years)	119.93	63.41	135.05	86.51
University (5 years or more)	140.35	90.74	152.27	128.70
Experience (years)	6.15	5.95	2.06	2.00
Experience^2	-0.09351	-0.09221	-0.02841	-0.03126
Weeks worked (each additional week)	3.37	3.53	4.10	4.35
Percentage of Variance explained ($\bar{R}^2$)	49.10	49.54	46.71	50.26

Source: Vaillancourt, *idem*, Table 1.

bilingual Anglophones earn no more than unilingual Francophones, while unilingual Anglophones earn 7.2 percent less than unilingual Francophones (in 1980). These figures mean a great deal: knowledge of English is no longer an economic advantage as such in Quebec, except for Francophones, as we have just said, and even for them it represents a very small advantage. In other words, and to reverse the argument, if unilingual Francophones earn less than Anglophones, it is not because they are Francophone or unilingual; it is because they are less educated on average and their occupational structure is less advantageous.

Indeed, as recently as 1980, 37.8 percent of bilingual Anglophone males had attended university, compared with 7.4 percent of unilingual Francophone males (Vaillancourt, 1988). However, 29.1 percent of bilingual Francophones had attended university. Disparities in education still exist, but they too have declined over the last few decades.

The same applies to occupational structure. In comparing the percentage of management positions held by bilingual males in Quebec, a discrepancy of 5.5 percentage points in favour of Anglophones was noted in 1970, but by 1980 this margin had been reduced to 1.7 points.

The type of position held was one of the reasons given for the difference in income; it is also a good indicator of the status of Francophones. Vaillancourt (1987) summarized the results of nine studies on the number of Francophones in management positions in Quebec between 1964 and 1984. These studies show without exception that Francophones have made great strides in this area. Traditionally, they were under-represented in management positions, but the latest data indicate that Francophones now hold about 80 percent of management jobs, which probably places them very close to the optimal position in view of the ownership structure of businesses in Quebec.

In fact, Francophones were traditionally farthest behind in the business world. In the 1950s, we described the Quebec economy as being fairly dynamic and very much integrated into that of the other provinces, but completely dominated and controlled by Anglophones and foreign nationals. With very few exceptions, Francophones were relegated to farms and small businesses. Sociologists could rightly state that French-speaking society was a truncated pyramid because of an almost total lack of French-speaking entrepreneurs.

What progress they have made since 1960! In the two studies we did on business ownership in Quebec, we determined the basic

Table 3. Ownership by language groups of various sectors of the Quebec economy in 1961, 1978 and 1987

Percentage of total employment under

Sector	Francophone control (Canadian)			Anglophone control (Canadian)			Foreign control		
	1961	1978	1987	1961	1978	1987	1961	1978	1987
Agriculture	91.3	91.8	87.5	8.7	8.2	12.2	0¹	0¹	0.3
Forestry	—²	33.4	92.3	—²	28.9	7.7	—²	37.7	0
Mining	6.5	17.0	35.0	53.1	18.1	40.4	40.4	64.9	24.6
Manufacturing	21.7	27.8	39.3	47.0	38.6	38.2	31.3	33.5	22.5
Construction	50.7	74.4	75.5	35.2	18.5	21.8	14.1	7.1	2.7
Transportation, communications and public services	36.4	42.2	44.9	55.3	53.4	50.2	8.3	4.4	4.9
Commerce	50.4	51.0	57.8	39.5	32.0	34.0	11.5	17.0	8.2
Finance, insurance and real estate	25.8	44.8	58.2	53.1	43.1	34.6	21.1	12.1	7.2
Services	71.4	75.0	75.7	28.6	21.2	21.6	0¹	3.8	2.7
Government	51.8	67.2	67.0	47.7	32.8	33.0	0.5	0¹	0¹
Total	47.1	54.8	61.6	39.3	31.2	30.8	13.6	13.9	7.8

Notes: 1. Hypothesis.   2. Not calculated.

Source: Vaillancourt and Carpentier (1989), "Le contrôle de l'économie du Québec...", (Montreal) Centre de recherche et développement en économique.

orders of magnitude (see Table 3). The yardstick used was the number of jobs in businesses controlled by Francophones, Anglophones and foreign nationals. For the economy as a whole, the respective proportions for the three categories of ownership were 47 percent, 39 percent and 14 percent in 1961. The same study conducted in 1978 showed a substantial rise in Francophone businesses from 47 percent to 55 percent, representing an increase of 8 percentage points or 17 percent. As the proportion of foreign-owned businesses remained at 14 percent, the increased Francophone ownership was achieved at the expense of Anglophone Canadians, whose share declined from 39 percent to 31 percent. In 1987, Francophone businesses had made further advances, to 61.6 percent, this time mainly at the expense of foreign-owned businesses, whose share dropped to about 8 percent.

The acquisition or expansion of businesses is, however, a very slow process. Progress should be measured in terms of generations rather than years. Francophone ownership in the manufacturing sector, for example, was still relatively low in 1987 at 39 percent despite an increase of 11.5 percentage points since 1978. In addition, Francophone companies are still smaller, less productive and more introverted, judging from the 1978 data.

On the other hand, although it takes a great deal of time, and perhaps because of that, the phenomenon of ownership and power is extremely important, as Albert and Raymond Breton showed in 1980. It determines in large measure and more than any other factor the socio-economic status of Francophones and the use of French in business. It provides an alternative to government intervention to promote the interests of the Francophone community — an alternative which, because it respects the rules of competition in the marketplace, raises none of the objections usually made about state intervention, particularly in the current context of liberalized trade and deregulation throughout the world.

In short, Francophones have stormed the world of business, just as they once swarmed into agriculture. Without waiting for sovereignty, they have become a normal community in a normal world.

Another traditional source of concern and tension was the lack of access for Francophones to the federal public service, access to services in French, and the use of French in the workplace. The situation that prevailed until the early 1960s was a shameful one in this respect. But things have changed. In the federal public service overall, Francophones now make up 28 percent of total strength (1986) — a proportion higher than their share of the population of Canada — and account for 36 percent of all federal employees in the National Capital Region. Although some under-representation still exists at senior management levels — and there is some doubt about this — it should be noted that 32 percent of positions staffed by order-in-council, which are at the highest levels, are held by Francophones. With regard to the use of French, it is much more widespread, especially since the creation of officially bilingual positions. Lastly, French is the language of work for all federal public servants in the province of Quebec.

In our view, the remarkable advancement of French and Franco-phones that we have outlined is mainly attributable to the Quiet Revolution in Quebec, which brought with it the secularization of institutions, education reform followed by a massive increase in schooling, the arrival of women in the workforce, self-affirmation, and a new dynamism amid rapid economic growth. This was primarily a cultural revolution based on the rejection of traditional values in favour of an alternative set of aspirations geared toward progress, wealth, technology, science and a broader horizon. These are the main reasons for the transformation of the occupational structure, income, business ownership and the socio-economic status of Francophones in general.

Raynauld's study focuses on changes in the relative status of Franco-phones in the areas of employment income and ownership of businesses in Quebec. Thus it is a useful measure of changes in the relatively dynamic sectors of the economy. A more nuanced picture emerges from an examination of other economic and social indicators. For example, Professors Marc Lavoie and Maurice Saint-Germain of the Economics Department of the University of Ottawa, in a brief to the Commission, described the results of an unpublished study of 1986 census data they conducted for the federal government. Among other things, they looked at differences between the status of women and men, and between Montreal and the rest of the province, and compared the results with 1981 census data. Here are some of their major findings:

• *Gross income disparities.* Total income, they note, is a better overall indicator of relative status than employment income, since it takes all classes of society into account, both those with a regular job and those who live on social welfare or derive their income from investments. In Montreal the average Anglophone male's income is 27 percent higher than that of a Francophone male, while outside Montreal the disparity is less than 10 percent. These disparities have changed little since 1980. A similar pattern exists for women, with one important difference: in terms of total income, Francophone women have not improved their status relative to Anglophone women since 1970.

• *Unemployment.* The unemployment rate of Francophone males in Quebec is twice that of Anglophone males (16.1 percent vs. 9.2 percent). Outside Montreal, the rates for Francophone males are comparable to those of Anglophone males in New Brunswick and Nova Scotia. Unilingual Anglophones have the lowest unemployment rate in Montreal. The unemployment disparities by language group are less for women, but in all regions of Quebec unemployment rates are higher for Francophone women than for Anglophone women.

• *Socio-economic status.* In finance and real estate, Anglophones have a greater per capita presence than Francophones (20-25 percent more for males, depending on the region). In the public service, the opposite is the case: Francophones have a much greater presence, except in Hull where both males and females in the two language groups are almost equally present. This suggests that the public service serves as a refuge or outlet for Francophones who cannot find equivalent employment in the private sector, the authors say.

In selected professions enjoying a high social status, male Francophones are under-represented, while female Francophones are over-represented. And in the management category, which contains only half as many women as men, Anglophones have almost twice the representation of Francophones in Montreal.

• *Education.* In Quebec as a whole, the relative number of Francophones who have completed secondary studies has improved over the last 20 years, but the relative standing in post-secondary studies has changed very little. In all regions and age groups, Anglophones are consistently more educated than Francophones. The education rates of women are generally lower than men's.

However, further analysis indicates that at the *same* education levels young Francophones are as well paid as young Anglophones – a dramatic change over the last 20 years.

• *Language transfers.* Outside Montreal, anglicization (a transfer from French to English as one's usual language) does not result in any net addition to income. In Montreal, however, it is profitable; regardless of educational level, the average income of an anglicized male (the data base for women is too limited to study) will be greater than that of an unassimilated bilingual Francophone.

Other studies indicate that in the area of language of work, despite the undeniable progress that has been made in recent years, many Francophones must operate in English during a substantial part of their working day. Conversely, in Montreal, the second-largest French-speaking city in the world, a majority of Anglophones still work predominantly in

English. The pattern is indicated in the following table, based on a study by sociologist Paul Béland for the Quebec government's Conseil de la langue française.

Percentage of workforce working in French, by mother tongue Private Sector, Metropolitan Montreal, 1979 and 1989						
	Francophones		Anglophones		Allophones	
Time working in French	1979	1989	1979	1989	1979	1989
90% or more	62	63	4	8	21	24
89% - 50%	30	30	24	37	35	39
49% or less	8	6	73	55	44	37
N	2,633	2,389	524	432	426	390

As the table shows, the "allophones" – those whose mother tongue is neither English nor French – are in an intermediary position between Anglophones and Francophones: 24 percent work essentially in French, 39 percent in both languages, and 37 percent work in English or some other language. However, the study also shows that barely half (52 percent) of the allophones agree that French should be the language of work in Quebec, and a majority express opposition to Quebec's language legislation, Law 101 (the *Charter of the French Language*).

This indifference toward French language rights on the part of the ethno-cultural minorities in Quebec is a source of concern to many Quebecers. In a brief to the Commission, University of Ottawa mathematics professor Charles Castonguay, an expert on demolinguistic trends, pointed to census data suggesting that the appeal of French began to decline among immigrants to Quebec after 1980. Although, in the 1970s, the majority of immigrants who chose one of the official languages as their language of home use chose French, English regained the upper hand in the early 1980s. Castonguay suggested that this trend might reflect the newcomers' perception, in the post-referendum period, of a loosened official commitment to "francize" Quebec, based on the provincial government's promise to restore bilingual signs and the strengthening of the federal *Official Languages Act*. The data, he said, revealed "the fragility of francisation in Quebec" and the need to "definitively remove the ambiguity surrounding the nature and powers of Quebec society in language matters".

Demographic trends continue to underlie much of the residual insecurity of Quebecers concerning their socio-economic status within Canada. As Professor Marc Termote of the Institut national de la recherche scientifique noted, in a brief to the Commission, "The issue is no longer whether Quebec will still speak French in a few generations, but also how many Quebecers will remain to speak it." The trends and resulting concerns are indicated in the excerpts from the brief of the Mouvement national des Québécois.

Mouvement national des Québécois (MNQ):

Demographic decline a burning issue

The Mouvement national des Québécois, founded in 1834 shortly before the Rebellion in Lower Canada, is a mass nationalist and patriotic organization whose motto is "Notre langue, nos droits, nos institutions, notre territoire" (Our language, our rights, our institutions, our land). Its brief to the Commission was presented on behalf of 12 local MNQ groups and two local chapters of the Saint-Jean-Baptiste Society (SSJB). The MNQ has been an active proponent of Quebec sovereignty since 1969.

In the late 1960s the SSJB, as it was then known, organized the Estates General of French Canada, which brought together prominent leaders and representative of grassroots organizations in French Canada to debate and propose solutions to the national question. It is an active participant in the fight for strong legislation to protect the French language, and in the 1970s was a founder, with the major trade unions, of the Mouvement Québec Français.

A major portion of the MNQ's 60-page brief was devoted to population policy, which it termed "the vital issue for Quebec's future". The following extracts are from this section.

Just when Quebec has never appeared so capable of achieving control over its destiny, when the perspective of a sovereign state seems near at hand, when a new generation of Quebec entrepreneurs can aim as high as it wants, when Quebec cultural productions are international hits, all the indications of a rapid population decline of disastrous proportions are making their appearance. If nothing is done to stem this decline, the effects will soon become evident, beginning with a rapid decrease in Quebec's relative weight in Canada and North America. Within Quebec, the aging of the population will produce a whole string of negative economic and social effects on the structures of this small society: declining regions, an insufficient critical mass of Francophones in Montreal to ensure the integration of immigrants, and a heavy burden of taxation and social costs on the economically active population.

We are not saying this decline is irreversible, nor are we suggesting that women should be forced back to the cradles. Some small countries such as Sweden have coped successfully with a similar challenge while providing women and families with remarkable opportunities to participate in society. But in our view it is urgent to document and openly debate the issues, to ensure that, whatever the solutions we adopt, we have the necessary constitutional means and political will. That is why the Mouvement National des Québécois has summoned its members, and invites the entire population, beginning with this Commission, to face up to the most troubling problem in our collective history: the problem of our survival. . . .

Population decline. First, we should recall that the evolution of the population is a function of births, deaths and migrations. The combined effect of these factors will long be felt, and it takes time to influence them.

Declining birth rate. There were 60,000 of us at the time of the Conquest, in 1759, and we are now more than six million in Quebec alone, after emigrations throughout North America. From 1608 to 1875, the fertility rate was high in Quebec: an average of 7.2 children per family, fairly close to the rate among other inhabitants of the continent, whether Canadians of British origin or Americans. Between 1870 and 1960, while the fertility rate in the rest of North America began to decrease, Quebec experienced its "revenge of the cradles", notwithstanding a slight decrease in its birth rate. But after 1960 it was a whole new story.

The trend is striking in comparison with Ontario's. From 1871 to 1891, fertility declined by 11 percent in Quebec and by 27 percent in Ontario. Between 1891 and 1921, Quebec was stable while in Ontario fertility was only half of what it had been in 1871. Until 1959 Quebec had a higher birth rate than the rest of Canada. After that, the curves cross each other.

The slowing of the birth rate in Quebec has combined with the high immigration to Ontario to produce a disparity in population trends between the two provinces. As Michel Demers of the ASDEQ wrote, in 1989:

> Quebec's population grew by 8.3 percent between 1971 and 1986, while Ontario's increased by 18.1 percent during the same period. Between 1981 and 1986, Quebec's rate of growth was 1.5 percent (94,000) while Ontario's was 5.5 percent (476,000). The disparity in population growth between Quebec and Ontario from 1981 to 1986 is therefore 4 percent. As the Conseil des affaires sociales says in its report, given the present

situation "the population that Ontario gains in one year, Quebec takes five years to achieve."

Higher life expectancy. While the birth rate was falling dramatically, the death rate was declining more rapidly than had been anticipated. After the 1976 census, it will be recalled, the demographers had based their projections for 1986-2001 on an average life expectancy of 73 years. But from 1981 on, it was actually 74 years in Quebec.

The consequences can be imagined from the following table:

Evolution in number of elderly, Quebec, 1951-1981			
	65-79	80 and over	65 and over
1951	200,666	31,431	232,097
1961	261,055	45,246	306,301
1971	346,870	66,140	413,010
1981	474,125	95,230	569,355

A small but recent net gain in migration. Not only has Quebec's birth rate decreased and death rate increased [sic], but a large number of Quebecers have left Quebec, and are leaving every year.

Since 1962 Quebec has suffered net losses in interprovincial population movement. The average number of people leaving Quebec for other provinces, primarily Ontario, was 15,522 between 1971 and 1976, and 31,299 from 1976 to 1981. Although the balance improved in 1985-86, to -3,415, it is still negative. Thus, from June 1, 1987 to May 31, 1988, 18,141 Ontarians settled in Quebec, while during the same period 26,322 Quebecers left for Ontario.

Fortunately, immigration from abroad with its annual positive balances has produced a modestly positive balance overall, but only since 1985: 2,400 in 1985, 11,600 in 1986 and 13,000 in 1987.

In 15 years, a decrease. The impetus provided by the baby boom coupled with immigration since the 1950s is such that Quebec's population will grow for another decade or so. . . .

It will reach 7 million, but then decline, even if immigration exceeds emigration. The slight increase in births of the last two years, although encouraging, cannot by itself change the anticipated trend. **A crucial period.** Our collective future depends on our ability to accurately analyze at this point the actual and foreseeable effects of the decline in population, and to indicate clearly to the people of

Quebec the possible courses open to them. If there is one historically meaningful expression in our history, it is the word "crossroads".
We are at one now.

Declining relative weight. As a small French-speaking people in
North America, can we look with equanimity on the possible
stagnation and decline of our population, while those of Ontario,
Canada and the United States continue to grow thanks to immigration and a higher fertility rate?

Already, from 1961 to 1981, Quebec's relative numerical influence
in Canada has declined from 28.8 percent of the population to 25.7
percent, and Statistics Canada demographers predict it will be 23.8
percent in 2006.

> Quebec is in fact the Canadian region that will post the lowest popula-
> tion growth rate during the period 1981-2006, less than 8 percent, while
> this rate will be as high as 25 percent for the entire area west of
> Quebec. The problem of population stagnation, and *a fortiori* the
> problem of depopulation, will not exist in English Canada for a long
> time to come. (Georges Mathews, *Le choc démographique.* Boréal, 1984,
> p. 150)

Whether within Canada or as a sovereign country, can we un-
flinchingly accept this perspective of a diminution in Quebec's
population? It is true that there are more than 60 countries with
less than 10 million inhabitants, and that Norway, for example, has
only a little more than four million, but can we count on the
relative and absolute decrease in population not having any political
consequences?

Can we accept as a consolation prize the fact that the proportion
of Francophones in Quebec is increasing slightly, to 83 percent, as
the 1986 census indicates? Can we be satisfied that an ever-larger
proportion of the Francophones in Canada is concentrated in
Quebec? . . .

A rapidly aging population. All of the specialists have been
dumbfounded at the sudden fall in fertility. Yet its effects will be
accentuated by another unexpected phenomenon, the increase in
life expectancy. The combined effect will produce an aging that is
unprecedented in the history of western civilization.

Population aging is not exclusive to Quebec. In fact, Quebec is
still one of the youngest societies in the West. But it is also among
those that are aging the most rapidly. . . .

In 2050, 26 percent of the population will be more than 65 years
old; there will be two women to every man among those 80 and
over; 30 percent of the voters will be over 65. Although 44 percent

of the population today is less than 35 years of age, by 2050 it will be 20 percent at most, according to Jacques Henripin.

Population of Quebec, by age, 1951-2001 (in thousands)				
	1951	1971	1991	2001
0-9 years	1005	1114	922	787
65 and over	232	413	767	939

Source: Census Canada and Statistics Canada

It is hard to predict all of the consequences, but researchers already point to the following: a lower productivity for the whole of society; substantial social costs in health, housing and pensions; and the burden of those expenditures falling on a dwindling number of individuals of working age. . . .

Evolution of population by mother tongue, Quebec and particular regions Montreal Census Metropolitan Area, 1981-1986					
Language	Island	Crown*	Total	Rest of Quebec	Total
Absolute differences					
French	9,247	87,718	96,965	82,379	179,344
English	-15,115	-6,754	-21,869	-1,848	-23,717
Other	21,437	3,088	24,525	2,390	26,915
TOTAL	15,569	84,052	99,621	82,921	182,542
Relative differences (%)					
French	0.86	9.43	4.83	2.42	3.31
English	-3.77	-5.14	-4.11	-0.99	-3.29
Other	6.74	5.02	6.46	4.41	6.21
TOTAL	0.87	7.48	3.41	2.27	2.78

Source: Michel Paillé, Conseil de la langue française, *Nouvelles tendances démolinguistiques dans l'Île de Montréal, 1981-86*, 1989, p.21.

---

* Montreal Census Metropolitan Area minus population of Montreal Island; similarly, "Rest of Quebec" is Quebec minus Montreal CMA.

Future of French at stake in Montreal. For more than 20 years Montreal has had the lowest fertility rate in Quebec. This is where the immigrants settle. Francophone couples are abandoning Montreal Island for the suburbs, as are the Anglophones emigrating to Ontario or Western Canada. In short, in Montreal we are talking not only about births, deaths and migrations, but about language, both mother tongue and home language, and language transfers. In 1986 metropolitan Montreal contained close to half of the Quebec population, 2,921,355 people, 1,752,580 of whom lived on Montreal Island.

Montreal has experienced very rapid population movements; some neighbourhoods are being depopulated while others are experiencing lightning growth. While the industrial base in traditionally Francophone East Montreal is being depleted, many sectors in the north of the Island, in the west end and in Montérégie, Laval and the lower Laurentians have been expanding. These economic redeployments will result in population displacements that in the next few years will challenge the majority position of the Francophones. . . .

––––––––––––

To combat the anticipated decline in the Francophone population, the MNQ advocates the adoption of coherent policies to encourage Quebecers to have children and facilitate the integration of non-Francophone immigrants into Quebec society. A family-oriented policy, its brief suggests, would include such measures as low-cost child care facilities funded in part by employer contributions; increased paid parental leave (of at least one year) with guaranteed re-employment; the provision of adequate low-cost housing and community services, and education of young people in the need for more equitable sharing of parental responsibilities between spouses.

Coercive language laws, the MNQ said, are not sufficient to promote the integration of immigrants. Quebec must obtain full control over all the powers it needs to determine its own immigration policy. And it must make Quebec society more hospitable to newcomers – for example by getting rid of its denominational schools system.

8.

Immigration and the clash of cultures

Much of the debate over the future of French and Francophones in Quebec revolves around issues related to immigration, and in particular how to integrate immigrants (particularly the "allophones") into Quebec society without the latter losing its French character. The MNQ brief, excerpted in the previous chapter, illustrated the demographic concerns of many Quebecers and indicated how the issue of the "ethno-cultural communities" has contributed to a larger debate over the definition of Quebec itself in the modern world.

Under the present Constitution, both the provinces and the federal government share jurisdiction over immigration, with federal paramountcy in the event of inconsistency or conflict between federal and provincial laws. Quebec was rather slow to occupy the field, however. In 1968 it established an Immigration Department. But the initial policy agenda was dominated by the issue of the language of education.

Most immigrants to Quebec, given the choice, preferred to send their children to English schools. English was, after all, the dominant language of business and therefore of economic success. And many immigrants objected to the Roman Catholic "confessional" character of most French schools. The issue came to a head in 1968 in Saint-Léonard, a Montreal suburb, when the local school board, reacting to a large influx of mainly Italian immigrants, ruled that all instruction in the board's elementary schools would be provided in French only. The Union Nationale government reacted by enacting Bill 63, which guaranteed immigrants the right to educate their children in English.

Bill 63 was very unpopular among the Francophone majority. In 1974 the Liberal government under Robert Bourassa enacted Bill 22, which restricted the right of immigrant children to attend English schools to those who could pass a proficiency test in that language. Bill 22 enraged the English, failed to satisfy Francophone nationalists, and alienated many immigrants who felt they and their children were being made the scapegoats of Quebec's linguistic ambiguities. Opposition to this legislation is generally considered to have been a major factor in the Liberals' defeat in the 1976 general election.

The new Parti Québécois government enacted Bill 101, the Charter of the French Language, which (among many other things) required all children, including immigrant children, to attend French schools unless at least one parent had received his or her elementary education in English in Quebec, or outside Quebec if the parent was domiciled in Quebec when the Act came into force in 1977 (the so-called "Quebec clause"). The PQ also moved to re-organize Quebec's educational system on the basis of language rather than religion.

The new legislation was largely successful in removing the language of education as an issue in the immigrant and majority Francophone communities. Much less successful, however, was the effort to secularize the school system. This issue, the topic of the next chapter, remains a central one in the debate on immigration policy.

Since the 1970s the debate has moved increasingly to cover a much broader range of issues raised by the clash of immigrant cultures with a Francophone majority culture that is rapidly changing its own self-definition. These issues were debated at length in many submissions to the Bélanger-Campeau Commission, although the Commission's report fails to acknowledge them with anything more than general platitudes ("efforts must be stepped up to ensure that Quebecers of all origins enjoy genuinely equal opportunities and participate fully in all spheres of activity"). The Commission itself contained no representatives of the ethno-cultural community, an omission that attracted much public criticism.

Many of those making submissions to the Commission argued that Quebec required full jurisdiction over immigration, if not sovereignty, in order to develop a comprehensive and coherent policy. Among these were the major union centrals. The comments of two of them are excerpted below.

Other witnesses were less inclined to identify existing constitutional arrangements as the problem. For example, Jacques Henripin, the noted demographer, was more concerned with the quality of French that is being taught in the schools. His written brief is excerpted below. Similar concerns were expressed by Fatima Houda-Pepin, a representative of the Centre Maghrébien de recherche et d'information, an organization of Francophone ethnic groups originating in North Africa. Excerpts from her oral testimony to the Commission are included in the final selection.

It should be noted that while the Commission was meeting, in December 1990, the Quebec government signed a comprehensive immigration agreement with Ottawa under which:

- Quebec is allowed to exceed by five percentage points its annual share of immigration, which is based on its proportion of the population. This would guarantee Quebec up to 30 percent of immigrants to Canada, if it so desired; in recent years it has taken less than 20 percent of the total.
- Quebec has full responsibility (with financial compensation) for the linguistic, cultural, social and economic integration of its immigrants.
- Quebec has exclusive responsibility for selecting its independent immigrants, i.e., those who are neither refugees nor applicants under the family reunification program. (The latter two categories account for about 40 percent of Canada's total immigration.)

The federal government will continue to set national standards and objectives; thus it will continue to determine overall immigration levels (in consultation with Quebec), to set medical standards, and to provide security screening of prospective immigrants.

The agreement, which became effective on April 1, 1991, incorporated but went beyond the Cullen-Couture accord of 1978, which would have become part of the Constitution if the Meech Lake Accord had been adopted.

✧ ✧ ✧

Goal is integration, not assimilation in a French but multi-ethnic Quebec — CEQ

Members of the Centrale de l'enseignement du Québec (CEQ), the province-wide teachers' union, have been front-line participants in some of the major debates over immigration. Perhaps for that reason, theirs was one of the few briefs presented to the Commission to explore at some length the concepts of race, ethnic group and nation, and to suggest how a French Quebec could be reconciled with a multi-ethnic, pluralist conception of a sovereign nation. Here are major extracts from their brief.

In the 19th century (and even the early 20th in some works, such as Lionel Groulx's in Quebec), the terms "race" and "ethnic group" were readily confused. For example, they spoke of the French and English races. Today the two terms have become specialized, and designate two different realities.

Race refers to a set of physical characteristics that are transmitted genetically. The concept is acknowledged to be of some use in animal breeding. Applied to the human species, it is of doubtful relevance. It can only be used to classify individuals, since there is no people that corresponds to a clearly determined race, no matter what characteristics one would use to define them (skin pigmentation, shape of skull, height, colour of eyes or hair, texture of hair, blood type, laterality, etc.). . . .

Race therefore designates no actual community; it is purely a category for classifying individuals. From a strictly scientific point of view, it is impossible to define a people from racial criteria. Ethically, it is generally acknowledged that legislative or administrative attempts to promote the purity or improvement of the race would be incompatible with democratic ideals.

Nor has race anything to do with culture in the anthropological sense of the word. It refers only to what is transmitted genetically. And the fact that one has common family antecedents does not necessarily mean that there is a strong genetic resemblance. . . .

However, an *ethnic group*, although it may be defined by dictionaries as "a group of families" and involve some common origin, has nothing to do in itself with physical characteristics or the genetic heritage of the individuals that it is composed of. Ethnic group refers to a cultural heritage and the affinities that are displayed between persons and families sharing that cultural heritage. Ethnic heredity is cultural, not genetic. One can find a great variety of physical types within the same ethnic group. . . .

Whether or not a particular individual belongs to a given ethnic group is determined by his or her correspondence to a cultural profile. The community of culture on which the ethnic group is based is one of likenesses between the individuals and families within it (e.g., the same mother tongue, religion, family customs, eating habits, way of dressing, memories of a common past, and the same hierarchy of values). The degree of likeness varies, of course, depending on the group observed and the way in which each ethnic group defines itself.

Because the ethnic group's underlying community of culture is one of individual likenesses, we use the word assimilation to designate the process by which an individual gradually abandons the characteristics of his culture of origin and adopts those of the dominant ethnic group of the community in which he lives.

A *nation* is defined essentially as a society having its own culture as a society, not as a group of people having similar cultural traits as individuals. As the *Petit Robert* says, it is "a human group, generally quite large, which is characterized by a consciousness of its unity and a desire to live in common." . . .

Ethnic culture is mainly transmitted by the family and the private institutions that gravitate around it. National culture is transmitted mainly by the national education system and through the operation of national institutions.

One's membership in a nation rests not on cultural characteristics inherited from the family milieu but on the implicit desire to live together, to constitute a true society, to share common institutions and adopt common standards of social life. In a normal situation this implicit desire is manifested by living in common in the same territory, defined in terms of the common culture erected on it. The nation is a work of reason and will, but a will renewed by successive generations — a synonym for historical continuity.

Human beings have not always lived in nations. In the days when they derived their food and fibre essentially from hunting and fishing, they lived in nomadic tribes, the unity of which rested primarily on ethnic affinities. With the invention of agriculture, they began to adopt sedentary habits, to combine and organize their collective life around the places in which they had settled and with those people who had chosen adjacent sites. Then came the creation of villages and towns, the development of industries requiring increasingly sophisticated and varied technical skills, leading to the need for public services such as the post office, the construction and upkeep of public roads, education, etc. These phenomena are the basis on which nationalities and nations are built. . . .

The Quebec nation. Insofar as the Quebec people defines itself as the entire population of Quebec, that is, all of the people who decide or agree to live permanently in Quebec and thus implicitly decide or agree to participate in its life and comply with its laws, it can be said to constitute a genuine nation. This people inhabits a territory that coincides with the sphere of influence of a distinctive national culture. It possesses a historical continuity going back to the 17th century. It has a national language that has accompanied it throughout its history and undoubtedly remains today the most easily recognizable aspect of its identity, to which it is very attached and with which it is spontaneously associated. It constitutes a distinct civil society, with its own codified civil law. It also has distinctive, original institutions — legal, political, educational, economic, cooperative, trade union, etc. And it is conscious that it constitutes an original society with a distinctive language, legal tradition and institutions.

The characteristics and attributes we have just referred to really belong to the entire Quebec society, to the Quebec people as a whole. Any Quebecer, even one who wishes it were otherwise, is affected and concerned by the fact that the society in which he lives has its own peculiar characteristics and a peculiar dynamic of social life. By agreeing to live in Quebec, no matter what one's origin, one accepts the laws of Quebec, short of helping to change them by becoming involved in the dynamics peculiar to Quebec's political and social context. To be a Quebecer it is not necessary to belong to the French-Canadian ethnic group, but to be a Quebecer regardless of one's ethnic affiliation is something quite different from being a Canadian or American. Quebec's national culture is the common property of everyone living in Quebec.

We said that the Quebec people indeed constitute a nation insofar as it is defined by the implicit will to live together and constitute an authentic civil, economic and political society. By this definition, we must acknowledge the special status of the aboriginal societies, which live collectively and to a large degree distinctly in the enclaves reserved for them in their own right. The Amerinds are ultimately subject to a law that applies only to them and imposes a particular political organization on them. Moreover, in many Amerind communities, and among the Inuit, there is a traditional political authority functioning parallel to the official political structure. Above all, in contrast to the situation of the other inhabitants of Quebec, their presence here cannot be interpreted *a priori* as a manifestation of an implicit will to share the institutions of the majority nation, since their societies already existed before the creation of ours. Their current societies are the extension of societies that never decided formally or implicitly to merge with ours. That is why we say that the native communities will only be part of the Quebec people to the degree that they themselves so decide. We recognize their right of self-determination and will demand that this right be inscribed in the Constitution of Quebec. . . .

The founders of New France did not simply open an area of immigration for Francophones from Europe; they created a distinct and original society. And not all of the immigrants who settled in New France were Francophones. Many in all probability spoke dialects or semi-dialects originating in the various provinces of France. Some were Italians, Spanish, German or Irish. The so-called "clash of dialects in New France" is comparable, in some respects, to the clash of ethnic languages in contemporary Quebec. The Quebec society of that day managed to integrate in French a linguistically diverse immigrant population speaking Norman, Poitevin, *gallo* (Breton), Picard and perhaps even Italian or Gaelic, and achieved its linguistic unity a century and a half before France.

From the very beginning of its history it sought to be a society with French as its common language, moving beyond the diversity of the languages of origin. Today's attempts to secure the integration in French, in the public schools and workplaces, of new Quebecers of every origin is consistent with the exemplary success achieved three centuries earlier.

The immigrants to New France came from provinces each of which had its own particular custom in the civil law. It soon became clear that the new society saw itself as a unified civil society with a correspondingly unified civil law. The *Coutume de Paris* was therefore recognized here as the ordinary law, laying the foundations of another major aspect of our national specificity. In the *Quebec Act* of 1774 the British conqueror recognized its Quebec colony as the juridical extension of New France by restoring the authority in civil matters of the *Coutume de Paris*, which it had vainly attempted to replace with the English common law 11 years earlier. The latter is still the basis of the civil law in the nine other Canadian provinces and most of the states in the United States. The legal and legislative specificity of Quebec, reconfirmed by the *Constitutional Act, 1791*, was maintained in this respect even under the Union of the two Canadas, from 1840 to 1867; in 1866, in fact, the Parliament of the United Canada adopted the *Civil Code of Lower Canada*, modeled on the French *Code Civil* and applying only in Quebec. Contemporary Quebec's demands for exclusive jurisdiction over family and commercial law expresses the desire to protect and complete the overall coherence of our distinctive civil law, an integral part of our historical heritage.

And not only the civil law. It is no accident that Quebec is often the only province to demand exclusive power to legislate in many fields. Its aspiration is to build a fully coherent society by enacting laws that correspond to its national culture.

The desire to promote one's distinct legal coherence normally implies a desire for political autonomy. In this sense, in particular, the right of self-determination and the idea of national independence are grounded on the existence of a nation and of its distinctive national culture. Quebec, a nation in every sense, is now ready of its own accord to take its place in history.

Need for a cohesive society. The Quebec people are a multi-ethnic nation, in the sense that they have a distinctive national culture with which several ethnic cultures, including that of the majority group, co-exist.

Census information indicates that Quebec is now about 83 percent Francophone and about 10 percent Anglophone. It appears that Francophones (defined by either mother tongue or language used in the home) will be in the majority for a long time to come. The percentage of Anglophones, on the other hand, has been declining for several decades. However, the percentage of persons whose mother tongue is English is declining more rapidly than the percentage of those for whom English is the main language used in the home.

In addition, many people and families in Quebec today have neither French nor English as their first language, and there will be many more in the future. The low birth rate and the high immigration rate we will continue to need mean that Quebec will be increasingly multi-ethnic. And, on the international level, Quebec has a moral responsibility to do its part to provide a refuge for persons and families in distress who come from other countries. If we consider the ethnic diversity from the standpoint not of first languages but of ethnic origin, it can be anticipated that the descendants of the inhabitants of New France will long remain the largest group numerically, but in five or six decades will no longer constitute an absolute majority of the population.

There is no need, in our view, to regard this possibility, in itself, as a threat. We think the survival of the Quebec people and the protection of its common culture are not jeopardized by the presence in Quebec of persons of various origins, mother tongues or ethnic cultures. They could be jeopardized, however, by an ambiguity in the relationships between the ethnic groups and a larger society that is insufficiently or not clearly enough defined. It is not a matter of indifference that immigrants feel they are joining a Canadian nation, rather than the Quebec nation.

What Quebec needs is not to be sheltered from immigration or to be protected against the ethnic diversification of immigration. What it needs is full control over the tools it needs to build and assert its cohesiveness as a society over and above its ethnic, religious and ideological diversity.

There are ideological movements that base their defence and promotion of the Quebec identity on ethnic homogeneity. They demand that immigration be limited solely to European Francophones, for example. And they recommend that the people of disparate ethnic origin already settled in Quebec be systematically and rapidly assimilated. We disagree completely with this approach, as you can imagine.

On the contrary, we think the diverse cultural contributions of the groups who join in the life of Quebec represent an opportunity for all Quebecers to enrich the national culture and open up to the world. We therefore advocate an open immigration policy that makes no distinctions on the basis of ethnic origin, without excluding, however, priority for those who, regardless of ethnic affiliation, already have a satisfactory knowledge of our national language. We also advocate a policy that values ethnic contributions, and promotes integration without assimilation. We support measures designed to promote the preservation of languages of origin. Finally, we support a policy of equal access for ethnic groups that suffer general discrimination in employment or are under-represented in specific jobs, for example in the public service.

A people's cultural dynamism is built not through levelling but through an emphasis on differences and building contacts between those differences and the common culture. Quebec's cultural dynamism needs all of the cultural resources of the peoples who make up its population. But it also needs to form a coherent society. Thus any policy of enhancing cultural differences must be accompanied by the promotion of a common culture and a common language. These two prongs of cultural policy are not contradictory, but complementary. . . .

Hence Quebec's immigration policy must be accompanied by greater efforts than before to francize all manifestations and aspects of our collective life.

It is not enough that a prospective immigrant has heard of Quebec's French character in his or her contacts with the bureaucracy, or that he or she is offered French courses. The immigrant must see, hear and feel this French character everywhere — in everyday life, at work, in shops, in public services, in signs, in product labels, in corporate names, etc.

The goal must be not only to facilitate the use of French for Francophones in all of their activities, but to establish French as the common language, in fact and in law, for all of the inhabitants of Quebec. The alternative is the cultural dislocation of Quebec.

Integration means more than learning French — CSN

All the unions appearing before the Commission supported expanded immigration to Quebec, as did virtually every business group. The unions, however, discussed a number of problems they had observed or experienced in the integration of immigrants. The comments of the Fédération des travailleurs du Québec (FTQ) are excerpted in its brief earlier in this book. The Confédération des syndicats nationaux (CSN) situated its discussion of immigration and the ethno-cultural communities within the broader context of employment policy and economic development. Here is what it said.

Independence will help clarify a number of problems. For example, it will be clear to people wishing to settle here that this is a French-speaking, not a bilingual country. But integration is not limited to learning French. To integrate in Quebec, one must be able to participate fully in all facets of Quebec life, and have the means to do so. In this sense, full employment is a decisive factor in any coherent immigration policy. In addition to helping integrate the new arrivals economically, the work environment is one of the places where prejudices and false perceptions of each other can be corrected. For our society, like many others, while open and welcoming, is not exempt from discrimination and racism.

A sovereign Quebec. In recovering full jurisdiction over immigration, Quebec will have to go much further than the policies and procedures established to implement the Cullen-Couture agreement of 1978. It will have to determine procedures for the reception of immigrants and refugees, criteria, immigration categories, and quotas.

Should the immigration issue be incorporated into an economic development policy? Should an independent Quebec give priority to Francophone immigration, or humanitarian concerns, or should employability be the primary consideration? These are issues around which a broad consensus must be developed. In our view, Quebec's immigration policy should maintain the present criteria of reunification of families, independent immigrants and humanitarian considerations.

The whole refugee issue will have to be reviewed and a new dimension given to the notion of "urgency and danger". For example, an independent Quebec might include among the endangered those fleeing famine, or women whose lives would be threatened by traditions in their country of origin if they were forced to return.

Quebec citizenship is another matter for substantive debate. What should be the qualifications for Quebec citizenship? Should they be broadened, as in some other countries, to allow anyone marrying a Quebec citizen to automatically obtain Quebec nationality?

Quebec might also adopt procedures to promote the settlement of new arrivals in outlying regions, by linking immigration with regional development policies.

The rights and obligations of immigrants and the obligations of the host society will also have to be clearly established. Quebec's immigration policy should contain precise procedures on such things as the comprehensive information on Quebec to be conveyed to anyone thinking of immigrating to Quebec.

French courses should be accessible to everyone, both new arrivals and those long established in Quebec who have not had an opportunity to learn our language. Furthermore, the school system will have to reflect the new realities. Secularization of the schools will help integrate students from different cultures and spread the underlying values of our society. Reception classes and intercultural educational programs should be systematized.

In addition, to facilitate access to the labour market it will be necessary to augment the number of equal access programs and facilitate the recognition of the educational training and occupational experience of new arrivals.

Immigration is a challenge to many peoples. The solutions Quebec must find will be decisive to its future. Can we be a welcoming and tolerant society?

Redefining Quebec to encompass racial and ethnic minorities

More than a dozen immigrant or ethnic groups addressed the Commission. Most represented groups of particular ethnic origins. A few were coalitions speaking collectively on behalf of many different organizations. One of these was the Comité de coordination sur la place des minorités ethniques et raciales au Québec,* a coalition of 80 organizations formed in July 1990 to "promote the full participation of groups in the cultural communities" in the proceedings of the Commission, whose formation had just been promised. The following is the major part of its brief.

---

* Coordinating committee on the place of the ethnic and racial communities in Quebec.

As of their first meetings, the members of the coordinating committee reached a consensus on four points:

1. Federalism as implemented before, during and after the Meech
Lake Accord has had its day, and we believe that there is an urgent
need to break the constitutional status quo that is poisoning federal-
provincial relations and deeply affecting the social climate.

2. The members of the coordinating committee recognize
Quebec's distinctive character and its right to self-determination.
This right was exercised during the 1980 Referendum. It is now
being exercised through this Commission on the Political and
Constitutional Future of Quebec. These two experiences, the
Referendum and the Bélanger-Campeau Commission, are very
reassuring with regard to Quebec's ability to define its future while
respecting democracy, freedom of expression and basic rights.

We should not forget, however, that the cultural communities,
which represent an important segment of the population, are
inadequately represented on the Bélanger-Campeau Commission.

3. Quebecers from ethnic and racial minorities are not a
homogeneous group, ideologically speaking. Like the majority, they
embrace a wide range of views. They have not reached a consensus
on a particular political option, but they do agree on the need for
a fair and equitable blueprint for society. We want a society that is
free of discrimination and racism, where minorities can participate,
as full citizens, in the development of society.

We are also concerned about the exclusion and marginalization
of other underprivileged groups, in particular young people, the
poor and women. We are deeply concerned about equal employment opportunities for racial and ethnic minorities and about the
presence and visibility of these minorities at all decision-making
levels.

4. We have noted, unfortunately, that Quebec's identity, as
defined by most public opinion leaders and the general public, does
not include ethnic and racial minorities. Although Quebec society
has evolved considerably over the past three decades, the concept
of Quebec's identity is still the product of a limited frame of
reference and is somewhat exclusive. Even today, some opinion-
makers refer to Quebec as a homogeneous society and talk about
immigration as if it were something new.

As for the coordinating committee, we believe that ethnic and
racial minorities are an integral part of Quebec society and that they
constitute one of its basic features. Quebec is currently a pluralistic
Francophone society and it will continue to be so in the future. It
is important to officially recognize Quebec's pluralistic character by

taking its intercultural, interracial and interdenominational nature into account. . . .

Quebec defines itself among its minorities, even after they have acquired citizenship and lived here for several generations, as a "host society". The participation of ethnic and racial minorities in public affairs is limited almost exclusively to invitations to sit on "ethnic" advisory committees. But when it comes to decision-making bodies or matters of national importance, these Quebecers are forgotten; they lose their status as full citizens and become "immigrants" again.

The composition of this Commission is a striking example of this.

In accordance with this exclusionary logic, the obstacles encountered by the ethnic and racial minorities, and the manifestations of racism, are reduced to mere isolated incidents. This leads to explaining racism and discrimination as human relations problems, and not as the operation of a system of values and practices that effectively exclude people on the basis of race, colour, religion, and ethnic or national origin.

That is why we are asking the Bélanger-Campeau Commission to extend the concept of Quebec identity, once and for all, to encompass the ethnic and racial minorities unequivocally. For, if Quebec is truly a distinct society, it is not only because of its Francophone character, but also because of its multi-ethnic, multiracial and multidenominational character, and its ability to integrate and promote this intercultural resource in French.

This concept of Quebec society is to us the central element in our legitimate desire to participate actively in public affairs, particularly in the political, economic, social and cultural fields. This Quebec society is also our society.

Recommendations. This Commission has an obligation to:

1. Recommend that fundamental economic and social rights, as provided by international agreements and the Canadian and Quebec Charters of rights and freedoms, be entrenched in all constitutional proposals.

2. Recommend that the multi-ethnic, multiracial and multi-denominational nature of Quebec society be entrenched in all constitutional proposals.

3. Identify the responsibilities of the different levels of government, both provincial and municipal, and create a constitutional obligation for all public and private agencies to eliminate systemic discrimination based on race, sex, religion, and ethnic or national origin.

4. Criminalize all racist acts and hate propaganda.

Is the Constitution the problem?

By Jacques Henripin

I suppose I am expected to discuss Quebec's outstanding population problems and indicate, to the degree possible, some ways to resolve them. The main problem can be summed up in two words: declining fertility. Two other problems related to migration are the substantial emigration to other provinces and the difficulty integrating a major portion of the immigrants from abroad. Let us take a brief look at each of these.

1. Fertility. By the end of her childbearing years, a Quebec woman now between the ages of 25 and 30 will probably have given birth to about 1.6 children (and not 1.4 as is often claimed). This is 0.5 children fewer than needed to ensure generational replacement — a deficit of close to 25 percent.

At this rate, two unwanted consequences will appear:

(a) A *substantial* aging of the population. This will become quite pronounced around the year 2010, and by 2030 about 25 percent of the population will be 65 and over. The proportion today is about 11 percent.

The only real remedy is an improvement in fertility.

Note: Contrary to what is often said, immigration does little to rejuvenate the population.

(b) By about 2030 Quebec's population will be well on the way to absolute decline. This decline will begin around the year 2000, then accelerate[1] and reach cruising speed shortly after 2030, resulting in a reduction of about 25 percent each quarter century. By 2080 Quebec will have about 4,000,000 inhabitants, or six-tenths of its present population.

These are problems faced to varying degrees by the entire industrialized world, including Japan. But they may be considerably more serious in Quebec, for two reasons: (a) the fertility is lower than elsewhere; (b) migratory trends, which are usually unfavourable, could accentuate the decline in population.

2. High emigration to other provinces. It is mainly the Anglophones who are leaving, with their possessions, that is, with their skills, their capital, and (this is never mentioned) a form of collective wisdom that is a useful complement to that of the French-Canadian majority. Between 1966 and 1986, 20,000 Anglophones and 9,000 Francophones left Quebec each year for some other province. In relative terms, 15 times as many Anglophones (and about 5 times as many allophones) as Francophones are leaving Quebec for the rest of Canada.

Let us also note that Quebec does a rather poor job of retaining its foreign immigrants: 40 percent leave within 10 years, 50 percent within 20 years, and 60 percent within 30 years. Obviously, this makes immigration from abroad a much less effective means to overcome demographic deficiencies. We need to take in close to three immigrants in order to keep one!

3. Difficulty integrating immigrants. The foregoing is itself an indication of the lack of integration. However, Quebec has a particular problem. Only 30 percent of immigrants whose language is neither English nor French, and who must, therefore, choose between the two dominant languages, adopt French. This does not come close to reflecting the distribution of the two dominant languages in the host population, which is the population not of Quebec but of Montreal, and which is about 70 percent Francophone (only 60 percent on Montreal Island). The disproportion is, therefore, less pronounced than is usually suggested. But it is nevertheless quite high, and there is no doubt that English exercises a very strong attraction.

Census figures indicate that in 1986, after nine years of enforcing Law 101, the relative attraction of English and French was about the same as in 1971. This is no cause for surprise, since schoolchildren are the only ones severely constrained by that law.

One might well wonder whether some advantage offered to adults might be more effective than the "stick" applied to the children. What kind of advantage? I think Quebec society as a whole and its public authorities in particular (including civil servants) are rather mediocre in their reception of strangers. We might achieve greater success by recruiting non-Francophone civil servants (provided they are competent, of course) than by prohibiting signs in any language other than French.

No outside jurisdiction prevents the Quebec government from recruiting non-Francophone civil servants or conducting educational campaigns to reduce what indeed should be called chauvinism.

We should mention, as well, that it has never been demonstrated — at least to my knowledge — that the survival of French is threatened by a sign that is one-quarter English or Italian.

Digression on a somewhat imaginary peril. Since we have just referred to the survival of French, let me use the opportunity to recall that it was long feared — and not without reason, incidentally — that the proportion of Francophones was diminishing in Quebec, and in Montreal in particular. These fears were belied by the most recent census findings, in 1981 and 1986, and there is no reason to think that things will change over the next decade and a half.

However, if Quebec were to dramatically increase its immigrant population, things might turn out quite differently in a quarter century. For example, if fertility were to be maintained at its current level, and we decided to compensate for the vacuum (which would necessarily result) by resorting to immigration from outside, the perspective would be completely different.

If there is any threat to French today, it is from the sorry state of the written and spoken language. And there is no use hiding one's head in the sand; this is not the fault of the English or of the Constitution! No doubt several factors are involved, but we cannot deny the enormous responsibility of the Quebec government and the teachers. I will be told that I am not an expert in the matter. My reply is that perhaps that is good: some experts used to defend *joual*! And in any case I have been in a good position to observe, for more than 35 years. I get the products of our schools, at the end of the line. And I can affirm that, of all the Francophone students I may have known, the French Canadians are those with the least mastery of their language. I would say, in fact, that close to one-fifth of the students in our French-language universities do not have sufficient mastery of their mother tongue to develop a logical thought.

It is this, above all, that threatens the vigour of French in Quebec. . . .

A comment on English. The concern to maintain French should not preclude some concern about the chances for survival of English. At this point I would not say that the English minority faces impending disappearance, but it is certainly heading that way. However, no one will deny that in Montreal (but only in Montreal) the English community is still full of vigour — and is beginning to speak French. So much so that in a few years it will be the Anglophones who are the real bilinguals! The Francophones will have lost this specialty, thanks to the shortsighted distrust of English that is fostered in the French-language school system. This is a fine example of the stupidity produced by protectionist ideology. If we want to give French some vigour, we will have to teach it correctly and with enthusiasm and firmness. And not look askance at English! . . .

And what about the Constitution? I don't quite know what to say. It seems to me that Quebec already has the necessary powers to deal with most of the failings I have pointed to. . . .

Give some content to independence

Fatima Houda-Pepin (Centre Maghrébin)

[Independence] mustn't be seen as a magic solution to solve all of our problems. If we don't give content to this independence, it will be difficult to sell it to the minority groups. One other comment I would make, Mr. Larose [CSN president Gérald Larose], is that there is an idea (which to my mind has no foundation) which questions the allegiance of the minorities to the Quebec government, because they have always been associated with the federal government, with multiculturalism, with a certain view of society. I believe that Quebec society must change this perception, because the minorities have no prejudices about the Quebec government or the political class in Quebec. Minorities are uneasy about ethnocentric nationalism; they fear it because they fear being excluded. If the society of the majority can demonstrate its ability to welcome them and consider them full citizens, the members of the minorities won't hesitate or won't necessarily oppose the plan for Quebec's independence, and in some cases will champion it. . . .

[A] Quebec identity would be pluralistic; a Quebecer is someone who wants to be one. It's up to us to make this identity happen, but the majority society must accept it. Let me give you some examples. I received a phone call from a government TV service that was preparing a program about marriages with foreigners. I asked them what they meant by "foreigner" and they told me it was someone who is an immigrant.

As long as you continue to see us as foreigners, there will be a problem in defining what a Quebecer is. I can give you many other examples. I attended a conference on education. One of those attending made a presentation on the problem of francizing the allophones, allophone children, and she made a speech that is completely in line with current thinking: French is in trouble because of the immigrants and allophone children. And, of course, she cited the example of Saint-Luc school.* That example makes me

---

* The Saint-Luc school is a secondary school in Montreal with 1,650 students, 90% of whom are of non-Quebec ethnic origin. They include 87 ethnic groups, 45 languages and 9 religions. The common language many of these students use to communicate with each other is English, although the school is a French-language school operated by the Catholic school board. The school is

furious. At one point, I asked a question. I asked if she could tell me the quality of the French, the state of the quality of French in schools having a high concentration of native-born Francophones. And do you know what I got by way of an answer? Silence, for several minutes. They realized that a fundamental question had just been asked.

It's very easy to blame the immigrants for their inability to speak French, but that doesn't improve the quality of French. If we really want to promote French, we have to promote the quality of French, of French education for all children, with no distinctions but with consideration of the specific needs of allophone children who have particular problems, of course. But the most interesting thing was that a few days later I met one of the people who was seated beside me at that conference, and who is known to be a very congenial nationalist. I asked him: "How did you react to my question?" I felt I'd embarrassed people. And he said to me: "You know, it's a little like having a child with bad manners; when you say it has bad manners, that's fine, but when an outsider says it, that's hard to take. So there we are, it's an automatic reflex, sometimes it isn't even intentional; it's built into us. For us, it stems in part from our idea of the Catholic French Canadian, and everything that doesn't fit this three-part mold can only be foreign."

So you can see we have some way to go: we're doing our part; for goodness' sake, do yours.

---

considered by many commentators in the Francophone media to be an example of the difficulty Quebec faces in integrating its immigrants.

9.

Quebec's frustrating struggle for a secular school system

A recurring bone of contention in some provinces is the continuing existence of publicly financed "denominational" schools and school boards propagating a particular set of religious beliefs. It is a particularly acute issue in Quebec, where opposition to the historic symbiosis of the Roman Catholic church and the provincial state has combined with growing attention to the role of the public school system in the integration of ethnic minorities. In many respects, the ongoing debate over school curriculum and structure mirrors the conflicting approaches within Quebec as it redefines itself as a pluralist and multi-ethnic society.

Most public schools in the province provide religious instruction, either Catholic or Protestant depending on how the school is defined. In fact, the Quebec *Charter of Human Rights and Freedoms* protects the right of parents to require that "public educational establishments" provide their children with "a religious or moral education in conformity with their convictions. . ." (s. 41), although the Charter also protects freedom of conscience as a fundamental right (s. 3).

Some groups appearing before the Bélanger-Campeau Commission challenged the very existence of religious instruction in the public schools. An example was the Mouvement laïque québécois, whose brief is excerpted below. But the particular target of a large number of briefs was the continued existence in Montreal and Quebec City of public school *boards* elected and controlled respectively by the Catholic and Protestant communities.

This sectarian system of education has traditionally been thought to rest in part on the Canadian Constitution. Section 93 of the *Constitution Act, 1867* provides that education is an exclusive provincial responsibility, but that no law shall prejudicially affect any right or privilege with respect to denominational schools that existed at Confederation, and that in Quebec

the powers, privileges and duties of the "dissentient" schools shall not be
less than those of the separate (Catholic) schools in Upper Canada
(Ontario) and their trustees at Confederation. In addition, s. 29 of the
Constitution Act, 1982 provides that nothing in the *Canadian Charter of
Rights and Freedoms* " abrogates or derogates from any rights or privileges
guaranteed by or under the Constitution of Canada in respect of
denominational, separate or dissentient schools."

At the time of Confederation, public school boards in Quebec were
structurally neutral — elected and funded without regard to religion —
although the boards were allowed to put a particular religious imprint on
the schools. If a board exercised this right, and most did, dissident
minorities were allowed to establish their own schools (religious or non-
religious) and receive public funding for them. Parallel to this system, in
Montreal and Quebec City, apparently because of the size of the
Protestant minorities in these cities, provincial legislation from the outset
established separate Protestant and Catholic school boards; the schools
administered by these boards, while teaching the respective faiths, were
nonetheless open to anyone regardless of faith. In practice, the children of
Catholics attended the Catholic schools, and all others attended the
Protestant schools. Most Catholic schools were French, and the Protestant
schools were overwhelmingly English.

This system endured without major crisis for over a century. But
postwar immigration began to put strains on it as the newcomers tended
overwhelmingly to send their children to Protestant — English — schools.

In 1966 the Parent commission on educational reform recommended
the creation of unified non-sectarian school boards throughout the
province. These boards, it was thought, would control immigrants' access
to English schools on a local basis. However, Bill 63 in 1969 guaranteed
parents' "free choice" of the language of education of their children
throughout the province. As explained in the previous chapter, this and
subsequent legislation in the early 1970s only exacerbated the problem.
Finally, in 1977, Bill 101 required immigrant children to attend French
schools. Today, close to one-third of the children in the French schools in
Montreal do not have French as their first language.

However, the schools are still organized along religious lines, and many
immigrants shun the Catholic schools. As a result, many immigrant children
are enroled in Montreal's Protestant French-language schools, which are
nevertheless under the control of boards dominated by Anglophones.
Nationalists argue that these schools present a misleading image of Quebec
society and prejudice the children against the Francophone majority.

Both of Quebec's major political parties favour scrapping the denominational schools system. The Parti québécois and Liberals are on record as
advocating separate school systems for Francophones, Anglophones and

the aboriginal communities respectively.* Other groups, such as the major trade unions, call for the creation of a single, unified common school system, without specifying whether this would exclude English schools for Quebec-born Anglophones. Their thinking is outlined in the excerpt from the CEQ's brief to the Bélanger-Campeau Commission.

An initial attempt by the Parti québécois government to restructure the education system by language rather than religion, Bill 3, was ruled unconstitutional in 1985 in a court challenge by the Protestant school boards. A Quebec Superior Court judge held that the legislation violated s. 93 of the Constitution by abolishing the Catholic and Protestant boards in Montreal and Quebec City.

Pressure then grew for the repeal of s. 93. The newly-elected Liberal government indicated sympathy but failed to raise the issue in the constitutional negotiations leading to the Meech Lake Accord. Instead, it withdrew its appeal of the Bill 3 judgment and introduced new legislation, Bill 107.

This bill would institute language-based school boards in most of the province, but (in an attempt to comply with the 1985 judgment) would retain the denominational boards in Montreal and Quebec City. Bill 107 would also retain religious education courses in the schools in accordance with the parents' beliefs.

Once enacted, Law 107 was referred by the government to the Quebec Court of Appeal for a ruling on its constitutional validity. In September 1990 the Court unanimously ruled it was constitutional. Furthermore, to the surprise of many, four of the five judges indicated that the government could have abolished all of the existing denominational school boards without violating s. 93. The purpose of that section, they said, was to protect freedom of conscience for minorities, not to give an automatic right of denominational schools to either Catholics or Protestants. The right to create dissentient schools was triggered only where legislation had made that necessary, through the prior establishment of a particular denomination's schools. "Theoretically," they said, "the legislature could decide to establish a system of secular education and prohibit any form of religious teaching in the public schools . . . there would be no need for the exercise of the right to dissent."

This judgment is being appealed to the Supreme Court of Canada by the Protestant school boards and the Montreal Catholic School Board, the CÉCM. Until the Court has handed down its decision the government is unlikely to move to re-organize the school system in Montreal.

---

* See Jean-Pierre Proulx, "Retour des remous linguistiques et religieux", *Le Devoir*, 10 April 1991, p. B-1.

Meanwhile, the CÉCM has become a key arena in the fight to "de-confessionalize" the schools. The Board has been controlled for more than a decade by the Rassemblement scolaire confessionnel (RSC), which aims to maintain and promote "the Catholic religious heritage" and "Christian and family values" among the pupils in its system. In the most recent school board elections, the RSC came within one seat of losing its dominant position to MÉMO, the Mouvement pour une école moderne et ouverte, which favours the creation of a language-based school board. MÉMO was organized in the mid-1980s by a coalition of community organizations, including the MLQ and activists in the teachers' alliance affiliated with the CEQ. Its brief to the Bélanger-Campeau Commission is excerpted below.

The RSC-dominated board received considerable publicity last year when it issued directives banning the use of languages other than French in the school yards. In its brief to the Commission, also excerpted below, it indicates its preference for immigrants "who share Judeo-Christian values with us".

Ironically, almost none of the 20 or so ethno-cultural minority organizations that addressed the Commission mentioned the schools issue. An exception was a coalition of Jewish groups that defended the network of Jewish private schools, while also supporting the concept of a public secular school system open to all.

Although the issue was raised in a great many other briefs submitted to it, the Commission made no mention of the language-versus-religion debate in its report.

Repeal of s. 93 an urgent priority — MÉMO

The Meech Lake process clearly demonstrated that there is not only a Quebec nation but an English Canadian nation as well. Although they were unwarranted, the profound fears aroused by the Meech Lake Accord (like the Free Trade Agreement before it), as a process threatening precious values, clearly, albeit negatively, reflected the existence of an English Canadian nation, although a nation lacking a focus equivalent to that of the government and political institutions in Quebec. In terms of education, it seems absurd to us that this English Canadian nation has nine different educational systems in which authority over such matters as adult education, occupational training, educational television and public education is parcelled out between two levels of government. A new constitutional relationship between the two nations should enable English Canada to rationalize its own system of education.

Our primary concern, however, is with Quebec, where the same problem exists, but the other way around. Quebec needs a single educational system, with jurisdiction over not only all issues affecting public and postsecondary education, but also child care, adult education and educational TV; a single system with jurisdiction as well over all aspects of occupational training and retraining, including unemployment insurance, to ensure consistency in all policies affecting the dissemination of knowledge and information in Quebec. That is why we hold that, in the negotiated redistribution of powers between Quebec and Canada — whatever the form finally adopted — Quebec should accept nothing less than full sovereignty over education.

Even in those fields in which it supposedly has exclusive jurisdiction over its public education systems, Quebec has been prevented from taking the necessary measures. Section 93 of the *British North America Act*, reinforced by s. 29 of the *Constitution Act, 1982*, hangs like a sword of Damocles over the Quebec education system. For close to 30 years, successive Quebec governments have attempted, without success, to secularize the structures of the public education system to make them conform to the realities of the late 20th century. Relying on s. 93, the courts have invalidated one reform after the other. The most recent attempt, Bill 107, may manage to pass muster with the Supreme Court of Canada — we don't know yet — but if so, it will only be on condition of maintaining the parallel existence of the denominational and linguistic structures. No one can predict the complexity or cost of a potential transition from the present denominational system, assuming the Supreme Court does give its approval. (Obviously, if MÉMO wins a majority of seats on the CÉCM, we will do all we can to facilitate this process.) Our major recommendation is, therefore, that Quebec make the abolition of sections 93 and 29, as they affect Quebec, immediate priorities in the constitutional negotiations to come.

This request is based not only on the fundamental principle of Quebec's sovereignty in education. It is also an urgent necessity. Francophone Quebec is making substantial efforts, in difficult circumstances, to integrate a large number of allophone immigrants not only into the French-speaking community but also into Quebec culture. The public schools constitute an important aspect of this integration process, as the experience of other countries clearly shows. This is especially true for a small Francophone nation within a North America that is predominantly Anglophone. In many neighbourhoods in metropolitan Montreal, the allophones constitute the majority of those attending school, and in many cases English is the common language of this majority. The challenge is therefore a substantial one, and is a challenge for which our school administrators and teachers are ill-prepared.

To assert ourselves collectively as a people, we must succeed in this process; our public schools must become places where new Quebecers are welcomed and where they can participate positively in the normal integration process. But the existing denominational schools system is an obstacle to this integration, and makes a process that is already very difficult even harder. Even if Quebec were composed only of native Quebecers, it would be difficult in a harsh economic context to educate our young people in a way that empowers them to successfully confront the challenges of a rapidly changing and increasingly technologically oriented society. Integration of the allophones adds a further complication; the sectarian structures make it practically insurmountable.

Furthermore, the parallel existence of four school systems in Montreal (English Catholic and Protestant; French Catholic and Protestant) produces an obvious waste of already limited resources. The result is a deplorable lack of financial resources, reflected in several phenomena: outdated textbooks, run down buildings, lack of equipment, lack of commitment among the teachers, etc.

Sectarian schools are a fundamental right — RSC

Since the establishment of school boards in Lower Canada in 1840, Catholic and Protestant parents and voters have been exercising, through these boards and in advance of their time, the rights guaranteed in the Universal Declaration of Human Rights, the Quebec Charter, and the international covenants.* It was these

---

*   The first part of the RSC brief quoted at length from international documents affirming the right of religious freedom and of parents to choose the kind of education to be given to their children. The RSC concludes from these that the "best way" to respect these rights would be "to ensure that the school transmits the same religious and

same rights, known as "natural rights", that were entrenched in the Canadian Constitution.

Prior to the establishment of the first school boards, the French Canadians had rejected the establishment of neutral schools and instead founded parish schools.

Even today, as a headline in *Le Devoir* reporting on a poll in 1988 put it, "a majority of Quebecers prefer the denominational school boards to language-based boards".

Since 1977 Montrealers have elected without fail a majority of board members supported by the Mouvement Scolaire Confessionnel, a provincial body composed of more than 1,000 organizations. In our view, Quebecers have more than demonstrated their attachment to the denominational school boards.

Consequently, these school boards cannot be eliminated on the pretext that they do not please other groups of citizens. It is the responsibility of the level of government with jurisdiction in the matter to serve the community fairly, and this government, seeing the appearance of groups with differing convictions (reflecting the evolution of the community) has a duty to secure the rights of these groups while maintaining the rights of those classes of citizens that have been present in this society since Confederation.

Thus, it is the fundamental right of Catholics and Protestants to control their own school boards, as expressed by s. 93 of the Canadian Constitution, and not a privilege from some past period. . . .

The role of tradition. The purpose of the international covenants is not to reduce national cultures and traditions to the same level but to promote human rights; that is why they do not spell out how the freedom of parents to educate their children in accordance with their convictions is to be secured. On the contrary, they provide full latitude to the sovereign governments to adapt the universal rights to the traditions of their respective nations. This apparent freedom does not exempt the leaders of any country from the moral obligation to treat their citizens equitably.

There is a strong temptation to avoid the problem by imposing a single system of neutral schools, in the belief that this will both fulfil human rights and satisfy everyone. The RSC maintains that this is a restrictive interpretation of the Declaration of Human Rights.

---

moral convictions". It appears that Quebec's human rights commission reads the same international covenants quite differently, as in fact affirming the separation of church and state (see the MLQ brief, below).

As a nation, we cannot refuse to grant certain privileges to new spiritual groups without running the risk of treating them as second-class citizens. On the other hand, we cannot abandon our own tradition in education on the ground that some groups are dissatisfied with it or that we need to abolish obstacles to the integration of immigrants.

For example, any proposal to impose a single language-based school structure on Quebec is a direct attack on the acquired and innate rights of the Catholics and Protestants to denominational school boards. Furthermore, these attempts are being perpetrated in the absence of public consultation.

With a denominational status adopted periodically by a vote of the parents in each school, the language-based school boards will not create the absolute fairness attributed to them. The imposition of denominational status, or any status, by a majority of parents will produce a dissatisfied minority.

What, then, can be said about schools that are wholly secular and devoid of any denominational status, except that they deprive both the founding and the new communities of the Quebec nation of their fundamental and innate rights.

At the other extreme, it would be unwarranted and even imprudent in this age of immigration to promote the unrestricted freedom to form schools. This could compromise cultural identity and the right to enforce the predominance of the national language, based on an excessively liberal reading of the Declaration of Human Rights.

The middle course is to respect the rights and established interests of the majority, who wish to build a future in continuity with their traditions, while providing an alternative to the minorities who so desire. . . .

Immigration policy. This Commission is also reflecting on Quebec's political future, and it seems clear there is a consensus on promoting a certain kind of immigration. This is an issue of the greatest concern to the Regroupement Scolaire Confessionel, since the Montreal Catholic School Board (CÉCM) receives a large proportion of the néo-Québécois students.

While it is legitimate and desirable to encourage Francophone newcomers, some thought should be given to the fact that people who share Judeo-Christian values with us would be applicants whose customs are closer to our own, and that people leaving their own country expect to have to adopt a new language but are more reluctant to change their spiritual values.

While advocating such a policy, the Regroupement Scolaire

Confessionnel is confident that parents of every origin and every religion, knowing the international reputation of the Catholic schools, will choose the CÉCM — especially if, relieved of its obligation to serve as a common school board by the presence of alternatives, but open to all by definition, it reaffirms the denominational character that is its trade mark.

Finally, we think that, if the government is thinking of taking in a large number of people in Quebec and keeping them here, it has every interest in providing a range of denominational and non-denominational school boards, the likes of which cannot be found anywhere else in North America. This is an advantage, which compensates for the obligation to learn and use French. For let us not forget that many expatriates arrive among us with America first in their minds.

Allophones are anglicized by sectarian schools — MLQ

The Mouvement laïque québécois was founded in 1976, although it continues the work of an earlier formation, the Mouvement laïque de langue française. In addition to its discussion of denominational schools, excerpted here, the MLQ was also critical of other infringements of freedom of conscience, such as the federal government's attempts to restrict choice in abortion, and what it viewed as impermissible state recognition of religion in such practices as the role of the clergy in officiating at civil ceremonies (e.g., the registration of births and marriages) and the recent decision to allow Sikh officers of the RCMP to wear turbans.

It is in the educational field that the religious discrimination engendered by the Canadian Constitution is most obvious and most acute.

The Constitution protects the denominational character of the public school system in Quebec. By allowing the confessionalization of the public schools, in violation of the right to freedom of conscience, s. 93 of the *BNA Act* effectively operates as a permanent "notwithstanding" clause.

Furthermore, the right to provide a denominational orientation to the public schools is granted only to Roman Catholics and Protestants. Similarly, the right of dissentience when the public school is denominational is also granted only to Catholics and Protestants where they are in the minority.

Section 93 opened the way to a series of sectarian laws in the education field, and this confessionality is highly discriminatory. For example, section 4 of the Regulations of the Catholic Committee of the Superior Council of Education provides that a Catholic school shall "incorporate the beliefs and values of the Catholic religion in its curriculum".

The same Regulations require that teachers must be of the Catholic faith to provide the religious education that is part of their duties. The Act therefore establishes job discrimination based on religious affiliation for teachers in public schools.

In such schools, a non-Catholic immersed in an environment tinged with Catholicism will necessarily feel that his or her freedom of conscience is being violated. This infringement of fundamental rights is so crude and obvious that the *Education Act* had to resort to the "notwithstanding" clauses in the Quebec and Canadian Charters to protect the religious sectarianism in the Act (ss. 726 and 727).

The Commission des droits de la personne spoke out against the proposed sectarian curriculum and the recognition of denominational schools, as well as the use of the "notwithstanding" clauses in the legislation. In its brief on Bill 107 amending the *Education Act*, the Commission pointed out that

> by allowing the existence of denominational public schools, the government is not adopting the solution imposed on it by the *Charter of Human Rights and Freedoms*, that is, the full exercise of the right not to suffer discrimination on the basis of religion. Nor is this approach consistent with the principles set out in article 13 of the International Convention on Economic, Social and Cultural Rights, to which Quebec has adhered. Moreover, article 26 of the Universal Declaration of Human Rights is to the same effect.

Accordingly, the Commission recommended "that the characterization of a school as denominational no longer be authorized" and asked for a "revision of section 93 to put an end to the rights and privileges granted to two religions". More recently, the Commission came out even more explicitly in support of non-denominational schools, which it sees as the only solution consistent with everyone's fundamental rights:

> In answer to the question that was put to us, which public school system would be most appropriate for Quebec — denominational,

neutral or secular — the Commission would choose secularization, which in other words would mean opposing sectarian instruction in the public schools, since in the words of a Supreme Court of Canada judgment of 1955: "Each person's conscience is a personal matter and no one else's business." (*L'exercise en toute égalité du droit à la liberté de religion dans les écoles publiques québécoises*, Haïlou Wolde-Gioghis, Research Branch, Commission des droits de la personne, March 1990)

In Montreal, the existence of two denominational school boards, each with a French sector and an English sector, leads straight toward the anglicization of allophones. Because the schools are denominational, close to 50 percent of them choose the French schools of the PSBGM. We know how francophobe that school board is. It is cultural suicide to entrust it with the francization of the immigrant communities.

Here again, Quebec's desire to adopt a language-based school system has continually collided with the sectarian provisions of the Canadian Constitution.

The influence of s. 93 is also reflected in the way the *Education Act* opens the door to the creation of schools for religious sects other than Roman Catholic or Protestant. A multi-denominational and factional approach prevails to the detriment of secularization. Prepared to maintain at any cost the sectarian privileges allowed the Catholics and Protestants, the government offers similar provisions to the other denominations, even if there is no demand for them.

This is exactly what any government wishing to retain some minimum consistency and social cohesiveness would avoid. You will never manage to grant equality to all sects by increasing the types of sectarian schools. Moreover, this splitting up of the educational system will lead to the isolation of the minorities in ghettos, when the school should be an institution promoting adaptation to the host society.

Finally, the sectarian nature of the public schools makes the state responsible for transmitting religious faith at its own expense. It is certainly not its duty to assume such a function, and by agreeing to do so it elevates the religions affected to the status of state religions.

There is a cost to all of this. According to a study by the Economics Department of the University of Quebec in Montreal, the denominational school system in Quebec costs more than $267 million a year, using 1980 data (*Les ressources économiques à la disposition de la confessionalité au Québec*, Michel Bergeron, October 1981). . . .

The solution: Independence and secularization. As we noted, secularizing the State will require some amendments to the

Canadian Constitution. Since its founding, the Mouvement laïque québécois has been seeking amendments to s. 93 of the *BNA Act* so Quebec could adopt a school system that corresponds to its needs. In 1980 we were not only the first to demand this, but the only ones. Today there is a consensus around this demand in Quebec and a number of ministers have stated that it should be included in the next round of constitutional negotiations.

A recent judgment of the Quebec Court of Appeal, on September 21, 1990, has upheld the privileges of sectarian dissentience accorded to Roman Catholics and Protestants by s. 93. These privileges will continue to be a constant threat to the language-based school system that Quebec has been trying to establish since the 1960s.

Thus s. 93 limits, as it always has, Quebec's power to legislate in the area of education. Quebec thereby has less power in this area than Newfoundland and Manitoba. It is imperative, therefore, that Quebec repatriate all jurisdiction over education, and this involves amendments to s. 93.

In addition, a secular state should not tolerate the monarchy or the deist preamble to the present Constitution [of 1982]. And freedom of conscience and religious equality should be better protected than they now are in this Constitution.

However, the sad fate of the Meech Lake Accord and the wrenching frictions that preceded its rejection have convinced us that it is impossible to amend the Canadian Constitution. If Canada was unable to accept the idea that Quebec be described as a distinct society, we dare not imagine the reaction if Quebec were to propose the abolition of the monarchy.

The Mouvement laïque québécois has, therefore, lost hope that Quebec will manage to achieve the amendment of s. 93 or any other provision of the Canadian Constitution.

But we shall not abandon the struggle for a secular state. The only realistic approach now, in our view, is for Quebec to adopt its own constitution completely independent of the Canadian Constitution — in short, that it proclaim its independence.

Such independence would be meaningless unless it were also the occasion to proclaim secularism as a fundamental principle of the Quebec state.

This is a time of historic choices. Beyond the choice between the Canadian federation and independence, Quebec must also choose between two conceptions of fundamental rights.

It can continue in the historical tradition and maintain more or less formal ties between Churches and State. Given the increasing pluralism, this road will lead it toward increasing sectarian divisions.

There are many unfortunate examples of societies that have been developed on the principle of religious or ethnic division. Lebanon, Israel, South Africa, Northern Ireland, and India offer us daily the sad spectacle of communities that are slaughtering each other because they do not accord the same freedom to everyone to exercise their fundamental rights.

Quebec, too, can break with tradition and join the ranks of those states that have made secularization one of the basic principles of democracy. Granted, secularization of the state will not lead magically to the disappearance of discriminatory attitudes such as racism or religious fanaticism. However, it does provide the necessary legal guarantees to ensure each citizen the same rights and the same possibilities of enforcing those rights.

CEQ favours single secular school system

The integration of immigrant children into Quebec society will be achieved to a large degree through the educational system. If the latter is to perform this role, it must provide pupils with a common school attended by the children of both established Quebec families and the various cultural communities.

Quebec is in an extremely fragile situation in this regard, given the incredible dispersal of the school system under the new *Education Act*. At present there are two systems of denominational school boards, which in turn are split into two language-based school systems. When the new Act comes into force we will have four school boards in each of Montreal and Quebec City: one Catholic, one Protestant, one Francophone and one Anglophone. The same model may be reproduced elsewhere in the province through the operation of the right of dissentience accorded to Roman Catholics and Protestants wherever one of the groups is recognized as a minority within a language-based school board. Within each denominational board there will inevitably be a French school system and an English school system. Within each language-based board there will be Catholic schools, Protestant schools and schools that are officially non-denominational. The result is a range of 10 types of public schools to provide education to a community that is multi-ethnic and pluralist in its religious orientations. And that's without counting the subsidized private schools, some appealing to specific ethnic clienteles and others (although not spelling it out *a priori*) attended almost exclusively by children from the French-Canadian ethnic group.

Under the combined provisions of the *Charter of the French Language* and the new *Education Act* when it comes into force, the children of immigrant families who are neither Roman Catholic nor Protestant will have to enrol with the French-language school board. Isn't there a danger that the denominational school boards and the private schools will become the refuge of French-Canadian pupils whose parents wish to shelter them from contact with other ethnic groups? The denominational alibi will be used to disguise racist or xenophobic motivations. As a result, the children of the ethnic groups may find themselves in schools where there are relatively few or too few children of Québécois origin. And this will complicate the integration process.

The dispersal of the education system is based in part, but not exclusively, on the requirements of the Canadian Constitution. Some aberrations go beyond the Constitutional requirements.

10.

Francophones outside Quebec
redefine their relationship

The Commission's terms of reference indicated it should address issues of concern to "French-speaking communities outside Quebec". The Report's one paragraph on the matter suggested that Quebec's institutions and government should "more actively support the initiatives of French-speaking people outside Quebec", without indicating what those initiatives were or what active support might entail.

A number of Francophone groups from outside Quebec made submissions to the Commission. The Fédération des francophones hors Québec (FFHQ), whose brief is excerpted here, is the umbrella organization for these groups. Created in 1975, it represents nine provincial and two territorial associations and four national sectoral associations (women, youth, media and culture).

In June 1991, several months after this brief was presented, the FFHQ changed its name to Fédération des communautés francophones et acadiennes du Canada. The new name, adopted unanimously at the federation's annual meeting, reflects the fact, as one delegate put it, that non-Quebec francophones are "tired of defining ourselves in terms of what we aren't". It also expressed their conviction that Quebec is no longer interested in the fate of the French-speaking communities in the rest of Canada.

The FFHQ brief is rather upbeat in its description of the condition of the Francophone communities outside Quebec – a reflection, possibly, of the Federation's recent decision to be less strident and "put greater emphasis on our accomplishments".

Perhaps the brief is unduly upbeat. Although it refers repeatedly to the presence of one million Francophones outside Quebec, this figure is disputed by some authorities. In a recent study using Statistics Canada data, Professors Marc Lavoie and Maurice Saint-Germain of the University of Ottawa report that in 1986 only 575,095 Francophones living outside

Quebec spoke French as their usual language at home. The same data indicated that 842,815 persons outside Quebec listed French as their mother tongue. "The difference between these two numbers", they say, "is largely caused by anglicization." Comparing language transfers over a ten-year period, they found assimilation rates of over 70 percent in Alberta and British Columbia; the lowest rates were in the Acadian parts of New Brunswick (8 percent) and rural Eastern Ontario (15.2 percent).*

. Nevertheless, as the FFHQ brief notes, non-Quebec Francophones have won some significant major victories in recent years. Most of these have been in the courts, where they have used Charter provisions on minority language educational rights to pressure governments to grant them their own schools and school boards where their numbers warrant.

These advances, however, have also produced some painful confrontations with Quebec. For example, in the recent *Mahé* case, the Quebec government intervened in the Supreme Court hearing to challenge the right of Francophones in Alberta to have their own school board. Quebec's concern is that judicial interpretations of the Charter provisions constitute an unwarranted federal intrusion on its right to determine its own education policies.

These irritants and tensions, to which the FFHQ brief alludes, underscore some of the ways in which the Francophone communities outside Quebec have been used as a political football in many of the constitutional disputes of the last 25 years. There were echoes of this around the Commission hearings, too. Commission member André Ouellet, representing the federal Liberal party, argued that there were two million Francophones outside Quebec, while author Yves Beauchemin, a sovereigntist, referred to Francophones outside Quebec as "a still-warm cadaver".

Generally, however, the Francophones outside Quebec have resisted the attempts to enrol them as footsoldiers for either side in the sovereignty struggle. They have tended instead to focus their efforts on fighting for services in their own language in their own communities, a struggle they must conduct in the face of considerable indifference, if not antipathy, on the part of English-Canadian society. Most see a stronger Quebec not as a threat but as an aid to their own efforts.

This approach was reflected in a joint statement by representatives of the Francophones outside Quebec and leaders of the sovereigntist

---

* "L'Assimilation des francophones hors Québec", *Le Devoir*, 22 March 1991, p. B-8.

movement in Quebec, issued in early February:*

> The recent recognition of Francophone rights by the federal government and some provincial governments, and the establishment of bilingualism policies, should not obscure the fact that it was the lack of recognition and the lack of such policies for more than a century that debilitated the Francophone communities and condemned some of them to a slow death. It was often in reaction to the rise of Quebec nationalism and Quebec's new strength that concessions were granted to the Francophone communities, frequently for strategic reasons.

The statement acknowledged that the "constitutional choices" of Quebecers and the Francophone communities outside Quebec might differ, but said both had a "fundamental interest in protecting the language rights and development of the Francophone communities". The sovereign-tist signatories undertook to ensure that a sovereign Quebec would, among other things, attempt to negotiate with English Canada a code guaranteeing the rights of their respective English and French language minorities, which might be incorporated in a treaty between the two states.

It should be noted, however, that the Francophones associations in Alberta and Manitoba, in their submissions to Bélanger-Campeau, argued that Quebec sovereignty would harm their own interests as a minority in English Canada.

Fédération des francophones hors Québec (FFHQ):

A new departure, as partners

Politically, the Francophones outside Quebec have been associated, despite themselves, with everything that has to do with bilingualism.

---

* "La souveraineté et l'avenir des francophones hors-Québec", *Le Devoir*, 6 February 1991, p. B-8. The document, prepared by Sylvain Simard, president of the Mouvement national des Québécoises et Québécois, was unanimously adopted at a meeting February 1 attended by leaders of the PQ, the Bloc québécois, the major union centrals, the FFHQ and Francophone provincial associations in Ontario and New Brunswick.

Not *la francophonie*, but bilingualism. This idea, in a thousand and one versions, has become a disquieting phenomenon to the people of Quebec. For many, it symbolizes a federal initiative that attacks the very foundations of Quebec culture, or at least dilutes it. How should one react? First, by taking one's distance, being on one's guard. Cooperate with the Francophones outside Quebec, granted, but not at any price and, above all, not on the basis of bilingualism.

So what attitude should Quebec now adopt toward the francophone community we represent? How should it position itself while preparing to define its position, not on new federal structures, but on the political and constitutional future of Quebec society?

We think it is important to answer these initial questions with some diligence. To do so, Quebec must understand where the Francophone community outside Quebec is coming from and where it is going.

A. The Francophone presence outside Quebec. So who were the first whites to settle on our continent?

It was the Acadians who founded a colony at Port Royal in 1605 and traced the first steps of *l'Amérique française.** . . .

Today, the Acadian community of New Brunswick enjoys a vast network of educational and social institutions, such as the University of Moncton, supported by a series of laws acknowledging the historic contribution of this French-speaking community in Eastern Canada.

Indeed, there are close to 300,000 Acadians in the Maritime provinces.[†] Even in Cap Saint-George, Newfoundland, there are Francophones with roots going back more than 10 generations.

These numbers have enabled the Acadian population to consolidate a significant economic network. The fishing industry, for example, once under U.S. and English control, is now controlled by Acadians. Pillars of the economy such as the Assomption insurance company are also controlled by the Acadian community. In Prince Edward Island, where there are a surprising number of Francophone cooperatives, they have developed the potato industry by forming a potato chip co-op using Quebec expertise.

The Acadian community in Nova Scotia, also known for its co-ops

---

[*] After establishing an encampment at Île Sainte-Croix in 1604 and a fort at Port Royal in 1605, the Acadians began to settle permanently in America around 1632.

[†] By itself this community is larger than the entire population of Prince Edward Island and the two northern territories combined.

in a number of fields, including the fishing industry, this year celebrated the one hundredth anniversary of the Université Sainte-Anne.

In contrast to the Acadians, the Francophones in Ontario and Western Canada almost all came originally from Quebec. When the history of *la francophonie* is written, it will be noted that many Quebec families, setting out for the Yukon or the Northwest Territories, ultimately settled permanently in that part of the country.

Going back a little further, it will be recalled that in British Columbia in the mid-19th century there was a Francophone community with its own network of institutions. At that time, no less than 60 percent of the province's population was French-speaking. . . .

From the early 18th century Alberta was populated by Francophones from Quebec, France and New England. They established political structures such as the Société Saint-Jean-Baptiste. . . .

Francophones have carved out a significant place for themselves in the entrepreneurial environment we still associate with this flourishing part of the West. The Desrochers and Allards are specific examples of our participation in the development of Alberta. In Saskatchewan the Francophone community of Zénon Park is developing new agricultural techniques involving the transformation of organic grains into edible oils. This is an example of economic innovation and diversification from which a number of other provinces may eventually benefit.

In Manitoba, the fur trade enabled the *voyageurs*, led by people like La Vérendrye, to found the first towns. This Francophone, and later Métis, presence became widely known through the demands of Louis Riel, which raised genuine issues of national interest. Riel's execution was bitterly denounced by the people of Quebec, leading the prime minister, Sir John A. Macdonald, to say that Riel "shall hang though every dog in Quebec bark in his favour!"

Around 1870 the population of Manitoba, at that time covering a very small area, was 50 percent francophone. Today there are still a number of Francophone concentrations, beginning with Saint-Boniface, of course. . . .

In Ontario, a number of towns and villages were also founded by Francophones. In 1912, when Regulation 17 prohibited education in French, the community reacted by established a clandestine French-language school system and founding a newspaper, *Le Droit*, which is still published daily in the Ottawa region. Today the Ontario Francophone community is quite large: half a million people. They have a large primary and secondary school system with about 300 institutions. In September 1990 the first Francophone college opened its doors: *La Cité collégiale.* . . .

Quebec may now ask itself, but where are all these Francophones? Let us acknowledge, first, that provincial boundaries have been extended and the populations substantially swollen. Massive immigration, particularly in the West, has decreased the relative weight of the Francophones. There is also, of course, an assimilation factor that was particularly strong during the periods when Francophone educational institutions were non-existent in some regions.

However, there remains a fundamental fact: there are at present one million Francophones outside Quebec.

One million Francophones is as many, if not more than, the population of six of the ten Canadian provinces. It is 20 percent of the Francophone population of Quebec. It is thousands and thousands of people who will speak for Quebec in the economic, educational and cultural domains. One million Francophones is an essential linguistic outpost for Quebec society.

Has Quebec realized that, beyond the setbacks, the declarations of unilingualism and the assimilation rates, there are still one million Francophones who share many of the cultural resources inherited from the French colonization? Has it realized that, without being forced to do so by sign laws, the whole of the Acadian peninsula in north-eastern New Brunswick advertises only in French? And is it aware that no fewer than 20 percent of the Francophones outside Quebec speak only French? We don't want to be judgmental, but these are simple facts that are often ignored.

We allow ourselves to ask, therefore: Is Quebec aware that a population equivalent to 20 percent of its Francophone community is living daily in French, and that this population has historically demonstrated its desire to continue to develop its own specificity in North America?

The Francophones outside Quebec are an historical reality in Canada going back more than three centuries. We are not, as some claim, a political fiction invented to slow down the development of the Quebec collectivity.

La francophonie is Quebec and it is also us.

B. Evolution of relations: 30 years of history. Before and after the Quiet Revolution: two periods, two types of relationship between Quebec and the Francophones outside Quebec. From *Maîtres chez nous*, which set the tone, to the painful Meech episode, the political confrontations of the last 30 years in Canada have inevitably left their share of scars.

How has *la francophonie* emerged from it all?

1. Before the Quiet Revolution. The historical background we have just sketched would indicate that relations between Quebec and the Francophones outside Quebec were particularly close during the period preceding Quebec's Quiet Revolution. There are a number of reasons for this.

First, the people of Quebec had a much closer feeling of belonging to a French-Canadian nation. Secondly, their government did not make a major issue out of Quebec's political status within the Canadian federation. Finally, Quebecers still thought of themselves generally as a minority in the country, and the fact that economic control was in the hands of the Anglophones was certainly not unrelated to this.

We find, therefore, that the period prior to 1960 is one in which the traditional religious and educational institutions in Quebec were particularly active in the French-speaking communities outside Quebec. We recall, for example, all those Catholic youth organizations that enabled many Quebecers to travel to symposiums across the country.

2. After the Quiet Revolution. The Quiet Revolution is still fresh in our memory. It was an unprecedented act of collective affirmation in which the French-speaking population of Quebec literally liberated itself and took control of its own territory. From now on Quebec would be defined as a society that was shaped, organized and controlled by its Francophone majority. Emerging from *la grande noirceur,* the days of obscurantism, Quebec began to act like a sovereign and independent community affirming itself beyond Canada's borders as America's *nation française.*

From then on the issue of Francophones outside Quebec became more remote: first, we organize ourselves! Quebec plunged into the whirl of events that comes with any *revolution:* institutional reform, the takeover of education and the health care, Trudeaumania, official language policies, the October Crisis, the rise to power of the Parti Québécois, the referendum and, finally, the period of the *beau risque.* It was a full agenda.

Overnight, our communities found themselves confused with those in Quebec. To many Anglophones outside Quebec, a Franco-Albertan was primarily a Quebecer. . . *a Frenchman.* The winds of factionalism and discord in the Quebec referendum reached the Francophones outside Quebec. "Are you French or Canadians?" many Anglophones asked. But the Francophones outside Quebec did not hesitate to recognize Quebec's right to define itself in its own way.

In New Brunswick the first Acadian premier, Louis Robichaud, opened the doors to a new era for Francophones outside Quebec. His government radically transformed the province's social system and in 1968 adopted the first *Official Languages Act* in Canada. The federal government followed suit one year later. Elsewhere in the country, the urbanization of Francophones accelerated and new methods of communication widened many horizons. *La francophonie* turned over a new leaf: it was now more contemporary, more mobile, more *official.*

The Francophones outside Quebec took advantage of the federal government's official languages policy. A political equation gained ground: if a provincial government resists the emancipation of non-Quebec Francophones, so what? The federal government is there, ready to up the ante, to establish the official languages coast to coast. The federal public service opened its creaky doors to *le fait français.* Who, outside Quebec, can fill bilingual positions? Why, the Francophones, of course!

The adoption of the *Canadian Charter of Rights and Freedoms* in 1982 also opened some horizons that historically had been jealously guarded by the provinces. For example, the provinces retained sole jurisdiction to legislate in the field of education, of course, but now there were conditions. Now the official language communities would be entitled to an education in their mother tongue. If the provinces resisted, the courts would decide. And that is what happened, since almost all of the provincial governments found themselves required in the years that followed to justify educational programs that were inappropriate to the needs of their French-speaking minorities. Quebec, for its part, denounced this unacceptable intrusion in a field so vital to it as education.

It was clear that while the interests of Francophone Quebecers now seemed to depend on the National Assembly, the interests of our communities depended directly on the increased power of the central government. Canadian Francophones, albeit despite themselves, found they were prisoners of the established structures.

There was a deep gulf in attitudes, well before Meech Lake.

Looking back, we will probably find that this constitutional *entente* simply reflected the profound uneasiness in the Canadian dynamic. The general population denounced a bargaining process that was completely beyond its control. It wanted to be more directly involved.

Quebec was surprised at the FFHQ's hesitation to support this document, which relaunched the constitutional talks that would probably deal with the situation of the minority-language communities.

But the Francophones outside Quebec had some serious reservations. While Quebec had alluded to direct reforms of the existing Constitution, our communities had to be content with an official recognition stating that, as Francophones, they were "also present elsewhere in Canada".

The Fédération gave its formal support to the agreement in February 1990 during its meeting in Manitoba. We had always recognized the legitimacy of Quebec's five conditions and the way they were incorporated in the Constitution, and the Fédération used its support to issue a public reminder of the importance of remembering the underlying purpose of the 1987 negotiations: to help get Canada out of the impasse in which it was stuck. We recalled that the Meech round was primarily the Quebec round.

The whole episode ended abruptly, and it is evident that the context was not one to promote a rapprochement between Quebec and the rest of the country, including necessarily our communities. **A new departure, as partners.** Quebec now finds itself building a new political relationship of forces. It is quite obvious that the people of Quebec have lost patience with the unwieldiness of the present federal system and, in practice, unanimously reject the status quo.

Our organization adds its voice to those who have already spoken out in favour of a re-ordering of the existing structures. . . .

From the economic standpoint alone, the Canadian provinces have managed to erect increasingly impenetrable barriers between themselves. Some examples that have directly affected the Francophone communities outside Quebec are the restrictions in the realm of services, such as in hiring policies or the refusal to recognize out-of-province diplomas, and the restrictions in communications. In fact, is it any surprise that the degree of economic integration inside Canada itself is less than within the European Economic Community?

For decades, however, Canada has been attempting to standardize the political status of its components, notwithstanding their disparate foundations. The equality of the provinces, for example, has been pushed a long way, a very long way. Similarly, the political structures have encouraged the standardization of policies in support of the official language communities. By trying to approach on the same footing the issues of Francophones outside of Quebec, Anglophones inside Quebec, and the mutual relationships between the Francophone communities, the federal government has certainly left itself little flexibility.

Likewise, the French language may well be the only language that is threatened with extinction in Canada, for obvious geopolitical reasons, but the present system is based on the Quebec-Canada duality, without distinctions.

To be a minority numerically is one thing; to be one politically is another. Obviously, Quebec is a Francophone society that is numerically a minority in Canada and especially in North America, where it represents only 2 percent of the total population. Yet Quebec has put aside the statistics to take control of and build a legitimate place for itself.

While taking advantage of the national policy on official languages, the Francophones outside Quebec have developed a reflex: to demand that the government give them *the right* to social and educational services. The idea has been that the state will protect Francophone culture outside Quebec.

Granting rights is an approach that does yield some results.* But when it is argued that Canada is a country founded on the existence of two major communities, can we limit ourselves to simply granting rights without ever granting genuine responsibilities to all of the members of these two components, no matter where they are located?

This systematic lack of Francophones outside Quebec at the decision-making levels has often obliged them to turn to either level of government. As one would expect, a form of dependency has developed. If something was not working, we had this systematic reflex of demanding, urging and protesting against governments.

Aware of the threatening trap, the Francophone communities recently decided to step back a bit and rethink this approach. We concluded that being Francophone means much more than being claimants, and we decided to put greater emphasis on our accomplishments and our collective potential. . . .

A partnership. In turning toward the future, Quebec must now put its mind to a basic question: does it think it has some interest in maintaining a close relationship with the Francophones outside Quebec?

---

* Section 23 of the Charter is an example of a right that has changed the face of the Francophone school system outside Quebec. Close to 10 years after the enactment of the Charter, and after many legal proceedings, this school system has improved appreciably.

In our opinion, this interest exists on both sides. But we are convinced that, if the relationship is to develop, it must be approached from a new standpoint, *that of a partnership*. The term is used here in its current sense, of a relationship based on the conviction that each party can contribute to the other's development and advance its own development through the relationship. . . .

1. Politically. If Quebec were to conclude, like us, that it has an obvious interest in maintaining a close relationship with our communities, then in our view its government should develop a new political discourse. . . .

The Quebec government's Secretariat for Canadian intergovernmental affairs already administers a program of assistance to Francophone communities, mainly at the administrative and financial level. From this standpoint alone, as we will point out more specifically, the criteria now being used shut out some assistance programs. It would therefore be appropriate to review these criteria. . . .

It should be emphasized, moreover, that the dialogue between our communities and the Quebec government has so far been kept off the public platform. Thus, while the Quebec government bureaucracy and our associations have built some bridges over the years, the elected representatives of the Quebec people have remained relatively excluded from this dialogue. As a result, the print and visual media pay little attention to it and the people of Quebec have few opportunities to learn about our situation.

The real problem is that the Francophone world outside Quebec is not yet an integral part of Quebec's reality. . . . To the degree possible, we should invest substantial efforts in making the concerns of our communities something in which Quebec feels directly involved; but as well, we should make some of the challenges facing Quebec society an exercise in which our communities can get involved.

If a clear need along these lines were to emerge, it would be appropriate for our Francophone associations, the Quebec government and the National Assembly to develop some structures that can respond to this reality. . . .

2. Economically. Our goal is clear: to make French a living language of daily use, and we know for a fact that this includes the economy, which provides the foundations for the development and prosperity of our communities.

With this in mind, we have provided ourselves with some economic tools. A pillar of our economic progress has been the cooperative movement, a form of organization widely used by the community because of the close association between its values and the *mentalité francophone*. The network is already a vast one: *caisses populaires*, worker co-ops, housing co-ops, food co-ops, health co-ops, distribution co-ops for cultural products, and childcare co-ops, fisher, financial, youth services, farm and consumer co-ops, to name only the major ones.

We also have coordination infrastructures in the form of the provincial and Canadian Conseils de coopération. During the last year, three groups of Francophone cooperators, the Fédérations des caisses populaires in Ontario, Manitoba and New Brunswick enroled as cooperative partners in the Mouvement Desjardins. The latter is recognized as a leader in Francophone solidarity across the entire country. Its leaders have always been motivated by a willingness to secure the prosperity of Francophones and make French a language of decision-making and the economy. . . .

It is also obvious that the partnership can be greatly expanded with regard to private firms. In the first place, for Quebecers we are a direct market of one million Francophones. Our linguistic and cultural needs are immense. In education alone, Francophones outside Quebec have invested tens of millions of dollars in recent years in the purchase of academic supplies from Quebec. This is an opportunity for Quebec entrepreneurs to do business in French beyond their borders and help break into the Anglophone market.

The same logic obviously applies to Francophones outside Quebec, in relation to the Quebec market. . . .

3. Education. At present Francophones outside Quebec can get a university education in French in New Brunswick, Nova Scotia, Ontario, Manitoba, Saskatchewan and Alberta. Needless to say, however, in some places the options are limited.

In our view, it is essential to establish a network of structured administrative and pedagogical exchanges between those involved at the elementary and secondary levels. This is especially relevant in that, during the last 10 years or so, a substantial number of French-language educational programs have been developed in our communities.

In this vein, it is important, we think, that Quebec adopt a clear political stance in favour of the right of Francophones to manage and control their own elementary and secondary educational institutions *through independent school boards.*

We note that in this respect as well there are precedents for Quebec collaboration with the Francophones outside Quebec. The advantages will become more obvious now that we can anticipate the formation of new French-language school boards in our communities in the wake of a recent judgment of the Supreme Court of Canada.*

At the French-language post-secondary level, many areas of specialization (such as architecture) or some that require enormous resources (such as medicine) remain closed to the Francophones outside Quebec. There are now agreements between Quebec and some provincial governments. We think it is essential that the Francophones outside Quebec be directly involved in this process.

For Quebecers, we offer access to programs that are likewise highly specialized. For example, the University of Moncton in New Brunswick and the University of Ottawa in Ontario provide courses in the common law in French that point to markets still relatively undeveloped by Quebec.

4. Literacy. In the struggle against illiteracy, the Francophone community outside Quebec is establishing a federation that will combine its associations with those of Quebec. Similar collaboration exists in the adult education field. . . .

5. Recreation and tourism. This is a socio-economic sector that deserves to be explored further. A major proportion of Francophones outside Quebec live in areas bordering Quebec. Yet these places, in Ontario and the Maritimes, remain largely unknown to Quebecers. They have much to offer, without the necessity of long trips. And, above all, many can be explored in French. . . .

6. Culture. For many years now the Francophones outside Quebec have penetrated the Quebec artistic market. The most recent ADISQ gala awarded Félixes to, among others, Daniel Lavoie, a Franco-Manitoban, and Roch Voisine, a native of New Brunswick, for their contribution to Francophone music. To artists like these, Quebec is much more than a market; it is an essential springboard for their careers.

However, there are many Francophone artists outside Quebec for whom Quebec and its training programs are relatively inaccessible. Yet, as many examples show, the artists in our communities open

---

* In the *Mahé* case, from Alberta, the Supreme Court ruled that section 23 of the Charter grants Francophone communities the right to manage and control their own school system. Since then, a number of governments (Manitoba, Saskatchewan and British Columbia) have established task forces to propose Francophone school systems. The communities in New Brunswick, P.E.I., Ontario and Yukon already have such school boards.

many horizons in Quebec and contribute a unique perspective to Francophone art in America. . . .

7. *Communications*. The significant growth of communications technology in recent years has been of great benefit to all of our communities and *la francophonie* in general. The TV-5 television chain, for example, is now distributed in more than one million homes outside Quebec. Our Fédération has already made many attempts to make such channels as *Canal famille*, *Musique plus*, *Le réseau des sports* and TV-5 accessible to more Francophones outside Quebec. . . .

Report of the Commission
on the
Political and Constitutional
Future of Quebec*

Introduction

Redefining the arrangements governing the organization and the
political relations of a society, a people or a nation is a quintes-
sentially political process. It is the firm belief of Commission
members that a clear expression of the will of the Quebec people
is the foundation of this political process.

The problems engendered by political relations between Quebec
and the rest of Canada are not new. Their sources can be found in
the past. The Royal Commission on Bilingualism and Biculturalism
(Laurendeau-Dunton Commission, 1963) and the Task force on
Canadian Unity (Pépin-Robarts Commission, 1978) focused on a
number of their causes and proposed solutions. Essentially, these
complex problems concern the political and constitutional expression of the relations between two linguistic groups, two majorities.
One province among 10, Quebec, holds the francophone majority.
The problems have been exacerbated by 25 years of constitutional

---

* The following is the whole of the Report with the exception of
chapters 1 (list of members of the Commission) and 2 (the Commission's mandate), and the various Addenda by individual members of
the Commission. Much of the omitted material is covered in the
Editor's Introduction or elsewhere in this book. The text follows the
official English translation of the Report as released by the Commission, with a few slight adjustments where necessary to ensure clarity
and conformity with the original French. — Ed.

debates which, for Quebec, have proven fruitless, by major constitutional changes which occurred in 1982 and to which Quebec did
not adhere, and by the decisive failure, in June 1990, of the 1987
Agreement on the Constitution.

In the wake of a quarter century of futile efforts, the Quebec
National Assembly has unanimously recognized that, at this point in
Quebec's history and development under the Canadian federal
regime, Quebec must redefine its political and constitutional status.
Why? How and to what extent must Quebec's political and constitutional status be redefined? These are the pivotal questions underlying the Commission's mandate and to which it will endeavour to
respond.

Let us turn briefly to various facets of the circumstances surrounding the redefinition of the political and constitutional status
of Quebec.

The world over, barriers to economic exchanges are toppling one
by one. Freer world trade has also led to the development of more
and more complete free-trade zones in Europe and America.

Any society seeking growth must belong to an economy which
extends well beyond national boundaries and participate fully in the
globalization of markets. The sweeping liberalization of trade has
encouraged states to associate more closely in order to open their
borders to trade and jointly seek development and economic
prosperity.

Quebec is no exception and is participating fully in this trend, as
witnessed by its broad-based support for the Canada-U.S. Free Trade
Agreement. Many Quebecers have taken up the challenge of
opening up their economy.

In redefining its political and constitutional status, Quebec is not
seeking to call into question the commitments as well as the
economic and financial ties it has established with foreign countries
or the rest of Canada, or to create barriers to the free movement of
persons, goods, services and capital within the Canadian economy.
The Commission noted a very firm consensus in this respect among
the various public and private parties who participated in its
deliberations, a consensus shared by all of the commissioners. The
interest and well-being of everyone concerned, in Quebec and
elsewhere in Canada, would benefit from maintaining the advantages ensuing from this freedom of movement. For either side to
relinquish the pursuit of such convergent interests would likely
engender economic damage that neither Quebec nor its Canadian
partners could risk incurring, no more than others elsewhere in the
world could.

In fact, discussions on the political and constitutional future of Quebec focus more on the existing political and constitutional arrangements governing Quebec's status and its relations with the other members of the federation.

Since 1867, Quebec has been a province within a federal State made up of 10 provinces and two territories. The federal structure, the arrangement of powers and the division of legislative and executive jurisdictions between the two levels of government have been set out in the Canadian constitutional texts and in other sources of constitutional law. From Quebec's standpoint, the Canadian federal regime was based at the outset on the Canadian duality and the autonomy of the provinces.

This Canadian duality, based on relations between French Canadians and English Canadians, is perceived as an underlying principle of the federal regime. The federal union is seen as a pact between these two peoples which may only be altered with the consent of these two parties.

As for the autonomy of the provinces, it rests on the exclusivity of the fields of legislative powers granted in 1867. Given its constant concern to maintain the autonomy of the National Assembly, Quebec has always denounced federal intervention and encroachment in its fields of exclusive jurisdiction. As the trend toward centralization grew, tension and conflict became inevitable.

The 1960s saw Quebec take charge of its development and affirm its uniqueness. Since then, Quebec has demanded the political and legal recognition of a special status and a far-reaching review of constitutional arrangements under the federation, especially with regard to the sharing of jurisdictions.

Quebec: A modern society, a distinct identity

With its 6.7 million inhabitants on an English-speaking continent of 275 million inhabitants, Quebec is the only political entity in North America in which a French-speaking majority enjoys autonomous democratic institutions. French is the language usually spoken or used most frequently in the home of 83 percent of Quebecers; English is used by 12 percent of the population, and the remaining 5 percent speak other languages.

Elsewhere in Canada, French is used by 4 percent of the population, English by 89 percent. If Quebec is included, French is used by 24 percent of Canadians, and English, by 69 percent. Today, nearly 90 percent of French-speaking Canadians live in Quebec.

Quebecers are aware that they form a distinct national collectivity: the language of the majority of Quebecers and their culture, which are in a minority situation in Canada, are unique across the continent. In their own way, Quebecers have always expressed the need to be masters of their own destiny. The 1960s marked a turning point in Quebec society's assumption of its own development. Quebecers' perception of themselves has changed, especially among the French-speaking majority. Before, French-speaking Quebecers were more inclined to see themselves as French Canadians and a minority. Now, they see themselves first and foremost as Quebecers and are acting more and more like a majority within their territory.

During this period, Quebec charted the course necessary to ensure the emergence of a modern, complete society open to the world. Various aspirations, a special national identity and specific needs found political expression and were reflected concretely in sweeping reforms in all spheres of activity, be they political, economic, social, cultural or educational.

The Quebec Government acted as a driving force and rallying point for the reconquering of political, linguistic and economic levers. Following the celebrated "Désormais. . ." uttered by Quebec Premier Paul Sauvé,* which set in motion the necessary reforms, the process gained momentum under the Lesage government in 1962 with the acquisition, through a public takeover, of the main electric utilities. The slogan "Maîtres chez nous" was launched. Created in 1944, Hydro-Québec was to play a key role in the economy. This initiative marked the beginning of a period during which the Government played an entrepreneurial role; many government corporations were set up and given mandates pertaining to economic development. Quebec set up the Quebec Pension Plan, a universal scheme whose funds are entrusted to the Caisse de dépôt et placement du Québec, which profitably managed them, while fostering Quebec's economic growth. All of these institutions gave French-speaking Quebecers access to senior management positions and hastened the emergence of a French-language business class which today plays an important role in the economy.

At the same time, major reforms were implemented in the public sector, e.g. government and administration, culture, education,

---

* "From now on...". Immediately after his appointment as Premier following the death of Maurice Duplessis, in 1959, Sauvé announced a series of political reforms, each preceded by this expression. — Ed.

health and social services, municipal affairs, economic and regional development. In its own fields of jurisdiction, Quebec confirmed its presence abroad, established a network of foreign delegations, engaged in exchanges and concluded agreements. Since the late 1960s and more recently, it has bolstered its international presence by participating in the institutions and activities of the French-speaking world.

This period of accelerated development, during which Quebec set up institutions and adopted public policies of its own, also fostered the emergence of a new vitality, a spirit of innovation, enterprise and openness to the world, still hallmarks of Quebec society. Today, its economic vigour hinges on the competitiveness of private sector firms. The Quebec government adopts or encourages policies which facilitate the adaptation of the economy to the demands of the globalization of markets. One striking example is its support for Canada-U.S. free trade.

Quebecers display a more deeply rooted desire to be, to affirm themselves and to live in French throughout Quebec and in all spheres of social activity. French has always been the language of the majority and its status is confirmed as the official language. The place of French in communications, the workplace, commerce and business is also reaffirmed and broadened.

This period, during which French-speaking Quebecers have acquired a new perception of themselves, shifting from that of a minority to that of a majority, also shows that they more strongly identify with Quebec political institutions when pursuing their economic, social and cultural development.

Ensuring the quality and influence of French, clearly a minority language in Canada and on the continent, challenges Quebecers to be equitable, open and just in two respects: first to English-speaking Quebecers, who historically are part of Quebec's reality, and toward the French-speaking population, whose efforts to protect and promote their language are legitimate. Both minorities are seeking to forge, between them, mutually respectful relations. The matter of the language used in public signs and commercial advertising largely coloured discussions concerning these relations. This question needs to be considered in its context, that of external signs and business advertising, and should not obscure the fact that individual and social activities, including commercial activities, are carried out in either language in Quebec.

The English-speaking community is tightly integrated by its institutions and the scope of its activities in the public and private domains. Its important contribution to the development of Quebec society is reflected in all spheres of activity, e.g. economy and finance, primary and secondary schools, colleges and universities, hospitals, the media, museums, architecture and so on. In the preamble of the legislation establishing the Commission, the National Assembly confirms the importance of respecting this community's rights and institutions.

Quebec society is also participating in the major currents of 20th century political thought. It displays a deep attachment to the basic values shared by modern, free, democratic societies. The parliamentary system, the functioning of political parties and the regulation of party financing, the *Election Act* and the *Referendum Act*, and procedures respecting representation in municipal governments and school boards reflect this attachment to democratic values and the guarantee of respect for such values. The May 1980 referendum, the campaign preceding it and its outcome all confirm the prominence accorded to the exercise of and respect for democracy in Quebec.

Moreover, Quebec shares with other free, democratic societies a commitment to protecting and promoting the enjoyment and free exercise of basic human rights and freedoms within its territory. The Quebec *Charter of Human Rights and Freedoms*, adopted in 1975 by the National Assembly, ensures recognition of and respect for basic human rights and freedoms, and guarantees the free exercise of such rights and freedoms in private relations as well as in relations between individuals and the State. Unless expressly stipulated, the guarantees enshrined in the Charter take precedence over all Quebec legislation and regulations. The Quebec Charter is among the most complete charters of human rights and freedoms adopted to date. It is the main means by which Quebec seeks to develop a pluralist society which respects differences.

The search for genuine equality between Quebec women and men is one of the fundamental values and objectives found in the Quebec Charter. A number of Quebec women stress that the desire for equality between men and women is one of the distinctive traits of the Quebec identity. Recent constitutional debates gave women an opportunity to stress this viewpoint and to apprise other Canadians of it.

As is the case in other Western societies, Quebec's population has diversified in recent decades: the guarantees of democracy, equality and freedom that it offers underpin the relations which are established between each newcomer and Quebec society. Full participation by Quebecers from all cultural communities and their contribution to Quebec's development are essential. They enrich Quebec society in a unique manner.

In the legislation which established the Commission, the National Assembly reaffirmed that Quebec recognizes the right of the Amerinds and the Inuit to preserve and develop their specific character and to assure the progress of their communities. The principles underlying Quebec's policy with respect to aboriginal issues were set out for the first time in a Cabinet Decision adopted on February 9, 1983, then in a Resolution of the National Assembly, adopted on March 20, 1985. During a Constitutional conference held on March 13, 1987, in Ottawa, Quebec reaffirmed that it favoured self-government for the aboriginal people. In Quebec, the Amerind population is made up of some 52,000 people belonging to 14 nations; there are roughly 6,200 Inuit. Regardless of Quebec's future political and constitutional course, agreements must be sought between the Quebec government and Quebec's Amerinds and Inuit.

Today, Quebec has all the attributes and characteristics of a modern, free and democratic, pluralist society open to the world. Through consensus and collective effort, it has developed a dynamic culture which animates its political, economic and social life. Recent history has witnessed the consolidation, marked by continuity, of a national identity in Quebec which has confirmed itself in all spheres of activity.

Moreover, Quebec society is an integral part of the major commercial and financial trends prevailing in North America and the world. It has developed special economic ties with the rest of Canada.

Starting in 1867, political leaders at the time sought to create an economic area which would consolidate the ties between the four former colonies. A protectionist trade policy and the development of east-west communication lines bolstered the initial economic area and spurred its subsequent expansion toward the West. Another factor which contributed to the development of these ties was the attribution to the federal Parliament, by the 1867 Constitution, of broad powers in economic areas such as currency, banks, interest rates and interprovincial trade.

Today, the Canadian economy encompasses over 26 million inhabitants; persons, goods, services and capital move freely in it. Corporations, individuals, institutions and all of the provincial governments, especially those of Quebec and Ontario, have established over the years a multitude of contracts, financial commitments as well as human and business relations.

The sharing of the same citizenship, a number of guarantees enshrined in the *Canadian Charter of Rights and Freedoms*, and the portability of entitlement to federal and provincial social programs facilitate the free movement of persons, who may settle and work wherever they wish, despite the existence of some barriers. The cost of integrating into a community of a different language undoubtedly curtails among French-speaking people wishing to move to other parts of Canada the complete enjoyment of this freedom of movement.

Available trade statistics reveal that Quebec sells 20 percent of its output to the rest of Canada, by and large the same proportion, on average, as that of all the regions of Canada , i.e. 17.5 percent. The markets of certain provinces are important to Quebec: 35 percent of its overall exports are shipped to Ontario, and 10 percent to the Atlantic Provinces. The opposite is also true: Quebec buys 20 percent of the goods and services Ontario exports and 24 percent of the goods and services exported by the Atlantic Provinces. In 1984, Ontario sold over 21 billion dollars worth of goods and services in Quebec, resulting in a trade surplus of over 3 billion dollars.*

However, foreign markets, especially the United States, have in recent years become increasingly important to Quebec. The proportion of Quebec's output sold on these markets rose from 9 percent in 1974 to nearly 15 percent in 1984. This shift in export markets reflects the trend toward the globalization of markets, and it should become more pronounced under the Canada-U.S. Free Trade Agreement. It also emphasizes the extent to which, in Canada as elsewhere, economic and political boundaries coincide less and less.

Other phenomena are indicative of the close ties between Quebec and the other provinces, e.g. the volume of air traffic between Montreal and Toronto or the extent of the interprovincial oper- ations of Canadian companies. Because any firm established in Canada can set up business, buy, sell and obtain financing wherever it wishes, many companies operating in Quebec also maintain branches elsewhere in Canada. Interprovincial dealings are especial- ly strong between financial institutions, which channel savings to private and public sector borrowers across Canada.

---

* Statistics Canada, Input-Output Division.

Toward the stalemate

In Quebec, as elsewhere in Canada, political visions and national aspirations and identities have emerged, on both sides, in a more striking manner over the past 30 years. The failure of the 1987 Agreement on the Constitution, which occurred on June 23, 1990, takes all its meaning in light of this evolution. This failure indicates that it is becoming increasingly difficult to reconcile these identities, aspirations and political visions within the constitutional framework of the Canadian federation.

1960-1985

The major reforms implemented in Quebec during the 1960s showed how important it was to review the division of powers, which changes in the federal regime had made problematical, and the financial resources of the federal and provincial governments. Quebec wanted to preserve and restore its autonomy in its fields of exclusive jurisdiction and, in a number of sectors, enjoy broader autonomy to ensure the development of Quebec society. In this respect, it affirmed itself as a distinct society and demanded recognition of its special status, aspirations and needs.

It was therefore necessary to specify new areas of jurisdiction which were not attributed in 1867 and halt overlapping and federal interference in sectors which Quebec deemed vital. Requests for discussions and review put forward by successive Quebec governments focused primarily on education, higher education, income security, health, taxation, regional development, language, culture, international relations, communications, the environment, immigration as well as federal spending power, and auxiliary, declaratory, residual and disallowance powers.

The constitutional discussions launched in 1968, mainly at the insistence of Quebec, showed that the concerns of the other governments in the realm of constitutional reform did not generally coincide with the issues that Quebec thought of as priorities. As for the division of powers, the constitutional conferences held since 1968 have not satisfied Quebec's requests.

On the eve of the May 1980 Referendum, when the Parti québécois government submitted to the public its proposal respecting sovereignty-association and the federal regime was called into question in Quebec, the then Prime Minister of Canada promised Quebecers that Canadian federalism would be renewed. Two years later, the other provinces and Ottawa introduced major additions and amendments into the Canadian political and constitutional order by proclaiming the *Constitution Act, 1982*, ignoring Quebec's traditional requests.

Pursuant to a political agreement reached in November 1981 between the federal government and the provincial governments, excluding that of Quebec, a charter of rights and freedoms was enshrined in the Canadian Constitution, along with language educational rights. These modifications imposed new constraints on the exercise of Quebec's legislative powers. With respect to language of education, Quebec's jurisdiction was curtailed.

The changes adopted in 1982 also repatriated from the British Parliament the power to amend Canadian constitutional documents through the enshrinement of an amending formula. Under such procedure, constitutional amendments likely to derogate from Quebec's interests could be contemplated without Quebec's consent being required. Moreover, the right to compensation associated with the exercise of the right to opt-out, should provincial powers be transferred to the federal Parliament, only applied in the fields of education and culture.

The *Constitution Act, 1982*, also constitutionalized the principle of the preservation and enhancement of the multicultural heritage of Canadians, thus imposing on Quebec a constitutional viewpoint which did not necessarily coincide with its reality within Canada: the latter was defined as a multicultural society, without constitutional recognition of the principle of "Canadian duality" and of Quebec's distinctiveness. The multicultural Canadian society, being predominantly English speaking, can easily become indifferent to Quebec's distinct identity and its unique linguistic and cultural position in Canada.

The federal government also agreed to include in the 1982 Act various provisions concerning regional disparities as well as jurisdiction over and taxation powers related to non-renewable natural resources, forestry resources and electricity, in response to specific requests from other provinces.

Thus, the 1982 Act introduced into the political and constitutional order of the federal regime a number of basic changes which curtailed Quebec's powers and derogated from its vital interests, without the Quebec National Assembly's consent and despite its opposition. Above all, the 1982 Act reflects the concerns and national priorities of the federal and other provincial governments. Far from revising the *Constitution Act, 1967*, the 1982 Act contains a new constitutional definition of Canada which has altered the spirit of the 1867 Act and the compromise established at that time. The original Constitution was based by and large on British constitutional principles and traditions, centred primarily on the supremacy of Parliament. In 1982, however, the Canadian Constitution drew closer to the American political culture, which tends to resolve major socio-political issues before the courts. Moreover, from a Constitution based on a political compromise which earned the support of representatives of the French Canadians in 1867, Canada shifted in 1982 to a Constitution adopted despite the opposition of a province where nearly 90 percent of French-speaking Canadians live and which accounts for over one-quarter of Canada's population.

While, in strictly legal terms, the 1982 Act applies in Quebec, it is void of political legitimacy as it has never received Quebec's full and free support. It should be recalled that, in October 1981, the Quebec National Assembly almost unanimously repudiated the federal government's proposed unilateral repatriation of the Constitution. It subsequently expressed its opposition to the agreement concluded in November 1981, in Quebec's absence, by Ottawa and the nine provincial governments, which led to the adoption of the 1982 constitutional changes. On September 4, 1990, the National Assembly unanimously reiterated its refusal to endorse these changes in the preamble of the legislation establishing the Commission. The absence of constitutional stability and the attendant uncertainty have persisted for nearly 10 years.

1985-1990

When it came to power in 1985, the new Quebec government set as its constitutional priority the conclusion of an agreement, with the governments of Canada and of the nine provinces, on the terms under which Quebec would adhere to the *Constitution Act, 1982*. It was a matter of seeking to reestablish the legitimacy of Canada's constitutional framework, to which all of the people governed by it must be able to subscribe. To this end, the Quebec government announced five conditions for its adhesion:

- explicit constitutional recognition of Quebec as a distinct society;
- constitutional guarantee of broader powers in the field of immigration;
- the limitation of federal spending power with respect to programs falling under Quebec's exclusive jurisdiction;
- changes in the constitutional amending procedure enshrined in the 1982 Act;
- Quebec's participation in appointing judges from Quebec to sit on the Supreme Court of Canada.

In the course of these constitutional deliberations, the approach emphasized, understood and publicly accepted by all governments concerned was to give priority to politically reintegrating Quebec into the Canadian constitutional order, which could have been made possible by a correction of the shortcomings inherent in the 1982 Act. Quebec's reintegrating the constitutional order was an essential prerequisite to any discussion of other constitutional issues. Quebec postponed discussing other matters of concern to it until later constitutional meetings.

The 1987 Agreement on the Constitution reflected the terms of the Meech Lake accord between Quebec, the federal government and the governments of the nine other provinces with respect to the five conditions set forth by Quebec. Despite unanimous agreement among the 11 governments, the accord was not ratified by a sufficient number of provincial legislatures to be proclaimed and come into force. It was not favourably received in general by Canadians outside Quebec. Yet, it was the first response ever given by the rest of Canada to constitutional initiatives launched 20 years earlier by Quebec. Its failure, following three years of public debate, raised the issue of the political and constitutional future of Quebec.

This setback and the ensuing stalemate have been spawned by unresolved political problems, exacerbated by social and political change in Quebec and elsewhere in Canada. The inflexibility of the constitutional amending formula and the political situation in Canada between 1987 and 1990 have only added to these problems. Public debates surrounding the 1987 Agreement on the Constitution have shown that it is becoming increasingly difficult to reconcile the various political visions, national identities and aspirations inherent in the Canadian federal regime.

These conflicts have increasingly fettered Quebec since the 1982 Act was adopted, as revealed by the failure of the 1987 Agreement. Were it not for these deeply rooted conflicts, the 1987 Agreement would have been accepted in the rest of Canada and ratified by all governments.

The *Constitution Act, 1982* and the principles it enshrines have indeed engendered a hitherto unknown political cohesiveness in Canada. It helped bolster certain political visions of the federation and the perception of a national Canadian identity which are hard to reconcile with the effective recognition and political expression of Quebec's distinct identity. The following principles reflect these political visions and this perception:

The equality of Canadian citizens from coast to coast and the uniqueness of the society in which they live.

This political vision, based on the *Canadian Charter of Rights and Freedoms* enshrined in the 1982 Act, perceives equality as having a strictly individual scope and applying uniformly across Canada: it does not make allowance for Quebec society to receive special constitutional recognition. The notion of a distinct Quebec society is thus understood as being a source of inequality and incompatible with the principle of equality of all Canadian citizens.

The equality of cultures and cultural origins in Canada.

This vision derives from the principle of multiculturalism, enshrined in the Canadian Charter, which promotes the objective of preserving and enhancing the multicultural heritage of Canadians. To many, the French language and French cultural origins are included among the numerous languages of origin and cultures which make up Canada's multicultural heritage. They are on the same footing with the other languages of origin and cultures and thus do not require special recognition or guarantees in the Canadian Constitution. Many Canadians feel that the notion of "linguistic duality" and of "two founding nations" do not reflect what they perceive to be the Canadian reality in which they recognize themselves.

The equality of the 10 provinces.

This notion has become one of the predominant political principles in Canada. It has been confirmed, to some extent, by the amending procedure enshrined in the *Constitution Act, 1982*, more precisely in the rule of unanimity and the so-called "7-50%" rule, which generally applies, with some exceptions. A constitutional amendment subject to the second rule requires the approval of two-thirds of the provinces representing together at least 50 percent of the population of Canada.

Pursuant to this principle of equality of the provinces, any constitutional change, prerogative or power obtained by Quebec must also be granted to the other nine provinces. Strict application of this principle has prevented Quebec from obtaining a special status.

Consequently, the principle of equality of the provinces implies uniformly decentralizing to all provinces any power or prerogative granted to Quebec, to which proponents of a strong central government object as they see in such decentralization a weakening of the federal government.

Given the combined effect of the principle of equality of the provinces and of the views which favour the centralization of powers in the hands of a single "national" government, it is hard to meet Quebec's needs and make room in the Canadian Constitution for the political expression of Quebec's uniqueness within the federation.

The vision of an exclusive national Canadian identity emphasizes the centralization of powers and the existence of a strong "national" government. This vision appears to have a levelling effect: an exclusive national Canadian identity centred on the equality of individuals actually becomes a prohibition for Quebec to be different as a society. It also overlooks the actual inequality, within Canada, of both linguistic majorities and their respective members.

Another reality has markedly altered the Canadian political context since 1982. A number of groups were given a voice with respect to constitutional matters during discussions leading to the *Constitution Act, 1982*. They now intend to be an integral part of any constitutional debate. This is, by and large, the case of women's groups, groups defending multiculturalism and, to a different degree, aboriginal groups. Various representatives of these groups strongly objected to the juxtaposition in the Canadian Constitution of visions or principles found in the 1987 Agreement which they deemed to compete or directly conflict with those which they succeeded in having included in the 1982 Act.

Moreover, all changes to the Canadian Constitution that Quebec might seek in the future would legally be subject to the amending formula adopted in 1982. To come into force, such changes would have to be ratified by the requisite number of provincial legislatures and the federal Parliament; the Senate enjoys a suspensive veto.

The constitutional amending formula adopted in 1982 makes it hard to contemplate any modification requiring the unanimous consent of the provincial legislatures. Unanimity is also required to alter the amending formula itself. Moreover, it is not unthinkable that constitutional changes be adopted without Quebec's consent. As it is the procedure adopted in 1982 which prevails, Quebec is not protected from possible changes which could jeopardize its interests.

In 1982, the Canadian constitutional order made possible the adoption of major constitutional changes in Quebec's absence and despite its opposition. Pursuant to the new rules adopted by the other provinces, a single province could, in 1990, prevent an amendment to the constitution of Canada intended to enable Quebec to regain its place in the federation. This new constitutional order, implemented in a manner unfair to Quebec in 1982, includes new rules whose application, in 1990, merely reinforced this lack of equity.

Furthermore, Quebec alone would be unable to prevent certain modifications which could be introduced under the general amending formula (7-50%) and which would affect its fundamental interests. Because unanimous consent would be required to grant Quebec a veto respecting amendments of this nature, any single province could prevent such a move.

The failure of the 1987 Agreement revealed the extreme inflexibility of the amending formula pertaining to the Canadian Constitution. It also showed to what extent the 1982 Act and the political visions prevailing elsewhere in Canada make it hard to obtain constitutional changes which would recognize Quebec's uniqueness and satisfy its particular needs.

Conflicting visions, aspirations and national identities.

In the course of discussions surrounding the 1987 Agreement, it was often said that Quebec's distinct character was obvious. Nonetheless, by virtue of one or another principle and vision evoked earlier, any political expression or significant recognition of this distinctiveness in the Constitution of Canada was rejected.

The conflict of visions, identities and political objectives revealed by the reactions to the 1987 Agreement is serious and restrictive for the future. It is not the prerogative of the Canadian political elite: ordinary Canadians across the country opposed the 1987 Agreement, except in Quebec.

The stalemate touches upon issues relating to national identities, which enable many people to define themselves and understand their participation as well as that of others in Canadian life.

The political principles and visions prevailing in Canadian politics could prevent Quebec from obtaining a constitutional arrangement which would satisfy its needs and aspirations within the federal system, for want of a fundamental change in its partners' attitudes toward it. Thus, it would appear that it is the ability to change that must be assessed.

After 25 years of constitutional debate, two federal commissions of inquiry, the major constitutional changes adopted in 1982 without Quebec's consent and finally the failure of a constitutional process which, for the first time, broached the political dimension of the Quebec problem from Quebec's standpoint, it is reasonable to ask, at the very least, whether the rest of Canada is capable of making choices which fully satisfy Quebec's own needs, aspirations and visions. Until now, such choices have been perceived or treated as being irreconcilable with other needs, aspirations and visions in Canada, or incompatible with the efficient operation of the Canadian federation.

The cost of the stalemate

The current stalemate is a source of instability and has economic, political and social repercussions which Quebec and Canada cannot endure indefinitely. This is one of the main messages which many Quebecers presented to the Commission.

Indeed, under the present political and constitutional regime, one province with over one-quarter of Canada's population does not adhere to the constitutional arrangements governing the federal regime of which it is a part, because these arrangements do not satisfy its needs. Allowing this situation to persist would be in itself a factor contributing to instability.

As far as the economy is concerned, political uncertainty may delay or modify investment projects and encourage lenders to impose higher interest rates on federal and provincial public debt. Indications to this effect have already appeared.

Moreover, globalization of trade imposes stiffer competition on the economy of countries like that of Canada which has heavy public debt and has recorded limited growth in productivity. These trends must be reversed if we are to create numerous and well paid jobs. Constitutional discussions over the past 25 years and, in particular, the current stalemate, are seriously hindering the ability to adopt the appropriate remedial measures as these debates are drawing widespread attention and draining the energies of politicians and governments. On the other hand, various representatives of organizations of the economic milieu pointed out to the Commission that it will be hard to put Canada's public finances in order as long as there persists a lack of precision in the division of powers as well as joint, inefficient federal and provincial government intervention in several fields of activity.

Constitutional problems and the attendant uncertainty also have political and social repercussions. In Quebec and elsewhere in Canada, public opinion is becoming increasingly polarized. The longer we wait to resolve these differences, the greater the social costs are likely to be and the harder it will be to find satisfactory solutions for everyone. Ongoing political conflicts are undermining the quality of relations between populations, as well as their ability and willingness to define and implement mutually satisfactory arrangements. Such conflicts also risk jeopardizing confidence in political leaders who fail to find grounds for agreement.

The Commission has noted the high expectations of the people of Quebec and their willingness to change. Many of them appearing before the Commission stressed the need to find durable solutions to Quebec's political and constitutional problems. The serenity in which the constitutional debate is now taking place is remarkable and it proves Quebecers' attachment to their values, democracy and social peace. Clearly, satisfactory solutions will have to be found soon.

Seeking solutions

Accepting the existing Canadian constitutional framework without modifications offers neither a solution to the current stalemate nor a valid option for Quebec. The legal and political order under the current federal regime fails to satisfy the demands for constitutional reform that Quebec has expressed over the past 25 years. The special needs and legitimate aspirations of Quebec society must normally be reflected in the fundamental law which governs it; Quebec society must be able to recognize itself therein and subscribe freely to it. Moreover, accepting the constitutional framework as it stands would mean that Quebec accepts and considers legitimate the *Constitution Act, 1982*. Quebec cannot adhere to this Act, failing major changes to the Constitution, without relinquishing at the same time the levers and guarantees it needs to protect and promote its identify and fundamental interests.

The vast majority of briefs received and testimony heard by the Commission emphasizes the unacceptable nature of the current constitutional arrangements and stresses the need to thoroughly alter the legal framework which establishes Quebec's powers and responsibilities, its political status and ties with the federal government and the provinces.

To break the stalemate and redefine its political and constitutional status, Quebec has only two choices. Under the first, Quebec would seek acceptance of the redefinition of its status within the constitutional framework of the Canadian federation. Such a course of action presupposes that its integration in the Canadian political system be maintained, but significantly modified. The second solution would entail Quebec's withdrawing from the constitutional framework of the Canadian federation, with or without the consent of the rest of Canada, with a view to acceding to full political sovereignty and becoming a State independent of the Canadian State, open to the establishment of economic ties with the latter.

The foregoing solutions are hardly new on the political scene, both in Quebec and Canada. In recent decades, the main political parties and successive Quebec governments have all sought to provide Quebec with the means of taking charge of its economic, social and cultural development. During this period, various Quebec proposals concerning political relations between Quebec and the rest of Canada have been formulated. All of them have focused essentially on either a thorough reworking of the federal regime of 1867, or the accession of Quebec to the status of independent State, combined with more or less formal economic ties with the rest of Canada.

A new attempt to redefine Quebec's status within the Canadian federal regime

The first solution would involve Quebec's seeking once again to obtain major changes within the federal constitutional framework. The outcome of such a course is uncertain: it depends on the political will of the federal government, the other provincial governments and other Canadians. Political and constitutional change in recent decades has shown that Quebec's conception of Canada and the federal system does not generally suit Canadians in the other provinces and territories as well as a number of their elected representatives. The proposal for new arrangements between Quebec and the rest of Canada is, perforce, contingent upon this situation.

A better understanding of what is at stake and a change in perceptions and attitudes with regard to Quebec's identity and place in Canada might make possible certain constitutional changes which are mutually satisfactory in areas of common interest and which respect differences.

Federalism, as a principle of political organization, is characterized by the flexibility of the arrangements and structures it makes possible. This is evidenced by the wide array of States with a federal constitution, e.g. the United States, Australia, Germany, Switzerland and Belgium, whose constitutional arrangements are markedly different. The Canadian federation is but one case of the application of federalism, numerous variations of which may exist. Between 1867 and the early part of this century, Canadian federalism changed a great deal, generally to the satisfaction of the parties concerned. Theoretically, the Canadian federal union could have continued to change in constitutional and political terms while respecting both the aspirations of Quebecers and those of other Canadians. In practice, the overall conception of Canada and the federal regime which now predominates seems rigid and clearly oriented towards the quest for uniformity and the negation of differences. Renewing the Canadian federation, while acknowledging and respecting Quebec's differences and needs, unequivocally means a thorough calling into question of the order of things in Canada.

The groups and individuals who commented on this solution indicated to the Commission the constitutional changes which they felt were necessary to redefine the political status and powers of Quebec. These changes vary in nature but have in common, among other things:

- the necessity of creating a new relationship between Quebec and the rest of Canada, based on the recognition of and respect for the identity of Quebecers and their right to be different;
- a division of powers and responsibilities which assures Quebec of exclusive authority over those matters and domains which already fall under its exclusive jurisdiction, which means among other things eliminating in these domains federal spending power and overlapping interventions;
- the exclusive attribution to Quebec of powers and responsibilities related to its social, economic and cultural development as well as to language;
- the transfer of tax and financial resources related to the powers and responsibilities which Quebec exercises;
- the maintenance of a Quebec representation in common institutions which fully reflects its particular situation in Canada;
- the guarantee that Quebec's consent be required with respect to any constitutional modification. However, it has been proposed that, where applicable, Quebec enjoy the right to opt out of a transfer of a jurisdiction to the federal government, with reasonable compensation. Such right to withdraw with compensation would replace the right to a veto in such instances.

It was also suggested that the right to withdraw from the federation be enshrined in the Constitution. Similarly, it was proposed that a specific jurisdiction be attributed to Quebec in matters of international relations, extending its internal jurisdictions. Several people stressed as well that the adoption by Quebec of its own constitution should accompany the redefinition of its relations with the rest of Canada.

The changes outlined above indicate that the current system raises many questions of an economic and fiscal nature. Overlapping actions by both levels of government have thus resulted directly, over the years, from the increasingly extensive use of the federal spending power. Similarly, the size of federal debt and deficits has reduced, in a manner costly to Quebec, federal transfer payments, often put in place by Ottawa to encourage provinces to undertake spending programs in their own fields of jurisdiction. The federal government's financial withdrawal has exacerbated Quebec's difficulties regarding its public finances. Moreover, the standards the federal government imposes, which it maintains in spite of its withdrawal, considerably curtail Quebec's ability to adapt to these financial constraints.

Many of the people who supported the solution under consideration noted that it would not be easy to put in place new arrangements in order to redefine Quebec's political and constitutional status under the current federal framework. The process of amending the Constitution is fraught with a plethora of pitfalls and problems and it is difficult to expect prompt, significant results. These difficulties centre as much on the process of negotiation between governments and on public participation as they do on the constitutional amending formula. An effective means to resolving these difficulties remains to be found.

Many Quebecers deem this solution to be a last-ditch effort. The risk of a new refusal, which would renew the stalemate and exacerbate tensions, was brought up on numerous occasions. Most of the parties appearing before the Commission underscored the importance of avoiding in the future that Quebec be in a position where the other members of the federation would reject its proposals without Quebec having an alternative.

Redefining Quebec's status within the Canadian federal system therefore raises various questions of political acceptability. The true scope of renewed federalism would be known to Quebec, and uncertainty dissipated, only when the governments and other political bodies, the various social groups concerned and Canadians, outside Quebec, indicate what they are willing to accept.

A reconciliation of Quebec's expectations and interests with those of the rest of Canada within the federal State would require a considerable effort on the part of the members of the federation.

Sovereignty

A number of individuals and organizations advocated Quebec's accession to the status of independent State. The attainment of sovereignty has been considered from two perspectives: for some, it is the only conceivable political course of action now open to

Quebec; for others, it is the only possible outcome should a new attempt by Quebec to redefine its status within the Canadian federal constitutional framework fail.

Be that as it may, in the minds of many Quebecers, sovereignty is a genuine solution to breaking the stalemate and easing the tensions between Quebec and the rest of Canada, as well as to renewing the political foundations of their relations.

Because attaining sovereignty would represent a fundamental change, it raises a certain number of questions related primarily to its very nature, the means of achieving it, and its possible economic consequences. For this reason, the issues examined are more numerous.

Were Quebec to achieve complete political sovereignty, its democratic institutions would have the sole right to adopt laws and levy taxes within Quebec's territory, and the power to directly conclude any type of agreements or treaties with other independent States and participate in various international organizations.

The Canadian Constitution makes no mention of the right of the provinces to secede, that is, to withdraw from the federation. The democratic expression by Quebecers of their clear will to become an independent State, along with Quebec's commitment to comply with the principles of international law, would establish the political legitimacy of Quebec's seeking to attain its sovereignty.

Were other members of the federation to consent to it, Quebec's accession to the status of independent State could be achieved by agreement. The necessary constitutional amendments could be prepared and various transitional measures negotiated prior to the official change in status.

Failing such an agreement, Quebec would have to secede unilaterally, on the basis of an unequivocal, clearly expressed will among Quebecers to do so. The success of such a procedure would reside in the ability of Quebec's political institutions to implement and maintain exclusive public authority over its territory. Under international law, other States would have to recognize Quebec as a sovereign State.

In legal terms, Quebec's accession to the status of independent State would involve transferring current federal jurisdictions, responsibilities and powers to the Quebec Parliament and government, signalling the end of the application of the Canadian Constitution as well as of federal laws and the levying of federal taxes. As soon as Quebec's new status came into effect, a Quebec constitution would govern the political and legal organization of the new State. Depending on the circumstances, the constitution could be transitional in nature, or a complete fundamental law. Various means of elaborating a new constitution could be envisaged, such as the establishment of a constituent assembly.

To ensure continuity in the legal system, the security of transactions and the maintenance of public order, legislation could then be adopted stipulating that existing federal laws would continue to apply in Quebec, as if they had been adopted by the Quebec Parliament, until such time as the latter deemed it appropriate to amend them. Provision would also have to be made for transitional measures which would clarify the jurisdiction of the Quebec courts, the handling of civil and penal cases before the courts and the execution of judgments rendered before the change in political status.

Possessing all the levers of a sovereign State undoubtedly represents a powerful instrument for change, even though sovereignty in itself would not solve all of Quebec's political, economic and social problems. Taking charge of these levers would make it possible, among other things, to review all matters of concern to the government and establish, without interference, public priorities and objectives. However, such an undertaking would occur against a backdrop of increased international interdependence and economic competition, which encourages other States to acknowledge the limitations of their sovereignty in this area. Adhering to international standards and different kinds of association with other States to jointly establish the principles and rules governing economic interventions increasingly confines State powers.

Certain questions raised by the attainment of sovereignty are complex. It would be wrong to underestimate or ignore them: a society must be well informed when making its choices. However, it would also be wrong to dismiss sovereignty *a priori* simply because it involves a major change. If the main difficulty of redefining Quebec's status within the Canadian federal regime is that of provoking a necessary change, sovereignty poses the problem of managing in an orderly fashion a change implemented on the basis of free choice. Successfully managing any change hinges upon a thorough knowledge of the ins and outs of the issue at hand.

At the international level, another question would be that of Quebec's succession to bilateral or multilateral treaties signed by Canada. International treaties dealing with the territory, such as treaties governing the Canada-U.S. border or the St. Lawrence Seaway, would automatically apply to a sovereign Quebec.

Succeeding to other treaties would be consistent with various principles, depending on whether bilateral treaties or multilateral agreements are in question, and depending on their respective purposes and objects. In the case of a treaty on which rests an international organization, Quebec should apply according to the rules of the organization in order to become a member.

Quebec's sovereignty also raises a number of economic issues. Two international treaties would be of particular importance to a sovereign Quebec adhering to the principle of openness to world trade: the General Agreement on Tariffs and Trade (GATT) and the Canada-U.S. Free Trade Agreement. In the case of GATT, whose foremost objective is to encourage freer trade, Quebec, recognized as sovereign by other countries, would likely be admitted retroactively to the date of its accession to sovereignty, should it so wish.

The Canada-U.S. Free Trade Agreement results from the will of Canada and the United States to minimize obstacles to trade between the two countries. An independent Quebec which would clearly indicate its intention to continue to participate in the movement toward freer trade on the continent should not meet with opposition from its partners; it would be incumbent upon Quebec and its partners to ensure that the mutual interests which led to the Agreement continue to prevail.

Though its participation in GATT and the continuation of free trade with the United States, Quebec would maintain the current terms of its economic relations with the United States and the rest of the world.

Maintaining the Canadian common market raises other questions. Despite certain flaws, individuals, goods, services and capital move without major impediments within the current Canadian economy. The common market undoubtedly contributes to the economic well-being of all Canadians and Quebecers, who thus have a mutual interest in preserving the market's basic components, regardless of their political and constitutional status.

Even if the North-South shift in Quebec and Canada toward increased trade with the United States were to continue, it would still be in the interests of Quebec and its immediate neighbours in Canada, the Atlantic Provinces and above all Ontario, to avoid fragmenting the Canadian economy, given their commercial and human interdependence.

Mutual recognition of their common interests and Quebec's acknowledgment that sovereignty does not in any way compel it to differentiate itself in all areas would make it possible to avoid this fragmentation. Under such circumstances, the issue of what type of institutional arrangements would coordinate common interests does not appear to be the leading question.

The economic performance of a sovereign Quebec is sometimes called into question in the event the rest of Canada refuses to formally and globally re-enter an economic association with Quebec. Such association is not the only means of maintaining the essential elements of the current common market: various measures could be contemplated in order to solve the problems likely to arise, without a general, formal agreement to associate.

In fact, following the accession to sovereignty, some of the main elements of the common market could be preserved by Quebec keeping in force most existing federal legislation and, subsequently, through some degree of harmonization. Competition, financial institutions and bankruptcy are important examples in this respect.

Similarly, in certain fields now under provincial or shared juris- diction, Quebec could continue to harmonize, as it has already done, much of its economic legislation with that of the other provinces or the federal government. Such harmonization could be achieved by renewing existing agreements, as is now the case in the field of road transportation, or by informal coordination, as is the case in the fields of taxation, securities and insurance.

Various government regulations have already been harmonized to a certain extent at the international level, or are about to be harmonized, through multilateral agreements, as is the case for example in the fields of industrial property, copyright and tele- communications. This is another way which could permit a certain harmonization of Quebec and Canadian legislations.

With respect to currency, the extent of trade and the number of contracts and financial obligations between economic agents in Quebec and those in the rest of Canada are such that keeping the Canadian dollar as the currency of a sovereign Quebec would be the best solution for both parties. It would avoid the need for busi- nesses and individuals in Canada and Quebec to make major adjustments and to bear substantial costs associated with transac- tions and exchange risks engendered by Quebec's adoption of another currency.

The use of the Canadian dollar could be maintained by the adoption of legislation to this effect in a sovereign Quebec. Each deposit institution in Quebec would be free to reach an agreement with one or another of the members of the Canadian Payments Association in order to procure cash and liquid assets.

It is hard to see what might prevent economic agents in a sover- eign Quebec from effecting their operations in Canadian dollars.

Obviously, under the circumstances, Quebec would not enjoy autonomy in terms of monetary policy. In any event, Quebec would have to relinquish such autonomy were it to adopt instead a foreign currency such as the U.S. dollar. The same would be true, at least for quite some time, if Quebec created its own currency as, in order to establish such currency's credibility, Quebec would have to closely tie it to the Canadian dollar or another foreign currency.

In the realm of public finances, a sovereign Quebec would recover within its territory all of the taxes levied and responsibility for current federal services. It would inevitably have to review the entire taxation system and government programs in light of its priorities, which might very well be one of the first benefits of sovereignty. The question would then be whether Quebec could maintain the level of current federal services by recovering all of the taxes now levied within its territory. According to the *Provincial Economic Accounts* prepared by Statistics Canada, not taking into account interest payments on federal debt, the tax revenues Quebec would recover would more or less correspond to the additional expenditures it would incur in order to ensure the maintenance of federal services.

However, a broad picture of the public finances of a sovereign Quebec cannot be established without knowing how the federal government's liabilities and assets would be divided, which means advancing a number of hypotheses. It must nevertheless be acknowledged that Quebecers are already bearing the burden of the federal debt and attendant interest costs insofar as they contribute to federal government revenues. If, after achieving sovereignty, they continued to assume the same proportion of the debt and interest charges, their level of debt would remain unchanged.

As for their foreign trade policy, Quebec and Canada could maintain the Canadian common market by pursuing existing free trade and applying the same trade policy to third parties.

Preserving a Quebec-Canada free-trade zone is entirely in keeping with the current trend toward freer trade in North America. Obviously, the mutual imposition of customs duties or other obstacles to trade would engender substantial economic losses for Quebec and Canada, and in the latter case especially for Ontario and the Atlantic Provinces, which carry on extensive trade with Quebec.

Furthermore, the failure to harmonize the external trade policies of Canada and a sovereign Quebec would make it necessary to implement a two-tiered customs inspection system at all land, sea and air entry points in Quebec from Canada, and vice versa. Given the extent of trade in goods and passenger movements between Quebec and the other provinces, often in transit, this situation would impose significant costs on individuals and businesses in Canada and Quebec.

It is not impossible that sovereignty may give rise to negative reaction from Canadian purchasers of Quebec goods and services. However, because current trade flows essentially reflect the free choice of the markets, such a reaction would result in additional costs and delays for these purchasers, and would not have a long-term effect.

Allowing the residents of Quebec and Canada to work freely throughout the territory would also make it easier to maintain the main elements of the Canadian common market. This would be to the advantage of Canadians and Quebecers, especially the non-French-speaking community in Quebec, whose mobility within Canada is much greater than that of their French-speaking counter-parts.

Be that as it may, Quebec should clearly indicate that it favours such mobility, provided that it is reciprocal. In this way, it could propose to the rest of Canada to maintain through new procedures the existing right to live and work anywhere, the transferability of entitlement to the main social programs such as unemployment insurance, social aid, government pension plans, old age security payments and health insurance, as well as to ensure to the same extent as at present the transferability of private pension plans. An offer to coordinate in the field of immigration could accompany these measures.

Although maintaining a single labour market in both States may be advantageous to Canadians and Quebecers, it is certainly not a prerequisite to the viability of sovereignty.

Therefore, a sovereign Quebec would have at its disposal a number of means to maintain its participation in world and North American trade, and the essential components of the current Canadian common market. Quebec's desire to act in this manner would rest on an acknowledgment that it has been advantageous in the past to open up its economy and that doing so is an essential condition for its active involvement in the concert of modern nations.

Conclusions

A commission such as ours could not confine its discussions to a narrow definition of the political and constitutional future of Quebec. One cannot examine the future political relations in the nation without inevitably focusing on the human, social and cultural facets of the life of the people. In drawing our conclusions, we would first like to stress a number of important dimensions of our future, on which light would not otherwise be shed through the main process we are proposing.

Quebec is a society open to social change, which enjoys a high standard of living. Even in such societies, not everyone has the same opportunity for social advancement; an extensive system of income support and social protection measures does not prevent the standard of living of some people from declining or others from experiencing sustained poverty. The problem of poverty in the cities and outlying regions, which are less prosperous in some instances, was stressed before the Commission. It was suggested that the problem should be solved before or at the same time that we redefine the political and constitutional status of Quebec. We believe that poverty and inequality are fundamental problems to which governments must respond with thorough reflection and enlightened action. However, we feel that there is nothing to suggest that such problems would be better settled were we to avoid discussing the constitution, no more than they would be by simply amending the current status or through a change of status. The dynamics of social change influences and is influenced by changes in modern democracies. While it may be slowed by authoritarian, closed regimes, it does not necessarily find an immediate solution in open systems such as ours.

In our society, Quebec women have achieved equality in principle; they must now strive to attain equality in everyday life. The political field has broadened considerably in the 20th century, drawing into the public domain what were hitherto deemed to be private matters. Women have been particularly affected by these changes. State intervention in the education and health sectors, among others, is a major political factor for women as it is tied to changes in the role of the family and the imperative of achieving equality between women and men. Several women's groups reminded us of this fact by emphasizing that it was time to halt the under-representation of women in political institutions.

The English-speaking community has historically been part of Quebec's reality. Its significant contribution to Quebec's development must be stressed and continue to be recognized. As a linguistic minority in Quebec, it is seeking, with French-speaking Quebecers who are themselves a minority in Canada, the development of respectful, harmonious relations, and this goal has largely been attained. A number of differences persist; both sides must endeavour to resolve them in a spirit of openness. With respect to the political and constitutional future of Quebec, it is important to maintain, in collaboration with the English-speaking community, legal guarantees which ensure the complete protection of its rights and institutions, and its full participation in Quebec society.

The issue of the rights and claims of the aboriginal peoples is a different matter altogether. The problems experienced by the 60,000 Amerinds and Inuit of Quebec may indeed be examined against the backdrop of social change. However, the problem is also political, and is tied to the existence of the historic rights of the descendants of the oldest inhabitants of our territory. The issues of concern to the aboriginal nations must be dealt with now. Indeed, the current arrangements governing the aboriginal peoples do not satisfy their desire for self-affirmation and self-government in regard to their internal affairs. This situation cannot be prolonged unduly while waiting for a final answer to the question of the political and constitutional future of Quebec. To the contrary, we believe it is urgent to specify the manner in which we intend to realize aboriginal self-government. Negotiations to this end must be conducted promptly and vigorously, in a spirit of openness and rigour, with representatives of the Quebec aboriginal peoples. Such negotiations, focused on the future, will only be more fruitful if a process for settling existing disputes is quickly adopted, in consultation with the aboriginal peoples.

The public hearings of the Commission took us all over Quebec and enabled us to better comprehend the diversity of Quebecers' concerns. However, we would like here to emphasize the similarity of viewpoints presented to us by individuals and businesses in the regions, by municipalities and other regional and local governments on the importance of drawing public administrators and Quebec residents closer together. Broader authority and more extensive resources are requested for the benefit of various regional organizations in the fields for which they are responsible; the reorganization of various structures is also demanded. We have decided not to include in our report recommendations concerning regional and local governments. While the question is indeed an important one, we feel that the situation can change more quickly and efficiently through normal democratic channels than it will if it is included in a constitutional debate.

It should be stressed that possible changes in the political and constitutional status of Quebec could have a particular effect on the Outaouais region in Quebec.* Indeed, were a significant number of federal sectors or services to become Quebec's responsibility, employment and economic activity in the region could be seriously affected. The same is true, undoubtedly to an even greater degree, were Quebec to attain sovereignty. Regardless of the course Quebec adopts, it will be necessary and urgent to implement specific programs aimed at maintaining employment and economic activity in this region.

One striking difference between the regions of Quebec is the concentration in the Montreal metropolitan area of the greatest proportion of Quebecers of non-French or non-British origin. A number of these cultural communities have been established for a long time in Quebec and have happily settled in, while contributing their customs, talent and vibrant creative energy to the social fabric. Others have arrived more recently and come from more remote regions, creating an even greater ethnic diversity. The principle of equal rights enshrined in the Quebec *Charter of Human Rights and Freedoms* must not mask the tensions, indeed the discrimination, which new Quebecers may feel. The Quebec cultural communities expressed their willingness to participate in Quebec society when they appeared before the Commission. In our view, in collaboration with members of the cultural communities, efforts must be stepped up to ensure that Quebecers of all origins enjoy genuinely equal opportunities and participate fully in all spheres of activity.

Elsewhere in Canada, French-speaking Canadians are often perceived as representatives of one of the many cultures which make up Canada's multicultural heritage, a culture which is entitled to preserve its ways and customs and speak its language in private, but which must in essence live socially in English, as do other cultural groups. The development of French-speaking people outside Quebec is thus limited in fact, wrongly no doubt, through the misunderstanding of multiculturalism as a reflection of social life everywhere in Canada. This development, while it is sustained namely by a number of provisions in the 1982 Constitution, is the object of constant legal battles. These conflicts before the courts, in

---

* The Outaouais is the region of Quebec adjacent to Ottawa; it includes the cities of Hull, Gatineau and Aylmer. — Ed.

which the federal government often appears as the sole source of support of French-speaking groups against the provincial governments, give rise to another misunderstanding. In the name of fraternity and a common culture, French-speaking groups would like Quebec to support their position. For reasons related to its own linguistic and constitutional position, it is not possible for Quebec to take up the cause of French-speaking groups in all of their legal undertakings. Were Quebec institutions and the Quebec government to more actively support the initiatives of French-speaking people outside Quebec other than through support before the courts, Quebec and Quebecers would contribute more fully to the vitality of the French-speaking community in Canada.

All of the matters we have just set out reflect concerns raised before the Commission. However, the very essence of the questions raised by our mandate demands that we focus exclusively on the political and constitutional status of Quebec, which we do in the following section.

History has witnessed Quebec society's long and patient pursuit of a political arrangement which accurately reflects its identity. Culture is at once the sum of the creative expression of a collective imagination and the actions, words, songs and accents which characterize the day-to-day life of a people. It is its culture, fed and sustained by creators and researchers, nourished by artists, experienced by one and all, which animates the identity of the people of Quebec. Through their culture, they are able to revive their roots and strive to surpass themselves, which demands that their political status reflect their identity. While defining Quebec's political future does not require indeed that we concomitantly define its cultural future, doing so requires that we clearly state that only a living, proud culture gives its people a sufficiently strong, distinctive face and spirit to sustain a promising future. This perspective has guided our reflection and given it all its meaning.

All Quebecers share a number of fundamental objectives: all of them want the society in which they live, Quebec, to enjoy freedom and prosperity, based on justice and fairness, a respect for differences, growth and openness to the world.

Various social and political models are put forward to serve as a foundation for the progress and development of Quebec society. When such models are discussed, any one of them may strike some people as inadequate; everyone seeks to highlight the advantages of the social and political framework he favours to gain the support of others. One fact remains: determining the political and constitutional framework of a society, of a people, is a political exercise, to the extent that democratic processes are imperative in the expression of fundamental choices.

Quebec's relationship with the rest of Canada, within the political system and the constitutional order which govern them, has reached a stalemate. After several years of constitutional demands which have expressed Quebec's fundamental needs and aspirations, Canada adopted a new Constitution Act in 1982, without the consent of the Quebec government and the National Assembly. This Act did not satisfy Quebec's requests. Moreover, for the first time since 1867 it meant that one province, Quebec, lost powers as a result of arrangements agreed upon by the other parties, in its absence and without its consent. In 1990, the minimal conditions Quebec put forward to ensure its formal acceptance of the *Constitution Act, 1982* were rejected.

It is pointless to refuse to acknowledge the current conflict: doing so will only cause the further deterioration of the political foundations of our societies and of the relations between Quebecers and Canadians. Allowing the situation to drag on will lead to the same result, thereby exacerbating dissatisfaction, uncertainty and instability.

Relations between societies are also of other types, for example economic. Quebec, like Canada as a whole, has an open economy fully integrated into the main world trends, especially North American currents. The close economic interdependence which characterizes Canada indicates that the reciprocal benefits of ensuring the free movement of persons, goods, services and capital are advantageous to everyone concerned and should, as far as possible, be maintained, regardless of the political and constitutional status Quebec adopts. Moreover, Quebec is not calling into question the economic and financial commitments and ties it has established with its Canadian and foreign partners.

With regard to political and constitutional relations, the consensus expressed during the Commission's deliberations is clear: profound changes must be made to Quebec's political and constitutional status. Regardless of the solutions adopted, they must promptly and permanently dissipate the uncertainty and instability resulting from the current stalemate.

Two courses are open to Quebec with respect to the redefinition of its status, i.e. a new, ultimate attempt to redefine its status within the federal regime, and the attainment of sovereignty. Some people feel that the first course must be adopted and, should it fail, that Quebec should achieve sovereignty. Other people prefer to adopt the second course of action immediately.

Should a final attempt to renew federalism fail, sovereignty would be the only course remaining. It is therefore important to focus immediately on all its implications and systematically specify the measures to be taken to efficiently implement it, especially should it be concluded that this is the only possible course of action, but also if it is deemed to be an imminent alternative.

The approach Quebec chooses must have two objectives. First, it must solve the political and constitutional stalemate and ensure that satisfactory, durable results are achieved in the near future: clear deadlines must be stipulated. Second, the choice and its outcome must be clearly spelled out by Quebec and made known to its partners in the federation. In this way, the rest of Canada will be able to accurately assess what is at stake with regard to the redefinition of Quebec's status and the seriousness of its process, and to make its own choices.

A final attempt to renew federalism cannot be meaningful unless Canada and the other provinces are prepared to participate effectively. It is incumbent upon them to inform Quebec of the contents of possible arrangements to which they would adhere. Quebec, free to determine its future, must ensure, without waiting to examine any offer or proposal whatever, that it is prepared to implement the option it chooses. Should the political climate so demand, preparatory measures would enable the process of acceding to sovereignty to be launched in an enlightened, orderly and predictable manner.

In this way, Quebec could take advantage of the time available to it and current arrangements to bolster its position, while strengthening its negotiating power. The continued presence within the federal system of a Quebec whose needs and aspirations are not satisfied and which is embarking upon fundamental changes is not the best guarantee for the smooth operation of the federal regime. This approach makes it possible to prepare for the attainment of sovereignty in a climate where there would be less uncertainty than if Quebec waited for the outcome of a possible referendum before proceeding. Similarly, Quebecers would be better informed of what is at stake, in anticipation of making a choice.

As long as Quebec maintains its current status and remains a province within the Canadian federation, its relations and those of Quebecers with the rest of Canada will continue to be governed by the Canadian Constitution. A positive, open attitude toward Quebec would preserve the principle of admissibility of any offer the rest of Canada might make.

For many Quebecers who appeared before the Commission, the question of their political future and status in relation to Canada and the rest of the world is tied to the exigencies of a global society, of a community which constitutes a distinct people.

The Commission has noted the extent and depth of the consensus expressed before it to the effect that the population of Quebec unequivocally rejects the current state of affairs.

For a significant number of Quebecers, Quebec's sovereignty is a concrete, economically viable alternative to Canadian federalism which, they believe, no longer efficiently contributes to Quebec's political objectives.

Quebecers have high expectations: they want Quebec to recover jurisdictions in all sectors, be they economic, social or cultural. They feel it is urgent to dispel uncertainty through a clear process which ends the stalemate and promptly produces results.

The Commission has also noted that Quebecers favour maintaining the reciprocal advantages resulting from various economic and financial commitments and ties between Quebec and the rest of Canada.

Under the circumstances, the Commission is of the opinion that Quebecers will have to express themselves on the matter of their political and constitutional future through a formal, democratic consultation.

Quebecers must consider the following: an unequivocal assessment, two equally clear solutions, one of which can only be adopted if Quebec's partners also wish to do so, and the other which must be prepared regardless of the choice made. Bearing in mind its strengths and weaknesses with respect to its geography and its physical and human resources, Quebec must now make a choice and implement it as quickly as possible.

Recommendations

The Commission recommends to the National Assembly the adoption, in the spring of 1991, of legislation establishing the process by which Quebec determines its political and constitutional future.

The legislation would contain three sections, that is, a preamble; a first part dealing with a referendum to be held on Quebec sovereignty; and a second part dealing with the offer of a new partnership of constitutional nature.

"Preamble

1. Considering the report, the conclusions and the recommendations of the Commission on the Political and Constitutional Future of Quebec;
2. Whereas Quebecers are free to assume their own destiny, to determine their political status and to assure their economic, social and cultural development;
3. Whereas Quebecers wish to play an active part in defining the political and constitutional future of Quebec;
4. Whereas the *Constitution Act, 1982*, was proclaimed despite the opposition of the National Assembly;
5. Whereas the 1987 Agreement on the Constitution, the aim of which was to allow Quebec to become a party to the *Constitution Act, 1982*, has failed;
6. Whereas it is necessary to redefine the political and constitutional status of Quebec.

Part 1 of the Act: Referendum on Quebec Sovereignty

The Act shall provide:

- that a referendum on Quebec sovereignty is to be held, either between June 8 and 22, 1992, or between October 12 and 26, 1992;
- that, should the outcome of the referendum be positive, Quebec will acquire the status of a sovereign State one year, day for day, after the date of the referendum;
- for the establishing of a special parliamentary commission of the National Assembly and for its membership to examine matters related to Quebec's accession to sovereignty;
- that the special parliamentary commission will study and analyze all matters related to Quebec's accession to full sovereignty, that is, Quebec's exclusive capacity, through its democratic institutions, to adopt laws, levy taxes within its territory and act on the international scene in order to conclude all manner of agreements or treaties with other independent States, and participate in various international organizations; that the commission will make recommendations in this respect to the National Assembly;
- that the commission will also be responsible, should the Government of Canada make a formal offer respecting an economic partnership, for studying and analyzing such an offer and making recommendations in this respect to the National Assembly;
- that the commission will be granted a budget and authorized to have studies prepared and conduct whatever consultations it

deems necessary, and to hear all interested persons and organizations.

Part 2 of the Act: Offer of a New Partnership of Constitutional Nature

The Act shall provide:
- for the establishing of a special parliamentary commission of the
  National Assembly and for its membership to assess any offer of
  a new partnership of constitutional nature made by the Government of Canada, and to make recommendations in this respect to
  the National Assembly;
- that only an offer formally binding the Government of Canada
  and the provinces may be examined by the commission;
- that the commission will be granted a budget and authorized to
  have studies prepared and conduct whatever consultations it
  deems necessary, and to hear all interested persons and organizations."

*The foregoing is a translation of the recommendations recorded in
the minutes of the March 25, 1991 meeting of the Commission held
in Quebec City.*

———————

On May 15, 1991 the Quebec government tabled Bill 150, *An Act
respecting the process for determining the political and constitutional
future of Québec*, in the National Assembly. The Bill embodied the
recommendations of the Bélanger-Campeau report: to hold a referendum
on the sovereignty of Quebec between June 8 and June 22, 1992 or
between October 12 and October 26, 1992; and to establish two parliamentary committees, one to examine matters relating to the accession of
Quebec to sovereignty, the other to examine any offer of a new
constitutional partnership.

However, the long list of "whereases" preceding these provisions
included, in addition to similar clauses in the Commission's report and in
Bill 90 establishing the Commission, the following:

> Whereas the Commission on the Political and Constitutional Future of
> Québec recognizes that a valid solution, other than the political sovereignty of
> Québec, would be a fundamental renewal of federalism through the establish-
> ment of a new constitutional partnership;
> Whereas Québec wishes to ensure that everyone should have a fair
> understanding of the changes that are necessary to make the Canadian federal

system acceptable to Québec and of the true definition of sovereignty and of its political, economic, social and cultural implications;

Whereas the Gouvernement du Québec retains at all times its full prerogative to initiate and assess measures to promote the best interests of Québec;

Whereas the National Assembly continues to hold the sovereign power to decide any matter pertaining to a referendum and to pass appropriate legislation where necessary;

The effect of these clauses, as *Le Devoir* publisher Lise Bissonnette noted, was "to tip the balance of the overall arrangement into the federalist sphere of influence, while the Commission refused to choose between the two options".[*]

Moreover, while the Commission said that, should the referendum outcome be positive, "Quebec *will acquire* the status of a sovereign State," s. 1 of Bill 150 states: "If the results of the referendum are in favour of sovereignty, they *constitute a proposal* that Québec acquire the status of a sovereign state one year to the day from the holding of the referendum."

Finally, the two parliamentary commissions, unlike the Bélanger-Campeau Commission, do not represent the sovereigntist and federalist options on an approximate parity basis. Instead, as s. 7 provides, "to reflect the numerical strength of the parties represented in the National Assembly", the committees are to be composed of the three party leaders, the Minister for Canadian Intergovernmental Affairs, nine Government members and three members of the Official Opposition (the PQ). Thus, Bill 150 formally ended the fragile consensus that had characterized the establishment and to some degree the operations of the Bélanger-Campeau Commission.

Bill 150 was adopted on June 20, 1991, by a vote of 65 to 29. Voting against were 26 PQ members, two Equality Party members, and one Liberal. Seven Liberal ministers, including Claude Ryan, the leader of the No forces in the 1980 referendum, were absent for the vote. It was widely rumoured that they were opposed to legislation requiring a referendum on sovereignty.

---

[*] "Considérant la dernière chance", Editorial, *Le Devoir*, 16 May 1991.

APPENDIX

Excerpts from the

Constitution Act, 1867, as amended
(formerly British North America Act)

VI. Distribution of Legislative Powers

Powers of the Parliament
91. It shall be lawful for the Queen, by and with the Advice and Consent of the Senate and House of Commons, to make Laws for the Peace, Order and good Government of Canada, in relation to all Matters not coming within the Classes of Subjects by this Act assigned exclusively to the Legislatures of the Provinces; and for greater Certainty, but not so as to restrict the Generality of the foregoing Terms of this Section, it is hereby declared that (notwithstanding anything in this Act) the exclusive Legislative Authority of the Parliament of Canada extends to all Matters coming within the Classes of Subjects next herein-after enumerated; that is to say, —

1. [Repealed]
1A. The Public Debt and Property.
2. The Regulation of Trade and Commerce.
2A. Unemployment insurance.
3. The raising of Money by any Mode or System of Taxation.
4. The borrowing of Money on the Public Credit.
5. Postal Service.
6. The Census and Statistics.
7. Militia, Military and Naval Service, and Defence.
8. The fixing of and providing for the Salaries and Allowances of Civil and other Officers of the Government of Canada.
9. Beacons, Buoys, Lighthouses, and Sable Island.
10. Navigation and Shipping.
11. Quarantine and the Establishment and Maintenance of Marine Hospitals.
12. Sea Coast and Inland Fisheries.
13. Ferries between a Province and any British or Foreign Country or between Two Provinces.
14. Currency and Coinage.

15. Banking, Incorporation of Banks, and the Issue of Paper Money.
16. Savings Banks.
17. Weights and Measures.
18. Bills of Exchange and Promissory Notes.
19. Interest.
20. Legal Tender.
21. Bankruptcy and Insolvency.
22. Patents of Invention and Discovery.
23. Copyrights.
24. Indians, and Lands reserved for the Indians.
25. Naturalization and Aliens.
26. Marriage and Divorce.
27. The Criminal Law, except the Constitution of Courts of Criminal Jurisdiction, but including the Procedure in Criminal Matters.
28. The Establishment, Maintenance, and Management of Penitentiaries.
29. Such Classes of Subjects as are expressly excepted in the Enumeration of the Classes of Subjects by this Act assigned exclusively to the Legislatures of the Provinces.

And any Matter coming within any of the Classes of Subjects enumerated in this Section shall not be deemed to come within the Class of Matters of a local or private Nature comprised in the Enumeration of the Classes of Subjects by this Act assigned exclusively to the Legislatures of the Provinces.

Exclusive Powers of Provincial Legislatures.

92. In each Province the Legislature may exclusively make Laws in relation to Matters coming within the Classes of Subject next herein-after enumerated; that is to say, —
1. [Repealed]
2. Direct Taxation within the Province in order to the raising of a Revenue for Provincial Purposes.
3. The borrowing of Money on the sole Credit of the Province.
4. The Establishment and Tenure of Provincial Offices and the Appointment and Payment of Provincial Officers.
5. The Management and Sale of the Public Lands belonging to the Province and of the Timber and Wood thereon.
6. The Establishment, Maintenance, and Management of Public and Reformatory Prisons in and for the Province.

7. The Establishment, Maintenance, and Management of Hospitals, Asylums, Charities, and Eleemosynary Institutions in and for the Province, other than Marine Hospitals.
8. Municipal Institutions in the Province.
9. Shop, Saloon, Tavern, Auctioneer, and other Licences in order to the raising of a Revenue for Provincial, Local or Municipal Purposes.
10. Local Works and Undertakings other than such as are of the following Classes: —
    (a) Lines of Steam or other Ships, Railways, Canals, Telegraphs, and other Works and Undertakings connecting the Province with any other or others of the Provinces, or extending beyond the Limits of the Province;
    (b) Lines of Steam Ships between the Province and any British or Foreign Country;
    (c) Such Works as, although wholly situate within the Province, are before or after their Execution declared by the Parliament of Canada to be for the general Advantage of Canada or for the Advantage of Two or more of the Provinces.
11. The Incorporation of Companies with Provincial Objects.
12. The Solemnization of Marriage in the Province.
13. Property and Civil Rights in the Province.
14. The Administration of Justice in the Province, including the Constitution, Maintenance, and Organization of Provincial Courts, both of Civil and of Criminal Jurisdiction, and including Procedure in Civil Matters in those Courts.
15. The Imposition of Punishment by Fine, Penalty, or Imprisonment for enforcing any Law of the Province made in relation to any Matter coming within any of the Classes of Subjects enumerated in this Section.
16. Generally all Matters of a merely local or private Nature in the Province.

Non-Renewable Natural Resources, Forestry Resources and Electrical Energy

92A. (1) In each province, the legislature may exclusively make laws in relation to
    (a) exploration for non-renewable natural resources in the province;
    (b) development, conservation and management of non-renewable natural resources and forestry resources in the

province, including laws in relation to the rate of primary production therefrom; and

(c) development, conservation and management of sites and facilities in the province for the generation and production of electrical energy.

(2) In each province, the legislature may make laws in relation to the export from the province to another part of Canada of the primary production from non-renewable natural resources and forestry resources in the province and the production from facilities in the province for the generation of electrical energy, but such laws may not authorize or provide for discrimination in prices or in supplies exported to another part of Canada.

(3) Nothing in subsection (2) derogates from the authority of Parliament to enact laws in relation to the matters referred to in that subsection and, where such a law of Parliament and a law of a province conflict, the law of Parliament prevails to the extent of the conflict.

(4) In each province, the legislature may make laws in relation to the raising of money by any mode or system of taxation in respect of

(a) non-renewable natural resources and forestry resources in the province and the primary production therefrom, and

(b) sites and facilities in the province for the generation of electrical energy and the production therefrom,

whether or not such production is exported in whole or in part from the province, but such laws may not authorize or provide for taxation that differentiates between production exported to another part of Canada and production not exported from the province.

(5) . . .

(6) . . . [Added in 1982]

Education.

93. In and for each Province the Legislature may exclusively make Laws in relation to Education, subject and according to the following Provisions: —

(1) Nothing in any such Law shall prejudicially affect any Right or Privilege with respect to Denominational Schools which any Class of Persons have by Law in the Province at the Union:

(2) All the Powers, Privileges and Duties at the Union by Law conferred and imposed in Upper Canada on the Separate Schools and School Trustees of the Queen's Roman Catholic Subjects shall be and the same are hereby extended to the

Dissentient Schools of the Queen's Protestant and Roman Catholic Subjects in Quebec:

(3) Where in any Province a System of Separate or Dissentient Schools exists by Law at the Union or is thereafter established by the Legislature of the Province, an Appeal shall lie to the Governor General in Council from any Act or Decision of any Provincial Authority affecting any Right or Privilege of the Protestant or Roman Catholic Minority of the Queen's Subjects in relation to Education:

(4) In case any such Provincial Law as from Time to Time seems to the Governor General in Council requisite for the due Execution of the Provisions of this Section is not made, or in case any Decision of the Governor General in Council on any Appeal under this Section is not duly executed by the proper Provincial Authority in that Behalf, then and in every such Case, and as far only as the Circumstances of each Case require, the Parliament of Canada may make remedial Laws for the due Execution of the Provisions of this Section and of any Decision of the Governor General in Council under this Section.

Uniformity of Laws in Ontario, Nova Scotia and New Brunswick.

94. Notwithstanding anything in this Act, the Parliament of Canada may make Provision for the Uniformity of all or any of the Laws relative to Property and Civil Rights in Ontario, Nova Scotia, and New Brunswick, and of the Procedure of all or any of the Courts in Those Three Provinces, and from and after the passing of any Act in that Behalf the Power of the Parliament of Canada to make Laws in relation to any Matter comprised in any such Act shall, notwithstanding anything in this Act, be unrestricted; but any Act of the Parliament of Canada making Provision for such Uniformity shall not have effect in any Province unless and until it is adopted and enacted as Law by the Legislature thereof.

Old Age Pensions.

94A. The Parliament of Canada may make laws in relation to old age pensions and supplementary benefits, including survivors, and disability benefits irrespective of age, but no such law shall affect the operation of any law present or future of a provincial legislature in relation to any such matter. [Added in 1964]

Agriculture and Immigration.

95. In each Province the Legislature may make Laws in relation to Agriculture in the Province, and to Immigration into the Province; and it is hereby declared that the Parliament of Canada may from Time to Time make Laws in relation to Agriculture in all or any of the Provinces, and to Immigration into all or any of the Provinces; and any Law of the Legislature of a Province relative to Agriculture or to Immigration shall have effect in and for the Province as long and as far only as it is not repugnant to any Act of the Parliament of Canada.

VII. Judicature.

96. The Governor General shall appoint the Judges of the Superior, District, and County Courts in each Province, except those of the Courts of Probate in Nova Scotia and New Brunswick.

101. The Parliament of Canada may, notwithstanding anything in this Act, from Time to Time provide for the Constitution, Maintenance, and Organization of a General Court of Appeal for Canada, and for the Establishment of any additional Courts for the better Administration of the Laws of Canada.

VIII. Revenues; Debts; Assets; Taxation.

121. All Articles of the Growth, Produce, or Manufacture of any one of the Provinces shall, from and after the Union, be admitted free into each of the other Provinces.

IX. Miscellaneous Provisions.

133. Either the English or the French Language may be used by any Person in the Debates of the Houses of the Parliament of Canada and of the Houses of the Legislature of Quebec; and both those Languages shall be used in the respective Records and Journals of those Houses; and either of those Languages may be used by any Person or in any Pleading or Process in or issuing from any Court of Canada established under this Act, and in or from all or any of the Courts of Quebec.

The Acts of the Parliament of Canada and of the Legislature of Quebec shall be printed and published in both those Languages.

Constitution Act, 1982

Part I

Canadian Charter of Rights and Freedoms

Whereas Canada is founded upon principles that recognize the supremacy of God and the rule of law;

Guarantee of Rights and Freedoms

1. The *Canadian Charter of Rights and Freedoms* guarantees the rights and freedoms set out in it subject only to such reasonable limits prescribed by law as can be demonstrably justified in a free and democratic society.

Official Languages of Canada

16. (1) English and French are the official languages of Canada and have equality of status and equal rights and privileges as to their use in all institutions of the Parliament and government of Canada.

(2) English and French are the official languages of New Brunswick and have equality of status and equal rights and privileges as to their use in all institutions of the legislature and government of New Brunswick.

(3) Nothing in this Charter limits the authority of Parliament or a legislature to advance the equality of status or use of English and French.

20. (1) Any member of the public in Canada has the right to communicate with, and to receive available services from, any head or central office of an institution of the Parliament or government of Canada in English or French, and has the same right with respect to any other office of any such institution where

(*a*) there is a significant demand for communications with and services from that office in such language; or

(*b*) due to the nature of the office, it is reasonable that communications with and services from that office be available in both English and French.

(2) Any member of the public in New Brunswick has the right to communicate with, and to receive available services from, any office of an institution of the legislature or government of New Brunswick in English or French.

Minority Language Educational Rights
23. (1) Citizens of Canada

(a) whose first language learned and still understood is that of the English or French linguistic minority population of the province in which they reside, or

(b) who have received their primary school instruction in Canada in English or French and reside in a province where the language in which they received that instruction is the language of the English or French linguistic minority population of the province,

have the right to have their children receive primary and secondary school instruction in that language in that province.

(2) Citizens of Canada of whom any child has received or is receiving primary or secondary school instruction in English or French in Canada, have the right to have all their children receive primary and secondary school instruction in the same language.

(3) The right of citizens of Canada under subsections (1) and (2) to have their children receive primary and secondary school instruction in the language of the English or French linguistic minority population of a province

(a) applies wherever in the province the number of children of citizens who have such a right is sufficient to warrant the provision to them out of public funds of minority language instruction; and

(b) includes, where the number of those children so warrants, the right to have them receive that instruction in minority language educational facilities provided out of public funds.

General
25. The guarantee in this Charter of certain rights and freedoms shall not be construed so as to abrogate or derogate from any aboriginal, treaty or other rights or freedoms that pertain to the aboriginal peoples of Canada including

(a) any rights or freedoms that have been recognized by the Royal Proclamation of October 7, 1763; and

(b) any rights or freedoms that may be acquired by the aboriginal peoples of Canada by way of land claims settlement.

27. This Charter shall be interpreted in a manner consistent with the preservation and enhancement of the multicultural heritage of Canadians.

28. Notwithstanding anything in this Charter, the rights and freedoms referred to in it are guaranteed equally to male and female persons.

29. Nothing in this Charter abrogates or derogates from any rights or privileges guaranteed by or under the Constitution of Canada in respect of denominational, separate or dissentient schools.

Application of Charter

32. (1) This Charter applies

(a) to the Parliament and government of Canada in respect of all matters within the authority of Parliament including all matters relating to the Yukon Territory and Northwest Territories; and

(b) to the legislature and government of each province in respect of all matters within the authority of the legislature of each province.

(2) . . .

33. (1) Parliament or the legislature of a province may expressly declare in an Act of Parliament or of the legislature, as the case may be, that the Act or a provision thereof shall operate notwithstanding a provision included in section 2 or sections 7 to 15 of this Charter.

(2) An Act or a provision of an Act in respect of which a declaration made under this section is in effect shall have such operation as it would have but for the provision of this Charter referred to in the declaration.

(3) A declaration made under subsection (1) shall cease to have effect five years after it comes into force or on such earlier date as may be specified in the declaration.

(4) Parliament or the legislature of a province may re-enact a declaration made under subsection (1).

(5) Subsection (3) applies in respect of a re-enactment made under subsection (4).

Part II

Rights of the Aboriginal Peoples of Canada

35. (1) The existing aboriginal and treaty rights of the aboriginal peoples of Canada are hereby recognized and affirmed.

(2) In this Act, "aboriginal peoples of Canada" includes the Indian, Inuit and Métis peoples of Canada.

Part VII

General

52. (1) The Constitution of Canada is the supreme law of Canada, and any law that is inconsistent with the provisions of the Constitution is, to the extent of the inconsistency, of no force or effect.

(2) . . .

(3) . . .

59. (1) Paragraphh 23(1)(a) shall come into force in respect of Quebec on a day to be fixed by proclamation issued by the Queen or the Governor General under the Great Seal of Canada.

(2) . . .

(3) . . .

The Institute for Research on Public Policy
L'Institut de recherches politiques

A national, independent, research organization
Un organisme de recherche national et indépendant

Créé en 1972, l'Institut de recherches politiques est un organisme national dont l'indépendance et l'autonomie sont assurés grâce a des revenus provenant d'un fonds de dotation auquel souscrivent les gouvernements fédéral et provinciaux ainsi que le secteur privé. L'Institut obtient en outre des subventions et des contrats des gouvernements, des compagnies et des fondations afin de réaliser certains projets de recherche.

La raison d'être de l'Institut est triple:

- Servir de catalyseur au sein de la collectivité nationale en favorisant un débat public éclairé sur les principales questions d'intérêt général.
- Stimuler la participation de tous les éléments de la collectivité nationale à l'élaboration de la politique d'État.
- Trouver des solutions réalisables aux importants problèmes d'ordre politique afin de contribuer à l'élaboration d'une saine politique d'État.

Un Conseil d'administration, chargé de la décision, et une Commission de direction, responsable d'éclairer le Conseil sur l'orientation de la recherche, assurent la direction de l'Institut. L'administration courante des politiques, des programmes et du personnel relève du président.

L'Institut fonctionne de manière décentralisée et retient les services de chercheurs en divers points du Canada, s'assurant ainsi que toutes les régions contribuent aux recherches.

L'Institut cherche à favoriser, dans la mesure du possible, la compréhension et la discussion publiques des questions d'envergure nationale, controversées ou non. Il publie les conclusions de ses recherches avec clarté et impartialité. Les recommandations ou les conclusions énoncées dans les publications de l'Institut sont strictement celles de l'auteur et n'engagent aucunement le conseil d'administration, la commission de direction ou les bailleurs de fonds.

Le président assume la responsabilité ultime de publier un manuscrit au nom de l'Institut. Il jouit à cette fin des conseils du personnel de l'Institut et de critiques de l'extérieur quant à l'exactitude et l'objectivité du texte. Ne sont publiés que les textes qui traitent de façon compétente d'un sujet digne de la réflexion du public.

Les publications de l'Institut paraissent dans la langue de l'auteur et sont accompagnées d'un abrégé dans les langues officielles du Canada.

, ⁻⁴

The Institute for Research on Public Policy
L'Institut de recherches politiques

A national, independent, research organization
Un organisme de recherche national et indépendant

Founded in 1972, The Institute for Research on Public Policy is a national organization whose independence and autonomy are ensured by the revenues of an endowment fund which is supported by the federal and provincial governments and by the private sector. In addition, the Institute receives grants and contracts from governments, corporations and foundations to carry our specific research projects.

The *raison d'être* of the Institute is threefold:

- To act as a catalyst within the national community by helping to facilitate informed public debate on issues of major public interest.
- To stimulate participation by all segments of the national community in the process that leads to public policy making.
- To find practical solutions to important public policy problems, thus aiding in the development of sound public policies.

The Institute is governed by a Board of Directors, which is the decision-making body, and a Council of Trustees, which advises the Board on matters related to the research direction of the Institute. Day-to-day administration of the Institute's policies, programs and staff is the responsibility of the president.

The Institute operates in a decentralized way, employing researchers located across Canada. This ensures that research undertaken will include contributions from all regions of the country.

Wherever possible, the Institute will try to promote public understanding of, and discussion on, issues of national importance with clarity and impartiality. Conclusions or recommendations in the Institute's publications are solely those of the author and should not be attributed to the Board of Directors, Council of Trustees, or contributors to the Institute.

The president bears final responsibility for the decision to publish a manuscript under the Institute's imprint. In reaching this decision, he is advised on the accuracy and objectivity of a manuscript by both Institute staff and outside reviewers. Publication of a manuscript signifies that it is deemed to be a competent treatment of a subject worthy of public consideration.

Publications of the Institute are published in the language of the author, along with an executive summary in both of Canada's official languages.